THE CHURCH
— IN —
ANGOLA

THE CHURCH
—— IN ——
ANGOLA

A RIVER OF MANY CURRENTS

LAWRENCE W. HENDERSON

THE PILGRIM PRESS
CLEVELAND, OHIO

Originally published as *A Igreja em Angola: Um rio com várias correntes,*
© 1990 by Lawrence W. Henderson and Editorial Além-Mar, Lisbon

The Pilgrim Press, Cleveland, Ohio
© 1992 by The Pilgrim Press

Biblical quotations are from the New Revised Standard Version of the Bible,
© 1989 by the Division of Christian Education of the National Council of the
Churches of Christ in the U.S.A., and are used by permission.

Book design by ediType
Cover design by Martha Clark

Printed in the United States of America
The paper used in this publication is acid free and meets the minimum require-
ments of American National Standard for Information Sciences-Permanence of
Paper for Printed Library Materials, ANSI Z39.48-1984

97   96   95   94   93   92   5   4   3   2   1

Library of Congress Cataloging-in-Publication Data

Henderson, Lawrence W., 1921–
    [Igreja em Angola. English]
    The Church in Angola : a river of many currents / Lawrence W.
Henderson.
        p. cm.
    Includes bibliographical references.
    ISBN 0–8298–0938–4 (alk. paper)
    1. Angola—Church history.   I. Title.
BR1447.25.H4613 1992
276.73—dc20   92-31494
                                               CIP

Contents

Part III
INDEPENDENCE AND CIVIL WAR, 1975–1991

Foreword

Just a decade before Columbus' voyage to the Indies, which planted Iberian Christianity in the Americas, Roman Catholic missionaries arrived on the west coast of Africa in what is now Angola. On Easter Sunday 1491 they performed their first baptism there, the first success of Angolan Christian missions, which have sometimes been glorious, sometimes exploitative and oppressive. Today 80 percent of the people of Angola are at least nominal Christians. A church has emerged through centuries of an often brutal colonialism and decades of tragic civil war into new freedom and a great opportunity for service to society.

This is an important chapter in the story of world Christianity, and Lawrence Henderson is an interpreter with unique qualifications for telling it. Immersed in the life of Angola through many years as a missionary, he has also been involved with that society and its churches as a teacher, scholar, and administrator, both in the United States and in Portugal. His book *Angola: Five Centuries of Conflict* (Cornell University Press, 1979) is a standard reference, and his shorter writings have highlighted particular individuals and strands of mission history. This new volume is informed throughout by a theological perspective that never interferes with the narrative but helps readers get beyond the extensive array of historical data to grapple with implications and meanings.

This is a past-breaking volume, the very first effort to write a comprehensive history of Christianity in one of the most interesting countries of Africa. The author tells the story as an account of what is essentially one Christian community in spite of the many obvious diversities and even tensions within it. One sees how the Catholic contribution over half a millennium has been enlarged and enriched by a century of Protestant missions and by more recent Pentecostal and indigenous messianic movements. As a Catholic reviewer has written, "Only a Christian notably cultured and ecumenical could describe The Church in all the churches with such respect and knowledge."

The life of the churches has been intimately bound up with the wider currents of Angolan history. After an initial flowering under an Angolan Christian king, the Catholic church became entrapped in the Portuguese "patronage." It became far too close to the colonial power, and its extensive exploitation of the local population, first through slave trade for the benefit of its Brazilian province and later through a brutal system of forced labor. Protestant missions brought a powerful and energizing version of the Christian gospel, and with it educational programs that helped prepare Angolans with skills and aspirations for liberation and self-determination. Comity arrangements among the major missions led to the development of Protestant churches identified to a considerable extent with native tribal groupings. With the rise of the Popular Movement for the Liberation of Angola (MPLA) and the National Union for the Total Independence of Angola (UNITA), the churches in some respects seemed to be these rival independence movements "at prayer." Such identifications reinforced both the drive for liberation and also the tensions that led to the tragic civil war of 1975–91.

Into his authoritative overview of the Christian story in Angola, the author weaves the hundreds of specific stories that provide its real and human substance. One learns, for example, of the successful collaboration of American and Canadian missions (United Church of Christ in the U.S.A. and United Church of Canada) in the Evangelical Church of Central Angola. Within that partnership, one of the most notable developments was the mission at Galangue, in which Henderson himself served for a time. For most of its first generation, it was staffed and supported by the African-American Congregationalists of the United States and involved some of the most creative missionaries of twentieth-century Africa, Henry Curtis McDowell, Samuel Coles, and Aaron McMillan.

In 1990, this book was published in Portuguese by the Catholic publishing house Além-Mar in Lisbon. That such a work by a Protestant writer should be issued by a Catholic press attracted considerable attention in that Catholic country. In Angola it has found a wide and eager readership. Publication of this English edition coincides with the first elections scheduled in Angola in September of 1992. The churches whose story it tells will play an important role in the electoral process. Their contribution will be even more crucial for the radical readjustments that must be made if Angolans are to achieve what they hope will be the first free and democratic society in their history.

David M. Stowe
Executive Vice President Emeritus
United Church Board for World Ministries

Acknowledgments

The older we get the longer the list of acknowledgments becomes. Since I have lived on three continents, my list not only grows in length but in width. To avoid being too tedious, let me name a few representative people through whom I am acknowledging many others who have helped me on the way to writing this book.

Professor Frank G. Williston, my major professor at the University of Puget Sound, transmitted to me his enthusiasm for history. Professor Kenneth Scott Latourette at Yale Divinity School showed me that to write church history, it is necessary to show the church as it relates to society and culture. Many other academics have also made essential contributions to my educational preparation.

In Angola the Chipenda family contributed immeasurably to my personal growth and my understanding of the church. Pastor Jessé Chipenda, who plays an important role in this book, taught me by his quiet commitment what it means to be a good pastor. The whole Chipenda family deserves mention, and they represent hundreds of other Angolans who should be acknowledged.

Jorge Sanches and Fernando Santos Neves, who introduced me to the Church of Vatican II while we were in Angola and who I have seen recently in Portugal, opened my eyes to the fact that the Church is One. Father Manuel Pinto, who made possible the publication of this book in Portugal in 1990, inspired me with his courage, and we felt bereft when he died suddenly at age 43.

Institutionally, I acknowledge the support of the United Church Board for World Ministries (UCBWM) since 1947 when Ki and I were commissioned to go to Angola. Having worked with the UCBWM as missionaries, staff, and members of the board of directors, we gratefully acknowledge its subsidy for the publication of this book.

My book, *Angola: Five Centuries of Conflict,* published by Cornell University Press in 1979, was dedicated to Ki. We are close to our fiftieth anniversary, so I am more and more conscious of the deep debt I owe to her encouragement of me in these literary efforts, but more importantly to her example by her life and love of what the Good News is about.

Presuppositions

Missionary memoirs or church history? That is a question raised by some who looked at the English manuscript or at the Portuguese edition of this book. It is probably a mixture of the two.

It contains reflections of our family's twenty-two years working as missionaries of the United Church Board for World Ministries (UCBWM) in Angola (1947 to 1969) and of the period from 1969 to 1977 when we were keeping in touch with the church in Angola from the UCBWM office in New York City. Memoirs gain new dimensions when they are rooted in the life of a family. Our four children, as they grew up in Angola, had experiences that gave their parents insights into Angolan life that we would not have had by ourselves.

Those who would prefer straight memoirs will find this book too impersonal. To them it will seem like a book of church history. Professional historians may find it not sufficiently academic.

My aim is to give a fair picture of the church in Angola at the end of the twentieth century. I base this description on our personal experience and the research done in various archives. This picture is also colored by at least four presuppositions that underlie it.

1. The church is one. We know from the earliest Scriptures that the church has been divided from the beginning. The Apostle Paul wrote to the Christians in Corinth: " ... it has been reported to me by Chloe's people that there is quarreling among you. ... What I mean is that each one of you says, 'I belong to Paul,' or 'I belong to Apollos,' or 'I belong to Cephas,' or 'I belong to Christ' Is Christ divided?" (1 Cor. 1:11–12).

The answer to the rhetorical question is no, Christ is not divided, but the one church has been divided from the beginning until today.

The affirmation that the church is one was made by the Catholic church in the Decree on Ecumenism of the Second Vatican Council: "The Church established by Christ the Lord is, indeed, one and unique."

My first presupposition is that Christ founded one church in Angola. The dissensions continue, and Angolan Christians say, "I belong to the Catholic church," or "I belong to the Methodist church," or "I belong to the "Kimbanguist church."

To describe honestly the church in Angola these divisions must be admitted and analyzed, but I still affirm that the church is one. To my surprise, in spite of the differences in organization, rite, and doctrine I found certain common patterns of implantation and growth in all parts of the church. The conviction that the church is one made me more aware of signs of this unity.

2. The church has two natures: human and divine. This presupposition is based on the biblical understanding that the church is the Body of Christ. The doctrine of the incarnation has its clearest expression in the phrase "The Word became flesh and dwelt among us" (John 1:14).

The "Word," which referred to God, became a human being in Jesus of Nazareth. The Constitution on the Sacred Liturgy of the Second Vatican Council echoed the words of John: "It is the essence of the Church that she be both human and divine..." (no. 1).

The church fought some of its fiercest doctrinal battles over the correct interpretation of the two natures of Christ. The difficulty of understanding this doctrine is reflected in analyses of the church. Secular authors tend to consider only the human dimension of the church and some even underestimate that aspect. On the other hand church historians or theologians are apt to focus on the divine nature of the institution and thus do not recognize the profound interaction between the church and economic, political, and social forces.

I do not claim to have succeeded in distinguishing these two natures of the church, but I am convinced that our understanding of the church will be deficient until we recognize that it does have both these dimensions.

3. The church is essentially a people or a community. The people of God require organizational structure, leadership, doctrines, and standards of behavior. These, however, function to serve the people and not the reverse. The people are not called to serve the institution.

This book describes primarily ecclesiastical institutions, but I hope that does not hide the presupposition that the church is essentially a community — the People of God.

4. The principal mission of Jesus was not to found the church, but rather to announce the coming of the Reign of God. The church, which constitutes the Body of Christ, pursues this mission.

This book focuses on the planting, growth, organization, and social activities of the church in Angola, which are really secondary to its primary mission of announcing the Reign of God and inviting all to repent and accept the gospel.

Angola and the rest of the world live between the proclamation of the coming of God's Reign and its final fulfillment. I hope that this description of the church in Angola, which is certainly incomplete, may at least be judged honest. I have faith that the church in Angola, although it suffers from the same sins that are common to all humanity, may continue, by God's grace, to break bread and drink the cup, announcing the Lord's death until he comes (1 Cor. 11:26).

Whether or not you agree with my presuppositions, I hope that the facts and interpretations in this book will give you a more complete and sympathetic picture of the Angolan people.

PART I

COLONIAL PERIOD
1866–1960

Chapter 1

The Soil in Which
the Church Was Planted

The first missionaries arrived at the mouth of the Congo River on March 29, 1491. They came from Portugal at the request of the Kongolese king Nzinga-a-Nkuvu. A few days later, on Easter Sunday, April 3, 1491, the first baptisms were performed in Angola. The same king who had invited the missionaries received holy baptism in his royal dwelling in the capital of the kingdom of the Kongo, Mbanza Kongo, on May 3.

How could these Angolans be prepared for baptism in such a few days?

The answer is found by a little historical research revealing that the first Portuguese explorers under the command of Diogo Cão had arrived at the southern bank of the mouth of the Congo nine years earlier in 1482. They contacted the king of Soyo, who ruled that region, and raised a monument to St. George. Diogo Cão sent greetings by emissaries to the king of the Kongo who ruled in his capital, Mbanza Congo, some fifty leagues from the coast. The Portuguese then continued south along the Angolan coast to Cape St. Mary.

On their return to Soyo they found that the emissaries had not returned from the Kongolese court, so Diogo Cão seized four young Kongolese who had audaciously approached the ships. He promised to bring the young men back when he returned to Angola in "fifteen moons."

Arriving in Lisbon these young men were given Christian instruction and were baptized. One, named Cassuta, became the godson of King John II of Portugal and the other three were made godsons of noblemen. After the promised fifteen moons Diogo Cão departed again for the Kongo and took the four youths, along with presents for the king of the Kongo, who received the expedition festively.

In return the king of the Kongo sent an embassy to Lisbon, headed by Cassuta with some other young men from leading Kongolese families that they might be taught and baptized. It was the king's hope that the number of Christians might be multiplied when these young men returned from Portugal. The king of the Kongo also requested that John II send priests to baptize him and all his kingdom and to give them the doctrine of salvation.

Presumably the other three Kongolese who were the first to be baptized in Lisbon began to teach their relatives as their colleague Cassuta returned to Portugal. In Lisbon the second group of young men was entrusted to the care of the Catholic order of Loios by whom they were instructed and baptized. They returned to Angola with the expedition of Gonçalo de Sousa, leaving Lisbon on December 19, 1490, with six missionaries, masons, carpenters, and the ornaments and utensils necessary to furnish a church. During that voyage both the commander, Gonçalo de Sousa, and Cassuta died.

So when the first Catholic missionary priests arrived on March 29, 1491, there were Angolans, including the king of the Kongo, who had learned the catechism and were ready for baptism.

The fact that the first evangelization in Angola at the end of the fifteenth century was done by Angolan lay Christians may be a historical oddity, but it will be seen as one of the main reasons for the growth of the church during the twentieth century.

Scholars differ concerning the characteristics and importance of the church in Angola during its first four centuries. Most historians judge the conversion of the kingdom of Kongo to Christianity to have been "superficial, diplomatically oriented, impure, dangerous to national sovereignty or rejected by the mass of the population." Historian John Thornton challenges that opinion, arguing that "although Christianity in Kongo took a distinctly African form it was widely accepted both in Kongo and in Europe as being the religion of the country."[1]

Why, then, does the title of this part suggest indicate that the planting of the church in Angola took place in 1866? It would, indeed, be more accurate to say that the arrival of the Catholic missionaries in 1866 was the *replanting* of the church. The main purpose of this book, however, is to describe the contemporary church in Angola, and for this it is sufficient to begin the story in the latter part of the nineteenth century.

This is not to belittle the first four hundred years of the church in Angola or to depreciate the value of the historical work being done on

---

1. John Thornton, "Catholicism in Kongo, 1491–1750," *Journal of African History* 25 (1984): 147–67.

that period. It is, however, fair to say that when the Catholic church was replanted in Angola toward the end of the nineteenth century and the Protestant churches were planted for the first time, there remained only memories and liturgical relics of the first four hundred years.

> For example, in San Antonio [Soyo] the people still sang the *Salve Regina*, the local king sprinkled water, preached, and gave his blessing with a crucifix; in San Salvador a royal "secretary" said "Mass" every Sunday, which seemed to consist mainly in moving a book back and forth on an improvised altar.[2]

The Name of the Land

What was the Angolan soil in which the seed of the gospel was replanted in the latter part of the nineteenth century?

In this chapter we will describe with broad strokes the geographic, political, economic, social, and religious soils in which the Catholic church was replanted and the Protestant churches were implanted for the first time.

Readers who study African geography during the colonial period (before 1960) when Zambia was Northern Rhodesia and Zimbabwe was Southern Rhodesia may well ask, "What was Angola's name before it became an independent nation in 1975?" It was always Angola.

The name had its origin in the Kimbundu word *jingola*, meaning a small piece of iron that became an emblem of political authority among the Kimbundu.[3] *Ngola* then was used as the royal title in the region from Luanda to the Malanje highland and the Portuguese referred to it as the kingdom of Ngola.

This kingdom was not a united political entity and had no recognized boundaries. The Portuguese referred vaguely to the coastal area of West Central Africa in which it had an interest as the kingdoms of Kongo, Angola, and Benguela.

When the Catholic and Protestant missionaries arrived in the Congo basin in the 1870s there were no official frontiers, but the whole area to which the Portuguese were laying claim was known as Angola. The treaty that set the northern boundary of Angola was signed by Portugal and the Congo Free State only on May 25, 1891.

---

2. Henry J. Koren, C.S.Sp. *To the Ends of the Earth: A General History of the Congregation of the Holy Ghost* (Pittsburgh: Duquesne University Press, 1983), 271.

3. Joseph C. Miller, *Kings and Kinsmen: Early Mbundu States in Angola* (Oxford: Clarendon Press, 1976).

Geographic Soil

The geography of Angola was favorable to the planting of the church. The topography of Angola facilitated the penetration of the interior by missionaries, since the Congo and Cuanza rivers gave access to the relatively populous Kongo and Kimbundu areas. Four natural harbors — Luanda, Lobito, Moçâmedes, and Porto Alexandre — provided ports of entry for the main regions of Angola.

The climate of Angola was also favorable for human habitation even though the whole country falls within the tropical zone. Both the high altitudes of the central plateau and the Benguela current moderate the temperature, the latter by bringing cold water from the Antarctic to cool the coastal plain.

Angola was a well-watered land, but like most of Africa it was subject to periodic droughts. The central plateau had an average rainfall of forty to sixty inches and the coastal plain from ten to twenty inches. The rainfall on the plateau fed a network of rivers that provided water for human consumption and agriculture and, later, became a major source of hydroelectric energy.

The moderate climate and adequate water supply contributed to an acceptable level of soil fertility in most parts of Angola. However agriculture was not easy because the underlying geological formations produced a soil of sharply angular sand grains that compacted easily. High temperature and abundant rainfall favored bacterial decay so that in areas of Angola with those climatic conditions, wastes were quickly decomposed and little humus accumulated in the soil. Nevertheless Angola's soil could produce a variety of crops from semitropical coffee, pineapples, and bananas to temperate wheat, corn, and peaches.

The geographic soil in which the church was planted was also rich in minerals. Iron has been important in the mythology and economy of Angola. Diamond deposits are widespread and currently petroleum is Angola's most valuable export. The church was planted in a favorable geographic soil.

Political Soil

The planting of the church in Angola in the last quarter of the nineteenth century coincided with the "scramble for Africa." The European nations clashed as they sought raw materials, markets, and colonial power in Africa after the slave trade was no longer profitable. Industrial capitalism needed workers in Africa to produce the raw materials for European and American factories, to build roads and railways, and to provide a market for European products more than it needed slaves to cultivate sugar, cotton, or tobacco in the Americas.

Angola was one of the vortices of the scramble for Africa as Portuguese, French, Belgian, German, and British interests clashed at the mouth of the Congo River. The Berlin West Africa Conference, called jointly by France and Germany, met from November 1884 to February 1885 and gave international dignity to the scramble. The announced purposes of the conference were to clarify the status of international trade on the Congo and of navigation on the Niger and to define conditions under which future territorial annexations in Africa might be recognized.

The church became involved in this international conflict as national rivalries between French and Portuguese missionaries impeded the work of Catholic missions. Religious tensions between British Protestant and Portuguese Catholic missionaries in the capital of the kingdom of the Kongo were exacerbated by the colonial rivalries between Portugal and Great Britain. Lutheran missions on the southern border of Angola with Southwest Africa became Catholic as Portugal won out in its conflict with Germany.

The international publicity given to the scramble for Africa has led to the erroneous conclusion that the church was planted in *Portuguese* soil in Angola. This assumption is false because during the last quarter of the nineteenth century Portugal had not established effective occupation of the territory that we know as Angola. Even at the mouth of the Congo where the Portuguese had arrived four centuries earlier, they did not exercise control in 1912, two decades after the frontier treaty was signed between Portugal and the Congo Free State. The governor of the district of the Congo in 1912–13 confessed that Portugal ruled only a narrow strip of land along the coast; hence the political soil of Angola was perhaps one part Portuguese and nine parts African.[4]

The African kings and chiefs did not exercise authority over large territories, but they wielded sufficient power locally to permit or impede the establishment of missions in their areas. The king of the Kongo exercised a strong influence on the Protestant and Catholic missions that established themselves in his capital, São Salvador, and the Umbundu confederation on the Benguela highland, although decentralized, affected the church through such strong kings as Ekuikui II of Bailundo and Ndunduma of Bié. The Kwanyama kings in the extreme south frustrated the Catholic missionary efforts for several decades.

---

4. Relatório do Governador José Cardoso, *No Congo Português: Viagem ao Bembe e Damba-considerações relacionadas*, September to October 1912, Luanda, 1911 (Imprensa Nacional, 1944), 42–43.

The political soil at the turn of the century was more African than European.

Economic Soil

In the fifteenth and sixteenth centuries the slave trade had poisoned the Angolan soil. By the end of the nineteenth century the slave trade had ended. Commerce in ivory, beeswax, and rubber had replaced it, but neither did this provide a soil propitious for the planting of the church. These trades required much travel and did not allow the creation of stable communities that could be nurseries of the new faith. The rubber trade, especially, created a mobile population. Gladwyn Childs describes the popular rubber caravans:

> Everyone who was able to carry a load joined a caravan. It had always been the custom to take boys on trading expeditions, as young as they could go — say, from their tenth year — as part of their education. Now girls were also taken and hardly any but the women stayed at home to raise the crops and provide rations for the caravans.[5]

Actually, women played the key role in the economy of Angola quite independently of the demands that the trading caravans made on other sections of the population. In most regions women set out for their fields at sunrise with baskets, calabashes, and hoes on their heads. On their backs some of the women carried babies; others led toddlers by the hand. When they arrived at their fields, the women hoed the mounds of manioc, corn, or millet. According to the region they also split pumpkins and dried the seeds in the sun or grubbed up the peanuts and spread them to dry. In late afternoon the women returned to their houses with baskets piled high with food, bundles of firewood, and calabashes of water. They and the young girls then prepared the main meal of the day for the family, which would be mush of manioc in the north, corn in the center, and sorghum or millet in the south.

Men also had their assigned economic responsibilities. While women provided vegetables and grains for the family, men supplied meat or fish. They built and repaired their houses and in some areas men were artisans — the most noble being the blacksmith.

Although hunting was part of the economy of all regions of Angola, it played a larger role in the economic life of the Lunda-Chokwe than in other groups in Angola. Among them everyone participated in the

---

5. Gladwyn M. Childs, *Umbundu Kinship and Character* (London: Oxford University Press, 1949), 209.

Map of Angola Showing Administrative Divisions

hunt, although the larger wild game was the special responsibility of
the men. The women's role was not less important in hunting, however,
since more of the meat consumed was from small game such as rabbits
and rodents.

Among certain peoples of the Ganguela group fishing was also a significant part of their economy. The Luvale especially followed an annual
cycle, adapting the kind of fishing to the flow of water in rivers and
streams.

Cattle raising was an important sector of the economy among the
Ambo, Nhaneca-Humbe, and Herero.

Social Soil

The church was planted in a social soil characterized by ethnolinguistic
groups. The word "tribe" is not used to describe the Angolans since it
has a pejorative sense for most Americans and Europeans. "People" will
be employed for the unit that in other writing might be called "tribe."
A people occupied a more or less defined territory, usually to the exclu-
sion of others by virtue of its common possession of and adherence to
a particular way of life and by its involvement in a coherent social system. A people spoke a dialect of a language that was also understood
by other peoples, with whom it formed an ethnolinguistic group. The
church was planted among ten ethnolinguistic groups: eight Bantu and
two non-Bantu. Wilhelm Bleek, a German linguist in South Africa, proposed the term "Bantu" in 1856 to refer to a family of languages that
used the root -*ntu* for "person": *muntu*, singular, and *bantu*, plural.

What follows is not a complete or systematic description of the
ethnolinguistic groups, but rather a brief sketch with a few of the chief
characteristics of each group.

We have followed the convention in English transliterations of dropping the prefixes to Bantu words except in the cases of the two largest
groups, which have a common root name, *mbundu*. Consequently, the
adjectival prefix serves to distinguish the Kimbundu, who occupied the
districts of Luanda, Cuanza North, Cuanza South, and Malanje, from
the Umbundu, who were concentrated in the districts of Benguela,
Huambo, Huila, and Bié.

The Kongo Group — from Kingdom to Clan

The Kongo ethnolinguistic group, with about 13 percent of the population, was the third largest in Angola. It included eight related peoples
who occupied Cabinda and the current administrative districts of Zaire
and Uige. Although two-thirds of the Kongo lived outside of Angola in

Ethnolinguistic Map of Angola

Congo (Brazzaville) and Zaire, the Angolan Kongo felt privileged because the ancient capital of the kingdom was in Angola. The Xikongo, the most numerous people in this group, occupied the area around the capital, Mbanza Kongo (São Salvador), about eighty miles south of the Congo River. The Xikongo, together with seven other peoples — Susso, Zombo, Sorongo, Iaca, Kongo, Pombo and Sucu — formed the Kongo ethnolinguistic group.

Persons of this area identified themselves most frequently as members of one of the eight peoples. However, their identity with the whole Kongo ethnolinguistic group was strengthened by the fact that the Kongo region had the only centralized monarchy in Angola.

The Kongo were also distinguished by a Catholic heritage, which they traced back to their hero-king, Afonso, at the beginning of the sixteenth century.

One important element in the social soil of Angola was the cohesion that provided a fertile field for the germination and growth of the church. The strongest social cohesion among the Kongo was provided by the matrilineal clan, *kanda*. A Kongo proverb stated that the person who left the clan was like a "locust who has lost its wings"; that person has crossed the boundaries beyond which security, solidarity, and affection are no longer guaranteed in all circumstances. The clan consisted of the descendants of a common line, "whether they lived underneath [the dead] or above [the living] the ground," who were bound together by a community of blood.[6]

Only women of free status carried this blood, which conferred membership in the clan. The mother and son were of the same clan, but the father remained a stranger in the clan sense, even though he did provide access to a paternal kinship, or *kitata*. The clan, which was represented and administered by an elder, regulated most social relations. It defined incestuous sexual relations, for the blood community forbade relations between a man and woman who bore the same clan name, and guaranteed access to the clan territory of which the ancestors, founders of the first settlements, remained "owners." The transmission of land rights and the line of descent operated from maternal uncle to nephew. The clan created the conditions for security and solidarity.

The Kimbundu Group — the Heart of Assimilation

The Kongo's immediate neighbors to the south, between the Dande and Cuanza rivers, belonged to the Kimbundu ethnolinguistic group, which had nearly twice the population of the Kongo. The Kimbundu spread from Luanda at the coast to the Kasanje basin in the eastern part of the district of Malanje. Twenty peoples belonged to the Kimbundu group: Ambundu, Luanda, Luango, Ntemo, Puna, Dembo, Bângala, Holo, Cari, Chinje, Minungo, Bambeiro, Quibala, Haco, Sende, Ngola or Jinga, Bondo, Songo, Kisama, and Libolo.

Linguistically the Kimbundu were not as divided as the long list of peoples might imply. The Swiss-American missionary linguist Heli Chatelain studied the Kimbundu language at the end of the nineteenth century and divided it into two main dialects: Luanda, used in the capital and coastal plain, and Ambaca, used on the plateau. This linguistic division coincided with political and social rivalries that have affected the Kimbundu group and the history of that part of Angola to the present.

The Ambaca-speaking people, or Ambaquistas, were proud of their long association with the Portuguese and their role in the subjugation

---

6. George Balandier, *Daily Life in the Kingdom of the Kongo from the Sixteenth to the Eighteenth Century* (New York: World, 1969), 181.

of Angola to colonial rule. Chatelain witnessed to the important colonial role of the Ambaquistas by affirming that "it is not the Portuguese nor the Germans or Belgians, but the black Ambaca people who have opened up the Kwangu, Kuilu, and Kasai basins."[7]

Another sign of the assimilation of the Ambaca people to Portuguese culture is the term *mundele*, which generally means "white person," but was used by surrounding peoples to refer to the Ambaquistas. In the interior, *mundele* could mean not only a European, but *um preto de sapatos*, a black wearing or owning shoes.[8]

The Kimbundu not only learned to speak Portuguese as they became assimilated, but also produced the first Angolan written literature. All the peoples of Angola had a rich oral literature — folktales, proverbs, poetry, and songs — but it was among the "Africans" who were located mostly in Luanda at the end of the nineteenth century that creative writing appeared. The word "Africans" referred in that context to a distinct cultural group of blacks and mestizos who were in close contact with Europeans. This Angolan elite, working mostly in commerce and public service in the capital, found journalism a vehicle for the expression of their literary talents. The first periodical edited by "Africans," *O Echo de Angola*, appeared in 1881, and during the next ten years several other periodicals using Kimbundu and Portuguese circulated in the capital.

The Umbundu Group — Villagers and Traders

More than a third of the Angolan population among whom the church was planted belonged to the Umbundu ethnolinguistic group. In spite of being the largest they were the most homogeneous group in Angola. In fact it was possible to classify the Umbundu as a people rather than a group of peoples.

The Umbundu were concentrated south of the Cuanza River on the central highlands in the most populous districts of Angola: Huambo, Benguela, and Bié. From this population center the Umbundu scattered to every district, so that this most homogeneous group was also paradoxically the most widespread of all linguistic groups. The Umbundu group was fertile soil for the planting of the church because of its homogeneity and also because the people lived in relatively large villages. The *imbo* (plural *ovaimbo*) was composed of ten to fifty households, which included one hundred to one thousand people. The village commonly bore the name of the founder of whom the current elder would probably have been a descendant. Only the village elder, *sekulu*, could speak

---

7. Heli Chatelain, *Folk Tales of Angola* (Boston: Houghton Mifflin, 1894), 14.
8. Ibid., 259.

of "my village" (*imbo liange*). For everyone else it was "our village" (*imbo lietu*). In Umbundu country, people did not build together in the same village unless they were blood relatives.

At the end of the nineteenth century the Umbundu were organized politically into a dozen kingdoms, the most powerful being Bailundo, Bié, Huambo, Chiyaka, Galangue, and Andulo. The kings exercised three principal functions: communicating with the spirit world, relating to other peoples, and dispensing justice.

The king was high priest for his people since the spirits of the king's ancestors were the principal communal deities. He and his medicine men sacrificed at the royal shrine to control the elements and ensure fertility and success in hunting. Closely related to these religious functions of the king was the use of magic, witchcraft, and divination to protect himself and his people. Fulfilling his second or diplomatic function, the king made agreements with other kings to promote trade, and to make war on neighboring peoples to provide his court with tribute and his warriors with plunder.

Although religious and diplomatic functions might have been regarded as his primary responsibilities, the Umbundu king spent more time dispensing justice than in any other activity. Proverbs appropriate for the judgment of cases at court were more numerous than any other category, except perhaps those used for the education of the young. The trials were usually lengthy and came to a close only when the king gave his judgment. "The advocate speaks; the king concludes or decides" (*O popia onganji; o malapo osoma*). The king was generally not arbitrary in his decisions, but was bound by the customs of his people as well as by the opinions of his councillors.

Each Umbundu king held authority over a number of subkingdoms, or *atumbu*. The largest kingdom, Bailundo, had about two hundred *atumbu*, and each *etumbu* ruled over three to three hundred villages. The Kongo, Kimbundu, and Umbundu accounted for about 70 percent of the population of Angola at the end of the nineteenth century.

The Ambo Group — Herders and Farmers

The Ambo, who composed less than 3 percent of the population, had most of Angola's cattle and were the principal suppliers of beef steers and young animals for the central highlands. Their economy should be called agro-pastoral because the Ambo depended on both agriculture and cattle-raising equally; however, the possession of cattle gave more status than successful cultivation.

The Ambo straddled the border between Angola and Namibia. In Angola the term "Ambo" has been applied to the ethnolinguistic group that included the Cuanhama, Cuamatui, Dombandola, Evale, and

Cafima in the area from 16° latitude to the southern frontier.[9] The Ambo did not live in villages as did the Umbundu. Rather the rural population was divided into communities or districts, *mukunda*, and each community consisting of one hundred to three hundred family units laid claim to a loosely defined area, or *chilongo*. An individual family unit occupied its own farmstead, *eumbo*, which was one large enclosure averaging from fifteen to fifty acres surrounded by entwined branches of thorn shrubs.

The Ambo were not only united in extended matrilineal families, as were the majority of Angolans, but were the only group with well-defined totemic clans. Such clans had a totem: an animal or plant by which the members were identified and which was considered their common ancestor. A taboo against the meat or fruit of the totem and exogamous rules between members of the clans were enforced. Among the twenty-odd clans were such totems as ox, dog, lion, hyena, and millet.

The Ambo did not have a centralized monarchy, but each people had its king. Among the Ambo in Angola the kings of the Cuanhama played a dominant role. The last powerful Cuanhama king was Mandume, whose capital was captured by the Portuguese in 1917.

The Nhaneca-Humbe — The Conservatives

The Nhaneca-Humbe, lying geographically and culturally between the Umbundu and the Ambo, accounted for about 5 percent of the Angolan population. They spread across the districts of Huila and Cunene from the towns of Chongoroi and Quilengues in the north to the border of Namibia in the south. Ten peoples compose this group: Muila, Gambo, Humbe, Donguena, Hinga, Cuancua, Handa of Quipungo, Quipungo, Qulengue-Humbe, and Quilengue Muso. The Nhanece-Humbe was the most conservative group of peoples in Angola. They had been less influenced than others by European culture even though a relatively large settlement of Portuguese invaded their territory in the middle of the nineteenth century. This conservatism, which resisted urbanization, caused Lubango (Sá da Bandeira) in the center of the Nhaneca-Humbe territory, to be the only city in Angola with a white majority.

The Herero — True Herders

The Herero group could dispute the classification of "most conservative" with the Nhaneca-Humbe, but the Herero peoples were so few in number that their place in the Angolan scene was less significant. The few thousand Dimbas, Chimbas, Chavicuas, Hacavonas, Cuvales,

---

9. Carlos Estermann, *Etnografia do Sudoeste de Angola* (Lisbon: Junta de Investigações do Ultramar, 1960), 1:78.

Dombes, Cuanhocas, and Guendelengos occupied the territory in the districts of Benguela, Moçâmedes, and Huila, reaching inland from the Namib desert.

Economically, the Herero were the most exclusively pastoralist of all Angolans. Neighboring groups, the Ovambo and Nhaneca-Humbe, valued their pastoral more than their agricultural wealth, but they also had long agricultural traditions. As recently as 1958 the oldest Herero could still remember the time before agriculture had entered their economy.

The Lunda-Chokwe — Proud Hunters

The peoples belonging to the Lunda-Chokwe group included the Lunda, Lunda-lua-Chindes, Lunda-Ndembo, Mataba, Cacongo, Mai, and Chokwe. In the hyphenated name of this ethnolinguistic group, "Lunda" refers to the great empire of Central Africa that sent political chiefs from Katanga/Shaba in Zaire to the most populous areas of eastern Angola in the seventeenth century. Among the peoples found by the Lunda chiefs were the Chokwe, who lived astride the watershed of the Kasi, Cuango, Zambezi, and Cuanza rivers in east-central Angola. The Chokwe sociopolitical organization was built around twelve matrilineal clans ruled by petty lineage chiefs. The Lunda imposed themselves as political chiefs over the local lineage heads and founded kingdoms on the model of the Lunda empire.

The Chokwe were the most aggressive and independent people of Angola at the end of the nineteenth century. They showed these qualities by refusing to send tribute to the Lunda rulers and about the middle of the last century began to expand westward into central Angola.[10]

Economic power strengthened their independence since the ivory, beeswax, and rubber, which were the central items of trade at the end of the nineteenth century, were mainly found in eastern Angola in areas controlled by the Chokwe. In their trading they had accumulated firearms and were skilled hunters. By trade or raid the Chokwe acquired many women slaves, or pawns, who not only added to the Chokwe population by their considerable number, but also were of child-bearing age.

During this expansive period the Chokwe attracted the attention and epithets of neighboring peoples and outside observers. "The Gypsies of Angola" and "Bohemians of Central Africa" were two phrases used to describe them.[11]

---

10. Joseph Calder Miller, "Chokwe Expansion, 1850–1900," M.A. thesis, University of Wisconsin, 1967.

11. Eduardo dos Santos, *Sobre a religião dos Quiocos* (Lisbon: Agência Geral do Ultramar, 1956), 16.

David Livingstone, after crossing Africa from the Cape to Luanda, classified the Chokwe as the most savage and least hospitable people he had met. These characterizations reflect the determination of the Chokwe to guard their own traditions and repel the domination of European culture.[12] The Chokwe, who were known as proud, independent hunter-warriors, were also famous as artists. Their sculptors carved fine human figures and ritual masks. Mural painting was another art in which they excelled.

The Ganguela Group — Fisher Men and Women

The Portuguese ethnographer José Redinha has classified the remaining twenty Bantu peoples in Angola into the Ganguela ethnolinguistic group, which accounted for perhaps 7 percent of Angolans: Luimbe, Luena, Lovale, Lutchazi, Bunda, Ganguela, Ambuela, Ambuila-Mambumba, Econjeiro, Ngonielo, Mbande, Cangala, Iahuma, Gengista, Ncoia, Camachi, Ndungo, Nhengo, Nhemba, and Avico. The American anthropologist George Murdock included most of these people in a Lunda cluster together with the Chokwe.[13]

The Ganguela group was the most heterogeneous in Angola. Each of the twenty peoples was so small and isolated that neither the peoples individually nor the group as a whole was fertile soil for the planting of the church.

The eight Bantu ethnolinguistic groups just described formed more than 95 percent of the population at the end of the nineteenth century. The two remaining peoples were non-Bantu: the Khoisan, representatives of the peoples who lived in Angola before the Bantu invasion, and the Portuguese, who played an important role in planting the church in Angola.

Khoisan — The Native Angolans

The Kung Bushmen in southern Angola call themselves *zhu twa si,* "the harmless people."[14] They call non-Bushmen *zosi,* which means "animals without hooves" because, they say, non-Bushmen are angry and dangerous like lions and hyenas. When the Bantu "animals without hooves" entered Angola four to ten centuries ago, they found hunting-gathering populations who were so harmless that they were soon dominated

---

12. Thomas Louttit, *Trial and Triumph in Chokweland: Central African Jubilee or Fifty Years with the Gospel in the "Beloved Strip"* (London: Pickering and Ingles, n.d.), 31.

13. George Peter Murdock, *Africa: Its People and Their Culture History* (New York: McGraw-Hill, 1959), 293.

14. Elizabeth Marshall Thomas, *The Harmless People* (New York: Knopf, 1959), 24.

and by the beginning of this century were represented only by a few thousand Khoisan and Vatua.

"Khoisan" is a compound of the Hottentots' name for themselves, Khoikoi, and their name for Bushmen, San. If there were ever Hottentots in Angola, they have been eliminated or removed.

At the end of the nineteenth century a few thousand Bushmen in small family bands wandered across southern Angola and into the Kalahari Desert. The slightly built, yellow-skinned Bushmen lived a nomadic life with no permanent settlements.

The Bushmen's social organization was simply the nuclear family, which seldom surpassed twenty people and may have consisted of an old man and his wife, their daughters, the daughters' husbands and children, and perhaps an unmarried son or two.

The Portuguese — Colonizers and Settlers

In 1900 only 9,198, or 0.2 percent, of Angola's population was white; of these the vast majority was Portuguese. In the nineteenth century few Portuguese went to Angola voluntarily: most were soldiers or exiled criminals, *degredados*, who were sent to Angola to serve their sentences rather than being jailed in Portugal. In 1881 of the 1,450 European residents in Luanda, half (721) were civil or military criminals and 394 were free men outside the army. A stable, growing white population would require an equal number of men and women, but in 1902 only a few more than a hundred European women were found in Angola, all but eight or ten of whom were *degredadas*.

Practically all the Portuguese were nominally Catholic, so the church assumed it did not need to plant itself in the white community, but only required priests who would make the church functional.

Mestizos

The small number of white women in Angola in the nineteenth century was the main cause of the relatively large mixed, or mestizo, population. In 1845 there were 1,832 whites and 5,770 mestizos. They performed important roles as middlemen in the slave trade and occupied key posts in business, the civil service, journalism, the military, and the church.

In summary, the Bantu population of Angola provided a social soil that was generally propitious for the planting of the church. Forming more than 95 percent of the Angolans, they all respected similar patterns of social unity based on kinship. Although the importance of matrilineal and patrilineal relations differed from group to group and even from people to people, in all cases kinship ties were decisive in establishing marriage patterns, economic responsibilities, access to land, local political authority, and spiritual well-being.

The church in the latter quarter of the nineteenth century found an Angolan society composed of peoples that had a strong sense of social cohesion.

The Religious Soil

When the missionaries arrived in Angola in the 1870s and 1880s they did not realize that they would plant the church in a rich religious soil. They dismissed the African traditional religion as superstition since it lacked the main features of Western religion: doctrinal statements, ecclesiastical structure, and Scriptures. However, as the missionaries learned the languages of the people among whom they worked, they were led directly into the world of African religion. They soon discovered that the people had a word for God. In Kikongo, Kimbundu, and Chokwe it was *Nzambi*. The Umbundu called the supreme being *Suku* and the Ambo referred to God as *Kalunga*. The Herero used the combined name *Nzambi-Kalunga*, and the Nhaneka-Humbe shared the name *Huku* (the same root as *Suku*) with the Umbundu and *Kalunga* with the Ambo. As the missionaries worked at the primary task of translating the Scriptures into the various Angolan languages, they all employed the names for God in common use in their regions.

Nzambi, Suku, and Kalunga were not only well known, but the characteristics attributed to the deity were not inconsistent with the Christian view of God. In fact some European missionaries or anthropologists have described the nature of the supreme being in African cultures in such terms of Christian theology as "omnipotent," "omniscient," and "omnipresent."[15]

Such attributes have been discovered in proverbs or ritual practices of the various peoples of Angola. For example, the Ambo describe God's omniscience in the proverb: "Kalunga has long ears, and his eyes can see in the dark."[16]

The Nhaneka-Humbe in south central Angola speak of a righteous God in such proverbs as *Ukamenekelwa na Huku, Ukapahulwa na Kalunga* ("You are to be greeted by God, you are to be visited by the Lord"). This is interpreted to mean, "Sooner or later God will punish your transgressions." The same people also say, *Wandinga tupu — tykale! Ekumbi limue*

15. Mário Malheiro, "A Religião nas tribos Angolanas," *Mensário Administrativo* (Luanda), no. 4 (December 1947), 15; John S. Mbiti, *African Religions and Philosophies* (Garden City, N.Y.: Doubleday & Co, Anchor Books, 1970), 39–49.

16. Raffaele Pettazoni, *The All Knowing God: Researches into Early Religions and Culture* (London, 1956), 35.

olyo Huku ha munkhwanya ("You did me wrong, let it go! But some day God will pay you").

According to Angolan traditional religion God not only knows what is going on in the world and judges our wrongdoings: the deity also protects his creatures as the Umbundu proverb states rhetorically, *Suku ka lavi viosi evi a panga?* ("Doesn't God care for all his creation?"). A Herero proverb affirms the same confidence in divine protection: *Hitu; mbi takamisiwa; Ndyambi-Karunga* ("I will not die, because God is protecting me").[17]

The Ganguela peoples of central Angola used sandgraphs as well as oral proverbs to describe their universe. To make the sandgraph a space is cleared on the ground so it has a smooth surface where dots and lines are drawn with fingers so that they trace a geometric form. For example, this figure represents God, "pregnant with creation," existing in eternity before any creation was brought into being. The upper curves with the enclosed dots represent the heavens while the lower curves with their dots depict the earth. The dots that are enclosed singly stand for God's attributes:

A hasi vuse.	He can do all.
A tantekeya viosi.	He knows all.
A mona viosi.	He sees all.
A li na ngozi.	He has goodness.

Emil Pearson, who recorded Ganguela sandgraphs, interpreted the four attributes as omnipotence, omniscience, omnipresence, and love.[18]

Whereas proverbs and sandgraphs indicate that Angolans believed in a benevolent God, their religious practices gave evidence that the supreme being was not an object of regular worship. Their cultic practices were directed toward a variety of lesser spirits that were influential in the daily lives of the people.

An Angolan named Cilela wrote an account of Umbundu religion in 1918 in which he noted that:

---

17. Carlos Estermann, *Etnografia do Sudoeste de Angola* (Lisbon: Junta de Investigações do Ultramar, 1960), 2:195.

18. Emil Pearson, *People of the Aurora* (San Diego: Beta Books, 1977), 21.

All the people know that there is God, the maker of everything, but they do not know how to worship him. They only worship the *olosande* and they say that the *olosande* are taking care of us every day.[19]

The Umbundu recognized various other spirits besides the *olosande* that affected their everyday lives, many of which were spirits of the dead called *ovilulu*. Ritual practices of prayer and sacrifice were frequently directed to the *ovilulu*, which could enter the living to harm or help. *Akisi* were the spirits of those who were long dead, and, having been entirely placated, they became guardians of the family.

At this point in our study it is sufficient to note that the church was planted in a culture occupied by countless spirits that affected all aspects of the people's lives from birth to death and beyond. The Angolans not only lived within a religious universe, but each human being was formed of both material and spiritual elements. The Kikongo identified four elements in each person: body, or *nitu*; two souls, the spiritual soul, *moyo*, and the perceptible soul, *mfumu kutu*; and the name, or *zina*.

Living within a spiritual universe, the Angolans developed a variety of rituals in response to the action of the spirits. Among the Umbundu certain rituals were enacted in the *etambo* — a small house constructed near the residence of the king or chief. This served also as a storehouse for valuable items such as trading goods: rubber, cloth, or ivory. Near the *etambo* was an *utala*, which at times was only two forked sticks on which hunt meat was hung, but it could also serve as an altar on which flesh sacrificed to the spirits could be placed.

Angolan traditional religion also recognized certain persons with special functions and authority. The *cimbanda*, or healer, was trained in the use of herbs and roots as well as secret rituals to invoke the protection of benevolent spirits or to exorcise evil spirits.

Some diviners used a basket in which they placed a variety of objects that were used to disclose the causes of misfortune. The importance of such an instrument was indicated by the testimony of a missionary to whom an African acknowledged: "It [the divining basket] is our book, we do not have any other; you read your book every day because you believe in it. We do the same."[20]

The functions of a diviner reveal much that is common in Angolan traditional religion:

The Ndembu diviner's task is the practical one of disclosing the causes of misfortune and death. His job is not to foretell the future,

---

19. ABC 15.1, vol. 19, no. 232.
20. M. L. Rodrigues de Areia, *Figuras antropomórficas dos cestos de adivinhação dos Quicos, Contribuições para o Estudo de Antropologia Portuguesa* (Coimbra) 9, no. 1, 7; citing G. Welter, *Les croyances primitives et leurs survivances* (Paris, 1960), 182.

but rather to scrutinize the past in order to identify the spiritual and human agents responsible for personal misfortunes. Since all human problems, such as infertility, illness, and trouble in hunting are ascribed to moral conflicts within the human community, the diviner's task is to disclose acts of immorality which have provoked the vengeance of the ancestors, and to reveal the destructive hand of witches and sorcerers.[21]

African traditional religion, known as animism, lacked a doctrinal statement, an ecclesiastical structure, and Scriptures, but it provided a fertile soil for planting the church. The Angolans believed in a supreme God. Lesser spiritual beings, many of which were ancestral spirits, were the objects of sacrifices and prayers performed to protect the living from danger and death and to seek favor and fortune. Religious wisdom and authority were vested in special persons such as healers, diviners, and sorcerers, and certain places and times were recognized as especially sacred.

The missionaries arriving in Angola at the turn of the last century came from societies where literacy, science, technology, and industrialism had produced what were considered the blessings of Christian civilization. From the perspective of Europe and North America the Angolans lacked health, education, good housing, clothing, and adequate food, because they had not received the Christian faith. The gap between European civilization and African culture was so great that they appeared to have few points of contact. Most missionaries did not perceive for some time that although European and African life were in sharp contrast, Bantu and biblical worldviews had many parallels.

European life had become increasingly individualistic, whereas Bantu and biblical cultures were communitarian. African society bound its people together by strong kinship ties among the living and also included the ancestors as respected members of the community. Many Western Christians could skip the "begats" in the Bible, but the Africans recognized the importance of the New Testament's beginning with the list of ancestors of Jesus Christ going back to King David and Abraham.

The first missionaries criticized ancestor worship among the Angolans, but quoted Jesus saying, " ... have you not read what was said to you by God, 'I am the God of Abraham, and the God of Isaac, and the God of Jacob?' He is not God of the dead, but of the living" (Matt. 22:32). In a curious but unrecognized reversal of roles, the first missionaries, who could not escape the secular corrosion of nineteenth-century Europe, were facing a "heathen" society with a biblical worldview. The Angolans in their traditional culture lived in a world surrounded and

21. Benjamin C. Ray, *African Religions: Symbol, Ritual, and Community* (Englewood Cliffs, N.J.: Prentice-Hall, 1976), 104.

penetrated by ancestors, angels, spirits, and mysterious relations with an invisible world.

The welfare of individuals and community depended from both Bantu and biblical perspectives on sound relations within this wider community. An immoral act such as violence toward a neighbor or lack of respect for an ancestor could not only cause an open conflict in the community, but produce illness in an individual. Finally, the Angolans were prone to ask the theological/philosophical question "Why?" rather than the secular/scientific questions of "What?" and "How?"

Conclusion

Historians also ask the question "Why?" *Why* during the twentieth century has the church grown more steadily and extensively in Africa south of the Sahara than in any other region of the world? From our century-long perspective we can suggest at least one answer: the soil was particularly propitious for the planting of the church in Angola at the end of the nineteenth century. However, we could hardly expect the pioneer missionaries to appreciate that fact as they were being decimated by disease, stammering to learn new languages, seeking reluctant guides and carriers to travel long distances with them on foot, laboring to build shelter for themselves and their families out of sticks, mud, and grass. To them the soil seemed indeed inauspicious. Yet this was an added challenge to their adventurous spirits and to their conviction that they were obeying God's call to persist in the arduous process of planting the church.

Chapter 2

The Planting of the Church 1866–1899

Our work as evangelists, no matter how productive and blessed it may be, will be incomplete and without guarantees for the future, if it does not have as its objective "the planting of the church."
— Dom Moisés Alves de Pinho

Kenneth Scott Latourette in his monumental seven-volume work, *The History of the Expansion of Christianity*, compared the spread of the Christian faith to a tide that rose and fell through the centuries.[1] The tide rose so high in the nineteenth century that he called the period from 1800 to 1914 the Great Century.

The Catholic Church in the Nineteenth Century

Catholic missions at the beginning of the nineteenth century were at ebb tide, with only 270 missionaries in the entire world.[2]

Italy, Spain, and Portugal, which had sent out most of the Catholic missionaries in the fifteenth to eighteenth centuries, suffered severe reverses at the end of that period and into the nineteenth century. However, the church as a whole recovered from these reverses because of the emergence of French ultramontanism, a reinvigorated papacy, and the creation of more new orders and congregations than in any other century.

---

1. Kenneth Scott Latourette, *The History of the Expansion of Christianity*, 7 vols. (New York: Harper and Brothers, 1937–1945).
2. H. Paul Johnson, *A History of Christianity* (New York: Atheneum, 1980), 450.

24

The Catholic church in Portugal, however, continued to suffer shocks that weakened it at home and reduced its mission outreach to the colonies. At the beginning of the nineteenth century Portugal was invaded by fifty thousand French and Spanish soldiers, who spread throughout the nation pillaging, robbing, arresting, and killing at will. The Portuguese government fled from Lisbon to Rio de Janeiro, Brazil, the richest part of the Portuguese empire; in 1922 Brazil declared its independence.

When the foreign troops withdrew, Portugal was torn by civil war between liberalism and absolutism — the Catholic church being one of the pillars of absolutism. Each battle won by liberalism, such as the decree of 1834 abolishing all monasteries and nationalizing their property, was considered a defeat for the church. Secular clergy became public servants paid by the state to perform public duties. A wave of anti-clericalism not only decreased the influence of the church, but from 1820 to 1840 reduced the number of secular priests in Portugal from twenty-four thousand to ten thousand. Another sign of the weakening of the church was the extinction of several dioceses: Aveiro (1837), Castelo Branco (1831), Leiria (1873), Pinhel (1838), and Portalegre (1833).[3]

The defeats suffered by the Catholic church in Portugal in the nineteenth century were reflected in Angola. The attrition of the clergy in the kingdom of the Kongo and the coastal cities of Luanda and Benguela continued through the seventeenth and eighteenth centuries and reached its nadir in the mid-nineteenth century, which Dom Manuel Nunes Gabriel, the archbishop of Luanda, called the "great Calvary" of the church in Angola.[4]

Statistically the decline of the church can be measured by the number of Catholic clergy in Angola:

1800	39
1840	18
1853	5
1863	16
1880	38

The five priests in 1853 were all natives of Angola — four were working in two parishes in Luanda and one in Benguela. Not a single mission was functioning in Angola.

The decadence of the church in the mid-nineteenth century was also reflected in the morals of the clergy. Bishop Moreira Reis, who arrived in Luanda in 1850, found the few clergymen "unfortunately not exemplary," but he could not punish them or he would have been left without any clergy. The result was that the people refused to attend church or receive the sacraments.

---

3. Oliveira Marques, *História de Portugal* (Lisbon: Palas Editores, 1976), 2:39.
4. *Portugal em África*, no. 137 (September–October 1966): 286.

The bishop pleaded with the Portuguese government to send help. In response the government published a decree authorizing the creation of new parishes in agreement with the ecclesiastical authorities. Applications to staff the new parishes were accepted from those who agreed to serve a minimum of eight years, and they were promised a substantial increase in salary. Eight priests were approved; arriving in Angola in 1858, they were sent to Bembe, Ambriz, Benguela, Golungo Alto, Cazengo, Pungo-Andongo, Huila, and Cassanje.

The Portuguese priests who came to resurrect the church from its great Calvary were not successful because of homesickness, disease, and death. Bishop Moreira Reis served in Luanda only from 1852 to 1855. His successor, Dom Manuel de Santa Rita Barros, disembarked in Luanda in 1861, but fell victim to yellow fever a year later. His successor spent only fifteen months in Angola before returning to Lisbon.

Congregation of the Holy Ghost

The replanting of the Catholic church in Angola was due primarily to the work of the Congregation of the Holy Ghost. This missionary community has been so important in the history of the church in Angola that we must record something of its roots to explain the orientation of the hundreds of its missionaries who served there. The Holy Ghost Fathers, or Spiritans, represented two features of the spread of Christianity in the Great Century: first, it was a new congregation formed during the period in which more new orders and congregations were formed than in all of Christian history; and, second, it was French, the result of a merger of two French congregations — the Congregation of the Holy Heart of Mary and the Congregation of the Holy Ghost.

The latter was founded in Paris in 1703 by Claude Francis Poullart des Places when he was still a seminary student. This missionary order consecrated to the Holy Spirit by the invocation of the Most Holy Virgin had as its purpose to "go to the savages and give itself to the most abandoned souls."[5]

The Congregation of the Holy Heart of Mary was founded by Jacob Libermann, who was born in 1802, the son of a conservative rabbi. Although prepared to follow his father's vocation, he never exercised it as he was converted to the Christian faith and baptized at the age of twenty-four. Libermann then changed his name from Jacob to Franz Maria Paul; later on he became a priest and founded the Congrégation du Saint-Coeur de Marie.

---

5. *Portugal em África*, no. 38 (1953): 239. Francisco Lopes, *Ao Encontro dos Pobres: Vida do P. Cláudio Francisco Poullart des Places (1679–1709)* (Lisbon, 1983).

Franz Maria Paul Libermann (1802–1852),
founder of the Congregation of the Holy Ghost, or Spiritans.
Courtesy of Província Portuguesa da Congregação do Espírito Santo.

Since the Congregation of the Holy Heart of Mary took the blacks as its special charge, the aims of these two orders were in harmony. In 1848 they joined to form the organization that played a major role in planting the church in Angola, La Congrégation du Saint-Esprit e de l'Immacule Coeur de Marie, popularly known as the Holy Ghost Fathers, or Spiritans.

Libermann wrote many letters in which he gave counsel and advice to the missionaries who were scattered all across Africa, South America, and as far as Oceania. In words that sound very similar to the twentieth-century missionary doctrine of identification, Libermann wrote:

> Leave your manner of being, your customs, and your spirit as Europeans; become Africans with the Africans, respecting them without imposing your opinions. Servants seek to adapt themselves to the habits and customs of their masters; very well, do likewise that you may perfect them, sanctify, and free them so that little by little they may become God's people. This is what St. Paul meant when he said, "I have become all things to all men, that I may by all means save some."[6]

Based on the foundations of saintliness and identification, the Holy Ghost Fathers helped build the church in Angola on three pillars: catechists, schools, and abnegation. Catechists, or village lay leaders, were the means to conquer souls; schools, the means to form a Christian community; and abnegation or renunciation the temper that was to guide and protect the missionary in his divine service.

Padroado and *Propaganda Fide*

The responsibility for planting the Catholic church in Angola was assumed by two entities: the *Padroado* and the *Propaganda Fide*. *Padroado*, or Patronage, referred to the treaty between the Catholic church and the Portuguese government, which gave special rights and responsibilities to the state for the spread of the faith within the territories it controlled.[7]

Propaganda Fide, or the Congregation for the Propagation of the Faith, in Rome, was entrusted at its creation in 1622 with the extension of the faith into all mission areas, and it considered Angola a mission area in the nineteenth century.

The agreement, or *Padroado*, between Portugal and the Vatican was first established by Pope Nicholas V in the papal bull *Romanus Pontifex* on January 8, 1455, and gave Portugal three main rights: (a) only its monarch could present names for bishops to be elected by the Vatican; (b) only missionaries sent by or recognized by the monarchs could evangelize in the territories of the *Padroado*; and (c) the king could take the

---

6. *Portugal em África* 14, no. 79, 51. The letters and other writings are gathered in the *Directoire Spirituel ou Instructions de Venerable F. M. P. Libermann aux membres de la Congregation* (Paris: Imprimatur, Maison Mere, 1910).

7. Patronage was the sum of privileges and responsibilities conceded by the Catholic church to founders of churches, chapels, or charities and to their successors. The system of patronage, which was widespread from the tenth to fifteenth centuries, was abolished by the Council of Trent with a few exceptions. One of the exceptions was patronage with kings. Portugal and the Catholic church in Portugal continued to insist on the validity of this arrangement right down to the 1974 revolution.

initiative in any alterations of the territories of the *Padroado,* such as the creation of new dioceses, relations with Rome, and the establishment of convents or monasteries.

The *Padroado* also imposed certain obligations on Portugal: to construct, repair, and conserve churches, monasteries, and diocesan residences; to support the clergy; to nominate enough workers for worship and pastoral care; and to provide necessary furnishings for the churches.

Parallel to the *Padroado,* the *Propaganda Fide* created districts called prefectures in missionary areas. In 1640 it established the Prefecture of the Two Guineas, which covered the whole west coast of Africa from Senegal to the Orange River and entrusted this huge missionary area to the Capuchins. Later this prefecture was subdivided and the part that included northern Angola was the Prefecture of the Congo. The Capuchins provided the missionaries for that area until the 1830s when they had to withdraw for lack of personnel. In 1865 the *Propaganda Fide* requested the Congregation of the Holy Ghost to assume the responsibility for the Prefecture of the Congo.

With both the *Propaganda Fide* and the Portuguese government charged with the evangelization of territories claimed by Portugal, more adequate resources should have been available for planting the church, but this division of responsibility also created friction and conflict on many occasions.

The Holy Ghost Fathers José Maria Poussot and António Espitallié with a lay brother, Estevão Billon, arrived in Ambriz on March 14, 1866, but they were unable to put down roots. Billon died six months after his arrival in Ambriz, and Poussot left for Europe because of illness. Espitallié and Father Fulgêncio Lapeyre, who replaced Poussot, soon left for Luanda, where one died in 1869 and the other in 1870.

Illness and death were not the only reasons for the failure of that first mission. National rivalries and the friction between the *Padroado* and *Propaganda Fide* also hampered the efforts to establish missions on the northern coast of Angola. These first Spiritan missionaries were French and thus suspect by the Portuguese since the political and commercial interests of France and Portugal frequently clashed in the 1860s and 1870s in the Congo basin. The problems between the *Padroado* and the *Propaganda Fide* were debated in the Portuguese parliament, and at times reason prevailed as the legislators recognized that Portugal could not enjoy the privileges of the *Padroado* unless it was prepared to assume the stated responsibilities.

The first effort to plant the church in Ambriz by the Holy Ghost Fathers failed, and the next venture in Moçâmedes was no more successful.

Father Charles Duparquet, a French Spiritan, was challenged by the needs and opportunities of Congo and Angola while he served as a missionary in Gabon. He went to Portugal with the intention of sailing for Angola, but in Lisbon he met the bishop of Angola and the Congo, Dom José Lino de Oliveira, who received him gladly and named him parish priest of Capangombe and other areas within the district of Moçâmedes. The energetic priest was not content to be confined to one parish as a priest, so he went inland and envisioned establishing a mission station in the interior. However, he ran afoul of the rivalry between the prefecture and the Portuguese hierarchy. This conflict was complicated by the charge that Duparquet favored British sovereignty over southern Angola. This suspicion was expressed in a letter written by the governor of Moçâmedes, Sebastião Nunes da Mata:

> It is being said that the French priest Duparquet is on a mission for the Catholic church to the east and beyond the Cunene carrying an English flag and preaching that those lands are part of British dominion and that a short time ago some of his group came to Mulondo and is in our territory on the right side of the Cunene and that there they showed their hostility so I believe that these facts well justify my apprehension.[8]

Though Duparquet was exonerated, the tension between Portuguese authorities and French missionaries continued. Duparquet left Angola in the middle of the storm. Deciding that since it was going to be difficult for French missionaries to work in Angola, he himself would train Portuguese missionaries for the work there. In 1867 he went to Portugal and opened the Casa do Congo in Santarem.

The Missions in Cabinda

The first four Spiritan missionaries sent to Angola in 1866 died before the end of 1870, but this did not dishearten the Rev. P. Ignatius Schwindenhammer, the superior general of the Congregation. He sent Fathers Duparquet and Carrie with Brother Fortunato to establish a mission at Lândana in Cabinda, where they arrived on September 9, 1873.[9]

Two commercial houses being for sale there, the missionaries bought them along with five to seven acres of land for their residence, schools, and dependencies. They also purchased from a chief named Peça Matenda the valley of Lândana for the price of two hundred bolts of cloth, two boxes of rifles, and two barrels of brandy.[10] Peça was unable to sign

---

8. A. da Silva Rego, *Curso de Missionologia* (Lisbon: Agência Geral de Ultramar, 1956), 302.

9. António Brásio, *Spiritana Monumenta Histórica* (Louvain: E. Nauwelaerts, 1971), 1:305–8.

10. Ibid., 309.

Catholic church in Lândana (constructed 1900–1904).
Courtesy of Província Portuguesa da Congregação do Espírito Santo.

his name on the contract, so he marked it with a cross. When Father Duparquet saw it, he was amazed and exclaimed: "But this is a cross." Peça agreed and said, "Yes, a cross, a Holy Cross."[11]

Brother Fortunato found seven men to help him cultivate the valley for its first planting. Father Carrie dedicated himself to studying the local language and without delay gathered the first catechism class among Fortunato's men and others from nearby villages.

Young men were offered bed, board, and clothing to study at Lândana. In order to help with expenses the missionaries wanted the students to do the planting in the fields. The chief objected saying, "A free boy should hunt, fish, get palm nuts, and trade. Only women cultivate the land." It took a long time to persuade the people that students should work in the fields.[12]

A more serious issue arose when the rains were late. The sorcerers took advantage of the situation by blaming the missionaries for the drought: "The spirits are unhappy with the arrival of the white man. They are punishing us because of the missionaries. We will die of hunger."[13] A plague of fleas aggravated the situation, only to be followed by a smallpox epidemic.

Finally, on November 2, 1874, Peça Matenda delivered an ultimatum to the mission:

> *Senhores Padres* — when you asked me for land to have a garden you deceived me. All the chiefs condemn me for having sold the land, thus causing the drought which now brought the plague of fleas. Since you have planted and harvested, you have received value for what you paid. Now you must leave and not plant any more or I will send troops to tear up everything and break down the house. I await an answer.
>
>   Chief Peça[14]

Father Duparquet did not reply. Peça's men came to the mission dramatically shouting and waving, but seeing that these threats did not produce the desired results, Peça decided to pacify the chiefs by giving them part of the price that the mission had paid for the land. Peça was the loser, for on the day that the ultimatum was to take effect rain came down in torrents, ending the drought that the missionaries were supposed to have caused.

Having overcome these severe tests, the Holy Ghost missionaries were able to proceed with establishing the first mission station during

---

11. Cândido Ferreira da Costa, *Cem Anos dos Missionários do Espírito Santo em Angola (1866–1966)* (Nova Lisboa, 1970), 70.
12. Ibid., 71.
13. Ibid.
14. Ibid., 71–72.

this new chapter in the history of the church in Angola. The Lândana mission sought to reach several classes of the population, even building a little seminary on the top of the hill for some mestizo students. In the field a school was built for young freed slaves who were under Brother Fortunato's care, while a community was formed for adults who were redeemed from slavery to form the nucleus of a Christian village in the valley.

Father Duparquet had plans to train African clergy from the first day on the mission, so he gave great attention to the moral teaching of the boarding school students in order to awaken clerical vocations. Two years after the foundation of the Lândana mission he was giving Latin lessons to a group of fifteen boys. On October 20, 1879, the minor seminary opened with fifteen students. Thirteen years later, on December 2, 1892, the first seminarian was ordained, Luís de Gourlet, the mestizo son of a Frenchman who worked in Lândana. He died two years later.

The Lândana mission also reached out to women of the area through the sisters of the Congregation of St. Joseph of Cluny, the first Catholic women missionaries to participate in planting the church in Angola. That congregation was founded in 1807 by Ana Maria Javouhey in France. She was a pioneer in the Catholic missionary expansion in the nineteenth century, beginning her work in Réunion and Guiana, followed by Senegal. In 1850 she was beatified.

One of the earliest and most distinguished sisters of St. Joseph in Angola was Mother Estanislau de Jesus Garnier, an Alsatian nun who arrived at the Lândana mission in 1890. There she worked for forty-five years with only one eight-month furlough.

It has been argued that one reason for the failure of the first attempt to plant the church in Angola in the fifteenth and sixteenth centuries was the absence of women missionaries. This is an argument that can never be proved, but it has certainly been true in both Catholic and Protestant missions that women have played a major role in planting the church during the nineteenth and twentieth centuries in Angola.

The second Catholic mission in the enclave of Cabinda was founded December 8, 1891, in the capital of the district by the Belgian Spiritan Father Emílio Callewaert. His first effort was to organize a boys' boarding school and teach the catechism. When the young men were judged to have learned enough so that they could go out and teach, each student was assigned to a village to which he went once or twice a week to teach the catechism. As they matured or after they married they established residence in the villages and continued teaching, still under the direction of the missionaries.

The sisters of St. Joseph of Cluny also accompanied the fathers and brothers of the Congregation of the Holy Ghost in establishing the mission in the city of Cabinda, arriving there in 1893.

Also in 1891 the Spiritans Frankoual and Paulus founded the third Catholic mission in the enclave of Cabinda at Lucula, three miles from the frontier with the Belgian Congo. In the planting stage the principal missionary at Lucula was Father Eugénio Bisch. As in all the Catholic missions the first effort was to build a boys' boarding school in order to prepare catechists. While Father Bisch was at Lucula the school had as many as 150 students. The directors of the mission considered closing it several times as five of the missionaries died in those early years, mostly from acute malaria.

Protestant Mission Societies

In this modern period of the history of the church the first Catholic missionaries were Spiritans who planted the church in Cabinda. The first Protestant missionaries in Angola arrived in São Salvador in 1878, having been sent by the Baptist Missionary Society (BMS) of London. The BMS is usually credited with being the first of the independent mission agencies to undertake the Protestant side of the expansion of Christianity in the Great Century.

Religious revival within Protestantism in the eighteenth and the early nineteenth centuries produced many organizations dedicated to spreading the gospel and planting the church. Just as France was the center of the greatest expansion of the Catholic church in the nineteenth century, so England organized the mission societies that made that country the main source of extension of Protestant Christianity around the world.

The first such organization was the Baptist Missionary Society of London, which was organized in 1792 at the inspiration of William Carey (1761–1834). Carey's father and grandfather had taught in village schools and were parish clerks in the English Midlands. William had a great liking for books of travel and developed a passion for geography and languages. Yet the family was in humble circumstances, and when Carey was fourteen, he was apprenticed to a shoemaker and cobbler. While an apprentice, through contact with dissenters, Carey "came into an earnest religious experience and a little later joined himself to the Baptists."[15] He earned a living by mending and making shoes and by preaching. The combination of his passion for geography and his warm religious conviction led to a growing concern for missions. He prepared *An Enquiry into the Obligations of Christians to Use Means for the Conversion of the Heathens,* in which he maintained that the New Testament command to "preach the gospel to every creature" was bind-

---

15. Latourette, *The History of the Expansion of Christianity,* 6:67.

ing not only upon the original apostles, but also upon Christians of the present time. He urged his fellow Baptist ministers to implement the plan he described and preached a sermon in May 1792 in that he used a phrase that his hearers were not to forget, "Expect great things from God. Attempt great things for God." As a result of the sermon and Carey's perseverance, a meeting was called at Kettering on October 2, 1792, and an organization was formed that later was called the Baptist Missionary Society.

In rapid succession two other missionary societies were formed by the evangelical movement in Great Britain: the London Missionary Society (LMS) in 1795 and the Church Missionary Society (CMS) in 1799. While these societies found their main support within denominational communities (BMS, Baptist; LMS, Congregational; CMS, Church of England), they were not organically related to denominational structures. Most of their support came from individuals or small groups who had a special commitment to the spread of the gospel and to planting the church in foreign lands. In addition to the regular small contributions given by supporters there were some donors who had both a deep commitment and substantial means.

One of these major donors challenged the BMS to enter Angola. Robert Arthington, an industrialist of Leeds, had given £5,000 each to the CMS and LMS to establish missions in East Africa. On May 14, 1877, Arthington wrote to the BMS Committee in London offering £1,000 if they would "undertake at once to visit these benighted, interesting people (in the Congo) with the blessed light of the gospel, teach them to read and write, and give them in imperishable letters the words of eternal truth. By and by, possibly we may be able to extend the mission eastwards on the Congo at a point above the rapids."[16]

In 1840, the BMS had sent missionaries to the island of Fernando Po in the Gulf of Guinea, about twenty miles off the Cameroon Coast, but the Spanish rulers soon forced the Protestant missionaries to leave. They then worked along the coast of Cameroon, but did not succeed in penetrating the interior. Therefore, when the BMS was challenged by Arthington to enter the Congo, it decided that George Grenfell and Thomas J. Comber, who were working in Cameroon, would be the best prepared to explore the new field of the Congo.

The BMS in São Salvador

In January 1878 Grenfell and Comber sailed on the SS *Elmira* for the Congo and spent a fortnight on the river before returning on the same

---

16. W. Holman Bentley, *Pioneering in the Congo* (London: Religious Tract Society, 1900), 1:59.

Dom Pedro V (Ntotela, Ntinu Nekongo), king of the Kongo.
Courtesy of the Baptist Missionary Society.

voyage to Cameroon. During this two-week period they went eighty-five miles up the river to Musuku (Nsuku) and from there they sent a letter to the king of the Kongo telling him that they would soon be visiting his capital.

Grenfell and Comber returned to the Congo in June 1878, and having brought a boat with them they made their way up the river with their small party: four men from Cameroon, two Kru men from West Africa, two small boys for personal service, and a good donkey, Jack. They finally arrived at the capital of the kingdom of the Kongo, São Salvador, on August 8, 1878, and were well received by the king, Dom Pedro, Ntotela, Ntinu Nekongo.

The vision that had inspired Arthington and the BMS was the Congo River as a great highway by which the heart of Africa could be reached with the gospel. Therefore, after only twenty days at São Salvador, Grenfell and Comber headed northeast toward the falls, seeking a passage to the upper river. Not finding a more suitable place for a base, however, they returned to São Salvador.

The king of the Kongo urged the missionaries to settle in his capital and they did make that their base. Comber wrote at the time:

> But it is not for its own sake so much that we wish to commence work at São Salvador...; it is chiefly as a base for inland operations, and we are most decidedly of opinion that it is the most suitable spot that could be found.[17]

Having thus decided on the base of the new mission, Grenfell and Comber made their way to the coast. The former returned to Victoria, Cameroon, and the latter went to England to report to the Baptist Missionary Society and to seek colleagues to help establish the mission.

Four new missionaries were recruited for the Congo mission: H. E. Crudgington, of Rawdon College, who had also studied medicine at the Leeds Infirmary; John S. Hartland; the Rev. W. Holman Bentley; and Miss Minnie Rickards, who married Thomas Comber.

The BMS Committee agreed that they should make São Salvador the base of operations and leave "no effort untried to reach as speedily as possible the Upper Congo river, near Stanley Pool, where, clear from all falls, cataracts, and rapids, the river is uninterruptedly navigable as far almost as Nyangwe, a distance of more than 1,200 miles."[18]

The party of Comber with his wife and three new colleagues stopped at Cameroon on the way to the Congo and were able to recruit an able helper, Misilina. He was born in Luanda, Angola, and had been taken from there as a slave to work on the plantations of São Tomé and Príncipe. There he married and managed somehow to escape to Cameroon in a canoe with his wife and two children. Misilina became an earnest Christian who had many qualities that made him a valuable worker in establishing the church in northern Angola. He spoke English and Portuguese as well as an African language similar to Kikongo; and he also knew something of stonemasonry and was generally handy.

---

17. Ibid., 84.
18. Ibid., 85.

Misilina, lay worker in the founding of the Protestant Mission of São Salvador (BMS).
Courtesy of the Baptist Missionary Society.

The party had to divide into two parts at Musuka, where they left the river to travel south to São Salvador since they could not arrange enough carriers to take the whole group and their freight. They arrived at their new base on July 25, 1879, but fevers plagued the party, and within a month the newly married Mrs. Comber succumbed to what the missionaries diagnosed as meningitis.

On the first several Sundays after reaching São Salvador the missionaries did not hold a public service, because they could not speak satisfactorily either Portuguese or Kikongo. They simply had their own service in English among themselves and the Cameroonians. On the fourth Sunday the king sent for the missionaries, and when they appeared he said:

> I do not understand the way in which you are behaving. You told me that you had come to teach me and my people about God, and yet you do not do so. You have been here four Sundays. You gather together on Sunday and read, and sing, and pray, but you never ask me or anyone else to join you; you never teach us. What sort of missionaries are you? You must teach us. This will not do at all.[19]

---

19. Ibid.,134.

The missionaries explained that they did not know enough Portuguese, much less Kikongo, and they intended to wait until they could speak Portuguese more fluently. This did not satisfy the king, because he noticed they were fluent enough to ask for carriers and conduct any urgent business they had. The king chided them and told them to at least try.

The next Saturday at sundown the royal drums were beaten and a herald announced that the morrow would be Sabbath so the people should not go to their farms and work, but should assemble in the king's compound as the missionaries were going to begin to teach. Sunday morning the drums were beaten again and a bugle was blown. When the king and crowd assembled, the missionaries and Cameroonians sang some English hymns. Misilina prayed in the best Kikongo he could muster. Then one of the missionaries told the story of the prodigal son in Portuguese, and Dom Garcia, the secretary of state, interpreted into Kikongo. The king repeated the greater part of the message and added further remarks of his own. He confessed that he could not do those things that were pleasing to God. The king begged the missionaries to hold regular services and also visit him frequently to teach him how to pray to God and become fit for heaven.

At the same time that Dom Pedro V was attending the Protestant services and requesting personal instruction from the Baptist missionaries, he wrote a letter to the governor-general of Angola and another to Father Antoine Carrie, the director of the Lândana mission, requesting that Catholic priests return to São Salvador to the "glorious Christianity of the ancient kingdom of the Congo."[20]

The BMS mission in São Salvador started with the encouragement of the king and found young people who were anxious to learn to read and write as steps to understanding the faith that motivated the missionaries, but it was still more than six years before the first convert was baptized.

Mantu had worked as a houseboy of Thomas Comber, who took him to England when Comber went home on his first furlough. While in England Mantu studied in a London school, and on his return to the Congo, having shown a real conversion, he was baptized on March 29, 1886, in the presence of a few friends.

Although Mantu had been baptized in 1886 the church in São Salvador dates its formation from December 4, 1887. On Friday, December 2, Thomas Lewis, after reading the story of Philip and the Ethiopian eunuch (Acts 8:26–39) and explaining the rite of scriptural baptism, baptized in the name of the Father, the Son, and Holy Spirit five converts: Nlekai, Luzemba, Kivitidi, Dom Álvaro Matoko, and Dom Miguel Nde-

---

20. Brásio, *Spiritana Monumenta Histórica*, 2:438–41.

langani, the last two being counselors of the king. The following Sunday the five converts and four missionaries took Communion together. The following comment by Lewis made some thirty years after the event explains the ecclesiastical orientation of the church that was planted in São Salvador:

> We did not impose any formal constitution upon this company of Christians. We were content to tell them that there was a New Testament which we had not yet translated (only a few portions were completed in 1887) and that it was to be the rule and guide of the Christian Church; and we left it at that, so that the native church might develop in its own way according to the African genius.[21]

W. H. Bentley also showed how the English Baptists had a commitment to the missionary principle of identification similar to that expressed by the French Catholic Father Libermann.

> In forming this new church we were careful to introduce as little as possible of what might be termed "European." We even had *kwanga* instead of our white man's bread at the Communion. Since then bread has become a part of the native food so we use it at the Lord's Table.... The term Baptist has never been used for we have always been known as the English Mission.[22]

Wavatidi

A week later, on December 11, 1887, seven other converts were baptized, including Wavatidi. Her story gives a personal dimension to planting the church. Wavatidi's mother, Cati Nkianienge, was involved in a serious dispute so she went to Dom Pedro V, king of the Kongo, to ask for protection and took her small daughter, Wavatidi, with her. The king granted his protection, but said that when Wavatidi became of age she was to become his wife. In the course of time, therefore, Wavatidi entered the royal compound to become one of the king's wives. He already had about a dozen others.

This happened shortly before the arrival of Grenfell and Comber. A few years later, when the BMS started work among the women of São Salvador, Wavatidi was one of the first (with other co-wives) to receive Christian instruction and was one of the earliest converts to be baptized.

The planting of the church produced conflict between the new and the old beliefs and practices. For example, on one occasion news came to São Salvador of a witchcraft ceremony in progress at a village only a mile or two away. Some of the Christians started off immediately in the hope

---

21. Thomas Lewis, *These Seventy Years* (London: Carey, 1930), 22.
22. Bentley, *Pioneering in the Congo*, 1:122.

of putting a stop to the proceedings. On arrival at the village they found the ceremony in full swing. A great crowd of practically naked people were dancing and gesticulating around the witch doctor who, although only scantily clad, was adorned with feathers and the red, white, and black markings of his trade.

The arrival of the Christians caused great consternation, and there was a slight pause as the people wondered what to do. Wavatidi seized her chance. She told the people that the good news of salvation had come to their land and asked them why they preferred to walk in darkness rather than in the light. As they pondered her words the witch doctor made his final bid for power. Quickly drawing a circle around himself and the little group of images he had with him, he defied anyone to enter the circle on pain of death.

Wavatidi did not hesitate. Not only did she step boldly into the circle, but stooping down, she picked up the images one by one and hurled them outside the magic ring. At that moment the missionaries arrived on the scene, but the battle had already been won, not by Christ's ambassadors from overseas, but by the very people who until so recently had been held in the bondage of superstition and fear.[23]

Nlemvo and Nekaka

Two Kikongo men, Nlemvo and Nekaka, made special contributions to planting the church among their people.

In 1880 the BMS missionary Holman Bentley was traveling to assist the king of the Kongo in ending a local war and passed through the village of Lemvo. The chief of the village, Dom Pedro Bidi, pleased by the white man, presented his son or nephew (records differ in this point), Ndundulu, to Bentley to be his "boy." The child, aged about twelve years, was dirty and ragged, but as Bentley needed someone to help him, he accepted him. Bentley thought that Ndundulu was not a "nice name," so he called him Lemvo after the town. It was only when Bentley acquired more of the Kikongo language that the prefix "N" was added which means "of," so the boy's name became Nlemvo, meaning "of Lemvo."

On April 30, 1882, when he was about fourteen years old, Nlemvo had a long talk with Bentley and then went away to meditate and to ask Jesus to be his Savior. He was not baptized, however, until six years later. Nlemvo did many things for Bentley, but his greatest contribution was in linguistics. He helped Bentley compile a Kikongo dictionary and compose a grammar. When Bentley went back to England in 1884 on his

---

23. Malvina J. Shields, *Congo Close-Ups* (London: Carey Kingsgate Press, 1960), 7–9.

Nlemvo, linguist and evangelist of the Baptist Church of São Salvador.
Courtesy of the Baptist Missionary Society.

first furlough, he took Nlemvo, then about sixteen years old, to complete the dictionary and grammar of the Kongo language for printing.

Having completed that basic linguistic task, Nlemvo worked with Bentley on translating the New Testament into Kikongo. The first book of Scripture printed was Mark's Gospel in 1888. The two men completed the New Testament in 1893, and it was published by the British and Foreign Bible Society. Bentley states in recognition of Nlemvo's contribution: "I cannot but regard him as raised up of God to help in this translation work."[24]

Nlemvo became an important evangelist and father figure of the Kikongo church, continuing his work even though he became blind. In 1905 he went to England to speak at the Baptist World Congress on "The Claim of Africa," drawing attention to the needs of Africa for the preaching of the gospel.

Nekaka was another man who played a significant role in planting the church among the Kikongo people. He was a Zombo from the Kibokolo district in the extreme north of Angola. As a youngster he was sold as a slave to another Zombo, who was one of the king's counselors in São Salvador. When passing the BMS school one day Nekaka decided to look inside while a reading lesson was in progress. The teacher was encouraging the pupils to give the correct response by offering a cookie to those who remembered the letters and how to spell their names. Tempted by this incentive Nekaka joined the class. His master made no objection to his attending school as long as his work was done properly. Nekaka became a Christian and was baptized on April 4, 1889. His contribution to planting the church in Angola was varied. As a stone mason he helped build the church and other mission buildings at São Salvador. He became an itinerant preacher, and after a few years of such work he was sent by the church as a teacher to the large town of Mbwela on the northern border of Angola where he built the first permanent church building outside São Salvador. His greatest contribution was the many hymns he composed or translated for the Kikongo hymnal.

The BMS maintained the goal of penetrating the Congo basin and did in fact establish more mission stations in Belgian territory than in Portuguese. Since we are limiting our study to the church in Angola, the various exploratory trips up the river made by BMS missionaries from São Salvador are not discussed here, but this activity may have detracted from the missionaries' efforts in Angola. At least that was the opinion of the commander of the Portuguese gunboat *Bengo*, who wrote, "These two missions [BMS and Livingstone Inland Mission] do everything except mission work; they are tireless travelers,

---

24. Bentley, *Pioneering on the Congo*, 1:447.

explorers, geographers... everything except missionaries."[25] The missionaries' peregrinations were noted also by the Angolans, who gave Comber the African nickname *Vianga-Vianga* (going-going).

The Catholic Mission of São Salvador

The Catholic hierarchy was aware that the Protestants settled in São Salvador in 1879, and the next year Bishop José Neto sent three secular priests — António José de Sousa Barroso, Sebastião José Pereira, and Joaquim da Anunciação Folga on the Portuguese gunboat *Bengo* to establish a permanent mission in the capital of the kingdom of the Kongo.

As the *Bengo* began to sail up the Congo River it stopped at Pinda, where Father Barroso disembarked and looked for the monument placed there by the first Portuguese explorer, Diogo Cão, in 1482. It had disappeared. Only a few ruins of the Capuchin monastery were to be found. The Catholic missionaries saw the ruins of the monastery and disappearance of the monument as an image of the spiritual situation of the Congo.[26]

Their arrival in São Salvador on February 13, 1881, was quite a contrast to that of the BMS missionaries in 1879. The Catholic missionaries traveled from Luanda to Noqui on the Portuguese gunboat accompanied by two military officers as ambassadors of the governor-general. They brought costly presents from the king of Portugal for the king of the Kongo, such as a piano, large silver tankards and cups, several kegs of rum, and large cases of gin. In contrast to the BMS missionaries who waited at the river to find carriers, the Catholic missionaries had 250 carriers sent to Noqui by Dom Pedro V to help them with their baggage.

Whereas the Baptist missionaries worked seven years before they baptized their first convert, the Catholic missionaries inherited the tradition that encouraged mass baptism of adults with little or no preparation. Father Barroso and his colleagues decided to require regular catechetical training before candidates were baptized, but the decision was difficult to enforce. The king complained to the bishop and demanded that the priests baptize all those who requested it, as had been done there traditionally.

A century earlier three missionary priests had made an excursion into the Kongo kingdom to try to revive the church that had been abandoned by the hierarchy. They performed two hundred thousand

---

25. Brásio, *Spiritana Monumenta Historica*, 2:544.
26. *Além-Mar: Revista dos Missionários Combonianos* 7–8 (July/August 1968): 18.

baptisms in four years from 1781 to 1785.[27] Taking into account the time required to walk throughout the region, it is obvious there would have been no time to prepare candidates for baptism.

Father Barroso, the superior of the São Salvador Catholic mission, was considered one of the most effective Portuguese missionaries. The missiologist António Silva Rego wrote that "Portugal owes its possession of the Congo to Padre Barroso."[28] He also impressed the people of the area with his honesty so that to establish the good faith of a commercial transaction they would "swear by the sacrament of Barroso."[29]

Planting the Church among the Kimbundu

To describe the planting of the church in Angola we could follow several orders: chronological, geographical, ethnolinguistic, or denominational. Each has its advantages, but it seems that at least during the period of planting, the ethnolinguistic order is the most significant. The ethnolinguistic approach also facilitates the localization of missions and churches on the map since during the nineteenth century and the first half of the twentieth each ethnolinguistic group was concentrated in a fairly defined region.

As we have seen, the church was planted among the Kongo peoples by both Catholic and Protestant missions by the end of the nineteenth century. As we noted in chapter 1 the Kongo region had the only centralized monarchy in Angola; therefore, the church had more contact with an African ruler than it had in other regions. Portuguese officials in the Kongo district were also particularly concerned about the political impact of the churches and missions since the Congo basin was the center of international friction.

We now move to the implantation of the church among the Kimbundu.

The Loge River divided the Kikongo to the north from the Kimbundu to the south. Luanda, which was to become the capital of all Angola, was the principal city in the Kimbundu area and the seat of the Catholic diocese of Angola and Congo. In Luanda the Catholic church never completely died out, but at its lowest point in 1853 it had only four priests in two parishes. The church had survived primarily in the Portuguese culture rather than among the Kimbundu even though the four priests in Luanda were Angolans.

---

27. Manuel Nunes Gabriel, *Angola: Cinco Séculos de Cristianismo* (Queluz: Literal, 1978), 138.

28. Silva Rego, *Curso de Missionologia*, 310.

29. *Além-Mar: Revista dos Missionários Combonianos* 7–8 (July–August 1968): 18.

The first Catholic missionaries to Luanda in this period were sent primarily to the Portuguese population. The Irmãs Franciscanas Hospitaleiras da Imaculada Conceição (the Franciscan Hospital Sisters of the Immaculate Conception) arrived in Luanda in 1883 with the specific pastoral responsibilities of assisting the patients at the military hospital and rehabilitating the Portuguese criminal exiles.

On January 28, 1887, two Holy Ghost fathers, Afonso Gauthier and José Foxel, arrived in Luanda to establish a residence for the congregation. They divided their time among chaplaincies at Maria Pia Hospital and São Miguel Fort occupied by 120 *deportados*, the asylum of Dom Pedro V, and a school that they had opened for forty pupils. Various missionaries were stationed in Luanda until the end of the century, but most remained for brief periods. Only Father Carlos Wunemburger worked in Luanda more than ten years.

From 1843 Portuguese traders resided in Malanje, 265 miles inland from Luanda, so Catholic missionaries made evangelistic visits there and a parish was organized. The Catholics of the area built a church dedicated to Our Lady of the Ascension, which was completed in 1890. After the expedition of Henrique de Carvalho into Muatianva (1884–88) and the exploration of Lunda the government in Lisbon proposed the founding of a mission in Malanje, which would be a base for the extension of Portuguese influence farther into the interior.

The Catholic mission of Malanje was established in 1890 and entrusted to the Congregation of the Holy Ghost. The first superior of the mission was Father Jorge Kraft (1890–98), having as colleagues Father Ferchaud and Brothers Adriano Macieira and Paul. Father Kraft was also named parish priest of Malanje. Father Vitor Wendling, a notable linguist, published a Kimbundo-Portuguese dictionary four years after he arrived in Malanje. The sisters of St. Joseph of Cluny, who had worked with the Holy Ghost Fathers in Cabinda, also collaborated, completing a decade of planting in Lândana (1883), Moçâmedes (1885), Huila (1887), Lubango (1888), Caconda (1892), Luali (1892), and Malanje (1893).

The Methodist Mission

The first effort by Protestants to plant the church among Kimbundu was made in 1885 by a group of Methodists under the leadership of the Rev. William Taylor, a colorful and creative Methodist minister who had served as a home missionary in California (1848–56) and later founded churches in India, Costa Rica, Peru, Brazil, and Chile. Aside from his commitment to holiness and his zeal for the spread of the gospel, Taylor is best known for his conviction that missionaries should be self-supporting.

William Taylor offered his services to the mission board of the Methodist Episcopal Church in the United States on condition that he could recruit his own personnel and be free from control of the board. According to Taylor's proposal the board would pay only the passages of the missionaries to the countries where they would work and an initial amount calculated to support the missionary and family for a short period until they could arrange a means of support. The board refused his proposal so Taylor established his independent Transit Fund in order to collect private funds to pay the passage of missionaries to foreign fields. He then realized that subsidies would still be needed to construct or rent buildings for missionary activities, so the complete name of his organization became the Transit and Building Fund Society of Bishop William Taylor's Self-Supporting Missions.

In 1884 the General Conference of the Methodist Episcopal Church meeting in Philadelphia elected William Taylor as bishop of Africa with the twofold responsibility of administering the organized Methodist work in Liberia for the Missionary Society and founding other missions any place in Africa following his self-supporting plan. Like other mission leaders Taylor had a vision of a series of mission stations stretching across the continent, and he decided to begin on the west coast.

For this venture Taylor recruited people who could support themselves: businessmen, doctors, teachers, mechanics, artisans, farmers, evangelists, and pastors. Forty-five Americans — twenty-nine adults and sixteen children — set sail from New York for Luanda in January 1885. All were Methodists with the exception of two Quakers.[30] Taylor reported that when they arrived at Luanda on March 20, 1885, they were kindly received by the governor-general of the province. However a few weeks later the governor wrote to the government in Lisbon a less than complimentary comment:

> A collection of fifty some Americans presided over by a Methodist Bishop Taylor arrived here. Their poor, miserable appearance makes it seem that they are composed of fanatics with an exaggerated religious spirit with their sick minds influenced by the most extravagant doctrines. They think that they can live here without help, maintaining themselves on the basis of "self- supporting missions," which will produce in practice — as I see it — complete disappointment. Beside the religious missionaries, strictly speaking, they brought musicians . . . mechanics . . . women and children, one being trained in medicine according to the homeopathic school.[31]

---

30. Emílio J. M. de Carvalho, *Ouço os Passos de Milhares* (São Paulo, Brazil: S. Bernardo do Campo Imprensa Metodista, 1978), 51.

31. Ibid., 54–55.

On their first Sunday in Luanda this band of missionaries, who were considered heroic pioneers by their supporters and poor miserable fanatics by others, organized the first Methodist church in Angola. This church was formed entirely of the foreign missionaries, since there had been no time to receive Angolans into the Methodist communion.

We have now seen three methods of church planting. The Catholic church considered the church replanted in São Salvador in 1881 when priests under the authority of the bishop were permanently stationed there. The Protestant church in São Salvador was planted on Sunday, December 4, 1887, when the first group of Angolan converts, who had been baptized on the previous Friday, sat down at the Lord's Table and were received into Christian fellowship. The Methodist church was planted when this group of American Christians, lay and clergy, gathered for worship for the first time in Angola.

While the BMS envisioned reaching the interior of Africa up the Congo River, Bishop Taylor dreamed of a line of missions south of the Congo basin running across the continent. He did not delay in starting to realize this dream. Two months after the party had arrived in Luanda Bishop Taylor sent a few men to explore for sites for the first mission stations. Although he had not included Dondo, at the head of steamboat navigation on the Kwanza River, in his plans because of its unhealthy climate, he was prevailed upon by the local Portuguese officials and businessmen to establish the first inland mission there. The missionaries in Dondo attempted to support themselves with a mechanic shop and a printing press. They attracted many to their religious meetings by using an organ — the first one to be heard there. Dondo's reputation for a morbid climate was proven accurate by the deaths of Dr. Mary M. Davenport on July 18, 1887, and later of Mary Estella Withey, daughter of the Rev. Amos Withey.

The Methodist missionaries' next stop on their inland trek was at Nhangue-a-Pepe, fifty miles from Dondo. Here the plan was to establish a tanning factory and trading house to support the missionaries. Karl Rudolph, the director of the mission, cultivated a plot of land with a McCormick plow and two yokes of oxen. The mission also started a primary school for the local children, who brought corn to pay their fees.

The third station in the line was at Pungo-Andongo about forty miles from Nhangue-a-Pepe. The rocks of Pungo-Andongo were so famous that David Livingstone on his transcontinental journey east from Luanda in 1854 made a detour south to visit them and to inspect the people's vegetable gardens, of which he had heard glowing accounts. Here the Methodist missionaries decided to start an industrial school as their means of support.

Under Bishop Taylor's dynamic leadership the missionaries pressed on another sixty miles to Malanje, where on September 14, 1885, the bishop formally organized the Methodist Episcopal Church with the Rev. Levin Johnson as its pastor, but again without Angolan members. Bishop Taylor left Malanje on September 16 and on September 23, 1885, he held the first district conference of the Methodist church in Nhange-a-Pepe.

The Methodist church in Angola was first organized by the missionary group in 1885 without any Angolan members, but Bishop Emílio de Carvalho, who has written several works on the history of that church, has registered the names of two Angolans who were converted in 1885: Bernardo Manuel Agostinho and his wife, Luzia Bernardo, of Malanje. He was a sawyer by profession, but after his conversion he taught near Malanje in Kimbamba kia Ngola. In 1895 the couple was nominated to work on an agricultural project in the Malanje circuit, and four years later they taught catechism and Bible in Pungu Andongo.

Bernardo M. Agostinho and Luzia Bernardo, when converted, had domestic slaves and they kept them until 1902, when Bishop Joseph Crane Hartzell wrote them insisting that they free themselves of this practice. Bernardo responded to the bishop:

> We accepted Christ in 1885, in the time of Bishop Taylor, and in this era of Bishop Joseph C. Hartzell we free ourselves of the vestiges of that spirit which still persisted in us to buy and sell slaves. . . . We wish to continue in the religion of Christ until we die.[32]

However, he did not actually continue his active Christian witness until he died, for in 1907 he was elected chief of Bango. The minutes of the West Africa Central Conference that year recorded that "his work as a preacher came to an end."

Bishop Taylor's Method

The whirlwind tour of Bishop Taylor's pioneers, establishing five mission stations in six months, was certainly the most frenetic church planting to take place in Angola, and serious questions have been raised about his methods. Is it possible to plant the church in Angola without a working knowledge of Portuguese and the regional African language? Is the self-supporting method feasible in the African economy? Were Bishop Taylor's missions actually self-supporting?

The first question regarding the languages could be answered easily in the negative, but the exception proves the rule. Among the pioneer missionaries of Bishop Taylor was the brilliant Swiss linguist, Heli Chatelain. He found in Malanje a young man, Jeremias, popularly known as

---

32. Emílio J. M. de Carvalho, *Heróis Angolanos do Metodismo* (Luanda: Igreja Metodista Unida em Angola, 1982), 11–12.

William Taylor, Bishop of the Methodist Episcopal Church in Angola (1885–96)

Jelemia dia Sabatelu (meaning Jeremias, the son of the cobbler), an apt teacher to instruct him in the Kimbundu language. Chatelain wrote: "I have a Kimbundu lesson with my shoemaker, Jeremias, and the next day I teach my students the first song in Kimbundu."[33]

Jeremias was so indispensable to Chatelain that in 1890 the two went together to the United States to continue their literary work in Kimbundu. Jeremias Álvares da Costa, as he was known in Portuguese, made such a significant contribution to the science of linguistics that he was honored by a statue that still stands in the Smithsonian Institution in Washington, D.C.

Under the tutelage of his Angolan teacher, within two years Heli Chatelain was able to publish a Kimbundu grammar and translate the Gospel of John.

The self-supporting method was judged by most observers and many participants to have been a failure. Ross Taylor, the bishop's son who came with the first party in 1885, was soon disillusioned and left Angola. Joseph Wilkes of Pungo-Andongo lamented that he had to repair whiskey distilleries, false scales, and billiard tables. James Duffy, a historian of Portuguese Africa, comments: "Self-supporting missions,

---

33. Alida Chatelain, *Heli Chatelain — l'Ami de l'Angola* (Lausanne: Secretariat de la Mission Philafricaine, 1918), 109–10.

though ardently championed by Taylor for their economic opportunities, were folly in Angola — as they were along most of the coast. They
made a little money but few converts, since the major exertions of the
missionaries went in to lumber mills and farms."[34]

The final question, whether Bishop Taylor's missions were actually
self-supporting, must also be given a negative answer. Bishop Taylor
spent a considerable part of his unbounded energy raising money for
his self-supporting missions.

By the time Bishop Taylor retired in 1896 his missions were ready
to abandon the self-support system and the Methodist Society in the
United States was prepared to assume financial and administrative
responsibility for the Methodist work in Angola.

Bishop Hartzell, who inherited the episcopal authority from Bishop
Taylor, abandoned the Dondo and Nhangue-a-Pepe stations. He found
scattered among the five remaining stations thirty-six church members, hardly more than double the number of missionaries. However
Rev. A. E. Withey, the presiding elder of the church under Bishop Taylor,
adopted Livingstone's view that the pioneer missionary's criterion of
success should not be "the conversion of a few souls, however valuable
these may be," but the diffusion of a general knowledge of Christianity
throughout the world.[35]

Planting the Church among the Umbundu

We have briefly sketched the planting and replanting of the church
among the Kikongo and the Kimbundu. We now move south to observe the planting of the church among the Umbundu, the largest
ethnolinguistic group in Angola.

In the last quarter of the nineteenth century the Catholic church
existed among the small concentrations of Portuguese population in
central Angola such as in Benguela, Bailundo, and Caconda, but Protestant missions were the first to reach the Umbundu people.

American Board of Commissioners for Foreign Missions

In 1806 students at Williams College in Massachusetts who held regular
prayer meetings became convinced that God was calling them to obey
the Lord's command to "go into all the world and preach the gospel to
the whole creation" (Mark 16:15). They persuaded the Congregational

---

34. James Duffy, *Portuguese Africa* (Cambridge, Mass.: Harvard Univ. Press, 1959), 125.

35. J. Tremayne Copplestone, *Twentieth Century Perspectives: The Methodist Episcopal Church 1896–1939, The Board of Global Ministries* (New York: United Methodist Church, 1973), 572.

churches of Massachusetts and Connecticut to form the American Board of Commissioners for Foreign Missions (ABCFM) in 1810, the first foreign mission society in North America. Two years later the ABCFM sent its first missionaries overseas — to India. It opened its first mission in Africa in 1836 in South Africa.

The BMS had had a mission in the Cameroons and the Methodists a mission in Liberia, from which they moved to establish missions in Angola among the Kikongo and the Kimbundu. The American Board had maintained a mission among the Zulus in South Africa, which led indirectly to the establishment of the mission among the Umbundu in Central Angola.

A retired British army officer, Major Malan, who worked as an evangelist in South Africa, was impressed by the American Board mission in Natal. In January 1878 he journeyed from England to the United States at his own expense specifically to lay a proposition before the Prudential Committee of the ABCFM: "It cannot be disputed that the field occupied by your mission in Natal is the best base of operations in Southern Africa for a mission to the interior."[36]

The board then set up a special fund for a Central Africa mission, but there were two problems to be solved before the Angola mission could be initiated. Additional funds would be necessary, and the actual location in Central Africa had to be decided.

Donations did arrive from friends, but it was a time of recession in the United States and finances were tight, until Robert Arthington of Leeds, who had challenged the BMS to go to the Congo, gave £1,000 to the ABCFM for this venture. Then, when the American Board received a legacy of one million dollars from the estate of Asa Otis of New London, Connecticut, the financial problem was solved.

The board asked its recording secretary, Dr. John O. Means, to present a report evaluating eight possible fields in Central Africa. He recommended not the East African entrance suggested by Major Malan, but a new field, the region of "Bihe and the Coanza." Dr. Means presented three arguments for his choice:

1. This area is not yet open to commerce. When the gospel has to follow trade, it has to face a double foe: not only the devils of paganism, which are bad enough, but the worse devils of an unprincipled and corrupt civilization.

2. This area, from which came many slaves, has a peculiar claim on American Christians because we supported slavery.

---

36. *Missionary Herald* (Boston, ABCFM) 74, April 1878.

3. Bihe and the Coanza is easily and cheaply accessible and healthful. Its compactness and permanency of the people and its relations to other tribes of the interior also make it a peculiarly inviting field.[37]

The board accepted the recommendation of Dr. Means and approved the establishment of the West Central Africa Mission in October 1879. One year later, October 5, 1880, the first three missionaries sailed from Lisbon on a royal mail steamer that left the fifth of each month, and after thirty-nine days, on November 13, arrived at Benguela, the port-of-entry for Bié.

The leader of this pioneer expedition, the Rev. William W. Bagster, was thirty-two years old, a grandson of Samuel Bagster, publisher of the Polyglot Bible in London. The Rev. William Henry Sanders, the second member of the party, was born in Ceylon in 1856 of missionary parents. The third, and first black missionary to Angola, Mr. Samuel Taylor Miller, was a teacher born in Virginia. His father and mother were slaves, and as soon as freedom came he entered school, completing his course at Hampton Institute.

The three men spent from November 13, 1880, to March 9, 1881, arranging a caravan in Benguela to take them up the steep escarpment leading to the mile-high plateau and on to Bié about three hundred miles from the coast. Travel was slow and tedious. Bagster rode an ox. Sanders and Miller started in *tipóias* (hammocks), but walked most of the way. Seven donkeys were in the caravan, but most of the baggage was carried by sixty men — each carrying sixty pounds. Including camp-followers, the caravan totalled ninety-five persons.

The Bailundo Mission

After twenty days they arrived at Bailundo, one of the Umbundu kingdoms, about eighty miles west of Bié. King Ekwikwi II of Bailundo received the missionaries cordially. However, the king of Bié was so eager for the missionaries to reach his capital that he sent his "secretary of state" to offer his hospitality.[38]

On July 29, 1881, the party left Bailundo for Bié, but because of the rivalry between the two kingdoms the king of Bailundo forced them to return to his village. The goal of the mission, as decided by the board in Boston was "Bihe and the Coanze," but the missionaries concluded that Bailundo would have to be more than a campsite on the way to Bié. Miller began building a school house and gathered a few pupils.

37. ABCFM, *Annual Report*, October 7, 1879. Bihe, which in Umbundu is Viye, or in Portuguese Bié, was one of the main kingdoms of the Umbundu group. Coanza (Kwanza) is a major river of Angola with its source in Bié and its mouth a few miles south of Luanda.
38. ABCFM, *Annual Report*, 1881, 26.

Sanders concentrated on mastering the Umbundu language and reducing it to writing, which was a necessary step for preaching the Gospel and planting the church among the Umbundu of Central Angola.

Since Sanders was making most progress with the language, he was chosen to explain to King Ekwikwi II the purpose of the mission. He had to wait considerable time for an audience since the king was preparing for war and did not have time for this thin, twenty-five-year-old white man. Finally King Ekwikwi sent for Sanders and asked him why they had come to his kingdom. The missionary replied that he and his colleagues had come to tell the king and his people about God. The king nodded for him to proceed and Sanders launched forth to prove to the king the existence of God and to go through the Ten Commandments that God had given to humankind. But suddenly Ekwikwi shouted, "Stop! If that is all you've come to tell us, you can go home because we know that already!" Recounting this interview to colleagues later Sanders said, "From then on like Paul, I knew only Jesus Christ and his Cross."[39]

So from the beginning the Bailundo missionaries recognized that the Umbundu already knew the creator God, *Suku*. Their task then was to tell the story of God's Son, Jesus Christ.

Bentley of the BMS made a similar point. "We are ... able to tell the people that we have not come to declare to them the God of the white man, but their own *Nzambi ampungu*, God, most high."[40]

Before becoming well established, the Bailundo station suffered two sharp blows. First, Bagster, the leader of the mission, died on February 22, 1882, less than a year after his arrival. Second, in 1884, on orders of King Ekwikwi the missionaries were expelled from Bailundo. The expulsion did not last long, primarily because of the intervention of a missionary of another Protestant community, the Plymouth Brethren. Frederick Stanley Arnot had spent three years in Central Africa and although only twenty-three years old when he sailed for South Africa, in 1881, he had learned much from his dealing with African chiefs and European traders. When he heard that the missionaries had been expelled from Bailundo, he hastened from Bié, where he was the guest of the Portuguese trader, Silva Porto, to speak to King Ekwikwi and to Braga, the Portuguese trader who had instigated the king to expel the missionaries. The young Scot's effectiveness is shown by the letter that King Ekwikwi dictated:

> To Mr. Sanders and Party, Missionaries: I wish you to return with all my heart. I have acted very badly to you and those with you. I have been as one turned, having received you as my friends and

39. Correspondence with Jean Collins, United Church of Canada missionary.
40. Bentley, *Pioneers in the Congo*, 1:248.

children, and then to turn you away as my enemies. Braga persuaded me in a way I could not resist. He told me, in short that to harbor those "English" was to be at war with the Portuguese; that you were people to be killed. I hear that you are now bound for Bihe. I will not stop you, as I did when you first came here three years ago. The whole country is before you: only return and be friendly with me. I will do my utmost to restore your things. I have eight bales of cloth, also tools, books, etc. belonging to you and your company. All shall be returned. My people are all crying. We are ashamed. Come back! Do not allow our name to stink everywhere because of Braga's deception.[41]

In a few months the missionaries returned to Bailundo and resumed their work. In 1886 Wesley M. Stover, who had arrived in 1882, reported, "I think the day is not far distant when I shall want to establish a class for catechumens, or in modern phrase an enquirers' class, to be instructed in the essentials of the Christian doctrine with a view to baptism and church membership."[42]

One year later in May 1887 fourteen candidates were baptized in the name of the Triune God and were formed into a Christian church by public profession of their faith and the adoption of a covenant of mutual love and devotion. Earlier we noted the BMS affirmation of the independence of the church from mission domination when the first congregation was formed in São Salvador, also in 1887. Stover's missionary policy was strikingly similar:

My purpose is to impress them with the idea that upon them now devolves the responsibility of Christ's work in Bailundu, that we are here only to guide and oversee. I do not deem myself the pastor of this church, nor do I allow them to regard me as such; I seek to impress it upon them that I am their elder brother — bishop, if that word is allowable — and that they are to have a pastor of their own number in due time.[43]

The Annual Report of the ABCFM for that year concludes: "Thus the Church of Christ in West Africa has become visible, and the work of the mission enjoys this precious seal of God's blessing upon it."[44]

In 1884 the ABCFM succeeded in founding a mission at Camundongo in Bié, which was its original goal when it sent its first missionaries to Angola in 1880.

---

41. *Missionary Review* 8 (May 1885): 220.
42. ABCFM, *Annual Report*, 1886, 27.
43. ABCFM, *Annual Report*, 1887, 63.
44. Ibid.

A third station was established by the ABCFM before the end of the century when the Rev. T. W. Woodside opened Sakanjimba in Bié, which was subsequently moved to Chilesso in Andulo in 1892.

The Congregational Foreign
Missionary Society of British North America

The second missionary agency to labor at planting the church among the Umbundu was the Congregational Foreign Missionary Society of British North America. It was organized in 1881 in Toronto, and for the first few years its work consisted chiefly of collecting money for other missionary societies. Later an arrangement was completed with the ABCFM for the Canadian Society to work through it, sending out missionaries under its auspices; it was agreed that the Canadian society should begin with one station in West Central Africa and become responsible for its work there.

The Canadian society appointed its first missionary, the Rev. Walter T. Currie, in 1885 when he had just been graduated from the Congregational College in Montreal. Currie spent the following months visiting churches in Canada to share his enthusiasm for the mission in West Central Africa, and to elicit support for the missionary society. On March 11, 1886, Walter Currie married Clara Wilkes of Brantford, Ontario, and the next month they set sail from Boston in company with Mr. and Mrs. W. E. Fay, who were ABCFM missionaries returning to Angola.

When the Curries and Fays landed at Benguela on June 4, 1886, Mrs. Currie was already ailing. She was carried up country in a prostrate condition to Bailundo, where she died on September 24, 1886.

Mr. Currie remained at Bailundo until he had mastered the rudiments of the Umbundu language and then, with a group of African helpers, he headed inland to select a site for the Canadian mission. Among the helpers was one young man who was to play a key role in the planting and growth of the church in Angola. His name was Ngulu.

Ngulu means "pig." Parents frequently gave offensive names to their children to protect them from hostile spirits who might consume their souls. Hostile spirits were the explanation given by the Umbundu for the fact that a majority of their children died in infancy. *Otulupokopoko*, or spirits of departed babies, were a particular threat to living babies, so parents tried to trick the spirits by giving the children the name of such a despised animal as a pig. Ngulu's older brothers and sisters had died in infancy so his parents decided to give their youngest son the name Ngulu to confuse the *otulupokopoko*.

Ngulu became Currie's strong right hand in constructing the new mission of Chissamba, in preaching the Gospel, and in witnessing in everyday life to what it means to be a Christian. His role as a hero of the faith in Angola will be more fully described in the next chapter on the growth of the church.

The presence of a lone white man roused many questions on the part of the Angolans living around Chissamba. Why is he here? What does he want? If we approach him, will he bewitch us? The people avoided the missionary for some time until in the nearby head-village, or *ombala*, of Chissamba an elder named Sanembelo decided to entrust his two sons, Kumba and Lumbo, to Currie. One of them, Kumba, delighted to relate the story of his first night spent in the hut of the missionary:

"I slept with one eye open and both ears," he relates. "I wasn't sure of the white man. Father bade me go. I obeyed. But my uncle said to me as I left our home village, "White men eat boys." I trembled. Morning light came. I was uneaten. The dawn was gladsome."[45]

Kumba became an orator among the church elders and evangelists.

A report from Mr. Fay, dated February 23, 1889, gives a picture of the young men among whom the church was being planted:

Kasoma, about 18 years old who worked for the Fays 1886–89, can read and write pretty well, but does not fully realize the relation between his [Christian] profession and his life.

Lumbo, about 18 is of average ability and plodding persistence. He reads and writes, but does best of all in arithmetic. [He became one of the great Umbundu preachers.]

Casinge, about 18 is the best reader and takes part in prayer.

Kafumbe, about 8 years old works in the house. A handier fellow could not be found. He reads and writes a little, but is not yet a professed Christian.

Cisipa is about 14 and steady.

Kandundu, 8 years old, is the brother of Cisipa and of average ability, but lazy.

Kopume, about 13 years old is small for his age and a slow learner.

Elundula, 20 or 21 years old learns rapidly, "the bull dog." He only needs the spirit of God to make him a sturdy Christian.

Kamundongo is 11 years old — smart and lazy.

Savihemba makes better prayers than some of the older boys and gives good evidence of a change of heart.

Sakawila is open hearted and willing.

Kanjila has only been with us a month.[46]

This list of thirteen young men on one mission station gives a profile of the kind of Angolans who were attracted to work with the missionar-

---

45. John T. Tucker, *Drums in the Darkness* (New York: George H. Doran, 1927), 82.
46. ABC (ABCFM archives, Houghton Library, Harvard University) 15.1, vol. 6, no. 206.

ies and among whom the church was first planted. Mr. Fay's comments reveal a peculiarly Protestant evaluation of the young men. Three characteristics appear essential for a young Christian: the ability to read so they could use the Scriptures, which were being translated and were considered the authority to guide individual faith and to form and inspire the church; a change of heart or conversion; and participation in voluntary prayer, which was evidence of personal piety and the priesthood of all believers.

Soon young women were attracted to the missions also, and Sarah Bell wrote from Kamundongo two years after Mr. Fay:

> We were counting over the other day how many have begun to pray within the last year: ten girls from Mrs. Sanders' school, three women from the village, and seven from among the boys on the place. Most of these have started in the Christian life within the last month or so.[47]

The Kamundongo church was organized in August 1890 with eight members: Cinyumba, Kasoma, Kakenge, Elandula, Sakanana, Cisapa, Lumbo, and Charlie. Mrs. Minnie Sanders, reporting the event to friends in the United States, added:

> Kamundongo and Cisunge of the boys and girls Lohema, Kasamua, and Duva were requested to wait. We all think them worthy of baptism, but those from Bailundo thought the boys were pretty young, and that best for all five of them to be better tested. The spirit in which they all bore the disappointment was good evidence of their sincerity.... Do pray for all these young people; that the Light may never grow dim here, but shine ever more and more until that perfect day, when this whole land shall know the Lord.[48]

At first, as each church was formed it was the ABCFM missionaries who admitted the new members, but soon thereafter the members themselves examined candidates for baptism and decided who should be received.

Another common practice showing that the church belonged to the people, or at least was entrusted to them as stewards, was self-support. The General Report of the Bailundo station for the year ending May 1890 observed:

> During the three years of its existence the church in Bailundo has received not a penny of mission money, and aside from the gift of a bell and of a Communion service, nothing from outside sources . . .

---

47. ABC 15.1, vol. 10, no. 8.
48. Letters of Minnie J. Sanders, vol. 2, 1887–91, 218.

regular contributions have been made each year to work abroad amounting this year to $6.35.[49]

Three years later the Protestant church in São Salvador, which was also self-supporting, decided to send its special missionary collection to work in China.[50]

Christian Missions in Many Lands (CMML)

A third Protestant group participated in planting the church among the Umbundu people of central Angola. It is difficult to determine the proper name to use for this community, because they resist adopting any designation that might imply that they are a denomination. To outsiders they are known most commonly as Plymouth Brethren.

The members of this movement are also known as Darbyites, from John Nelson Darby, who was born in 1800 and became a curate of the Church of England in Ireland. In 1827 he wrote a tract, *The Nature and Unity of the Church of Christ*. According to Darby, the established church in Great Britain was cold and corrupt, needing revival and purification. As most reformers, Darby started his agitation within the church in which he was nurtured and did not intend to separate from it. However, he did finally leave the Church of England and became one of the recognized leaders of a new movement of evangelical Christians.

Missionaries sent from this very evangelical, though small community to other countries needed an incorporated body to identify them when governments required legal identification. Therefore Brethren in North America formed an agency known as the Christian Missions in Many Lands, Inc., for such official purposes. The Brethren are quick however, to explain that this is not a "mission board" and has no authority over missionaries or the institutions or assemblies that result from their work. We have already mentioned Frederick Stanley Arnot, the Plymouth Brethren pioneer who was instrumental in opening the door of the Bailundo mission after it had been closed by King Ekwikwi II. After seven years in Africa Arnot returned to England and recruited several more Brethren to work in Central Africa. They arrived in Benguela in 1889. As the American Board missionaries were aiming for Bié but founded their first mission in Bailundo, so the Brethren were looking toward Garenganze, later called Katanga and now Shaba, but they established their first mission station in Bié. Arnot was a friend of Silva Porto, a Portuguese trader who also represented the Portuguese government and indicated the site for a mission at

---

49. ABC 15.1, vol. 9, no. 1.
50. BMS Church Minute Book, no. 1, December 25, 1893.

Kuanjululu, a short distance from the *ombala*, or African capital, of Bié. This was considered a way-station to serve missions to be established later in the interior. However, the missionaries Charles Albert Swan and Frederick Thomas Lane began to perform the traditional functions of a mission — preaching, teaching, and healing. Thus they planted the church with its particular Brethren style among the Umbundu. In 1894 the mission was moved from Kuanjululu to Chilonda. In the same year a second "Brethren" station, Hualondo, was founded in Bié by George Richard Murrain and his wife, Elizabeth, with their four children — a black family from Jamaica. The first Angolan believers who became leaders of the new Christian community, or "assembly" as the Brethren called it, were Ricardo Hama, António Amélio, Silva Canguende, Sabino Cossengue, Raimundo Silivondela, and Alberto Sanjimba.

Philafrican Mission

The fourth Protestant mission agency that came to plant the church among the Umbundu was an offshoot from Bishop Taylor's mission in Luanda.

Heli Chatelain, the linguist with the Taylor mission, resigned from that organization and formed a new missionary society in his adopted country, the United States of America, in 1897. The society's goal of aiding freed slaves in Angola was embodied in the title, Philafrican Liberators' League. Chatelain still accepted the self-supporting principle of Bishop Taylor, and his first recruits were an agriculturalist and a carpenter with their wives and a single doctor. They founded a mission station among the Umbundu in the Kalukembe area and called it "Lincoln," after Abraham Lincoln. Four years later Chatelain cut his ties with the American supporters and founded a Swiss-based agency called Mission Philafricaine en Angola. Some small subsidies were sent first from America and later from Switzerland, but the missionaries were primarily dependent on their own labor for their maintenance.

The first five catechumens were baptized in Kalukembe in 1912 after fifteen arduous years.

Four Protestant missionary societies planted the church among the Umbundu in the last quarter of the nineteenth century: American Board of Commissioners for Foreign Missions, Congregational Foreign Missionary Society of British North America, Plymouth Brethren, and Mission Philafricaine en Angola.

Catholic Missions among the Umbundu

Catholic missions were slow in entering the most populous section of Angola even though the government requested the Catholic church to establish missions in Bailundo and Bié.[51] The Catholic hierarchy complained that the government was not prepared to provide funds, which would have been necessary for such initiatives.

A rather weak effort was made in 1884 when two Portuguese secular priests who had just arrived from Lisbon were appointed missionaries, and the next year they were sent to Bié. However the location of the mission was twice changed at the order of the government and finally the two priests were separated — one staying in Bié and the other being sent to Bailundo according to orders of the civilian authority, without any intervention by the diocese.

They opened schools and went about their ministry, but the two young missionaries were not able to organize their missions properly without help from the diocese. The bishop had appointed the personnel requested by the government, but then depended upon the civil authorities to assume responsibility for the missions.

The Bié mission continued until the end of 1890, and the Bailundo mission closed in December 1889. The closing of the Catholic mission of Bailundo was under strange circumstances. The bishop of Angola and Congo, Dom António, wrote on January 30, 1890, to Father Ernest Lecomte:

> The people of Bailundo destroyed the Portuguese mission, the chapel and the school, robbed them, forced the missionary to flee to Bié; then the people joined up with the Protestant mission. The African chief told the military commander that this had happened because of the bad behavior of Father Bernard.[52]

The bishop added that he suspected that the Protestant mission was behind the people's action since the people went over immediately to the Protestants. So the bishop asked Father Lecomte to investigate the matter, and he replied from Caconda that it was impossible for him to travel to Bailundo at that time because of the rains and lack of carriers. He also stated that it was a question for the civil authorities to resolve.[53]

The first successful attempts at a "true Catholic missionary occupation" of Bié began in 1890. The Catholic church felt the urgency to move into Bié because three Protestant missions, Camundongo, Chissamba, and Chilonda, were "exercising great influence" in the district.[54]

---

51. Gabriel, *Angola: Cinco Séculos de Cristianismo*, 288–89.
52. Brásio, *Spiritana Monumenta Histórica*, 6:7–8.
53. Ibid., 9–10.
54. Ferreira da Costa, *Cem Anos dos Missionários do Espírito Santo em Angola*, 296.

Three Portuguese military explorers — Artur de Paiva, Paiva Couceiro, and Teixeira da Silva — imprisoned the Biéan king, Dunduma, in the Camundongo mission, which the Catholic missionaries took as a signal of the "pacification" of Bié. They concluded that the door was then open to plant the church in that region.

Father Lecomte left Caconda to look for a suitable site for a Catholic mission in Bié. At first he had in view Sacassenhe, which was nine miles from the *ombala* of Ecovongo on the Cuquema River. However, that area was too much under the influence of the Protestant mission of Camundongo, so Lecomte decided to establish the mission at Cachingues, sixty miles south at the border between the Umbundu and Ganguela peoples.

It was in this mission that Father Lecomte died of black water fever on September 9, 1908, at the age of forty-six. During his twenty-three years of service in Angola he was apostolic prefect of Cimbebasia and played key roles in founding the mission stations of Catoco, Caconda, Cachingues, Matadiva, and Bailundo. With his administrative responsibilities of the Cimbebasia prefecturate Father Lecomte was almost always traveling, usually by oxen. However, this time was not lost as he used it to write catechisms and lessons to teach Portuguese as well as to write a life of Jesus in Ganguela and to translate the Old Testament in the same language.

During this time in which the Catholic missions were being frustrated in Bailundo and Bié, Caconda became the first successful planting of the Catholic church among the Umbundu.

Father Folga had been serving the Portuguese parish of Caconda since 1882, but in 1889 Father Ernesto Lecomte arrived and began a serious effort to reach into Angolan culture. Lecomte established a printing press and produced readers, catechisms, hymnals, and prayer books in the Umbundu, Ganguela, and Kwanyama languages, which he had mastered. After ten years of teaching catechism the Caconda mission baptized the first adults and founded the first rural school in 1900. In 1895 Caconda had three priests and five lay brothers and was teaching ninety-five boys, of whom twenty were learning the arts of carpentry, metalwork, woodwork, and masonry. Four nuns of St. Joseph of Cluny were teaching eighty-nine girls.

The bishop of Angola and Congo wrote to the Portuguese overseas minister on June 10, 1895, pleading for a larger subsidy for the Caconda mission because of its key position. He called it the "Mother Mission" for new stations to be founded on the Bié and Benguela highlands and out toward the Zambeze. The bishop reinforced his argument by reminding the minister of what was happening in southern Africa: England had occupied Bamanguato and Barotze, German troops were in Ondonga, and even a part of Portuguese Kwanyama was about to be occupied by Germans through two Protestant missions established there.

If we wish to secure our dominion of these areas and gain these people for the Catholic church we must send missionaries right away who will peacefully attract and civilize them and not let them go after the mirage with which the Protestant missionaries blind them so that we may attract them to our sphere of influence.[55]

At the same time that the bishop made his plea to Lisbon for support of Caconda, Father Lecomte was writing a glowing report of the reopening of the Bailundo mission. He rejoiced because he had never been in a place where whites were received so readily. He attributed this to the fact that Catholic missionaries had come to teach the Catholic religion, the Portuguese language, reading, writing, arithmetic, and all those things that people wanted. According to Lecomte the people lamented the fact that until then they had only had an American Protestant mission, which taught them "only Bible reading accompanied by native songs of doubtful inspiration."[56]

Lecomte promised in this same letter to publish a revised edition of his study of the Umbundu language so it would help new missionaries coming to plant the church among the Umbundu.

Planting the Church among the Nhaneca-Humbe

Before the end of the nineteenth century the church was also planted in the less populous areas of the south and east of Angola.

The Huila Catholic mission was founded in 1881 and was entrusted to the Spiritans, who were authorized to administer the sacraments and preach the word of God in the district of Moçâmedes. They were thus charged with both mission and parish work, except where a parish priest might be installed.

The mission worked mainly among the Muila people, who belonged to the Nhaneca-Humbe ethnolinguistic group. However, many of the first students in the boys' and girls' boarding schools were redeemed slaves or orphans of internecine warfare. As they left school they had no place to go since many of them did not even know where they had come from or where their families were. The missionaries decided to seek productive land to start Christian villages for these orphans and redeemed slaves, some of whom had married one another. Land was found in Jau and Chivinguiro, which accounts for the establishment of these missions in 1889 and 1892.

The Huila mission became the mother-mission of the Catholic church in the south of Angola. There were boarding schools for both

---

55. Brásio, *Spiritana Monumenta Histórica*, 6:287–89.
56. Ibid., 296.

boys and girls, and the bishop of Angola transferred the only Catholic seminary in Angola from Luanda to Huila. The mission also developed a large agricultural program and soon had twenty-five thousand head of cattle, later reduced to one thousand when a bovine epidemic spread through the region.

The Muila people were averse to Europeans and the gospel so although the Huila mission had impressive institutions and talented missionaries, such as José Maria Antunes and Mário Bonnefoux, it had little impact on the people of the area.

The arrival of two groups of Europeans in the Huila area constitutes at least a footnote to the planting of the church in Angola.

Three hundred Boers arrived in 1880 on the Huila highland after a five-year trek from Mafeking, South Africa, to escape British rule. After journeying across the desert of Bechuanaland and South West Africa with their wagons and cattle, the Afrikaners were well received by the Portuguese, who gave them extensive tracts of land at Humpata as well as Portuguese citizenship and freedom from taxes for ten years. The Portuguese had hoped that these rugged Protestants would help subdue the rebellious Angolans and also develop the rural economy by agriculture and cattle raising. The Portuguese were disappointed because the Boers did not integrate into the very small white population nor did they become Catholic. They had periodic visits from Afrikaner dominies, who came from South Africa to provide them with their religious services.

The second group of Europeans who arrived in that area at the end of the last century were colonists from the Portuguese island of Madeira. About three hundred families were sent by the Portuguese government to establish themselves in Lubango, Humpata, and Chibia in 1884. Their spiritual care was entrusted to the Holy Ghost Fathers of the Huila mission.

Planting the Church among the Ganguela

Catholic missionaries led by Father Charles Duparquet left the Humbe area in southwest Angola to explore across the Cunene River in 1883. They decided to establish a mission in the area of Cassinga and a site was chosen on the Cului River at Kakele nine miles south of Cassinga. The first two priests, Hogan and Lynch, died of malaria in 1885, and so the mission was moved to Cassinga in 1887. In its first twenty-eight years twenty missionaries died in this mission, mostly of acute malaria.

The second mission among the Ganguela was founded some sixty miles north of Cassinga at Catoco near the Cubango River in 1888. Planting the church among the Ganguela was not only hindered by disease but also by violent opposition. During the early years the Kwanyamas made periodic attacks on the Ganguela peoples, including the missions. Monsignor Alfred Keiling, the Alsatian priest who was the superior of the Cubango prefecturate from 1908 to 1936, has written a detailed and dramatic account of the violent founding of the Cubango Mission in his book *Quarenta Anos de África*.

Father Lecomte went north from Cassinga with two brothers, Nicásio and Narciso, and thirty boys who were redeemed slaves. The latter were to help in constructing the mission and to be the future founders of Christian villages. With his usual enthusiasm and creativity Lecomte wrote words in Ganguela to which he adapted French music, and the people enjoyed learning the truths of the catechism as they sang. They requested a school, but when it opened only two students appeared — Ngunda and Tchyango, sons of the king of Catoco, Tchyihwaco, who prohibited other young men from attending because he wanted only his sons to be educated. This caused tension between the missionaries and the king. Another issue was raised by Tchyihwaco: why had the missionaries not asked him for permission to establish the mission in his area? He claimed that all the whites in his area — missionaries, traders, or soldiers — were responsible to him and could only remain at his pleasure.

In that region the Portuguese had two small forts: Princess Amélia near Catoco and another at Dongo twenty-five miles west. At about this time Princess Amélia was closed and troops were withdrawn to Dongo. Commander Francisco da Silva Marques entrusted the Portuguese flag to Father Lecomte and charged him to see that Portuguese sovereignty was respected, promising to send support if it were necessary.

As Tchyihwaco's people became more and more attracted by the services of the mission, the king saw his power and influence being threatened. So when the rains that usually arrived at the beginning of October had not started by mid-December, the king accused the missionaries of having caused the drought by their magic. He pointed to the ditch that the missionaries had dug from the Utombe River to provide an adequate water supply for the mission while others had no water with which to cultivate their fields.

The diviner was consulted and confirmed that the mission was the cause of the people's distress, so Tchyihwaco said he was going to expel the white men even if it were necessary to fire upon them. Hearing the rumors of such an attack, Father Lecomte went to Dongo to tell Captain Marques and sent a messenger to inform the Cassinga mission.

The soldiers at Dongo who, except for the captain, were natives of the area, refused at first to march against the king and his people, but being intimidated by their officer they finally went. The white men assumed that the presence of the troops would terrorize the king and he could be captured with the help of some people disloyal to him.

Captain Marques sent to Dongo for a cannon, which Brother Nicásio dragged through the woods with an ox team. Setting it up and aiming it at the king's village during the night, the soldiers expected that in the morning the village people would realize the danger and surrender. However, by his spies the king knew what was happening, and so during the night his men put the ill-trained artillery men under heavy fire. At the same time the king sent groups of men to destroy the abandoned Fort Princess Amélia and attack the mission. The Portuguese cannon resounded three times and the noise of the artillery, far from terrorizing the king's village, only told everyone in the area that something was happening and many neighbors ran to the village. The cannon failed to fire again, and before dawn the Africans in great numbers had surrounded the government forces. Just then a torrential rain caused the Africans to withdraw. The firing began a little later, but the government troops were relatively few and they were reluctant to fire on relatives and friends.

Lecomte decided on negotiation with the king, but as soon as he crossed the river he was tied up and abused. He calmly said that he had come to arrange a cease-fire, to which the king and his advisers finally consented. Three men were named to go with Lecomte, two sons and a nephew of Tchyihwaco: Kakola, Tchyipandeca, and Lilu. As they were leaving Lecomte was faced by a witchdoctor with a rifle. He pulled the trigger, but the firing pin stuck, so the priest ran to the river where a boat was sent for him. Lecomte refused to enter the boat saying he had come to arrange a cease-fire. The captain said he would rather die than survive such an affront, since the honor of the Portuguese flag demanded it. However, the captain finally agreed and withdrew.

Lecomte surprised Tchyihwaco and his men, who did not expect him to return. Lecomte was stripped of his clothes and tied to a tree. Then, fortunately for Lecomte, the king remembered that he could get oxen as ransom for his hostage. The king demanded withdrawal of all whites and substantial indemnity of twenty oxen, though in the end he agreed to two oxen, a barrel of brandy, a keg of gun powder, a fine rifle, four bolts of cloth, and other articles of less value. When leaving Lecomte did not say goodbye, only "See you later," indicating that he would return. The government would not allow the revolt to go unpunished.

Tchyihwaco complained to the captain in Caconda, the highest authority he knew, but Lecomte went to Lisbon, where he spoke to political leaders and the minister of colonies. At the minister's orders the governor-general of Angola, Guilherme Brito de Capelo, went to Humpata to organize an expedition under the command of Artur de Paiva, which arrived in Cubango on October 2, 1889. After heavy artillery fire across the river the column entered the king's village and found fifty dead. Among prisoners taken was Lilu, Tchyihwaco's nephew, who according to Ganguela tradition should have been the king's successor. Soon Tchyihwaco himself was captured and deported to Cape Verde. It was rumored that he threw himself into the sea as he was being taken to the islands.[57]

The Plymouth Brethren also planted the church among the Ganguela group when they established the Cavungu mission in 1891 and the Cazombo mission in 1899 among the Lwena. The Gospel of John was translated into Lwena in 1902 and published privately.

Planting the Church among the Ambo

In 1883 Father Duparquet founded the first mission among the Kwanyama, one of the Ambo peoples, at Cauva, twenty-five miles north of Njiva, the capital where Namadi reigned. At first the king appeared favorable to a mission in his territory, but soon he became antagonistic and Duparquet decided to move farther north. In 1885, however, before the mission was moved, the king suddenly died of unknown causes and people blamed the missionaries for his death and attacked the whites. When they pillaged a commercial establishment near the king's residence, the proprietor and a companion fled to Humbe to save themselves. Brother Lúcio and Father Delpeuch were unable to flee and were murdered. The third missionary, Brother Geraldo, escaped by hiding in a well with water up to his neck. Thus ended the first effort to plant the church among the Ambo.[58]

After an interval of fifteen years the Holy Ghost Fathers made a second attempt to plant the church among the Kwanyama at Matadiva, not far from Cauva. This site lacked a good water supply so they sought a more favorable location near the kingdom of Evale farther north. King Cavanguelwe was antagonistic to the mission and attacked it on December 2, 1903, when Brother Dionísio was fatally shot.

The mission then moved to Oupiacadi in 1904, where the missionaries were well received. However, that was not the end of opposition to the church. In 1912 the last powerful king of the Kwanyama, Mandume, hearing that the mission was to be handed over to the government as a fortress, ordered it burned. In 1913 the mission again moved farther north to Nacaheque at the base of the Mupa mountain. Next came an attack from nature as drought and famine decimated the people of the area, and the missionaries left the Ambo territory.

---

57. Monsignor Alfred Keiling, *Quarenta Anos de África* (Braga, 1934).
58. Ferreira da Costa, *Cem Anos dos Missionários do Espírito Santo em Angola*, 366–67.

Only in 1923 was the church finally planted among the Ambo. However, during the previous forty years so many missionaries died that we could apply the oft quoted saying "The blood of the martyrs is the seed of the church" to this area of Angola especially.

The church was planted successfully among the Ambo and Herero by the Protestants south of the Angolan border in South West Africa, and since the Ambo were seminomadic cattle people they brought the church into Angola. In fact, there were three German Lutheran mission stations on the Angolan side of the border at Njiva, Omupanda, and Namakunde. These Protestant missions in the disputed district between the areas claimed by Germany and Portugal became a matter of contention between those two nations. A Portuguese official noted that the Protestant missions could not be supervised by the Portuguese because it was in disputed territory, "therefore, it cannot fail to be damaging to our sovereignty and also to our nationalization."[59]

When the Portuguese drove the German troops from Angola during World War I, the Lutherans were forced out of Omupanda. In 1928 that mission was taken over by the Catholic church, becoming the center for its work among the Ambo.

Conclusion

Jesus told the parable of the sower and the seed that fell on different kinds of soil and then described what happened to the seed that fell along the path, on rocky ground, in shallow soil, and in rich soil. The missionaries, Catholic and Protestant, who sowed the seed of the gospel in the major ethnolinguistic groups in Angola during the last quarter of the nineteenth century did not know what would happen to their sowing. However, they planted with much faith and many fertilized the soil with their lifeblood; most died of disease, though some were victims of violent attacks.

In the perspective of a hundred years the planting in Angola fits into what seems a master plan to evangelize the world during the Great Century. Yet at the time the interests and intentions of the various mission agencies not only seemed uncoordinated, but at cross-purposes.

The Catholic missions were united in a common allegiance to the pope but suffered in Angola from the friction between the *Padroado* and the *Propaganda Fide* as well as from the national rivalries between Portuguese and non-Portuguese missionaries.

---

59. A. Torres Neiva, "Angola, sob o signo do Protestantismo," *Portugal em África* 19 (1962): 140.

The six Protestant mission societies represented a spectrum of polities and doctrines, but all shared roots in the evangelical, pietistic current that was strong in European and North American Protestantism in the nineteenth century. They had little opportunity for friction and rivalry among themselves since they followed an unofficial comity arrangement by which each society sought an unevangelized region in which to work. Comity is "the division of territory and assignment of spheres of occupation including the delimitation of boundaries on one hand and noninterference in one another's affairs on the other."[60]

The Protestant mission agencies did not enter into formal agreements to divide Angola into spheres of occupation, but in practice each mission became a territorial proprietor. The BMS established itself in São Salvador, the capital of the kingdom of the Kongo, and that became its territory, or perhaps it is more accurate to say that the Bakongo became its people. The ABCFM was in part persuaded to enter the central highlands of Angola because the territory was easily accessible and healthful and the Umbundu were concentrated in the area where there was no other mission at work. The Methodist mission under Bishop Taylor came almost immediately to occupy the territory between the Kongo and Umbundu peoples.

These first mission agencies occupied the regions of the three largest ethnolinguistic groups. The missions that followed created some overlapping, but this did not cause serious friction because the areas were so large and the Portuguese government restricted the entrance of new missions after the 1920s.

In this chapter of the history of the church in Angola the alliance between the Portuguese state and the Catholic church was *ambivalent*. The church benefited at times from the support and protection of the state, but in other cases the Angolan rulers identified the missionaries with the colonial government, which prompted violent attacks on the missions.

The Portuguese government feared the denationalizing influence of the Protestant missions, because the missionaries were foreigners and their religion practically unknown in Portugal. However, the Portuguese presence in Angola was so thin that the Protestants were more preoccupied with establishing good relations with the Angolan people and their rulers than they were concerned about Portuguese anti-Protestant attitudes and actions.

Certain differences in emphasis appeared between the Catholic and Protestant missions from the beginning. The Catholic church placed more emphasis on the role of the clergy and therefore on the voca-

---

60. R. Pierce Beaver, *Ecumenical Beginnings in Protestant World Missions: A History of Comity* (New York: Thomas Nelson and Sons, 1962), 15.

tion and training of the ordained ministry. The *Boletim* of the diocese of Angola and the Congo in 1937 commented:

> Our work as evangelists, no matter how productive and blessed it may be, will be incomplete and without guarantees for the future, if it does not have as its objective "the planting of the church" ... and the church is composed not only of the multitude of the faithful: it has an essential and even the principal element, the hierarchy established by its Divine Founder.[61]

In contrast, the Protestants gave a more important role to lay leaders. The BMS depended upon Misilina, the Angolan who had been converted in Cameroon, and on Nlemvo, who was a key worker in literature and translations. Ngulu labored side by side with Currie in planting the church in Chissamba.

Related to the central role of the laity was the Protestant emphasis of placing the Scriptures in the hands of all members. The Protestant missions therefore considered scriptural translation as an essential first step in planting the church. The Catholic missions did not agree with the Protestants in their policy of entrusting the Scriptures to ill-prepared people. However, there were gifted linguists among the Catholic missionaries who mastered languages and produced Christian literature, especially in catechetical form.

Still, Protestant and Catholic missionaries used essentially the same methods. They chose strategic sites and with the agreement of local Angolan chiefs or kings they built simple residences and schools of stick-and-mud or adobe bricks with thatched roofs. A few young men helped in the first tasks of cutting down trees, building houses, or cultivating fields. In most cases they lived on the mission stations, receiving room and board for their services as well as instruction in the rudiments of the Christian faith. Not only were individuals converted to the Christian faith, but Christian communities were formed.

Mindful of other attempts to plant the church in the early centuries of our era in North Africa, and in the fifteenth and sixteenth centuries in the Congo basin, it is premature at this point in our study to conclude that the church had taken root in Angola by the beginning of the twentieth century.

Thus we shall focus now on the germination and growth of the seed sown in Angola in the late nineteenth century and the early twentieth century.

---

61. *Boletim da Diocese de Angola e Congo* 3, no. 15 (May–June 1937): 67.

Chapter 3

The Growth of the Church
1900–1960

A sower went out to sow. And as he sowed, some seed fell along the path, and the birds came and devoured it.... And other seed fell into good soil and brought forth grain, growing up and increasing and yielding thirtyfold and sixtyfold and a hundredfold.
— Mark 4:3–4, 8

The church was planted among the largest ethnolinguistic groups in Angola in the last quarter of the nineteenth century, but this process never ends. Not only were there many areas where the church had not yet been planted, but the seed of the gospel must be sown anew in each generation. By the turn of the century a new phase in the history of the church in Angola began: the growth of the church.

During the first six decades of this century the church grew in a variety of ways:

1. Local congregations grew in membership.

2. New communities were started by evangelists and catechists.

3. New mission stations were established to plant the church in unevangelized areas.

4. More Catholic missionary organizations entered Angola.

5. Seven more Protestant mission agencies began work in Angola.

6. New means of communication spread Christian teaching within the church and beyond.

7. Angolans became increasingly the subject of church growth instead of the object, as more Angolan leaders were trained and ordained.

8. Schools played a central role in evangelization.

9. Medical work made the gospel more real and attractive.

10. Church structures were shaped and developed.

The first seven types of growth will be described in this chapter while the last three will be subjects of later chapters.

Growth in Membership of Local Congregations

Church statistics are difficult to interpret since denominations use various criteria to determine membership; they also differ in the efficiency of keeping records and in the manner of reporting statistics. The Catholic church counts all baptized persons as members and, since it baptizes infants, the membership list includes persons of all ages. The Protestant churches in Angola — whether they practiced infant baptism or not — usually did not include infants in their membership statistics; rather they included only baptized adults and young people after they had been confirmed.

A pattern of steady growth, which was common in most populated areas of Angola, is shown by the statistics of the church in Cabinda, the site of the earliest Catholic missions. Lândana, founded in 1873 by the Holy Ghost Fathers, had several schools to train young men to become village leaders or catechists. The system worked and in 1927 catechists were leading Christian communities in thirty-six villages belonging to the Lândana church. By 1966 the number of communities had doubled, and in a total population of 20,363, 70 percent, or 14,263, were counted as Catholics.[1]

The Holy Ghost Fathers founded a second mission in the city of Cabinda, capital of the enclave. Church growth is shown by the regularly increasing number of baptisms each year:

1901	63
1906	94
1910	369
1917	359
1924	800

---

1. Cândido Ferreira da Costa, *Cem Anos dos Missionários do Espírito Santo em Angola (1866–1966)* (Nova Lisboa, 1970), 69–74.

This growth continued until the 1966 statistics recorded that 92 percent of the total population of 16,542 was Catholic.[2]

Lucula, the third Catholic mission in the enclave of Cabinda, was located less than three miles from the frontier of the Belgian Congo, which restricted its extension, but within its geographical limits the church growth was considerable, with 71 percent of the 6,400 people being Catholic in 1966.[3]

According to the official 1960 census 85 percent of the population of the Enclave of Cabinda was Catholic and 11 percent Protestant.

The Catholic church based its membership statistics on the number of baptisms performed each year. For example, during the decade of the 1930s the Catholic church in all Angola registered an average of 35,350 baptisms per year. The Catholic membership was determined at the end of each year by adding the number of baptisms and subtracting deaths.

Protestant churches have followed a more personal process of calculating membership. For example, the São Salvador church registered 573 members in good standing on January 1, 1907. During the year it received seven members who had been under discipline and were restored to active status. Two members were received by transfer from another church and 121 "believers" were received by baptism. This was an increase of 130 members. However, 37 were removed from the rolls: 17 by death and 20 were under discipline. This resulted in a net gain of 93 members, so that the total active membership on December 31, 1907, was 666.

The Jubilee Celebration at Bailundo in 1930 was a great occasion for Protestants of the central highlands, because it came at the peak of rapid growth in the church established by the ABCFM/United Church of Canada. After twenty-five years of work, in 1905, only 283 church members could be recorded. At the Jubilee the churches of the area reported 9,000 church members and 6,000 catechumens distributed among 822 outstations.

Twelve thousand Angolans as well as Portuguese officials and friends and visitors from churches in the United States and Canada attended the Bailundo Jubilee from May 16 to 25, 1930. People from Chilesso, Kamundongo, Dôndi, Elende, and Galangue had prepared speaking, acting, and singing parts of the program and arrived at Bailundo a few days early to have a complete rehearsal of a drama entitled *The Three Crosses*. The theatrical production was presented in a natural outdoor amphitheater with one act each day.

The First Cross — the Cross of the Diviners — was represented in two episodes by the Kamundongo and Elende missions acting out the

2. Ibid., 85–88.
3. Ibid., 89–91.

establishing of the Bié capital at Ekovongo and the choosing of Chilulu as king of Chiaca (Elende) with the counsel of the diviners.

The Second Cross — the Cross of the Explorers, or the Value of the Lusitanian Race — showed Prince Henry the Navigator at Sagres in Portugal in 1435–38 discussing with other Portuguese noblemen that the main purpose of exploration was the spread of the Christian faith. In the second act, first scene, King John II sends Diogo Cão to continue exploration of the west coast of Africa, and the second scene showed Diogo Cão and his crew landing at the mouth of the Congo River.

The Third Cross — the Cross of Jesus Christ in Our Life — dramatized the founding of Protestant work in Bailundo, Kamundongo, Chissamba, and Galangue.

The climax of the Jubilee was the singing of the sacred cantata *Esther, the Beautiful Queen* by a 540-voice choir from all the churches, under the direction of Arthur Steed of Chissamba with Henrique Kapiñala at the organ.[4] Fifty years later at the Centennial celebration of the churches in central Angola selections from that cantata were still being sung.

New Communities Started by Evangelists and Catechists

Less than six months after the Protestant church in São Salvador was formed in 1887 it adopted the suggestion made by the missionaries "to select one of its number to undertake the work of an evangelist to visit the neighboring towns; believing this to be he best method of bringing the people to the knowledge of Jesus Christ the Lord."[5] The monthly meeting of the São Salvador congregation then voted that Kavitidi be appointed to the above post and that the church pledge itself to support him by their free will offerings. He would work three days a week as an evangelist and the rest of the time as a carpenter for the BMS.

The founding of a new congregation usually started with a visitation program to one or more villages near the mission station. The Angolan evangelist explained the missionary work and led the worship services. He would also teach those who wished to prepare themselves to become members of the new church. The congregation in São Salvador took the next step in church growth in 1892 by deciding to send a young convert, Nlekai, to reside in the village of Mawunze on the following terms:

---

4. Words by C. M. Cady, music by William B. Bradbury. Translated from English to Umbundu by J. Arthur Steed.

5. Baptist Missionary Society, *Church Minute Book*, no. 1 (Angola, May 27, 1888).

1. that he be an agent of the church supported wholly by the church;

2. that on no account whatever he is to engage in trade so that his whole time is devoted to teaching in school and preaching in the district;

3. that his salary be fixed at the rate of eight guns [the medium of exchange in the Congo at that time] per month which is understood to be sufficient in the event of his getting married; and

4. that he be allowed one month holiday every year to be taken as he pleases.[6]

Nlekai did not undertake this job because he proposed to marry a girl, Bwingidi, who was judged improper to be a teacher's wife. However, this was the pattern followed by the BMS churches.

In central Angola the teacher-evangelist was not supported wholly by the church: rather, he was sent to a village where the people would agree to provide him a plot of land and give a day or two each week in his field. The rural church leader, whether called catechist, evangelist, or deacon, was expected to support himself and his family, basically by his agricultural work, but with some labor and monetary contributions from his people to supplement his income.

Mission stations were the nurseries in which the church was planted, but very soon new offshoots, called outstations, were scattered around the missions with the number constantly increasing. In 1915 the ABCFM annual report commented: "The important of the outstation work is illustrated in the Bailundo report that 9/10ths of the 119 new members received during the seventeen months came from the outstations."[7]

Church Growth

The way in which the church grew can be illustrated by episodes from the life of the Rev. Jessé Chiula Chipenda, one of the church leaders in Angola during the mid-twentieth century.[8]

Pastor Jessé was born in 1903 during the Bailundo War, which signaled the effective Portuguese occupation of the central Angolan highlands. His father, Chipenda, was a successful trader during the heyday

---

6. Ibid., July 25, 1892.

7. ABCFM, *Annual Report*, 1915, 59.

8. These episodes in the life of Jessé Chiula Chipenda are taken from two main sources: the autobiographical statement and theological credo presented at his ordination in 1938 and a brief sketch of his life written by Marie Crosby, ABCFM missionary. Both are unpublished mimeographed reports. Facts also come from the personal knowledge of the author.

of the beeswax and rubber trade. The name Chipenda comes from the Umbundu verb *oku penda* — to open a path — and means trailblazer.

At the turn of the century the Portuguese not only occupied central Angola militarily, but they controlled it economically. By early 1902 Portuguese merchants had established five hundred stores on the highlands so Chipenda abandoned trade and settled down as chief of Lomanda, one of the subkingdoms owing allegiance to the king of Bailundo.

Cawoli, one of Chipenda's eighteen wives, bore two of his fifty-one children, a daughter and a son. The son, later to be known internationally as the Rev. Jessé Chiula Chipenda, was simply called Chiula as a young boy.

Chiula had strong-willed parents, and when he was ten years old Chipenda angered Cawoli so she left the village of Lomanda. The daughter went with Cawoli to her home village of Timiha while Chiula stayed with his father at Lomanda. Two years later Chiula asked his father's permission to visit his mother, to which Chipenda agreed. Chiula was frightened when he arrived in Timiha to discover a Protestant school, for he knew that his father did not like these new schools, and Chiula was particularly disturbed because his sister was attending it. He protested to his mother, pointing out that Chipenda would be angry, but Cawoli responded simply, "She's going." The girl shared a desire for education with the thousands of other Umbundu youngsters of that period. From 1910 to 1920 the number of pupils registered in the ABCFM schools of central Angola increased from 4,176 to 12,596.

Chiula's curiosity overcame the fear of his father and one day he accompanied his sister to a worship service at which the hymns particularly impressed him. In his personal testimony at his ordination service years later he recalled one of those first hymns sung to the tune of "Massa's in the Cold Cold Ground"; it had these words:

Nda ove wa yongola omuenyo	If you wish life
Una kopui pua	That life which never ends
Ka tambule ndopo Yesu	Go, receive Jesus now
Eye o ka ku yovola.	He will save you.

During the first service that Chiula attended, a visiting elder preached on Luke 15, explaining how God mercifully seeks all men, women, and children. The parables of the lost coin, the lost sheep, and the prodigal son touched Chiula very deeply, although he was only twelve years old. He saw himself as the lost sheep and as the son who had squandered his inheritance. Walking out of the stick-and-mud school house, he said to his companions, "Today, I believe in Jesus."

The next day Chiula asked his mother for a little corn so that he could buy a book. Even at that early stage in the development of the Protestant

Christian community in Angola, to believe and to read were part of one process.

Cawoli gave Chiula a basket of corn, which he exchanged for a penny with a local trader. Taking the coin to the nearest Christian leader with a supply of literature, he bought a booklet of New Testament epistles in Umbundu. His sister, who had started to read earlier, helped Chiula. By the time he returned to Lomanda he was not only half way through the book, but he also had learned to pray. In his father's village Chiula could not read openly, but only when he was alone during the day or by a small fire at night, for Chipenda would have burned his son's book if he had found it. Although his father had not seen the book he did notice some changes in Chiula's behavior: for example, he no longer practiced the sacrifices according to the traditional religion.

In that same year, 1915, the Bailundo church sent to Lomanda a catechist named Job, who began a Christian village on the opposite hill. Chiula was overjoyed as he attended classes and services, making good progress in reading, learning hymns, and other lessons for new Christians.

During the Week of Prayer in January 1916 Cawoli died. Chiula visited the village of Timiha to pay his respects to his mother and then returned to Lomanda with his sister. As they pounded corn or washed at the river in Lomanda, Chipenda's other wives expressed their fear that Chiula had killed his mother by witchcraft. They believed that people could not learn to read unless they had sacrificed life to clear their vision. The women worried about their children going to the new school thinking, "Our children may kill us so that they can learn to read."

The teacher, Job, had resisted receiving Chiula into the catechumen class because he was too young and his small stature made him seem even younger. However, Chiula was finally admitted and showed his enthusiasm not only by attending classes regularly, but by inviting his friends to come to church to hear God's word and by helping his brothers learn to read. Chipenda disapproved, but he did not find any good reason to punish Chiula as he was always obedient and hard-working. Frequently on Sunday Chipenda sent all his children away on errands so they could not go to church.

When Chipenda realized that most of his children and even some of the slaves in Lomanda were going to school in the new Christian village on the other hill, he called his people together. The angry chief put his son in the center of the gathering and said, "Chiula, today you must choose where you belong. If you want to go to school, move to the village. I will never see you again."

That evening Chiula struggled with the decision. He was fourteen years old and had grown up at his father's knee, never depending on anyone else. At the same time he remembered the words of Jesus, "No man is worthy of me who cares more for his father and mother than for me" (Matt. 10:37). That night Chiula made a decision that shaped all the rest of his life. He would leave his father's village and dedicate himself completely to his new master, Jesus Christ.

In the morning Chiula moved over to the "school." The teacher knew of Chipenda's anger, but he courageously received Chiula not only into the school, but into his home.

Chipenda sent word to the catechist, "If you receive my son, I will have you sent away to the army." The chief did not carry out his threat against the teacher, but everyone took seriously the threat made on Chiula's life, "If I meet my son, I will kill him. I will not stand for a son of mine being subject to the orders of anyone else." Chipenda's other children stopped going to school, because they would have been forced to make the same decision to leave their father's village.

These episodes from the life of the Rev. Jessé C. Chipenda illustrate how the growth of the church in Angola depended upon a combination of personal decisions and the formation of Christian communities.

The Angolan church at first grew as people moved on to the mission stations and were converted and baptized, forming Christian communities. The next stage of church growth was the formation of many outstations or Christian villages such as Lomanda within a fairly short radius of the mission stations. The missionaries supervised these communities and for the first decades they had to travel on foot, which required that the villages not be too widely scattered.

New Mission Stations

The third means of church growth was the founding of new mission stations. In 1900, 41 mission stations were scattered across Angola: 25 Catholic and 16 Protestant. By 1965 the number of mission stations had grown to 190: 134 Catholic and 56 Protestant. In addition the Catholic church had 69 parishes, fully organized churches under the direction of a priest.

The BMS, which established the first Protestant station in 1878 at São Salvador, founded two more missions among the Kongo. The Zombo resented the Xikongo alliance with the Portuguese at Mbanza Kongo (see p. 11) and rebuffed the first explorations made by the BMS missionaries in their area. However, the missionaries succeeded in winning their confidence and established a mission in one of the most populous districts of the Congo at Kibokolo, which was estimated to have had about five thousand people while São Salvador had between fifteen hundred and two thousand.

The third BMS mission station in the Portuguese Congo was Bembe.

A mission had been founded in Mabaya, south of São Salvador, in 1905, but after epidemics of smallpox and sleeping sickness had decimated the population of the area and one of the missionaries had died of sleeping sickness, the BMS ordered Mabaya closed. The Kikongo requested urgently the reopening of a mission station in the Bembe area, to which the BMS agreed. The Portuguese authorities permitted the reestablishment of the mission, but insisted that it not be at Mabaya. For convenience of sanitary and administrative surveillance, a site was chosen about a mile from the town of Bembe in 1930.

The Methodist missionary society that assumed responsibility for Bishop Taylor's missions and missionaries among the Kimbundu did not continue to maintain all the stations that the bishop had hurriedly established in 1885–86. The missions at Dondo, Nhangue-a-Pepe, and Pungo-Andongo were closed, leaving but three Methodist stations: Luanda, Malanje, and Quéssua. Later the Methodist church attempted to establish a mission on Fazenda Isabel in the Dembos, but the government refused permission to transform the farm into a mission station. Nevertheless, the Methodist church grew in that area and missionaries were placed in Salazar/Ndalatando in 1960, but were withdrawn the next year because of the outbreak of the War of Independence.

Among the Umbundu the ABCFM and the United Church of Canada founded four new missions: Elende (1906), Dôndi (1914), Galangue (1923), and Lobito (1924). Around each mission grew a strong self-supporting church.

Galangue Mission

Galangue was the first and only mission in Angola to be pioneered entirely by black missionaries. The idea for such a mission traces its roots to the American Missionary Association, which founded and supported many schools for freed slaves in the South of the United States and inspired the establishment of many Colored Congregational churches.[9]

Three men who received their education in AMA schools conceived the idea of establishing a station in Africa where American black youth could work as missionaries "among their own people." H. H. Proctor of the First Congregational Church of Atlanta, Georgia, the Rev. W. L. Cash of the First Congregational Church of Thomasville, Georgia, and William H. Holloway of Columbus, Ohio, sent $100 to the ABCFM in 1915 as a nest egg for an African mission.

The ABCFM agreed to establish such a mission if the Colored Congregational churches would assume entire responsibility for recruiting

---

9. The Congregational churches that founded the Galangue Mission were organized in the Council of Colored Congregational Churches.

personnel and for their full financial support. However, the mission would be under the general supervision of the American Board.

The first recruit was Henry Curtis McDowell, who had just graduated from the theological department of Talladega College in Alabama. His fiancée, Bessie Farnsville, who was teaching in Athens, Georgia, agreed to marry McDowell and accompany him to Angola. In August 1919, they sailed for Lisbon with nine-month-old son, Curtis.

The McDowells worked at the Chilesso mission for three years, where they learned Umbundu and became acquainted with the Angolan church. After exploration in an unevangelized area south of Nova Lisboa, the missionaries chose a site, Bunjei, eighteen miles north of the king's village of Galangue. The Galangue mission was established January 15, 1923, by the McDowells. Later the same year Samuel Coles, another Talladega graduate, arrived at Galangue with his wife, Bertha. In 1931 Dr. Aaron M. McMillan, a physician and surgeon, came with his wife, Wilina, and daughter, Helen, to direct the medical work and build the Willis F. Pierce Memorial Hospital.

The Galangue mission had a missionary team distinguished not only by its race, but by the exceptional gifts of an evangelist-church administrator, an agriculturalist-industrialist, and a physician-surgeon.[10]

Although Galangue was the area of the most concentrated influence of black missionaries on the church in Angola, other mission societies sent black personnel also. The Methodist mission sent four black women to Angola. The first was Susan Collins, who worked in the Natumba mission near the port of Banana at the mouth of the Congo River. In 1902 she was sent to the Quéssua mission to work at the girls' school. She retired in 1921. The second black missionary in the Methodist mission was Martha Drummer from Atlanta, who arrived in Luanda in 1906. She taught at the girls' school in Quéssua while Susan Collins was dean. Miss Drummer had to leave Angola in 1922 due to poor health. Alberteen Ware and Rose C. Thomas, the other two black missionaries in the Methodist mission, were short-term appointees in the late 1950s.[11]

George Murrain, a black Plymouth Brethren missionary from British Guiana, started the Hualondo mission in Bié.

Catholic Mission of Galangue

The Catholic church was aware that Protestant missionaries from Dôndi were exploring the area south of Nova Lisboa to find a suitable site for a

---

10. Lawrence W. Henderson, *Galangue: The Unique Story of a Mission Station in Angola Proposed, Supported and Staffed by Black Americans* (New York: United Church Board for World Ministries, 1986).

11. Emílio J. M. de Carvalho, *Ouço os Passos de Milhares* (São Paulo, Brazil: Imprensa Metodista, 1978), 158–61.

mission station, so "obeying . . . the urgent necessity of counterbalancing the Protestant action" the Catholics began a mission in the area of the post of Galangue in February 1922.[12]

The official government approval for the Protestant mission of Galangue was dated January 15, 1923, and the Catholic mission July 4, 1923.

The Congregation of the Holy Ghost admitted that the Galangue mission was started without proper preparation, but they argued that it was necessary to start a "national" mission before the Protestant foreigners became established. It is true that the founders of the Protestant station had English names — McDowell, Coles, and MacMillan — but the pioneer missionaries in the Catholic mission also had foreign-sounding names: Keiling, Blanc, Breitenstein, Baur, Scherring, Hablitz, and Sanders. Yet the Catholic mission was "national" in the sense that it received regular financial support from the Portuguese government each year beginning in 1923.

The Benguela Railway

The city of Benguela, founded in 1617 by Cerveira Pereira, was the site of the first Catholic church in southern Angola and in 1619 was the only parish in central-southern Angola. The parish priest was also one of three vicars general in Angola, the other two being in Congo and Luanda. At the end of the nineteenth century a parish was created in Catumbela, but it soon was left without a priest and was restored only in 1939.

In central Angola all the Protestant missions founded in the first four decades were rural since there was only one city, Benguela, and it had a very small African population. However, in the early 1920s the Bailundo church recognized the need to reach out to a new city, Lobito, which was developing at the coast and attracting many Bailundo people.

The Portuguese realized the necessity of penetrating the interior of Angola if they were to establish effective control over their West African colony. As long as commerce into the interior depended on African carriers, the Portuguese could not control Angola. The first railroad in Angola was built from Luanda and reached Lucala in 1899 and Malanje in 1909. The aim was ultimately to reach Lunda, but the line was beset with financial problems and never went beyond Malanje.

Although the Portuguese saw the advantage of building a railroad from Benguela east along the old slave and rubber trails, the final impulse for construction came from Katanga in the east. Robert Williams, a Scot, who had arrived in Africa in 1891 and was associated with

---

12. Ferreira da Costa, *Cem Anos dos Missionários do Espírito Santo em Angola*, 392.

Cecil Rhodes, explored for minerals between the Zambezi and the Congo rivers. To do this Williams had to obtain a concession from King Leopold of Belgium, who controlled that area. Leopold not only gave the concession, but contributed toward the cost of exploration. Extensive deposits of copper were discovered and the British and Belgian interests combined to form Tanganyika Concessions, Ltd., in 1901.

Williams then had to negotiate with Portugal, which was still very angry with Britain because of the ultimatum Britain had issued in 1890 demanding that Portugal abandon its claim to a strip of land across Africa connecting Mozambique and Angola. When the Portuguese people heard that their government was negotiating a contract with a British company to construct a railroad across Angola they foresaw a further capitulation. In spite of public protest the contract was concluded and signed.

Because of its natural harbor Lobito was created as a city to serve the port and terminal for the Benguela Railway. To build the docks and warehouses and prepare the roadway for tracks labor was needed. Local labor was not available since the desert strip along the Atlantic coast was inhabited by only a few nomads. Kroos and Senegalese from West Africa, as well as two thousand Indians from Natal, were contracted. Only after the line was one hundred miles inland were Umbundu workers found to furnish an adequate labor supply. After the first stretch of road was laid from Lobito to Benguela and from Benguela on across the coastal desert, most of the imported labor returned home.[13]

The Lobito Protestant Mission

In January 1923 Pauling and Company, the British contractor that had built the Benguela Railway, began the construction of the port of Lobito. Instead of seeking labor outside Angola, the Portuguese used the system of forced labor, euphemistically called "contract labor." Hundreds of men were taken from the Bailundo area to work on the docks. The Bailundo Protestant church sought a Christian leader to serve the church members and catechumens who had been taken to Lobito and also to tell the good news to the many non-Christians working on the docks. The church decided that Jessé Chiula Chipenda was the best person to minister in Lobito.

After Chiula, who was now called Jessé, completed primary school in the Bailundo mission, he was sent in 1920 to Currie Institute in Dôndi. That school was started in 1914 to train Christian leaders for the increasing number of villages that sought Protestant catechists or teachers. In

---

13. Muriel W. Henderson, "The Historic Background and the Construction of the Benguela Railway," unpublished paper, Northwestern University, 1965.

1924 Jessé was graduated from the institute and received a certificate enabling him to teach. He joyfully returned to Lomanda. His father, Chipenda, had recently become reconciled to Jessé when he saw the value of education in dealing with the Portuguese. All the children, even slaves, were allowed to go to worship and to school. Before Jessé could begin teaching, however, the call came from the Bailundo church for him to go to Lobito.

The thought of going to the coast frightened Jessé since he had never been away from the Bailundo-Dôndi area. The church assured him that he had been chosen after much prayer and they also reminded Jessé of the promise made at his baptism that he would serve wherever needed. Jessé, now twenty-one years old, responded: "If it is God's will, I will go."

The Rev. William C. Bell, director of the Bailundo mission, drove Jessé C. Chipenda to Lobito where they arrived on September 11, 1924. The two men went to the government administration office to request an identity card for Jessé so that he could work legally as a catechist. According to the law the catechist had to be presented by the director of a recognized mission and be able to speak Portuguese.

After the catechist card was issued, Bell and Chipenda went to the warehouse that served as the office for Pauling and Company. The construction company agreed to hire Chipenda part-time and provide a room for him with other laborers. He started working each morning on the dock as a carpenter, a trade he had learned at Currie Institute, but because of his education and reliability he was soon foreman of a warehouse and worked on payrolls and invoices. In the afternoons he taught children, and each evening he led hymns, preached, and conducted a night school for adults.

Soon Jessé Chipenda had gathered congregations in Lobito, at the sugar plantation in Catumbela, and twenty miles south in the old city of Benguela. Legally these were outstations of the Bailundo mission, two hundred miles away, but progressively, as the churches and schools grew, they became recognized as the Lobito Mission and the coast church, tracing their founding to the arrival of the young catechist, Jessé Chipenda, at Lobito in 1924.

The Church among the Lunda-Chokwe

The period of planting the church in Angola coincided with the process of "pacification," which allowed Portugal to claim administrative control over the whole colony. The last area to be occupied in the terms of the Berlin Conference was the region of Moxico along the eastern border, which was organized into an administrative district only in 1922. This was the home of most of the Lunda-Chokwe in Angola.

The Plymouth Brethren missionaries Thomas Louttit and William

Maitland from the United States were the pioneers from the Protestant community in planting the church among the Chokwe people. They arrived in Angola in 1904 and established a mission at Boma the following year. In 1908 Mr. and Mrs. Cuthbert Taylor and Leonard Gammon opened the Luma-Cassai station.

T. Ernest Wilson, a Brethren missionary with experience among both Chokwe and Umbundu peoples, wrote:

> The Chokwes are a proud, independent, outspoken race who despised the Ovimbundu as the slaves of the white man. They were the old highway robbers of Central Africa, plundering the trade caravans as they went to and from the coast. All the young men had the prefix "Mwa" attached to their name. It means a prince of royal blood. But then all Chokwe blood was royal blood.[14]

With this attitude the Chokwe refused to do the physical labor of building the first mission stations, so the missionaries had to bring in Ganguela workers. Soon, however, the Chokwe began to listen to the Christian teaching and in the fourth year of work at Boma a few Chokwe made a profession of faith. The seventh year saw three baptized.

The Catholic church did not send missionaries to that area before 1933, but Manuel Avelino Mavinga, a student from the Catholic school in São Salvador from the time of Dom António Barbosa Leão (1906–8), had built a small chapel and worked zealously as a catechist in Luso. In 1933 before the first missionaries arrived Bishop Moisés Alves de Pinho visited Moxico, where the catechist prepared everything for his visit including a throne like one he had seen when a previous bishop had visited São Salvador some twenty-five years earlier. The first parish in Moxico was created canonically in Vila Luso in 1956.

Motive for Founding New Stations

Mission stations were established primarily to promote the spread of the church, but secondary motives were also involved as indicated in the founding of the Catholic and Protestant stations of Galangue. At times rivalry between two parts of the church influenced the location and timing of the establishment of new missions.

The founding of new Catholic missions in the Malanje area illustrates other motives. The frontier between Angola and the Belgian Congo in the region of the Cuango River was not yet defined in 1900, so the Portuguese government was interested in having a Catholic mission established that could prove that Portugal had effectively occupied the area. This political motivation coincided with the apostolic desires of

---

14. T. Ernest Wilson, *Angola Beloved* (Neptune, N.J.: Louzeaux Brothers, 1967), 32–33.

the Holy Ghost Fathers in Malanje, so in July 1900 two priests and two brothers set out on a three-hundred-mile trek from Malanje to the post of Loremo.

The Mussuco people were the most easterly of the Kongo ethno-linguistic group. The king of the Mussucos at the turn of the century was Quipacassa upon whom the missionaries depended for carriers to bring supplies from Malanje. In addition to the usual pioneering tasks of building houses and cultivating gardens and fields, the missionaries had to learn new languages, compose catechisms, and translate the Gospels. During the first decade of the Mussuco mission the church recorded 467 baptisms.[15]

As in Mussuco, a variety of motives contributed to the founding of the Bângalas mission in 1913. The Catholic missionaries saw as their goal the conversion of the Bângalas, the Bondos, and the Haris. They also wanted a new mission as a bridge between Malanje and Mussuco, which were about two hundred miles apart. The round trip took at least a month. The government supported the location of a new mission to strengthen Portuguese penetration of the Cassange basin and the expansive Lunda district to the east.

Reopening Old Stations

In some cases the new mission stations in the early twentieth century were old stations that were reopened, such as Dembos and Zaire.

Italian Capuchins had worked in an area called Caculo-Cahenda in the Dembos district in the seventeenth century. The only vestiges of that work were a village named Iglesia (church) and the cult of St. Anthony. In 1913 an attempt was made to establish a Catholic mission in the Capitania-mor dos Dembos in the district of Golungo Alto. Because of the wars of occupation and lack of personnel, however, that effort was abandoned and the mission was closed in 1919.

In the 1930s Father Isalino Alves Gomes, the legal representative of the Congregation of the Holy Ghost in Luanda, traveled periodically on foot or by hammock from Luanda to Quibaxe, about a hundred miles, accompanied by a catechist from Caxito. In spite of the little time that Father Isalino was able to devote to that work, it bore fruit with 250 baptisms and 36 weddings. He placed four catechists in the areas of Quibaxe, Panga, Tonio-Angola, and Cabanga. In 1938 the Dembos mission was officially reopened.[16]

While the Catholics were building an impressive station with church, school, boarding school, and annexes, as well as many chapels and

---

15. Ferreira da Costa, *Cem Anos dos Missionários do Espírito Santo em Angola*, 135.
16. Ibid., 101ff.

schools in the area, the Methodist mission was also requested by some of the local people to establish a station in the Dembos. The Methodists did purchase a property and started a school, but the government refused their request to open a mission there. The Catholic mission of Santo António do Zaire was first established by the Holy Ghost Fathers in 1881, but met such local opposition that it was closed in 1885. In 1930 it was reopened and by 1966 it reported that of a total population of 16,625, "baptized Christians" numbered 12,814.[17]

New Swiss Mission Stations

The Protestant mission society that opened the greatest number of new stations in this period of church growth was the Mission Philafricaine, popularly known as the Swiss Mission. Previously it had opened only the Kalukembe mission in 1897.

The Kalukembe church, which was born with the baptism of five Angolans in 1912, did not show the growth of the other churches planted among the Umbundu. Three reasons have been given for this relative stagnation.[18] First was the failure of the self-support mission method. Chatelain, the inspirer and organizer of the Swiss mission, was a member of Bishop Taylor's mission and a faithful disciple of his self-support principle. This had not worked well in the north among the Kimbundu as it was practiced by Bishop Taylor's Transit and Building Society, and it did not work in the southwest region of Angola. Second, Chatelain and his colleagues were dedicated to fighting slavery (the original name of the Kalukembe mission was Lincoln), and therefore directed evangelistic efforts to slaves and nomads in the Kalukembe area, ignoring the local Umbundu and Mbali. Third, Chatelain and his colleagues did not form a good team. He was an intellectual and internationally known linguist-anthropologist, while his colleagues were stolid Swiss artisans who had no academic preparation for missionary work.

The Swiss mission received a group of new missionaries after World War I, which gave new life to the church. Two new stations were founded: Ebanga in 1927 and Sussangue in 1930. However, even with these two new stations the growth of the church in areas served by the Mission Philafricaine was minimal.[19]

The Rev. Eliseu Simeão, president of the Evangelical Church of Southwest Angola, considers 1928 an important date in the growth of the church planted by the Swiss mission. That year many of the people

---

17. Ibid., 170.
18. Rodolphe Bréchet, *J'ai ouvert une porte devant toi: Essai sur l'histoire de la Mission Philafricaine* (Lausanne: Alliance Missionnaire Évangélique, 1972), 15–16.
19. Ibid., 25.

who had lived near Kalukembe returned to their homes in the extreme south, leaving the villages around the mission practically empty. But on the positive side the mission took a step that enhanced the growth of the church. A council of elders was chosen to work with the missionaries in the development and orientation of the church. Three elders were chosen: Daniel Kanyanga, secretary, Benjamin Kassoma, and David Chiñuli. This step was taken in part in response to a comment by John T. Tucker from Dôndi who used the Umbundu proverb, *Unene wongandu kovava* ("The strength of the crocodile is in the water"), that is, the missionaries need the cooperation of the Angolans if the work is to progress.[20]

The church at that time must have had about five hundred members, and although it seemed to have positive responses from villages being visited, the reports being sent to Switzerland by the missionaries related mostly the difficulties of the work. This prompted the committee in Switzerland to send its president, Dr. Pierre de Benoit, and vice-president, Pastor Henri Monnier, to study the situation at first hand in 1938. They first visited the Dôndi mission and several of its centers and then proceeded to Kalukembe. A direct acquaintance with the work persuaded the president that the Mission Philafricaine should turn over its work to another mission in Angola. However, Dr. John T. Tucker, director of the Dôndi mission and general secretary of the Evangelical Alliance, who accompanied the Swiss visitors challenged them by pointing to the vast unevangelized region of Hanya to the west of Kalukembe. The officials returned to Europe much encouraged and determined to give Kalukembe new life.

The great turning point in the history of the church in Southwest Angola was the arrival of Dr. Rodolphe and Anny Bréchet in 1943. For almost forty years Dr. Bréchet shaped the structure, theology, and political orientation of the church. Under his strong leadership the mission took several steps that promoted the growth of the church.

Dr. Bréchet showed his skill as a diplomat by opening two new stations shortly after his arrival: Jamba, north of Cubal, and Catala, north and west of Quilengues. In each case the local Portuguese authorities supported the founding of the new stations, because Dr. Bréchet promised to provide medical assistance for the sufferers of leprosy in the area.

Dr. Bréchet was president of "the field" and moved immediately to unite the two major stations, Kalukembe and Ebanga, and their respective churches. They had developed disparate styles in discipline, the Ebanga church being lax and Kalukembe very rigorous. For example,

---

20. Eliseu Simeão, "Igreja Evangélica do Sudoeste de Angola: Resumo Histórico," mimeographed, Kalukembe, 1982, 28.

in Kalukembe catechumens were at times required to wait as long as six years before being baptized. To overcome the differences Dr. Bréchet called two missionary meetings a year so they could establish priorities and set common standards for the whole field. Although the missionaries were all Swiss they did not have a common mother tongue so they used Portuguese in these meetings.

The Swiss mission then moved vigorously into new areas. Dr. Bréchet presented the first catechists to Portuguese officials in Ngola in the district of Quilengues southwest of Kalukembe. Evangelism was also encouraged in the Hanya and Kanyala regions to the west and north.

From 1900 to 1965 the church in Angola grew in part by the establishment of forty new Protestant mission stations. This required not only a constant supply of missionary personnel and financial resources, but also permission for new stations and outstations from the Portuguese colonial government, which was reluctant to see the Protestant work expand.

Rapid Catholic Growth

During this same period the Catholic church opened 109 new mission stations. It too needed to recruit missionaries, but the Portuguese government was committed to furnish financial support and gave not only permission but encouragement to the Catholic church to establish new stations.

There was a brief period at the beginning of the twentieth century when the growth of the Catholic church was slowed by two political issues: internal ecclesiastical tensions between the *Padroado* and the *Propaganda Fide,* and the conflict between church and state after the proclamation of the Portuguese republic on October 5, 1910. The tension between church and state will be discussed more fully in chapter 9.

The Salazar regime, which was inaugurated in 1926, provided both political and financial security to Catholic missions; twenty-nine new stations in Angola stimulated the growth of the Catholic church in the 1926–40 period.

Arguing the necessity for new mission stations Monsignor Keiling wrote to the superior of the Holy Ghost congregation on May 6, 1933:

> Missionary stations that serve fifty thousand Christians are not, properly speaking, missionary stations, but missionary "counties" whose direction becomes impossible materially and spiritually. We don't know what to do. We find ourselves enmeshed in a way that willy-nilly we are carried along. Although we say that we cannot increase our work, the rate of conversions is such that in spite of

all the resolutions to the contrary, we are obliged to do it. If your Excellency could see the great crowds around the confessionals, the distribution of Communion for hours, or the priests leaving the confessionals at midnight or 1 A.M., and this for weeks at a time, not being able to stay up any longer, certainly you would pity us. And what do you think of these good Christians who, after a three-day walk, have to wait three or four days in order to confess, because of the multitude that fills the churches from 4 o'clock in the morning. Needless to say, they do not all come at the same time: they push and shove each other wanting to be the first to say confession.[21]

In order to respond to this rapid growth the Catholic missions subdivided their areas and created new stations. For example, the Bailundo Catholic mission founded in 1896 reached out into the populous area of the central highlands. As the church grew the area was divided and five new stations were created in the area once served by one: Bimbe (1929), Mungo (1948), Cumbira (1950), Pucusso (1951), and Caimbuco (1958).

The Bailundo Protestant mission established in 1881 also fostered a growing church, but it was prohibited by the government from founding new stations, so in 1960 the same area served by six Catholic missions had only one Protestant mission.

This comparison may be misleading, because the Protestant church had established sixteen pastoral centers in this area. The staff of each center included an ordained minister, several licensed teachers, and a nurse, all Angolans. The physical facilities of the Protestant pastoral centers could not compare with the buildings and equipment of the Catholic missions. The sun-dried brick and thatched buildings of the Protestant centers were constructed entirely by the financial contributions and volunteer service of church members. No foreign funds were received by the centers. In contrast, the Portuguese government subsidized both physical plants and personnel of the Catholic missions and these government monies were complemented by contributions from European churches and missionary societies.

If the Protestant mission agencies had been permitted by Portuguese authorities, they might have turned some pastoral centers into full mission stations. However, in the long run, the church was strengthened in these centers where the people themselves developed financial and spiritual self-reliance. In 1960 the Bailundo Protestant church registered 17,355 communicant members and 7528 catechumens in 571 villages.

Catholics were urged to visit their rural mission stations on the first weekend of the month so that they could go to confession, attend Mass, and receive Communion. However, many did not regularly reach the

---

21. Brásio, *Spiritana Monumenta Histórica* (Louvain: E. Nauwelaerts, 1971), 5:607–8. Translated by author.

mission for reasons of health, work, or lack of motivation. To provide religious services to these Catholics, missionary priests felt obliged to visit each Christian village in their areas at least once a year, for only the clergy could administer the sacraments.

Augusto Maio, a Catholic seminarian, used a vacation to visit the Cubango Mission and made a three-week visit to outstations between the Cubango and Cutato rivers in 1940. The seminarian and Father Pedro mounted on a bicycle and a donkey started out with seven carriers. They stopped first at Catala, the first location of the Cubango Mission where Father Lecomte almost lost his life (see p. 66). Maio described the church in Catala: "There are many Christians here, but sadly the good ones are rare, if any. Almost all have returned to their old pagan ways." Father Pedro suggested that perhaps if they abandoned the village it would wake up, and added, "There is no gain in just having a school open. In fact, the school-chapel is in ruins and translates well the state of those souls in relation to Christianity!"[22]

Most village visits included some catechetical instruction, listening to and giving solutions for moral and social problems, hearing confessions, saying Mass with popular songs, giving Communion, and administering baptism. Such a program took at least twenty-four hours. At the end of the visit the villagers presented gifts to their priest, usually chickens and eggs.

The catechist was the key person in each Christian community and some were exceptionally dedicated and effective, such as António in Vicungo who taught himself to read, write, and count. His father, Kalungulungo, a non-Christian, was the founder of Vicungo. He was anxious to be baptized, but was separated from António's mother, who was a Christian, and he was living with another woman. Kalungulungo could not be baptized unless his first wife died or he was separated from his second wife. This was a common problem.

New Catholic Missionary Organizations

In an exact sense every Christian is a missionary, but in the present context we are using the term to refer to non-Angolan, full-time church workers who played a major role in the planting and growth of the church during the colonial era.

The Portuguese church and state wanted to keep control of the missions, but they could not supply sufficient Portuguese personnel. The Spiritans worked out a *modus vivendi* with the religious and civil authorities, but they too were not able to supply the needs of the rapidly

---

22. Augusto Maio, *No Coração da África Negra* (Lisbon: Editorial LIAM, 1947), 14–15.

growing church. As the lack of Catholic missionaries became more acute the civil and ecclesiastical authorities agreed that they should call on other missionary orders to supply workers. From 1900 to 1960 twenty new missionary orders sent personnel to Angola. In the 1930s the Benedictines arrived and were given responsibilities in the district of Moxico. In rapid succession they established four new stations: Moxico-Velho (1933), ten miles from Luso/Luena; Cazombo (1934); Dilolo (1936) on the Zaire border; and Santa Cruz do Cuando (1939). They also opened the College of San Bento, which was the only secondary school in the Moxico district for many years. In 1960 thirty-six Benedictines worked in Angola.

A German Benedictine order of women also came to Angola in the 1930s and worked among the Ganguelas at Cubango, Galangue, and Cuchi. The Dorotéias, a Portuguese teaching order, opened girls' schools in Moçâmedes, Benguela, and Sá da Bandeira, having its headquarters in the last-named city. In 1936 the first group of the Sisters of the Most Holy Savior, an Alsatian nursing order, arrived to work in the Cuando and Bimbe missions in the district of Huambo. These new orders brought the total number of Catholic missionaries in 1940 to 395:

Male Missionary Personnel		
	Priests	Brothers
Secular	32	
Spiritans	124	76
Benedictine	11	1
	167	77

Female Missionary Personnel		
	European	African
St. Joseph of Cluny	62	40
Franciscans	8	1
Benedictines of Tutzing	3	
Dorotéias	20	
Most Holy Savior	17	
	110	41

Source: Manuel Nunes Gabriel, *Angola: Cinco Séculos de Cristianismo* (Queluz: Literal, 1978), 382–84.

Two vigorous Catholic orders of men initiated work in Angola in the late 1940s: the Swiss congregation of LaSalette and the Italian Capuchins. The LaSalettes, perhaps attracted by a terrain similar to their mountainous homes in Switzerland, settled in the most rugged area of the Benguela highland, where they were given charge of the Ganda and Quilengues missions that had been founded by the Spiritans. Another reason for their placement there may have been to give some competition to the Protestant Swiss mission that was expanding its work in the same area.

The LaSalette Fathers pioneered in the formal training of Catholic catechists. Catechists, or local lay leaders, were the key figures in the planting and growth of the church in Angola, but the Catholics had provided little or no formal training for these essential workers until the LaSalette Fathers organized their courses. They also formed the Pia União de Santa Catarina to train Angolan women to help with catechetical teaching and other apostolic activities.

The Capuchins had been the principal Catholic order in Angola from 1640 to 1830. In 1948 the province of Venice of the Capuchins was invited to reenter Angola. This order had personnel available as some of the missionaries in Ethiopia were interned during World War II and were without assignment after the war. So in 1948 six Capuchin priests and two lay brothers arrived in Luanda. In addition to serving parishes in the capital they were given responsibilities in the districts of Cuanza North and the Congo, where they founded the stations of Damba and Camabatela. The Archbishop of Luanda asked the Capuchins to replace secular priests in São Salvador, Maquela de Zombo, and Sanza Pombo. In addition they founded the Quiculungo mission in Cuanza North and the Bembe and Quimbela missions in the Congo. By 1960 the Capuchins had thirty priests and nine brothers working in Angola.

Three new orders of women entered Angola just after World War II, providing teachers, nurses, and social workers. The Benedictines of Bethany began work in Luso; the Reparadores do Sagrado Coração de Jesus went to Dumbi in Cuanza South and Kazanga near Luanda. The congregation of St. Teresa of Jesus worked in the mission of Bela Vista and in 1957 opened the first women's teacher training school.

In the 1950s four orders of men and six of women entered Angola for the first time. The Redemptorists were called by the bishop of Silva Porto, the first group arriving in 1954. They took over the Spiritan mission in Cuchi and were given charge of the vast Cuando-Cubango area. The Redemptorists created new stations in Vouga in 1955 and in Serpa Pinto-Menongue in 1959. Very soon the Vouga mission became known all over the country for its large hospital, which served both Africans and Europeans.

Spanish missionaries of the Trappists (Order of Cistercians of Strict Observance), a contemplative order, came to the diocese of Nova Lisboa in 1959. Monks were installed near Bela Vista where they built a monastery not far from the large Protestant Dôndi mission.

In 1958 Father José Maria Mollier of the Little Brothers of Jesus, who had worked with Bushmen in Namibia, moved north of the border to Xamavera in the administrative district of Dirico. During this same decade the lay teaching congregation of Marists began work in Angola, first at the government secondary school in Sá da Bandeira/Lubango and then at new schools in Silva Porto/Cuíto and Salazar/Ndalatando.

In the 1950s six orders of women brought a group of dedicated, skilled, and experienced missionaries to reinforce the work of the church in fields of education, health, and welfare. A Spanish congregation of the Amor de Deus, which had been working in Portugal for twenty years, sent its first group of sisters to Angola in 1954 and established a girls' school in Vila Nova de Seles/Uku. Years later they started a school in Carmona/Uige. Portuguese Dominicans of St. Catherine of Siena founded a school in Salazar/Ndalatando and expanded their work into various schools as well as providing a residence for university schools in Luanda. The women Spiritans came to Angola in the 1950s, undertaking teaching and nursing ministries in the dioceses of Benguela, Nova Lisboa/Huambo, and Silva Porto/Cuíto. The Medical Missionaries of Mary, an Irish order, began in Chiulo near the Namibian border what Archbishop Gabriel called "the first missionary hospital in Angola." He ignored all the Protestant hospitals that had been functioning for years.

The Dominicanas do Rosário arrived in 1954 to work at the hospital in Santa Comba, now called Waku Kungo. That same year the Sisters of Mercy came to establish communities in Luanda and Uige, dedicating themselves to pastoral, health, and social work.

Seven Additional Protestant Mission Agencies

While Catholic missionary personnel were being reinforced by twenty new orders during this period of church growth from 1900 to 1960, seven new Protestant missionary agencies began to send personnel to Angola: the Evangelical Mission of Angola, the North Angola Mission, the Canadian Baptist Foreign Mission Board, the South Africa General Mission (SAGM), the Portuguese Baptist Convention, the Pentecostal Mission, and the Seventh-Day Adventists.

The Evangelical Mission of Angola

The earliest successful planting of the church in Angola in this modern period was by Catholic missionaries in the enclave of Cabinda at Lândana in 1873. The first organized Protestant work in Cabinda was established by Matthew Zachariah Stober in 1901. Stober's father was a Jamaican who went to Scotland in service of the Duke of Edinburgh and married a Scottish woman. Matthew was born in 1875 and his father died when he was quite young. His widowed mother struggled to bring up her son and two daughters.

Matthew was converted at an early age and, encouraged by his mother, decided to give his life as a missionary in Africa. Much later his daughter wrote, "As white people had brought his father's ancestors away from Africa as slaves, he felt that he, in particular, had a great responsibility to help people of Africa in every way that lay in his power."[23]

After an exploratory visit to Angola Stober decided in 1901 to return to England to arouse interest and support for a new mission in Angola. Six volunteers responded to his call, sailing with him from Liverpool on June 20, 1903. Six weeks later the party reached Ambrizete on the northern coast of Angola and began seeking a place for mission headquarters. Cabinda was chosen, and a large wooden house on forty acres of fertile land was discovered for sale by a Dutch trading company. Stober agreed on a price of £1200 sterling to be paid on March 26, 1904. He sent out an urgent appeal to friends in Great Britain for help; the small band of missionaries prayed fervently, but by March 17 they had only £520. On March 26, however, they were able to praise God, because by then they had received £1245, 11s, 5d.[24]

The first three converts were baptized on November 4, 1904, but the Evangelical Mission of Angola was officially established in 1910. From then until Stober's death in 1951 it founded six stations in addition to Cabinda: Ambrizete, Ambriz, Mucula, Mussera, Quimpondo, and Tomboco, all south of the Congo River.

Since this mission was nondenominational and Stober had not developed another network of support, its income was uncertain. This was reflected in the physical characteristics of the stations, some of which were less impressive than pastoral centers of other Protestant missions and also had fewer followers.

In addition, the numbers of personnel of the Evangelical Mission of Angola fluctuated. In the 1920s the mission had sixteen missionaries, but usually fewer. Some missionaries came to Angola to work with Stober but stayed only a short time, either returning home or moving to another mission. The Rev. Archibald Patterson left the Evangelical Mission of Angola to start his own North Angola Mission.

North Angola Mission (NAM)

The detailed history of the North Angola Mission founded by the Rev. Archibald Patterson is difficult to reconstruct; some documents indicated that it was established in 1922 and others that the proper date is 1925. Both dates are significant.

Archibald Patterson worked with Matthew Stober of the Evangelical Mission of Angola beginning in 1910. He was stationed in Ambrizete

---

23. Harrison H. Pike, "History of Baptists in Angola," unpublished M.Div. thesis, Central Baptist Theological Seminary, 1971.
24. H. S. Hilyer, *Being Sent Forth* (Toronto: Canadian Baptist Foreign Mission Board, 1959), 32.

and became enthusiastic about the possibilities of evangelization of that region. Patterson and Stober had some disagreement over mission policy, and so in 1912 Patterson left the Stober mission to return to England. Before departing he visited the area of Uige to the east of Ambrizete and discovered an area that at that time had no Christian witness. Patterson stayed ten years in England and shared his concern for the evangelization of the Uige area with other Christians. In 1922 he returned to Angola and was given permission by the Portuguese authorities to establish a mission at Kikaya, ten miles southeast of Uige, where he sowed the first seed of the gospel in that area. The church that grew from that seed considers 1922 as the date of the founding of the North Angola Mission.

In 1925 the North Angola Mission was organized in Liverpool, England, and also in that year a Swiss missionary, Ernest Niklaus, joined Rev. Patterson in Kikaya. A leaflet published by the office in Liverpool says that "the North Angola Mission was established in 1925."

Patterson planted many acres of coffee for a cash income and a variety of crops to provide food for boarding school students. In 1934 the North Angola Mission established a second station at Kinkuni near Sanza Pombo. Twenty years later the NAM founded another mission station at Kimbele.

When the NAM was started in the Uige area Kimbundu was the dominant language, but as the work spread it reached more Kikongo-speaking people, so the hymnbook was published in both languages as well as Portuguese.

The Rev. Mr. Patterson was Anglican in England, and although he came to work with Stober, who followed many Baptist practices, Patterson still used the Book of Common Prayer in Portuguese in the services of the church that he established.

Canadian Baptist Foreign Mission Board

Before Stober's death in 1951 he "willed" his work to the Baptist Missionary Society (BMS). This act showed two facts about the Evangelical Mission of Angola: although it called itself nondenominational, it was for all intents and purposes Baptist, and, second, it was a personal venture and there was no missionary or ecclesiastical organization to make decisions about the future of the work. Everyone involved accepted that Stober had the authority to turn his mission stations over to the BMS.

The BMS entered into negotiations with the Canadian Baptist Foreign Mission Board (CBFMB), which previously had worked only in India and Bolivia but had decided that it should undertake further responsibility in the evangelization of the world. The administrative wheels turned, and in October 1953 the CBFMB took action to accept the responsibility from the BMS for the work of the Evangelical Mission of Angola on January 1, 1954.

Mr. and Mrs. Howells, a missionary couple who had worked many years with Stober, remained in Ambrizete until the first Canadian Baptist missionaries could arrive. Since the missionaries had to be recruited, to be given special training, and to have a period of language study in Portugal, the first couple, the Rev. and Mrs. Jack Lockwood, did not arrive in Angola until July 1957. They were the first of a wave of twenty-four young missionaries to arrive in Cabinda and northern Angola in the next two years: nine couples, one single man and five single women. Their youthful vigor, training, and dedication promised to revive the many Christian communities that had grown up around the stations of the Evangelical Mission of Angola. Before these young missionaries could learn the local languages and produce much fruit, however, the colonial war broke out in 1961, directly affecting the area in which they were working.

The South Africa General Mission (SAGM)

The informal comity agreement among Protestant missions had left the territory from the fourteenth parallel south unoccupied. This was changed in 1914 when the Rev. A. W. Bailey, an American sent by the South Africa General Mission (SAGM), crossed over from Northern Rhodesia. The SAGM was founded in Cape Town, South Africa in 1889. Its first president was Andrew Murray, a Scottish evangelist and well-known Dutch Reformed minister and author. From Cape Town the mission spread to Swaziland, Pondoland, the Transvaal, Nyasaland, the Rhodesias, and then Angola.

Bailey built a temporary house on the Luanguinga River among the Luchazi. He worked alone for some time under great difficulties, but was encouraged when a large group of ex-slaves, Umbundu Christians from Bié with their wives, arrived bearing letters from Dr. Robert George Moffat of the Chissamba mission. Given their freedom by a Christian chief, they were on their way eastward to a new life in the Congo, but decided to settle with Bailey. This gave the work a great impetus as they spread out to villages where Angolan chiefs had requested teachers, offering food and promising to construct school buildings.

In 1916 Bailey saw the conversion of the first Luchazi and also completed the translation of the Gospel of John in that language. In the same year the mission suffered a setback as a result of an uprising by the local population in which a number of white traders were killed and the missionary's life threatened.

A permanent site on the Muié River was finally chosen for a mission station and building commenced. But it was clear that in order to plant the church in such a huge area Bailey needed help, so when he went to America on furlough in 1919 he recruited new people. In 1920 he sailed for Africa with eight North Americans, being joined later in Cape Town by two workers from England, one of whom was a doctor. From Cape Town they traveled to Livingstone and thence by barge up the Zambezi and over the border into Angola.

The caravan was composed of a thousand carriers, and each day the lead carrier went ahead in African fashion carrying a flag that could be seen from afar so the other carriers might follow. The flag used by the caravan was a piece of white calico with a red cross painted on it. Every morning one of the missionary women, Daisy Pearson, sounded a cornet for all to get up, breakfast, and break camp.

The place and style of entering Angola aroused the suspicions of the Portuguese. An article in the *Jornal de Benguela* reflected this suspicion by raising a series of rhetorical questions: Who are these people? Do we want South Africans anyhow? What are they here for? Why did they come in military formation? Why did they sound military bugles? Why did they hoist and carry the British (or American) flag on Portuguese territory? Why did they have a school for teaching English?

When Bailey and the new recruits arrived at their destination they discovered that the outstations that had been established with Angolan lay leaders had all been closed by the Portuguese authorities. The young missionaries opened several new stations in the 1920s: Ninda, Cunjamba, Cassoango, and Cuelei, but they were all either refused official permits to function or were closed by the authorities for lack of a Portuguese teacher or for some other technicality. It was only in 1932 that the Catota station in the Chiumbo district of Bié was successfully opened and became the central mission of the SAGM during the colonial period with a school, a church, a well-equipped hospital, and a Bible Institute. Missionary personnel were placed in Sá da Bandeira/Lubango in 1946 and in Moçâmedes in 1950.

Several reasons can be cited for the difficulties the SAGM had in planting the church in its area and the slowness in its growth. The area that comity ascribed to the SAGM was vast, covering a swath of territory across the thousand-mile width of Angola. This territory was sparsely populated by very disparate peoples even though many of them were classed together by scholars as belonging to one ethnolinguistic group, the Ganguelas. At one time (1932) the SAGM was working among ten different peoples: the Chokwe, Mbunda, Luchazi, Mashi, Nkangalala, Mbundu, Luimbe, Chimbanda, Songo, and Nyemba.[25] It

---

25. John T. Tucker, *Angola: Land of the Blacksmith Prince* (London: World Dominion Press, 1933), 73.

was the Protestant experience that the church grew most rapidly in those areas where one mission society could concentrate on one ethno-linguistic group, such as the BMS among the Kongo, the Methodists among the Kimbundu and the ABCFM/Canadian mission among the Umbundu. Without even one well-established station the SAGM attempted to work among ten different peoples belonging to several ethnolinguistic groups.

The area served by the SAGM lacked highways and railroads, making transportation difficult, and the sparse European population meant there was little pressure on the government to provide a communications network. Another impediment to the implantation and growth of the church in eastern Angola was the constant exodus of the local population. Angolans who lived near the frontiers fled from the contract labor system, which forced men to work under almost slave conditions. A large proportion of the converts and adherents of SAGM churches left annually for Northern Rhodesia/Zambia. While many of them joined churches there, it was a loss to the Christian community in Angola.

The Portuguese Baptist Convention

The conviction and conversion of Manuel Ferreira Pedras, a tinsmith from Valença in the extreme north of Portugal, were the first steps toward the entrance of the Portuguese Baptist Convention into Angola. Pedras was condemned for a common crime and sentenced to prison, which at the turn of the century frequently meant exile in Angola. At that time half the white population of Luanda was composed of exiled prisoners, or *degredados*. Before Pedras was sent to Angola he was converted in Oporto, and so as a newborn Christian in Angola he developed a concern for the evangelization of the colony.

Upon completion of his prison sentence he returned to Valença and was baptized in the River Douro at Cabedelo in 1926. Then as a layman he began to work at the evangelization of his community. In 1928 a Baptist church was organized in Valença, and Pedras requested that it send one or more missionaries to Angola, suggesting that for a year the church pray daily that God might indicate someone to go." Always in his heart Pedras kept hearing the voice saying, 'You go.' "[26] The church had not taken action on Pedras's request, but since he felt the Lord's call, he prepared to go to Angola on his own. He gave his tinsmith shop to a Christian brother who had no means of support, and in 1929 Manuel Ferreira Pedras and his wife, Justina das Dores Pedras, emigrated to An-

---

26. Harrison H. Pike, "History of Baptists in Angola," unpublished M.Div. thesis, Central Baptist Theological Seminary, 1971, 34.

gola, settling in Nova Lisboa/Huambo. He supported himself and his wife by tinsmithing, but his main task was to give "Baptist witness in Angola."

In 1931 the Pedrases returned to Valença, and he was ordained. This church, which had been organized with only seven members in 1928, now in 1931 was sending out its first missionaries.

In 1928 Matthew Stober of the Evangelical Mission of Angola had visited Portugal looking for Portuguese Evangelicals who would work with him in Angola and unsuccessfully tried to persuade Pedras to go with him. Again in 1931 before going back to Angola as a missionary pastor Pedras refused another invitation from Stober. Pedras "wanted to do Baptist work," using the Baptist name instead of the generic term "evangelical," which Stober used.

Pedras changed his mind, however, and in October 1931 accepted Stober's offer to work in Cabinda with the Evangelical Mission of Angola for six months. After that period Pedras said goodbye to Stober and returned to Nova Lisboa, where he had already "sown the seeds of the gospel."

Pedras was disappointed that the Portuguese Baptist Convention would not undertake missionary work in Angola, his only support coming from the tiny church in Valença. Finally in 1934 the Portuguese Baptist Convention meeting in Leiria recognized Pedras as a missionary worker, but he still had to support himself and his work as a tinsmith.

His first convert was an Angolan, Paulo Chirunda. On May 21, 1933, the First Baptist Church of Nova Lisboa was organized by receiving the letters of transfer of six Angolan Christians who had been baptized previously by Pedras into the fellowship of the Valença church, although they had never been to Portugal.

In 1937 the Baptist church of Etunda, a suburb of Nova Lisboa, was organized and other preaching points were established around the city. In 1959 the building of the First Baptist Church was completed. When Manuel Ferreira Pedras retired in 1963, the small Baptist community of Nova Lisboa with both white and black members was active and growing.

The Pentecostal Mission

The church in Angola grew also during this period through the efforts of the first Pentecostal mission in Angola. The Church of God, with headquarters in Cleveland, Tennessee, began missionary work in Angola in 1938 with the arrival of Edmond and Pearl Stark. Before her marriage Mrs. Stark had worked briefly as a missionary in China and Liberia with Baptists and Assemblies of God; in the latter community she "received

100 Colonial Period, 1866–1960

the fullness of the Spirit."[27] When she and Edmond Stark were married in 1937, they both felt called to go to Africa.

Shortly after arriving in Angola the Starks attended the annual meeting of the Angola Evangelical Alliance, and in conversation with other Protestant missionaries from all over Angola they learned that there was no Protestant work in Cuanza South, except the Namba station of the Seventh-Day Adventists who did not participate in the Alliance. Since neither the Starks nor the Church of God had permission to open a station in that district, they accepted the invitation of J. E. Bodaly, a Plymouth Brethren missionary of the Chitau mission in Bié, to live in an abandoned missionary house, which they repaired. In March 1939 Mr. Stark became ill with malaria, and because faith healing is one of the tenets of the Pentecostals, they did not seek medical help immediately. When a missionary doctor did arrive, it was too late, and Edmond Stark died on March 22, 1939.

Still there was no government permission to open a mission station and World War II had begun. The Church of God mission board advised Mrs. Stark to return to the United States. After the war in 1946 the Church of God asked permission for Mrs. Stark and four other missionaries to enter Angola, but it was refused. Finally, Mrs. Stark alone went to New York and requested a Portuguese visa, which was granted. She sailed from New York on February 7, 1948, and landed three weeks later at Lobito Bay, where Bodaly, who had befriended her and her husband ten years earlier, met her. For a year she worked with the Bodalys at the Chitau mission and then received word that Joaquim António Cartaxo Martins, his wife, Joana, and two daughters, Portuguese Pentecostal missionaries, were arriving in Angola.

Although they still did not have official permission to open a mission station, the authorities recognized Cartaxo Martins's right as a Portuguese citizen to evangelize. Mrs. Stark and the Cartaxo Martins moved to Vista Alegre in the Cuanza South district. The Portuguese couple was young and enthusiastic, attracting many Africans to their school and preaching services. They worked for four years and were seeing the results of their labors when it was decided that the Martinses and Mrs. Stark should have a furlough for rest and also to visit churches in Portugal and the United States. In 1953 T. D. Mooneyham and his family arrived from South Africa to replace Mrs. Stark and Martins; Manuel Cartaxo Martins, brother of Joaquim, also came from Portugal to help.

In a few months, however, Mrs. Stark received word that the authorities accused the mission of violating the permission given to Joaquim Cartaxo Martins, so the Mooneyhams were denied residence permits.

---

27. Douglas LeRoy, *Pearl Stark Wilson: "I Had to Take up the Torch"* (Cleveland: Pathway Press, n.d.), 4.

When Mrs. Stark and J. C. Martins returned to Angola in 1954, they found the institutions closed, but individual believers were meeting for prayer and Bible study in their homes. Opposition from civil and religious authorities continued, and on August 7, 1957, the governor-general of Angola ordered all mission endeavor to cease, the Vista Alegre mission to close, and the Martinses to leave the area within ninety days. Still in 1959 the Church of God reported that it had 98 pastors and evangelists, and 1,633 communicant members in a total Christian community of 6,358 in Cuanza South.

Seventh-Day Adventists (SDA)

So far we have sketched the activities of the Roman Catholic church and eleven Protestant agencies. In the Introduction we stated our assumption that the church is one, and to this point we have implied that all the various missions were planting this one church, even though they used differing names and a variety of forms.

The entry of the Seventh-Day Adventists raises seriously the question of the boundaries of the church in Angola. The Seventh-Day Adventists deny by their teachings and practices that they are a part of this one inclusive church. They teach that the prophetic Scriptures reveal that God acted in 1844 to prepare for the end of the world, and furthermore "Seventh-Day Adventists believe that to them has been entrusted the sacred task of cooperating with divine agencies to prepare a people to meet their Lord."[28] The SDA are, according to their doctrine, the remnant separated from the rest of the church that has not properly interpreted what happened in 1844 and is therefore not being faithful to its divine calling.

Consistent with this teaching is the stance of the Seventh-Day Adventists in holding themselves aloof from other Christians who do not share their interpretation of prophetic Scriptures. The SDA was the only Protestant church that did not affiliate with the Angola Evangelical Alliance during the colonial period, and rather than using the generic term "Evangelical" for their missions as did the other Protestants, they called themselves "Adventists."

Nevertheless, we are including the SDAs in "the church" for the purposes of this book since we believe that God is no more offended by the explicit exclusivity of the SDAs than by the implicit exclusivity of most of the other branches of the church in Angola.

The first Seventh-Day Adventist missionary to enter Angola was W. H. Anderson, who came from South West Africa in 1922 to explore

---

28. Gerald J. Christo, "Born to Be a Prophetic Movement," *Adventist Review* (June 30, 1985): 4 (692)–5 (693).

the country and to study the possibilities of establishing mission work. The next year Anderson returned with two colleagues and opened the first SDA mission station at Bongo, ten miles from Lepi on the Benguela Railway west of Nova Lisboa/Huambo. Bongo soon had the standard tripartite Protestant mission program of church, school, and hospital and became the central SDA station for Angola. In August 1925 O. O. Bredenkamp opened the Luz mission in northeastern Angola in the Lunda district.

The Seventh-Day Adventists added to the growth of the Protestant community by opening in rapid succession several more stations: Nova Lisboa (1927), Namba in Cuanza South (1928), Quicuco (1931), Lucusse in Moxico (1932), Cuale in Duque de Bragança (1934), and Quilengues (1962).

Among the Protestants the Adventists had the most aggressive program for evangelizing Europeans. In 1945 a Sabbath School was organized in Benguela for Europeans under the direction of Luisa Bastos, who had heard the Adventist message in the Bongo hospital. Manuel S. de Castro was sent there as a full-time worker in 1947, and a temple was dedicated in 1955. In Nova Lisboa/Huambo the Adventist work among the Europeans began in 1948 when Pastor A. J. Rodrigues began weekly visits from Bongo. European congregations were organized successively in Moçâmedes (1950), Luanda (1951), Sá da Bandeira/Lubango (1953), and in Lobito.

The Angolan Union of Adventists counted 54 churches in 1961 with 13,554 members.[29]

New Methods of Communication

Three years after his consecration as bishop of Angola and the Congo Moisés Alves de Pinho launched two publications: the *Boletim da Diocese de Angola e Congo* for the clergy, which was to come out every two months, and a popular weekly newspaper, *O Apostolado*. The latter combined the teaching of Christian doctrine with commentary on secular news. Both publications responded to the growth of the church and sought to inspire further growth. The first director of *O Apostolado* was Father Abílio de Costa Reis Lima who served until 1947. In 1953 the paper became a semi-weekly.

In 1954 *O Apostolado* began a campaign to open a Catholic radio station. The director of the paper, Father José Maria Pereira, wrote:

In Angola and especially in the capital there is a lack of churches, and we have heard that it might be more urgent to build churches.

29. *Seventh-Day Adventist Yearbook 1961.*

Far be it from us to counter this opinion. The construction of new churches is impelling and is a matter that equally deserves the attention of Catholics, and the radio station will not replace them. It will, however, assist prodigiously the action of the reduced number of missionaries, which God knows how many years will have to pass before they are sufficient.

Let there be no hesitation. Let us do everything we can so that on December 8 we can dedicate to the Immaculate Virgin, the Patroness of Portugal, not just a small temple to serve the believers in a special locality, but an immense cathedral that will cover the skies of Angola, that will be a transmitter, sending to those who live in the cities as well as those who live in the most remote savannas the comforting message of the church.[30]

Catholics of Angola responded, and on December 8, 1954, *Radio Ecclesia* broadcast for the first time with a fifty-watt transmitter. Year by year it added to its equipment and installations until it became the only radio station broadcasting twenty-four hours a day to all points of the colony. Regular religious and liturgical programs as well as secular news, music, and special features were included in its broadcasts.

In addition to these colony-wide means of communication each diocese had its own information bulletin. About the same time the *Apostolado* was first published, the Protestants began *O Estandarte* in Luanda. The founder and editor during most of its life was a Methodist minister, the Rev. Gaspar de Almeida. It aimed to serve the whole of Angola, but the lack of an effective Protestant network made it difficult to reach that goal.

Several Protestant missions and churches broadcast fifteen-minute weekly radio programs on private stations in Benguela, Lobito, Nova Lisboa, Luso, and Sá da Bandeira.

More Angolan Leaders — Lay and Clergy

The increase in the number of missionaries was an essential element in the growth of the church, but probably more important was the increase in the number of Angolan leaders — lay and clergy.

Catechists

The key lay leaders were called catechists. As this classification had a legal base in governmental decree No. 77, there was more uniformity in

---

30. Ferreira da Costa, *Cem Anos dos Missionários do Espírito Santo em Angola*, 118–19. Translated by the author.

the work and qualifications of these leaders than there was in such titles as teacher or evangelist:

> Art. 5. Missions are not allowed to establish branches or schools to be in charge of Natives, or to entrust Natives with the work of religious propaganda without such Natives being in possession of a recognized identification card granted by the respective administrator or military officer when they shall have been presented by the principal of the mission.
>
> (1) Whenever an outstation with a school is under consideration the identification card cannot be given unless the native teacher is able to speak the Portuguese language.[31]

With the issuing of Decree 77 in 1921 the government required that catechists prove their competence in Portuguese, but passing such a test did not mean the person was equipped to teach the essentials of the Christian faith.

All churches recognized that catechists were the key persons in church growth whether quantitative or qualitative. As bishop of Malanje Dom Manuel Nunes Gabriel wrote a comprehensive pastoral letter on religious instruction. In it he emphasized the importance of catechesis, religious instruction, by quoting Cardinal McGuigan:

> A priest whose only job is religious instruction would do much more in his parish than another who perfectly fulfilled all his other duties, neglecting religious instruction. While the first would prepare for his successors a generation of Christian believers, the second would leave them for inheritance a generation of baptized pagans.[32]

The bishop suggested that the church sponsor regional schools for catechists so that they would reach a minimum level of third grade in primary school (able to read, write, and do simple arithmetic), a knowledge of catechism and sacred history, and the ability to teach the catechism to children and adults. Until such an ideal could be reached, each mission should have an intensive course in religion and the Christian life each year.

The training of Catholic catechists faced the dilemma of preparing more competent workers for new Christian communities or placing as many workers as possible regardless of training in order to compete with the Protestants. The bishop of Silva Porto/Cuíto in his *Circular on Missionary Work* advised that the most productive use of time and money was to prepare catechists, but then he went on to urge the sending of catechists

---

31. Tucker, *Angola*, 175–76.
32. Dom Manuel Nunes Gabriel, "Pastoral Sobre Instrução Religiosa," *Boletim Eclesiástico de Angola e S. Tomé* 20 (1960) (Luanda: Missão Católica, 1961), 77.

to as many villages as possible even it they were not well prepared, for "this sign of our presence will be sufficient to impede the entrance of Protestants."[33]

This sense of rivalry was evidenced in the same circular as the bishop recognized that the missions should not neglect raising the standard of living of the people for "in this the Protestants set an example for us."[34]

The Protestants shared the conviction of the bishop concerning the importance of the catechist, and faced the same problem as the Catholics in finding personnel and resources to give adequate training. It was common practice to have a short intensive course for catechists during the dry season, May through September, when the catechists were freer from their agriculture. These courses included not only Bible study and worship leadership, but also a broad spectrum of classes to equip the catechists as community leaders in public health, agriculture, music, and community development.

In the 1950s missions related to the American and Canadian societies with headquarters in Dôndi considered establishing a central catechist school, but the idea was rejected in favor of using whatever funds could be arranged to have larger courses on each mission station. One incentive for catechists to attend was the provision that they would have their tax paid if they attended a one-month course. This was attractive not only because of the amount of money, but because Catholic catechists were exempt from the head tax and the Protestant catechists saw this as a recognition of their work, in a sense putting them on a par with their Catholic counterparts. In the light of the social disruption caused by the colonial war (1961–74) and the civil war that began in 1975, this decision in favor of a decentralized program was proven wise.

The bishop's pastoral letter also dealt with the questions of maintenance for catechists. The bishop believed that it was neither possible nor advisable to pay a salary for their support lest they be considered government servants or employees of the church. The ideal would be that the catechist be also the teacher. This would be a favorable situation for the Catholics since their teachers were paid by the government. The bishop then suggested that teachers should not be hired to teach in mission schools unless they were willing to be catechists also. If teachers were not available as catechists, then it would be advisable for the catechists to support themselves and their families by agriculture, carpentry, tailoring, or another honest trade to give a good example. The Christians should develop the practice of helping catechists in their work or providing a small monthly or annual subsidy.

---

33. *Boletim Eclesiástico* 23, 24, nos. 123–30 (1933–34): 141.
34. Ibid.

Ordination

The number of Angolan leaders of the church grew significantly during the period from 1900 to 1960: catechists, both Catholic and Protestant, multiplied around each mission station, and the churches ordained an increasing number of men as priests and pastors. Although Catholic and Protestant catechists received the same official authorization to teach religion and occupied similar positions of authority and responsibility, the meaning of ordination was quite different in the two communities.

In the Catholic church ordination is a sacrament: "An outward sign of inward grace, ordained by Jesus Christ, by which grace is given to our souls." Ordination is the sacrament by which a man who is called by God is empowered by the laying on of hands to share in the priesthood of Christ. The basic and primary power of the priesthood is concerned with the "real body" of Christ, and is known as the power of orders. In virtue of a man's ordination he shares in Christ's great priestly act, the consecration of His body and blood at the offering of his great sacrifice — the offering that he commended his friends to do in remembrance of him and that the priest obediently performs when he celebrates Mass.

Ordination in the Catholic sense also gives the power of jurisdiction over the faithful, that is, the "mystical body of Christ" with which the priest admits persons to God's grace by baptism, strengthens them by confirmation, and absolves them by the sacrament of penance. The sacrament of ordination gives the *magisterium*, or teaching authority of the church, to the priests as well.

The Catholic church in Angola ordained an increasing number of men to assure its survival, for without priests empowered by the sacrament of ordination, the church, did not exist.

The Protestant churches ordained an increasing number of men during this period, but not with the same urgency, for they believed in the priesthood of all believers, the Reformation principle that was taught most explicitly by Martin Luther:

> Here we take our stand: There is no other Word of God than that which is given to all Christians to proclaim. There is no other baptism than the one which any Christian can bestow. There is no other remembrance of the Lord's Supper than that which any Christian can observe and which Christ has instituted. There is no other kind of sin than that which any Christian can bind or loose. There is no other sacrifice than of the body of every Christian. No one but a Christian can pray. No one but a Christian may judge of doctrine. These make the priestly and royal office.[35]

---

35. Robert S. Paul, *The Church in Search of Itself* (Grand Rapids: William B. Eerdmans Publishing Co., 1972), 135.

Since all Christians are priests, ordination among Protestants is the rite by which certain persons are empowered to act in the name of a community of believers.

The growth of the Catholic community — from the establishment of the first mission station in this modern era at Lândana, Cabinda, in 1873 until the signing of the concordat by Portugal and the Vatican in 1940 — was impressive, reaching more than half a million according to the official census.[36] However, the increase in the number of Angolan priests did not accompany this growth: the church was dependent upon European priests. In fact, in 1940 out of 167 priests there were only eight Angolans, which was only three more than in 1853, the lowest point in the history of the church. During the twenty-five years (1882–1907) that the Catholic Seminary was in Huila, only six men completed the full course and were ordained. Three were still serving as diocesan priests under Dom Moisés (1932–66). One entered the Congregation of the Holy Ghost.[37]

In 1934 Moisés Alves de Pinho celebrated his first ordination of an Angolan, Father Abel, in the Cubango Mission. The meaning of the ritual was explained in Ganguela. After the service Father Abel came to say farewell to the archbishop who embraced the new priest. Many in the crowd were amazed and enthused for such public expression of affection between European and African which was not common at that time.[38]

The record of Catholic ordinations in Angola followed the same pattern as that in other African nations. The Congregation of the Holy Ghost, the largest missionary order in Angola, reported that in all of Africa between 1840 and 1924, it had succeeded in producing a total of only thirty-seven priests. The turning point in the bleak outlook was reached only in the 1930s. The statistics for 1935–36, for instance, show that although the number of African priests was still small (only 32 for 21 Spiritan vicariates and prefectures on the continent), there were 130 senior seminarians. Then the development became more rapid, and in 1960 the figure showed more than 330 African priests and nearly 300 seminarians preparing themselves for ordination.[39]

The turning point in Angola was the creation of the new dioceses by the concordat in 1940 and the subsequent creation of diocesan seminaries. Following this the number of ordinations increased dramatically. The *Anuário Católico de Portugal — 1968* shows that in the twenty-eight

36. Gabriel, *Angola: Cinco Séculos de Cristianismo*, 328.

37. Moisés Alves de Pinho, *Memorias: Recordação duma vida que o Senhor quis longa* (Lisbon: n.p., 1979), 252.

38. Ibid., 254–55.

39. Henry J. Koren, *To the Ends of the Earth: A General History of the Congregation of the Holy Ghost* (Pittsburgh: Duquesne University Press, 1983), 465.

years after 1940 the number of Angolan priests increased from eight to seventy-one.

Protestant Ordinations

The Protestant churches in Angola had a variety of titles and categories for their ministerial leadership. They all had catechists, since that was a status determined by law and regulated by the government. All except the Plymouth Brethren ordained pastors to lead individual congregations or series of congregations. The Brethren chose two or more elders to give ministerial leadership to each assembly.

The Methodist system was the most complex and the Methodists were the first Protestant church to give ecclesiastical status to its Angolan leaders. On April 29, 1911, the West Central Africa Mission Conference received Mateus Pereira Inglez, João Garcia Fernandes, and João Leão Webba as "members on trial." The first two were ordained as deacons and presbyters on the same occasion.

Bishop Emílio de Carvalho gives brief sketches of these three Angolan heroes of Methodism, recording actions by which the conference recognized the dedicated service of these three pioneers. On his retirement in 1926 the conference noted the long connection of Mateus Pereira Inglez with the missions, his fervor for the Bible, and the humility that led him to confront such difficulties as hunger in spite of the riches that he possessed in Ambaca. João Garcia Fernandes was considered the best Angolan preacher during the first years of the Methodist church. Rev. Herbert C. Withey called him "the Nestor of our Angolan workers." The last of the three to die was João Leão Webba, who was described in the *Estandarte* as "one of the noblemen most devoted to the evangelical cause in Angola."[40]

By 1920 the leadership of the Angola Mission Conference had grown to eighty-five preachers and exhorters plus thirty pastors of whom only five were missionaries.

The churches planted by the ABCFM and Canadian Congregationalists in central Angola raised the question of ordination in the mid-1920s. In its annual report for 1927-28 the Bailundo church stated:

> Everyone knows that Abrahama Ngulu is the greatest single force in the Bailundo church. Most of the cases of discipline are settled in consultation with him and many are never brought to the missionaries save as he reports them later. He has done a deal of travelling among the outstations this year and some preaching in new regions, but we are trying to spare him an undue amount of

---

40. Emílio J. M. de Carvalho, *Heróis Angolanos do Metodismo* (Luanda: Igreja Metodista Unida em Angola, 1982), 16, 21–22, 25.

First pastors of the Evangelical churches of Angola. Seated: Israel Cassoma (Bailundo), Abraão Ngulu (Bailundo), António Chico Wambu (Dôndi). Standing: Lumbu (Chissamba), Paulino Ngonga (Elende), Jorge Chilulu (Dôndi), Horácio Rodrigues (Bailundo), Enoch Salupula (Chilesso), Chiwale (Bunjei), Albeto Catema (Chissamba)

foot travel. Were he ordained, his position would not be of much greater responsibility than at present, but we feel that some special recognition is due to him. We therefore urge the Mission to carefully and earnestly consider this case, and if it finds itself of like mind with us, to proceed to the ordination of Abrahama Ngulu at the earliest opportunity.[41]

The time indeed seemed opportune for the ordination of the first pastors, and the churches were invited to send their nominees for ordination to the Umbundu Church Council, which met on May 25, 1929, and was attended by forty representative elders from seven churches and by four missionaries. Elder Lumbo of Chissamba presided and Paulino Ngonga Liahuka of Elende as secretary recorded the names sent by the churches: Abrahama Ngulu, Bailundo; Umbombo Samose, Kamundongo; Lumbo, Chissamba; Enoch Salapula, Chilesso; Henrique Chilulu, Ndondi; and Chiwale, Galangi [sic]. The Elende church later sent the name of Paulino Ngonga Liahuka.

The council agreed that the salary of pastors should be 160$00 angolares (about $7.50) per month. "It further agreed that it should not be their work to pass upon the names of those who are to enter the church,

---

41. ABC 15.1, vol. 21, no. 255.

but that this should remain the work of the church elders, even as has been the case while the missionaries from abroad have had charge."[42]

Abrahama Ngulu was the first pastor ordained by the churches established by the ABCFM and the United Church of Canada; the ceremony took place at the Bailundo mission in September 1929. The others were ordained between then and the Jubilee of the mission celebrated in May 1930.

The process of choosing leaders, ordaining them, and deciding on their responsibilities was very democratic, emphasizing the priesthood of all believers and the authority of the laity.

The church planted by the Swiss mission ordained its first pastors in 1944 and sent them to their respective charges: Daniel Canyanga to the Kukala church on the Kalukembe mission station; Benjamim Cassoma to the large parish in Noni; David Chinguli to Cuilu; and Filipe Alves to the Viyonga church.[43]

The Church Becomes Missionary

A sign of the spiritual growth of the church in Angola was the initiative taken by several churches to send missionaries out and beyond the usual limits of their activity. The Bailundo church acted maturely in 1923–24 when it named Jessé Chiula Chipenda to go as their representative to serve the many men from the highland who were being forced to work on the coast or were attracted to the urban centers of Benguela, Catumbela, and Lobito.[44]

Jessé Chipenda not only gathered congregations in the three coastal towns, but also was responsible for sending the first catechist among the Chissanji people in the Bocoio area, a little over sixty-two miles inland from Lobito. His missionary work also took him to the fisheries south of Benguela, where many men from "up country" were on contract, a euphemism for forced labor. Dombe Grande, the site of a sugar plantation owned by the Companhia de Assucar de Angola, was the center of the largest number of contract laborers along the coast south of Benguela. Pastor Jessé visited these workers, but the company, which was very Catholic, refused the Protestants permission to worship or establish a congregation there. A colporteur, Florindo Dombe, as well as Pastor Jessé, visited Dombe Grande and the fisheries, but his work was also severely restricted.

The attitude of the Companhia de Assucar changed in 1941 as the

---

42. Ibid., no. 142.
43. Bréchet, *J'ai ouvert une porte devant toi*, 38.
44. In 1931 Jessé Chipenda studied at high-school level in Luanda, after which he moved to Benguela. In 1937–38 he did the theological course in Dôndi and was ordained in September 1938.

result of a special service held in the British consulate in Lobito on the occasion of the fall of France. John T. Tucker participated in the service and hundreds of Portuguese attended this gathering, which was widely reported in the press of the colony. Dr. Tucker wrote: "The meeting disabused the minds of many, ridding people of the fears entertained of our work."[45]

The sugar company, which was represented at the service, agreed that the Evangelical church could place a worker in Dombe Grande, and the Dôndi church chose the Rev. Macedo Pina of Chiumbo. So in December 1941 Dr. Tucker and Pastor Jessé went to Dombe Grande with Pastor Macedo, who, with the agreement of the company, established a church and school there and began regular visitation to the neighboring fisheries. The churches of central Angola organized a missionary committee to supervise the work and supported it with special missionary contributions, which were in addition to the regular financial support given by church members.

In 1944 three Protestant churches in central Angola reported the following total offerings:

Bailundo	$2,209.35 (dollars U.S.)
Chilesso	3,179.06
Elende	2,006.00

These sums were in direct cash gifts and did not include offerings for special purposes or gifts of labor and love. The dedication of these Christians to the work of the church is particularly impressive when it is known that average wages were at that time from three to six cents per day against which the government levied taxes amounting to the cash earned by fifty to a hundred days' labor per year.

In 1952 the Evangelical Alliance responded to the call for pastoral leadership from the Evangelical church in São Tomé. The first Angolan missionaries to be sent were the Rev. and Mrs. Joaquim José Cristiano of the Methodist church. They were replaced in 1960 by the Rev. and Mrs. Júlio Francisco from the Chilesso church.

The story of the founding of the Evangelical church in São Tomé illustrates that "God works in mysterious ways his wonders to perform." During World War I a young man, Samusili, from the village of Kamapenda in lower Sambo was impressed by a labor recruiter to go to São Tomé and work in the cocoa and coffee plantations. At that time "São Tomé" was a synonym for death, destruction, and hell for Africans.

One day a new Angolan worker at the plantation on São Tomé told Samusili about a new way of life. He mentioned the name Yesu (Jesus) of whom Samusili had never heard and told him about a good book that

---

45. ABCFM *Annual Report*, 1942.

had pleasant but piercing words, words that reached the heart. While the two men were together Samusili began to learn the ABCs, but his teacher was soon transferred to another plantation.

As Samusili was emptying bags of beans from Angola into a large bin, to his astonishment and delight, a book fell out. Samusili snatched it up and later carried it to his sleeping quarters: the longed-for book had appeared. On its cover he recognized eight letters — O V I K A N D A — (epistles). Inside the book the same word was printed and at the bottom of the page was "Bates Memorial Press, Kamundongo."

Samusili recognized the book was in his own Umbundu language. Some of the words were difficult, but he persevered, spelling out the words letter by letter. After many days he had actually reached Romans 1:16, and Samusili recounted: "I felt that God had spoken to me, and that he had given me a new heart."[46]

At this juncture help arrived for Samusili, as two Angolan Christians, Chitumba from Chilesso and another from the Methodist church in Malanje, were placed briefly at his plantation. The three men met regularly for prayer. When the two were transferred, Samusili was alone, but not silent or idle. Calling the other workers in the shed together after the day's work was done, he told them what he had found. Great rejoicing followed. Everyone wanted to be able to read the book and to learn to write. Samusili wrote scores of ABC books while the men saved their pennies to buy paper and pencils.

The plantation manager got wind of what was going on. Raiding the school one night, he burned the papers and pencils. Samusili was flogged and put in irons, but as soon as he was released he started preaching and teaching again. The manager forbade any singing, reading, or teaching, and the next time he caught Samusili, he had him beaten on the hands so he could not work, but his pupils did his stint of work for him. After many years when Samusili was finally given permission to return to Angola, he refused, saying, "Here in São Tomé I found Christ; here I remain for the rest of my life to help others know Him."[47] For the rest of his life Samusili was a pillar of the church in São Tomé. With his wife and family he was happy that someone had lost a book that later fell into his hands.

Silivondela, an elder of the Hualondo church, was another founder of the church in São Tomé. He took his hymnbook and portions of the Scriptures with him when conscripted for work in São Tomé and met the same kind of resistance and opposition as Samusili. But he too remained

---

46. John T. Tucker, *A Tucker Treasury: Reminiscences and Stories of Angola, 1883–1958*, selected and prepared by Catherine Tucker Ward (Winfield, B.C.: Wood Lake Books, Inc., 1984), 212.
47. Ibid., 214.

firm in his faith and through him scores of men were converted and added to the church in São Tomé.[48]

The stories of Silivondela and Samusili have been written down as permanent chapters in the history of the church. The spread of the church in São Tomé and to the far corners of Angola was due as much to men and women whose names are lost to our records, but who are known to the Lord of the Harvest.

A Broader Vision

The maturity of the church in central Angola was shown by its vision of its place in the Church Universal. The Umbundu Church Council meeting in Bailundo in August 1941 with over a hundred delegates closed its report with these words:

> The time is ripe for a colony-wide meeting of African Christians. Our people are traveling widely and standards should be compared. It is also desirable that some time in the future a still wider conference should be held which would include Christians from the Congo, the Rhodesias and Damaraland. We are building a church for Africa, not an Umbundu church, nor an Angolan church, but a church working in Africa, a branch of the universal church a church truly catholic.[49]

The 1941 vision of these Umbundu Christians was obviously shared by other African Christians, because in July 1946 Africans from central and southern Africa gathered in Leopoldville, capital of the Belgian Congo for a memorable missionary conference. The church in Angola was represented by three ministers: Gaspar d'Almeida, Filipe de Freitas, and Jessé Chipenda, as well as by Álvaro Lutucuta, a professor from Bailundo.

Conclusion

The church in Angola grew in many ways from 1900 to 1960. Local congregations in rural and urban areas grew in membership. Evangelists and catechists established new Christian communities around the pioneer missions, and new stations were established to extend the church in unevangelized places. Several more Catholic missionary organizations sent personnel to staff the increasing number of stations and seven more Protestant mission agencies added to Protestant strength. For the future

---

48. Wilson, *Angola Beloved*, 224–46.
49. ABCFM *Annual Report*, 1942, 42.

life of the church in Angola the most important sign of growth was the increase in the number of Angolan leaders — lay and clergy.

To close this chapter we compare the numerical estimates of the church constituency in 1960, recognizing that a qualitative measurement would be more important but also more difficult than this quantitative census.

Official Census
Religious Population of Angola — 1960

District	Total	Catholic Total	Catholic Percent	Protestant Total	Protestant Percent	Non-Christian Total	Non-Christian Percent
Cabinda	58,547	49,964	85%	6,519	11%	2,064	4%
Zaire	103,906	67,422	64%	35,537	34%	947	2%
Uige	399,412	196,206	49%	197,981	49%	5,225	2%
Luanda	347,763	262,594	75%	59,443	17%	25,726	8%
Cuanza North	263,051	222,938	85%	34,259	13%	5,854	2%
Cuanza South	404,650	240,318	59%	19,283	5%	145,049	36%
Malanje	451,849	150,795	33%	37,517	8%	263,537	59%
Lunda	247,273	20,877	8%	8,375	3%	218,021	89%
Benguela	487,873	300,259	62%	43,487	9%	144,127	29%
Huambo	597,332	411,245	69%	135,186	27%	50,901	4%
Bié	452,697	198,277	44%	135,562	30%	118,858	26%
Moxico	266,449	44,469	17%	33,252	12%	188,728	71%
Cuando-Cubango	113,034	19,163	17%	1,505	1%	92,366	82%
Moçâmedes	43,004	20,596	48%	728	2%	21,680	50%
Huila	594,609	249,278	42%	49,457	8%	295,874	50%
Total	4,830,449	2,454,401	51%	800,091	17%	1,575,957	32%

The church grew largest in areas of densest and most homogeneous populations. In the districts of Cabinda, Zaire, Uige, Luanda, Cuanza North, and Huambo more than 90 percent of the population were considered Christian. In Cuanza South, Benguela, Bié, Moçâmedes, and Huila, 50 to 75 percent were classified as Christian. In four districts, Malanje, Lunda, Moxico, and Cuando-Cubango, the majority of the population was non-Christian.

In the whole of Angola the official religious census considered 51 percent of the population Catholic, and 17 percent Protestant, with 32 percent non-Christian.

The *Anuário Pontificio* a Vatican publication, reported a Catholic population of 1,950,000 (40 percent), which placed Angola in second place in the percentage of Catholics in African territories and near Switzerland and Holland.[50]

The *Atlas Missionário Português* published in Lisbon by the Missão para o Estudo de Missionólogia Africana in 1962 reduced even more their estimation of the Christian population of Angola, calculating that 33 percent of Angolans were Catholic and 11 percent were Protestant.

---

50. *Portugal em África*, no. 137 (September–October 1966): 277.

The estimates of church constituency in Angola in 1960 varied from a high of 68 percent to a low of 44 percent. The higher percentage was probably accurate if it measured the persons who had been significantly influenced by the church. If the standard were that of a "practicing Catholic" or a Protestant in "full communion," then the lower figure was without doubt closer to the truth.

The difficulty of making an accurate religious census is illustrated by an anecdote told by John T. Tucker. An old man came to him in Dôndi and begged for a teacher for his village. "We are all Christians now. Ñala Kole [Dr. Currie] once slept in our village and when we awoke, we were all Christians." "Christians?" Dr. Tucker asked, "Christians? Do you not still follow fetish faith?" "Yes, indeed we do," came the earnest reply, "We are all children of God walking in the darkness."

Chapter 4

Growth Deterred

Kimbanguism

The steady growth of the church from 1900 to 1960 was deterred by two movements that overflowed south from the Belgian Congo/Zaire into Angola: Kimbanguism and Tocoism. (The word "deterred" is applicable to these movements only in the colonial period of 1900 to 1960. As we will see in chapters 14 and 15 after independence in 1974–75 Tocoism and Kimbanguism have been considered as two among many Protestant churches.)

Such movements were not as important in Angola during this period as they were in other African countries. *Schism and Renewal in Africa* by David B. Barrett analyzes six thousand independent religious movements.[1] The "historical" churches, which we have been describing, have generally looked with disdain or hostility on these independent movements. But is it possible that the Zulu scholar Absolom Vilakazi is correct and that the independent church movement is an "African reformation?"

Kimbanguism and Tocoism are examples of *Kingunza*, "Kongo prophetism," which has appeared in the region of the Lower Congo since the seventeenth century. Of those early prophetic movements the best known was the Antonian sect of the early 1700s, led by the prophetess Beatrice, which affected almost the entire kingdom of the Kongo.

In the period covered by this book the first major prophetic movement disrupting the growth of the church in Angola was started by Simon Kimbangu. He was born in 1889 in the village of Nkamba, Zaire,

---

1. David B. Barrett, *Schism and Renewal in Africa: An Analysis of Six Thousand Contemporary Religious Movements* (Nairobi: Oxford University Press, 1968), 163.

a few miles from the BMS mission of Ngombe Lutete in the district of Thysville/Mbanza Ngungu. His father was a *nganga,* or magician-diviner. Simon attended the Baptist school in his village and then studied at the BMS station of Ngombe-Lutete (originally Wathen), where he was a houseboy for the missionary H. R. Phillips. Simon Kimbangu studied the Bible and served for a time as a catechist in the local Baptist church. He married Mwilu Maria, and they had three sons: Daniel Mbuta Kisolokele, Paul Dialungana, and Joseph Diangienda.

Accounts differ as to when and where the young man began to have visions and dreams and when he responded to the call to become a *ngunza,* "prophet." One report says that in 1918 Kimbangu heard a voice say, "I am Christ, my servants are unfaithful, so I have chosen you to testify and convert your brothers."[2] Kimbangu replied that he was not wise and that there were pastors and priests for that work, but he kept hearing the same call for two years. Finally, he decided to flee to Leopoldville/Kinshasa to get away from that voice. However, he did not find peace there either, so returned to his village, Nkamba. In early 1921 the call to become a prophet — preaching and healing — was more and more insistent. April 6 is accepted as the official beginning of Kimbanguism. Dialungana, Kimbangu's second son, described the historic events, more as a disciple and adoring son than a historian:

> In Nkamba a man appeared who had never studied at a mission station, but he was a believer and had learned to read and write a little from a village teacher. His name was Simon Kimbangu. He raised the dead, caused the paralyzed to stand upright, gave sight to the blind, cleansed lepers, and healed all the sick in the name of the Lord Jesus. But he chased away those who practiced witchcraft. In the twinkling of an eye this news spread, and the whole country went wild. Like dust the news spread that in Nkamba had appeared a Prophet who was raising the dead. From that time Nkamba was called the New Jerusalem.[3]

> 1. The Prophet
> 2. The New Jerusalem

> Think well on both of them. When the prophet was revealed, the dead in stretchers and the sick of all kinds were brought to the Prophet of God. But in everything, whether raising the dead, healing the sick, or giving a blessing in the name of Jesus, first there must be prayer, then hymns, and then a teacher must read the Bible

---

2. François Choffat, "Notes sur le 'Kimbanguisme,' " *Cahiers de la Réconciliation* (Paris), no. 5–6 (May–June 1966): 4.

3. Wyatt MacGaffey, *Modern Kongo Prophets* (Bloomington: Indiana University Press, 1983), 33–34.

and teach the doctrines that change hearts, in order that all men should leave their wickedness; for if that does not happen, then these blessings you have come to get become as fire to you. Believe in the Lord Jesus, he who saves you from your sins. For I am in obedience to him.

Now God our Father and his Son Jesus Christ are returned to us, so cease your wickedness. Every day the doctrine of repentance must be taught, and when it is finished, the sick will be healed and the dead raised.

Now see how all the villages hastened to abandon their fetishes: see all the roads littered with fetishes of all kinds. People confessed their sins. Drums were broken, dancing forsaken. People struggled to seek out teachers. Churches were built overnight in all the villages. Those who had not cared to pray to God fought for places in church, and those who had no use for schools fought to enter the classroom.

Thus the words of Jesus were fulfilled, when he promised: And I will pray the Father, and he shall give you another Comforter, that he may abide with you forever; Even the spirit of truth; whom the world cannot receive, because it seeth him not, neither knoweth him (John 14:16–17). See now the power of the Lord Jesus revealed in his Servant, Simon Kimbangu, he having said: "Verily, verily, I say unto you, He that believeth on me, the works that I do shall he do also; and greater works than these shall he do, because I go unto my Father." (John 4:12).

Because Simon Kimbangu obeyed the voice of Jesus, all things promised by Jesus were fulfilled in him, the work of Jesus was revealed, and the names of God the Father and of the Lord Jesus were glorified. Since the coming of the missionaries, it had never happened that the dead arose, the lame walked, and the blind saw; or that people of their own free will threw away their fetishes, or wanted to pray to God. And only then did we the people of Kongo know that God and Jesus remembered us. The grief and suffering of ours fathers were wiped away in Kongo.

Missionaries and colonial rulers recognized that something unusual and powerful was happening at Nkamba. The local administrator, L. Morel, visited there on May 11, 1921, and his report was summarized as follows:

From a distance he saw, in a little plateau where the village was built, the noise of an excited crowd. He saw coming towards him a strange group, yelling and gesticulating: two young men and two girls surrounding the principal figure, dressed in red trousers and a white shirt, and holding in his hand the prophet's staff —

Kimbangu himself! All five trembled ecstatically.... A crowd of people of all ages milled through the village, with the sick lying among them. No more dead bodies had been brought since God had told the prophet to forbid it.... Kimbangu and his group continued to surround the white man with cries and gestures, and then the prophet, Bible in hand, read aloud the story of how David felled Goliath. To make quite clear what he meant, one of the girls showed the administrator a picture of the giant laid low.[4]

On May 18, 1921, the BMS missionary R. L. Jennings visited Nkamba and accounts of his reactions differ. Popular traditions say that he saw Kimbangu's miracles, broke into tears, and confessed that Europeans at home exercised the same powers although in Congo they denied them. The missionary's own report affirms that he saw no miracle, but rather folk who appeared demented, and was satisfied of the falsity of it all. He went on to say, "I was asked to address the people, and kind words were spoken of me as their missionary who, with others had brought to them the light of God's word."[5]

The government became alarmed at the strength of the movement as patients left their hospital beds to go to Nkamba to be cured; workers did not report at the cement factory at Lukula, and the Matadi-Leopoldville Railroad had to put on additional cars to carry the thousands of pilgrims to Nkamba.

On June 6, 1921, the Belgian administrator, accompanied by twenty soldiers went to Nkamba to arrest Simon Kimbangu. The prophet had given instructions to his followers; "If they arrest and beat me, you should not use force."[6] Yet there was a skirmish with some shots fired and one child killed. Kimbangu was led to his house and put under guard, but he succeeded in escaping and hid out in the village of Nsanda near Leopoldville/Kinshasa. All the people knew that Simon Kimbangu was in Nsanda: only the Belgian officials were ignorant of his whereabouts. Many pilgrims made visits to the prophet during the next three months.

Then on September 10 Kimbangu decided to return to Nkamba and give himself up. The administrator heard of Kimbangu's reappearance and on September 14 rearrested him and took the prophet, Bible in hand, to Thysville/Mbanza Ngungu, accompanied by a great procession. On his arrival a multitude of sympathizers ran to greet Kimbangu, including the director of the local Protestant mission.[7]

---

4. Ibid., 38.
5. Ibid., 39
6. Efraim Andersson, *Messianic Popular Movements in the Lower Congo*, Studia Ethnographica Upsaliensia 6 (Uppsala, 1958), 64.
7. Eduardo dos Santos, *Movimentos proféticos e mágicos em Angola* (Lisbon: Imprensa Nacional-Casa de Moeda, 1972), 86–90.

On October 16, 1921, Simon Kimbangu was charged before the War Council in Thysville with threatening the security of the country by inciting public disorders, conflict between black and white, nonpayment of taxes, and refusal to work. In his defense statement some prayers of Simon Kimbangu were presented to prove that he did not incite public disorder or conflict, and it was shown that "false prophets" not connected with Simon Kimbangu were taking advantage of the emotions at that time to preach subversive doctrines of which Kimbangu was being accused. However, the council found him guilty and sentenced him to death. King Albert of Belgium commuted the sentence to life imprisonment and exile to Katanga. Kimbangu was transferred to Elizabethville/Lubumbashi where he died on October 12, 1951, after thirty years in prison.

Some say that near the end he was baptized by a Catholic priest and died a "good death." Kimbanguists, however, claim that this is not true and that he died peacefully after reciting the Twenty-Third Psalm.

But what does all this have to do with the church in Angola? Most Angolans north of the eighth parallel were Bakongo, and the border between the Belgian Congo and Angola was not a significant barrier. Family members lived on both sides of the border, and while thousands of young men went to Leopoldville to seek work or adventure, the Bakongo north of the border still looked to São Salvador as their traditional capital. In 1921 when thousands of people trekked to Nkamba to be cured, the Baptist hospital in São Salvador was depopulated.

The São Salvador church meeting on June 7, 1921, took a cautious attitude toward the prophetic movements. They referred to the Acts of the Apostles, chapter five, which describes how the Jewish council imprisoned the Apostles who were preaching and healing. Gamaliel, a teacher of the Law who was much respected by the people, advised the council not to persecute the Apostles: "I tell you, do not take any action against these men. Leave them alone! If what they have planned and done is of human origin, it will disappear, but if it comes from God you cannot possibly defeat them. You could find yourself fighting against God."

The first official reference to Kimbanguism in Angola was a letter from the High Commissioner of Angola, Norton de Matos, alerting the BMS missionary Carson Graham to the dangers of these prophetic movements and informing him that the Portuguese would be no easier on them than the Belgians. In the same year fourteen catechists of the BMS mission of São Salvador were arrested for implication in a subversive movement, and the government acted against other Baptist leaders, giving them five months of forced labor.[8]

---

8. René Pélissier, *Resistance et revoltes en Angola (1845–1961)* (Lisbon: Editorial Estampa, 1982), 2:961–62.

During the 1920s, 1930s, and 1940s Kimbanguism was a part of the prophetic movement in the Kongo and not a distinct organization. Leaders in the movement:

> differed widely in their beliefs and practices. There is no doubt that some of them held reasonably orthodox beliefs but others held very "way out" views and not a few of the "ngunzas" or prophets, who claimed to be followers of Simon Kimbangu, were little different from the traditional "ngangas" (witch finders).[9]

The 150th Annual Report of the BMS in 1942 lamented the fact that "for at least ten years our work continued under heart-breaking opposition and the church and school work was largely destroyed by the Prophet Movement."

As the 1950s came to an end Kimbanguism moved toward a new stage in its development. In 1957 the Belgian colonial authorities gave permission for public demonstrations that were purely religious. This allowed seventeen leaders of Kimbanguism, using the name the Church of Jesus Christ on the Earth by the Prophet Simon Kimbangu (IJCSK), to petition the Belgian prime minister to recognize the movement. They argued that the charges that it had disturbed public order and that its followers were xenophobic were false. They claimed that the imprisonment in 1921 of the founder of Kimbanguism was due only to the fact that the religion he had just created was competing with the Catholic and Protestant religions. In December 1959 the Belgian government decreed freedom of religion in the Congo and recognized Kimbanguism.

As the religious movements moved back and forth across the border between the Congo and Angola at the end of the 1950s, so did political ferment:

> It was at this period 1959–60 that a number of men who claimed to be Kimbanguist prophets came into Angola secretly from the Congo/Zaire and began to preach in the villages. At the same time agents of UPA (Holden Roberto's Angolan political organization) were in the villages collecting subscriptions from the people. Portuguese authorities made no distinction between the two movements and wherever possible arrested them and any local people they suspected of association with them. Two of our teacher-evangelists were arrested and later killed. Because of this, one of the main concerns of the mission and the church was to protect the people from the Portuguese authorities. So we made a

---

9. F. James Grenfell, "Some Impressions of the Kimbanguists between 1955 and 1980," mimeographed.

point of warning the people of the dangers of becoming involved with the "ngunza" prophets or the political agents.[10]

Grenfell reported that the prophets from the north made little impact on the Baptist church during the 1950s for two reasons. First, most of the prophets were semiliterate and were unable to impress the people as being in any way superior to the Baptist teacher-evangelists. Second, the São Salvador people who belonged to the royal clan of the old Kongo kingdom were inclined to be contemptuous of movements from what they regarded as the "provinces." "The missionary efforts of the Kimbanguist *ngunzas* in Angola came to nothing except in two small villages in the Nkanda Hill country where the church did not have strong leadership."[11]

Other sources indicate that Kimbanguism had attracted some adherents in northeast Angola in the districts of Pombo and Kimbele.[12]

Kimbanguism did not attract a significant number of members from churches in Angola during the period of growth, 1900 to 1960, but it served as a deterrent to the growth of the Protestant churches particularly. It also added to the suspicions of Portuguese officials that religious activity and political subversion were closely linked; this increased government oppression of Protestant churches, especially in the Kongo area.

Tocoism

The second prophetic movement appearing during this period affected the church in Angola more widely and directly. Simon Kimbangu was born and lived his whole life in the Belgian Congo, while Simão Toco was a native of Angola and his greatest impact was in his homeland, although his experiences in the Belgian Congo shaped his ideas and actions.

Simão Gonçalves Toco was born on February 24, 1918, in the village of Sadi Kibango in the district of Maquela do Zombo, about six miles from the border with Zaire. He attended school at the BMS station of Kibokolo, where he finished his primary education and then was sent by the Baptist church to Luanda, where he did the first cycle of secondary school in the government *liceu*. While in Luanda Simão Toco participated in the life of the Methodist church. In 1937 he returned to Kibokolo, where he taught for a year, and then was transferred to another BMS station, Bembe, where he taught from 1939 to 1943.

---

10. Ibid.
11. Ibid.
12. Pélissier, *Resistance et revoltes en Angola*, 962.

Toco left Angola in 1943 for the Belgian Congo for reasons that have been diversely defined. His departure has been attributed to a dispute with BMS missionaries over salary, to a sense of having paid his debt to the mission and so being free to leave, to a desire to earn money for a dowry, and just to the urge to go to "the city." One acquaintance reported a conversation with Simão Toco in 1943 in which he asserted that he was going to Leopoldville/Kinshasa to start a church that would be an Angolan national church as Kimbangu had founded a Congolese national church.

In Leopoldville Simão Toco became active in the Baptist churches and was invited to organize a catechism class and choir among the many Angolans from Maquela do Zombo. He began with twelve members, and soon there were several hundred. His leadership qualities were also recognized, for he took responsibility for the delegation from Leopoldville that went to celebrate the jubilee of the Kibokolo mission in 1949.

A variety of influences played upon Simão Toco: Baptist teaching, Kimbanguist prophetism, Salvation Army organization, and Jehovah's Witnesses, but it is impossible to measure accurately the relative strength of each.

The event that marked the initiation of Tocoism as a distinct movement occurred on July 25, 1949 in Leopoldville. As Simão Toco led his choir in prayer, suddenly he felt a wind, and some singers began to shake and speak strange languages, quoting biblical passages principally from the Acts of the Apostles chapters 2–4. The choir members, frightened by the strange happenings, cried out and asked Simão what this meant. He told them to open their Bibles and read from the Old Testament book of Joel 2:28:

> And it shall come to pass afterward that I will pour out my spirit on all flesh; your sons and your daughters shall prophesy, your old men shall dream dreams and your young men shall see visions.

Believing that something wonderful had happened, Toco and the choir went to his house, where they continued praying and singing until morning.

When the BMS missionaries heard of the event they called Toco and interrogated him about what had happened and what literature he had been reading. Discovering that he had Watch Tower (Jehovah's Witness) books, they scolded him, saying that these books contained false teaching, and such literature was banned by the Belgian government. The missionaries prohibited Toco from having his evening prayer service at the mission. He then met with his choir at his house, and several times the experience of July 25 was repeated.[13]

On November 22, 1949, Toco and his followers were arrested, and on December 8 orders were given for expulsion from the Belgian Congo. They were charged with disturbing the public order by preaching that a new order under the reign of a new Christ would depose the present authorities and take their place, ruling with justice.[14]

Eighty-two persons, including sixty-six men, two women, and fourteen boys, were placed on the Angola frontier at Noqui.[15] The Portuguese authorities received them and placed Toco and the unskilled members of the party at Bembe in the colony of Vale do Loge, where they were to make a road. Why was this place chosen? One observer assumed that the Portuguese government hoped that being near his old mission would help Toco see the error of his ways.[16] Another, to the contrary, thought this was a way to undermine the work of the Baptist church by letting their apostates return to them.[17] Probably the decision was motivated neither by such hope or malevolence, but rather by a desire to dispose of a minor problem in a practical way.

The skilled people (office clerks, tradesmen, house boys) were sent to a camp near Luanda and were given work in the city at half-pay, but were obliged to return to the camp at night. John Marcum, a historian of the Angolan revolution, reports on the basis of correspondence with the BMS missionary David Grenfell, who visited the Luanda camp, that the Tocoists remained defiant. When the government demanded that they pay their taxes the Tocoists refused on the grounds that they were earning only half-pay.[18]

Young Marxists in Luanda contacted the Tocoists, but found them unprepared to project their religious heresy into organized political protest.

> Simão Toco's Bazombo disciples spoke Kikongo, little Portuguese, and no Kimbundu, and even more to the point, they spoke the language of a dislocated, rural peasantry, not that of a politically sophisticated urban intelligentsia.[19]

When the government recognized that the eighty-two Tocoists were more of a problem than was expected, Simão Toco was separated from

---

13. J. M. da Silva Cunha, *Aspectos dos Movimentos Associativos na África Negra*, Estudos de Ciências Políticas e Sociais 23 (Lisbon: Junta de Investigações do Ultramar, 1959), 2:29–68.

14. dos Santos, *Movimentos proféticos e mágicos em Angola*, 375.

15. Ibid. 376.

16. Ibid.

17. Pélissier, *Resistance et revoltes en Angola*, 972–73.

18. John Marcum, *The Angolan Revolution*, vol. 1: *The Anatomy of an Explosion (1950–1962)* (Cambridge, Mass.: MIT Press, 1969), 80.

19. Ibid.

his disciples and sent to a *colonato*[20] in Caconda near the Swiss mission of Kalukembe late in 1950. Toco was given the job of tractor driver. A Catholic assistant was assigned to keep him under surveillance and report to the colony officials the smallest sign of religious activity. The assistant became Toco's first convert there.

Shortly after Toco's arrival, word reached the church and mission of Kalukembe that a stranger was at the colony who preached wonderful sermons. Without knowing who he was, they invited him to Kalukembe, but he did not respond. After a few weeks the mission learned that the stranger was none other than Simão Toco.[21]

Toco held clandestine meetings at night, and many followers were attracted to the prophet because of his strong personality, his religious passion, and the fact that he was an educated African proud of his race and head of his own religion. Toco appealed especially to folk who had already some Bible knowledge, and Tocoism "spread like fire in straw over the field of the Philafricaine mission — one of the strange revivals in which the African continent is so rich."[22]

Some who heard Toco's messages saw visions; others heard voices and transmitted to "galvanized" audiences the messages received from the prophet. Great scenes of confession, absolution — always at night — were followed by singing and dancing. Rumors of miracles circulated. The Protestant church in the area was thrown into confusion, and three or four Kalukembe villages went over to the new sect. Some Tocoist practices were introduced into Protestant services. The pastors and missionaries of Kalukembe sought for some solution to the problem in prayer, and they recognized that condemnation was not enough. They were involved in a spiritual battle.

Simão Toco received authorization to spend a day at Kalukembe mission, but a long conversation with him did not give the mission any satisfaction. The prophet spoke reticently and was vague regarding his doctrine. He told the story of his life, affirming that while in prison in the Congo he had read literature of the Jehovah's Witnesses. Privately Toco asked Pastor Daniel Canyanga why he was willing to be a slave of the whites.

Dr. Bréchet concluded that the Tocoists emphasized a limited number of biblical passages, and they tried to demonstrate that the missionaries came to Angola with the intention of hiding the greater part of Christian teaching, thereby leading their adherents into error.

---

20. A Portuguese government agricultural settlement in Angola for Portuguese or Cape Verdian immigrants.
21. Rodolphe Bréchet, *J'ai ouvert une porte devant toi: Essai sur l'Histoire de la Mission Philafricaine* (Lausanne: Alliance Missionnaire Évangélique, 1972), 68–69.
22. Ibid., 69.

The concern over what Kalukembe missionaries termed the "Tocoist heresy" and other problems in the Kalukembe church led the missionaries and pastors to invite some leaders from the East African Revival to visit them in 1952 and lead services in the hope that a revival would renew the Kalukembe church the way it had awakened many churches in East Africa since the 1930s. Dr. Bréchet reported many testimonies to the blessings received through the ministries of their visitors, Dr. Joe Church and William Nagenda, but the revival did not have the desired effect on the Tocoist movement, which continued to grow in the Caconda-Kalukembe area.

In 1952 Portuguese authorities, upon receiving complaints from both Catholic and Protestant missions, transferred Toco from Caconda to Jau. However, the Tocoist groups survived the absence of their leader. A Swiss mission magazine published in January 1954 expressed concern over the continuation of what was considered a heretical sect. The author, Heini Schmid, reported the testimony of a young man of noble family who was an alcoholic and had found deliverance only with the Tocoists. Similarly, an old man who had been present at the founding of the Kalukembe mission testified that he had received more from the Tocoists than from the mission and that the moral life of the new Tocoist villages was superior to that of the mission villages.

In 1954 Simão Toco was transferred from Jau to Cassinga and the following year to the lighthouse at Ponta Albina on Baia dos Tigres about twenty miles from Porto Alexandre. He stayed there until 1961, when he was sent to São Miguel in the Azores.

By moving Simão Toco and his disciples from one place to another the Portuguese government did not achieve its goal of squelching the movement, but facilitated the spread of Tocoism all the way from the northern border of Angola to the extreme south in Porto Alexandre. By 1958 Tocoist congregations were reported not only in the Maquela do Zombo and Bembe areas, which would be considered Simão Toco's home territory, but also in Luanda, Moçâmedes, Porto Alexandre, Benguela, Caconda, Malanje, Salazar, and Uige. In 1957 the Luanda congregation reported 299 members: 126 men, 46 women, 60 boys, and 67 girls.[23]

As the number of congregations increased, the problem of maintaining common beliefs and practices also became greater. To establish a common identity, cards were prepared for church membership, marriage, and child dedication, all with the name, *Igreja do Nosso Senhor Jesus*

---

23. Eduardo dos Santos, *Movimentos proféticos e mágicos em Angola*, 378. Alfredo Margarida gives a smaller figure for Tocoists in Luanda in 1958, reporting only 118 (Marcum, *The Angolan Revolution*, 1:82).

Cristo — *Ebundu dia Mfumuetu Yeso Klisto* (Church of Our Lord Jesus Christ).[24]

The doctrine of Tocoism is difficult to define since it is a combination of Baptist teaching in which Toco was educated, some Jehovah's Witness concepts, which came from their literature, inspiration from Kimbanguism and Kongo prophetism, mixed with certain elements of African traditional religion.

Simão Toco closed the door to any organizational tie with the Jehovah's Witnesses in the mid-1950s when a dissident group of his movement allied itself with Watch Tower Bible and Tract Society. John Cook, an American representative of Jehovah's Witnesses, having heard that there was a group of Angolans using Watch Tower literature, visited Angola in 1955. He succeeded in interviewing Simão Toco in government offices in Sá da Bandeira/Lubango with a Portuguese official present. Although the conversation seems to have been pleasant, it became clear to both sides that Toco would not join the Watch Tower movement.

G. Phillips, the secretary of Watch Tower in South Africa, wrote a certificate affirming, in part:

> We understand that at one time several of those connected with the group of Jehovah's witnesses at Baia dos Tigres were connected with the movement led by Simão Toco. That was before they became Jehovah's Witnesses and before they were recognized by us as such. We are satisfied that Mr. João Mancoca and those associated with him at Baia dos Tigres are no longer associated with the Simão Toco Group. In view of that fact we believe you will agree that they should not be placed under the same restrictions as have recently been imposed upon members of the Toco group.[25]

This separation between Simão Toco and Jehovah's Witnesses is confirmed by a letter from Toco to the dissident congregation in Baia dos Tigres and a second to the Tocoist congregation in Benguela.[26] In an interview with Silva Cunha, Toco declared that his doctrine did not differ from the Protestants' since he also taught the Bible. When Silva Cunha observed that if anyone could read and understand the Bible, it was not necessary to have someone teach it, Toco responded that was not true. It is necessary to know how to take from the Scriptures that which is helpful. He quoted 1 Corinthians 6:12: "All things are lawful for me, but not all things are helpful."

On insistence by Silva Cunha, Toco admitted that he preferred to use

24. Silva Cunha, *Aspectos dos Movimentos Associativos na África Negra*, 48 opposite.
25. Ibid., 39.
26. Ibid.

Bible passages that dealt with the future and especially the apocalyptic texts such as Revelation and Daniel that gave the people hope.[27]

On reading a report of that interview Father Carlos Estermann opined that it was not surprising that Toco could not readily explain his doctrine:

> It does not appear to us that an individual no matter how intelligent, with the preparation of Toco, consisting of an elementary catechist's course and the first two years of secondary school... would be capable of constructing a well-articulated system of beliefs.[28]

The liturgical practices of the Tocoists were similar to those in regular Protestant services centering on singing and reading and interpretation of the Scriptures. The sacraments of Communion and believers' baptism by immersion also followed common Protestant practices.

The central role of the Holy Spirit in Tocoism led to practices characteristic of Pentecostalism, such as praying in tongues, shaking with emotion, and raising hands in prayer. The relation between these ecstatic experiences in the regular religious services and the all-night sessions of singing and dancing was not clear in the 1950s. As the movement spread across Angola some writers have affirmed that the night events included nude dancing, depilation, and sexual orgies. Silva Cunha, however, who investigated this extensively, confessed that "in spite of all our diligence we have not succeeded in obtaining proof of these practices."[29] David Grenfell, BMS missionary in Kibokolo, did write a letter dated February 1, 1966, that he had to break up a dancing session in front of his house and to take "one young man up to the Posto who was running around our house in the nude."[30]

Although worship practices and beliefs were not always clear or consistent throughout Angola, the Tocoists could be identified by their emblem — a white star on a red background. The star took various forms, which some explained as representing the parts of the chorus: soprano, alto, tenor, and bass. However, such a relation between chorus and emblem was not consistently evident. The emblem, worn by both men and women, was also used to decorate churches and private homes.

Several lists of rules for Toco's followers have been distributed, some

---

27. Silva Cunha, *Aspectos dos Movimentos Associativos na África Negra*, 45.
28. Carlos Estermann, "O Tocoismo como fenómeno religioso," *Etnografia de Angola (Sudoeste e Centro)*, Colectânea de Artigos Dispersos 1 (Lisbon: Instituto de Investigação Científica Tropical, 1983), 464.
29. Silva Cunha, *Aspectos dos Movimentos Associativos na África Negra*, 61.
30. Marcum, *The Angolan Revolution*, 1:80.

lengthy and detailed and others more concise. Following is a resumé of some of the more succinct lists of rules:

1. *Ten Commandments* (as in Exodus 20:3–17).

2. *Obedience and respect* to be shown to Simão Toco and other church leaders, to employees and government officials.

3. *Dress:* Wear white clothes with star emblem. Cut hair short with part in middle. Women should cover head with red or white kerchief. Should not wear jewelry. Should not put oil on hair.

4. *Cleanliness:* Wear clean clothes and shoes when outside. Before going to church service, wash mouth or take a bath.

5. *Prohibitions:* No smoking. No drinking alcohol. No eating pork.

6. *Work:* Be conscientious at your job. Seek skilled work.

7. *Education:* Send children to school. Learn to read and write Portuguese.

Most of the rules were supported by Scripture passages.

Discipline was strict in the "Church of the Lord Jesus Christ" and was enforced by expulsion or corporal punishment. The latter was administered at times by the "hand-paddle," or *palmatória*, which was in common use by Portuguese officials.

The discipline could be enforced because the hierarchical structure of the church identified those who had authority in the local groups and in the whole movement. Although Simão Toco was moved at least six times during the 1950s and was under constant surveillance by colonial officials, he was the undisputed chief of the movement. He was assisted by a council chosen by him from among some of his first disciples. Toco divided Angola into two districts, with the northern headquarters in Vale do Loge and the southern in Luanda. Each congregation had two catechists, or teachers, who were responsible for initiation and indoctrination, worship leadership, and discipline. Each congregation also had an elders council of men and women, which was the final authority on questions of discipline.

Observers have emphasized the influence of Kimbanguism, Jehovah's Witnesses, and African traditional beliefs on Simão Toco and his movement. Perhaps because they are less esoteric they underestimate influences that were affecting all churches in Angola. For example, Simão Toco was much impressed by the conference sponsored by the International Missionary Council in Leopoldville, July 13–24, 1946, in which he participated. The Rev. Gaspar d'Almeida, a delegate to the conference from the Methodist church in Luanda and director of the Protestant paper *O Estandarte*, mentioned in his report the presence of

Simão Toco, who was at that time, he wrote, a part of the Salvation Army.[31]

Simão Toco showed the importance he attributed to the 1946 meeting in Leopoldville by writing about it twenty years later to António Domingos Afonso Pereira of Taia Nova, Maquela do Zombo.

The Protestant Missionary Congress... dealt with many things — general education of Africans, the growth of civilization, law, etc., and finally the increase of the Light of the Gospel of Christ in the period of a few years. I, too, was invited to attend the Congress. Really, I saw and met blacks coming from various parts of the world, some we didn't understand because they spoke other languages and it was necessary to have an interpreter if we wanted to talk with a brother of another country. I met also black brothers from North, South, East, and West of Angola....

Before the end of the Conference... from the Angolan natives two were chosen to pray to God.... The first black prayed to increase instruction, education, progress, the right to unify blacks and whites, etc., etc. That black was Rev. Gaspar de Almeida of the Evangelical Episcopal Mission in Luanda.

The second black was told by his missionaries, Dr. Tucker of the Dôndi mission in Nova Lisboa/Huambo, now deceased, and Dr. Bréchet of the Philafrican mission of Caluquembe not to repeat a lot in his prayer, but to ask only for the Holy Spirit and God to convert the African people; that the power of the Holy Spirit in Africa should continue and that this prayer could not be led by a foreigner; it should be led by one of the Africans chosen by the missionaries who brought the word of God to Africa. That second African prayed asking only for the power of the Holy Spirit in Africa and the increase of the Word of God. That black was named Simão Gonçalves Toco.[32]

It is easy to see how Toco could interpret his experience of July 25, 1949, as an answer to the prayer that he led three years before.

The way in which the heretical and subversive influences on Simão Toco were emphasized by both church and state is shown in a confused report linking the Leopoldville conference to Toco's contact with the Jehovah's Witnesses:

Among the participants were delegates, black and white, from many parts of the world, including the United States of America and Liberia. In the Congolese capital was also the wife of the

31. Rev. Gaspar d'Almeida, *Congresso Evangélico Missionário da África Ocidental: Diário de uma Viagem* (Luanda: Edição do "O Estandarte," 1948), 27–28.
32. dos Santos, *Movimentos proféticos e mágicos em Angola*, 371–72.

famous singer, Paul Robeson. We do not know of her connection with Watch Tower or who of that organization spoke with Simão Toco. The Rev. Reinolds of the BMS supposed that it was the black American Cowes who introduced Simão Toco to Watch Tower.[33]

Eduardo dos Santos, the author of the above quotation, added a footnote identifying Cowes as an ABCFM missionary at an all- black mission station. Then he concluded, "In any case the information about the missionary Cowes appears correct." [34]

To be more accurate, the black missionary was not "Cowes," but Samuel B. Coles, the agricultural-industrial missionary at the Galangue mission described earlier (p. 80). Certainly it would not have been Sam Coles who introduced Simão Toco to the Jehovah's Witnesses. Nor would there have been any relationship between the Leopoldville conference and that organization which was seen as a heretical sect by the International Missionary Council/Foreign Missionary Conference that sponsored the Conference.

If the Belgian and Portuguese colonial officials had not been so paranoid about African pride and self-assertion, Simão Toco might have found a place in one of the Protestant churches, where he could have shared his religious experience and expressed his missionary zeal.

Kimbanguism and Tocoism impeded the growth of the church in Angola during the period from 1900 to 1960 politically and religiously. Politically they made officials in Angola even more convinced that religious activity directed by Africans was a cover for political activity. Religiously the two movements attracted hundreds and perhaps thousands of men and women who were adherents of other churches and converted even some local leaders.

Other Movements

We have given most space in this chapter to Kimbanguism and Tocoism, because they were the two prophetic movements that had the most influence during the 1960s, 1970s, and 1980s. However, there were other movements that merit some mention.

Lassyism, founded by Lassy Simon Zepherin in Congo-Brazzaville, spread into Cabinda in 1953. The prophet was given permission by the Portuguese authority in Mussabi to cleanse his area of fetishism. At the same time Lassy attracted many people as he travelled from village

---

33. Ibid., 384.
34. Ibid.

to village, gathering fetishes and preaching. When the Portuguese authorities perceived that he was forming a new church they prohibited his entering Cabinda, but by 1957 he is reported to have had 10,400 adherents.[35]

In central Angola in the 1950s a movement appeared known as *Olosanto*, the Saints. In the beginning the Catholic missions of the region welcomed the Olosanto because they promised to rid villages of fetishes. The Saints also sought to annihilate the fetishists. When the Catholic missionaries recognized that the Saints were a sect that used magic, they denounced to the government those whom they originally welcomed. The Saints included women as well as men. In 1955 about two hundred Saints were arrested in central Angola.

Most of the Saints were Catholic and they claimed various appearances of the Virgin Mary with a "black God" at her side. A Catholic catechist who was a part of the movement declared in 1955 that "if the Whites had a religion made for them, the natives could make a religion for their use."[36]

One of the teachings of the Saints that most disturbed the Portuguese authorities was that the people should kill all black domesticated animals because they were used in fetishism. The Saints also urged people to destroy their fields and not plant again, for manna would fall from heaven for the people as in Bible times. The sect especially sought as disciples young girls between the ages of fifteen and twenty whom they would dress in white in a way similar to nuns. The movement also contained apocalyptic doctrines that promised a new world in which whites would have no place or would be under control of blacks.

The Saints' movement did not seem to have any centralized organization as did the other movements described in this chapter, and it did not last beyond the mid-1960s.

Conclusion

The prophetic movements were a deterrent to the growth of the church in Angola during the period from 1900 to 1960, but they were also a challenge. In the first chapter we noted the difference between the European and African worldviews and the similarity between the Bantu and biblical cultures. The African prophets cited Scripture as interpretations of their own experiences, not, as colonial authorities believed, to disguise subversive political intentions. It was true, however, that the prophetic

35. Ibid., 485.
36. Ibid., 496.

movements expected that as imminent changes occurred they would affect political, economic, and social realities as well as religious.

Simon Kimbangu interpreted his April 6 experience by quoting Jesus' instructions to his disciples (Matt. 10:8): "Heal the sick, raise the dead, cleanse lepers, cast out demons. You received without paying, give without pay." Simão Toco quoted Joel 2 to explain what happened to him and his choir on July 25, 1949.

David Barrett confirms the observation of Catholic critics who say that the Protestant action of putting the Bible in the languages of the people was a major factor in producing independent Christian movements. This is not surprising because of the parallel nature of Bantu and biblical cultures.

In the periods of transition from colonialism to political independence and then during the adaptation to the new society and civil war, prophetic or independent Christian movements have grown in Angola. Are such movements necessarily a deterrent to the growth of the church or could they be a stimulus to its renewal? Is it to be expected that as the roots of the Christian church reach deeper into the Angolan soil the church will become more African in its liturgy, beliefs, and style?

Chapter 5

The School:
The Principal Means
of Planting the Church
and Promoting Its Growth

A church without a school is like a couple without children.
— A Methodist report

In 1880 there were only twenty-seven schools in Angola, all supported by the Portuguese government in administrative centers. Of the
twenty-seven regular teachers, fourteen were priests and four were
women who taught sixty-two girls in four schools. In the other twenty-
three schools, 525 boys studied, and these schools were scattered across
the western part of Angola as indicated on the map.[1]

The statistics do not indicate the racial composition of the 587 students, but since all the schools were in Portuguese administrative centers, we can assume that whether white, mestizo, or black, the pupils
were part of the Portuguese community and were able to study in that
language.

---

1. Michael Anthony Samuels, *Education in Angola, 1878–1914: A History of Cultural
Transfer and Administration* (New York: Teachers College Press, 1970), 24, 59.

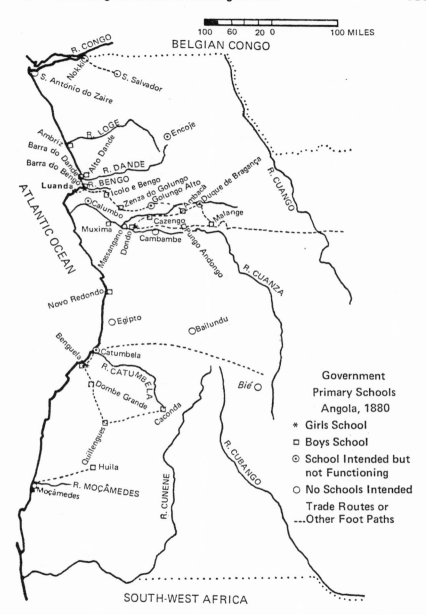

Government Primary Schools, 1880. Reprinted by permission of the publisher from Michael Anthony Samuels, Education in Angola, 1878–1914: A History of Cultural Transfer and Administration *(New York: Teachers College Press, © 1970 by Teachers College, Columbia University; all rights reserved), 59.*

Purposes of Missionary Education

Protestant missionary societies did not expect schools to be an important feature of the initial missionary effort. The ABCFM in Boston stressed conversion as the primary objective of the mission: "Do not be in a hurry to teach the natives many things until the one thing needful has been learned and received in the heart."[2] At first the missionaries agreed with this advice from the mission board, as shown by William Sanders's comment in 1885 that education had "no practical benefit to the people."[3] Two years later, however, he recognized that "school boys are Christianized as outsiders are not. The school is the most powerful Christianizing agency."[4]

This change in mission theory and practice was produced by a basic missionary experience. As the missionaries arrived in any area they were dependent upon Africans for many services. First they needed carriers to take their baggage from the port to the site chosen as a mission station. Then they needed people to help them clear land, cut down trees, build stick-and-mud houses, cultivate garden plots, carry water, and gather firewood. To achieve all this required that missionaries learn the local language. As they wrote down new words the Africans recognized that the white people's magic was a key to his wealth, power, and mysterious communications across oceans and generations, so they wanted to learn to read and write.

The major task of the Protestant mission, after survival, was translation of the Scriptures into the vernacular. The missionaries and young men who gathered around to serve their physical needs were bound together as they exchanged informal lessons in Kimbundu, Kikongo, or Umbundu for classes in reading and writing.

The Bible and the school — both in the vernacular — were the two foci of the Protestant church as it was planted and grew. The BMS began to teach Kikongo by stenciling words on white cloth as soon as their first school opened in October 1880.[5] Holman Bentley and his African colleague, Nlemvo, translated the Scriptures, and by 1893 Mrs. Bentley had prepared primers in Kikongo for the school: *The Peep of Day, The Congo Primer, More about Jesus, A Bible History,* and a three-part arithmetic book with 1550 problems.[6]

---

2. ABCFM Annual Report 1880, 30.

3. Letter, Sanders to Smith, February 6, 1885 (ABC 15.1, vol. 7, no. 64).

4. Letter, Sanders to Smith, October 8, 1887 (ABC 15.1, vol. 7, no. 89). This same pattern was noted by Professor J. F. Ade Ajayi of the University of Ibadan in *Christian Missions in Nigeria 1841–1891: The Making of a New Elite* (Evanston: Northwestern University Press, 1969), 133–35.

5. Holman Bentley, *Pioneering in the Congo* (New York: Fleming Revell, 1900), 1:215.

6. The *Missionary Herald*, BMS, February 1888, 39.

The missionaries from Great Britain and North America were tempted to teach English to the students. After a few years, however, prodded by pressure from Portuguese authorities, the missionaries and mission agencies recognized that teaching English was counterproductive. Holman Bentley, writing from the Congo Free State, warned his fellow missionaries in São Salvador, "If we do not stop the teaching of English we stand a good chance of being restricted both on Free State and Portuguese ground. At San Salvador Portuguese should have preference over English."[7] His warning was not accepted fully though, and in 1897 the mission board in London wrote a private series of regulations stressing that "missionaries should not seek to make the people Englishmen."[8]

In 1914 the ABCFM Annual Meeting passed a motion declaring it "inadvisable to teach English at this time."[9]

Catholic schools used the Portuguese language earlier and more consistently than did Protestants for several reasons. In the early years of establishing and developing the church and schools there were no Portuguese Protestant missionaries while about one-half of Catholic missionary personnel was Portuguese. Catholic missionaries, whether Portuguese or foreign, were supported by the Portuguese government, which considered its investment in Catholic missions not only a religious duty, but a means of transmitting Portuguese culture and language to the African population. Finally, Catholic schools had as their primary goal the preparation of clergy; this required secondary and higher education, which was available only in Portuguese or another European language.

Difference between Catholic and Protestant Educational Policies

This last reason for using Portuguese in the Catholic schools points to the fundamental difference between Catholic and Protestant mission schools. The Catholic schools were seminaries founded to stimulate vocations and promote education for the priesthood. The Protestant schools, on the other hand, had as their basic purpose the teaching of reading and writing so that the mass of Christians could read the Scriptures and participate in the life of the local congregations, which were led by lay men and women.

By present standards the early mission schools in Angola hardly deserved the name "school." Most missionary teachers were well enough

---

7. BMS Archives A/32, April 23, 1888.
8. "Regulations for the Future Conduct of the Mission," BMS Archives H/28, September 30, 1897.
9. ABC 15.1, vol. 18, 1914.

qualified, but they had a variety of other responsibilities, which allowed them scant time for preparation and teaching. The pupils also worked in construction, farming, and domestic services and were in class only a few hours a day. Moreover, lesson materials were very scarce.

The General Report of the Protestant Mission of Bailundo, May 1, 1899, recognized that at that time the schools' primary role was evangelistic:

> The schools of the station are really a branch of the Evangelistic work, their only aim being to get hold of the children and teach them the truths of the gospel, and to prepare those who are sufficiently instructed in Christian life to carry the gospel to others. It is only by accommodation of terms that the work done in our schools can be called "Educational."[10]

Under the pressure to train more teachers and raise academic standards the missions established boarding schools at stations and outstations. These provided pupils with more time for class and study since they did not need to walk back and forth to their villages each day. The mission station also furnished an atmosphere that missionaries judged more propitious for developing Christian character than that of the non-Christian villages from which the students came. Yet, even in boarding school, the students only spent a half-day in class and study. The other half was spent in various chores that contributed to the support of the school: cultivating fields to produce food for the students, gathering firewood, preparing and cooking food, fetching water, and the many other tasks necessary for the maintenance of school and station. Even so, the boarding schools were seldom completely self-supporting, depending partially on some outside subsidy.

Protestant missions subsidized their boarding schools by funds received from overseas supporters. Catholic missions depended on the Portuguese government for the basic support of their boarding schools, but the missionaries also received contributions through their congregations or from individual donors. Catholic missions were allowed by the government to engage in commercial operations to help support their schools and other programs. The talents and interests of the missionary personnel and natural conditions dictated whether Catholic missions grew coffee, made tiles, or operated printing presses to add to the basic support that came from the government. The government prohibited the Protestant missions from engaging in commercial activities.

---

10. ABC 15.1, vol. 9, no. 122.

Training Schools

As the demand for catechists and teachers for new Christian communities increased there was pressure on the Protestant missions to establish special teachers' training schools. As early as 1909 the Annual Meeting of the West Central Africa Mission (ABCFM) voted to found an institute that would have as its aim:

> To train approved Christian young men for more adequate service as helpers in Industrial, Educational, Medical and Evangelistic mission work among the Ovimbundu and other tribes.[11]

A committee composed of Walter Currie, chairman, William Sanders, and T. W. Woodside was appointed to formulate a plan that could be placed before the ABCFM and the Plymouth Brethren.

Study of the proposal continued among the missionaries in Angola and in correspondence with the boards' offices in Boston and Toronto. All parties agreed that such an institution for young men was advisable and the American and Canadian boards promised support. The Plymouth Brethren were unable to give organizational approval, but they did send some students.

Dôndi, a site that was central to the ABCFM and Canadian mission stations just north of Bela Vista/Katchiungo on the Benguela railway, was chosen for the project. The school was officially opened on October 5, 1914, and received its first class of young men. Six churches sent twenty-five students:

Elende	*Chissamba*
Paulino Gonga Liahuka	Jorge H. Chilulu
Madaleno Chipa	Henrique Chali Sicato
Paulo Canhimi	Doutor Gungo Canjundo
Raul Cavita	Stanley Songuila
Quinhentos Nhani	Álvaro Heque

Bailundo	*Camundongo*
Horácio Rodrigues Arão	Moises Umbondo
Jorge Chingano	Ferminão Seinja
Edouardo Miller	Tomas Dindimo
	Enoque Gomes Sacamana

Chilesso	*Chissamba*
Pessoa Canganjo	Canguende
Israel Chitumba	Siquete
Bene	Chissungui
Valeriano Dundo[12]	

---

11. ABC 15.1, vol. 14, no. 7.

12. John T. Tucker, *A Tucker Treasury: Reminiscences and Stories of Angola, 1883–1958* (Winfield, B.C.: Wood Lake Books, 1984), 187. The name of the Chissamba church is repeated and the name of one student is missing.

The size of the school increased each year: 1914, 25; 1915, 44; 1916, 60; 1917, 70; 1918, 75; 1919, 82; 1920, 100.[13]

The 1916 Annual Meeting gave the name Currie Institute to the new central boys' school, honoring Walter Currie, the chairman of the committee that proposed the institution. Some would have preferred the name Kachivungo to recognize the African name of the location.

The three-year curriculum was divided into three sections: academic, Bible, and trades. The first included Portuguese, history and geography, science, and mathematics. Bible was required each year. In addition to agriculture Currie Institute offered courses in carpentry, masonry, and tailoring. All students were required to take agriculture and two other trades for one year. Specialization in one of the trades for two more years was needed for graduation. Lessons were also given in pedagogy, and this later developed into a special department, as did a pastoral training course.

All graduates were expected to serve the church in some capacity. Many of the young men became teachers or nurses, receiving a small salary supplemented by income from one of the trades that they had learned at Currie Institute. Those who did not become professional church workers still made significant contributions as volunteer church leaders, whether they held catechist cards or not. Dôndi men improved the quality of life in Christian villages by building better houses and furniture, planting vegetable gardens and fruit trees, and sharing their knowledge of public health.

The institute constantly raised its academic standard. In 1921 two Protestant couples were recruited from Portugal to teach at Dôndi: Eurico and Clotilde de Figueiredo and Jaime and Celeste Raposo. The latter couple worked for twenty years as teachers in Protestant schools in Angola. In 1922 seventy-five students passed the most elementary government examination, *primeiro grau*, which corresponded roughly to the fourth grade in American schools. The next year ten students passed the exam for complete primary education — the sixth grade, or *segundo grau*, in the Portuguese system.

Dôndi attracted attention not only for its academic achievements, but for its agricultural innovations. Sawimbo and Essinde of Chissamba demonstrated the proper handling of the plow and other farm implements, which not only provided improved crops in subsequent years, but also gave a valuable lesson to the Africans about the immense value of scientific agriculture. Responding to these initiatives, the government distributed new varieties of seed to the institute and through it to people of the area. Strawberries were introduced by the mission, and from this beginning there developed an industry that brought a certain renown

---

13. Ibid., 187–93.

to the region. The Rhode Island Red breed of chickens raised in Dôndi was also shared with the neighboring people.

The central school for girls was opened on the Dôndi property in 1916. It was named after John O. Means, the ABCFM secretary who made the original proposal that a new work be started among the Umbundu in central Angola. The Means School curriculum also had three sections: academic, Bible, and home economics. Girls were required to have finished village and station schools before entering Means School. They not only studied all aspects of home economics — laundry, sewing, child care, and agriculture — in class, but they also carried their lessons into the practice cottages in which they lived. In the early years only a few Means women entered professional fields, but practically all became wives of Currie men and mothers of second-generation Christians in central Angola.

From the founding of Currie and Means until 1950 the educational system in the churches planted by the ABCFM and the United Church of Canada was a hierarchy based on hundreds of village day schools where pupils studied three or four years, learning the rudiments of reading and writing in Umbundu, simple arithmetic, beginning Portuguese, and Bible knowledge. Those who were successful next entered a boarding school on a mission station; there they completed in three or four years what would correspond to an American primary education. Then the best students and those judged to have a good character reached the apex of the pyramid at Dôndi — Currie Institute for boys and Means School for girls.

In the 1930s and 1940s Currie and Means were considered the foundation of a future university of Angola.

The steady stream of leaders coming out of the two central schools was one factor in strengthening the educational program of the Protestant church in central Angola as shown by the increase in students in ABCFM schools in the annual reports of the West Central Africa Mission:

1910 . . . . 4,176 pupils enrolled
1920 . . . . 12,598 pupils enrolled

Like all schools, Currie Institute and Means School were instruments for planting the church and promoting its growth. Students scattered out on Sunday mornings to conduct services in neighboring villages, sometimes accompanied by the agricultural instructors, Sawimbi or Essinde of Chissamba, or one of the carpenters, Chitumba of Chiuka, Ndumbu of Chissamba, or Njamba of Bailundo. John T. Tucker and William Bell often joined the students on their hikes to take the gospel to villagers who were anxious to hear the Word.

The workers at the central institutions who had come from other churches settled down in Dôndi and felt the need for their own church.

Thus the Dôndi church was organized in 1920, and the first twenty members were almost entirely professors and workers of the institute with their families. The names of the charter members were:

Paulo Bonga	Kapuka	Siluano	Maundi
Chikumbu	Nahossi	Victoria	Josefe
Madaleno Chipa	Kalandula	Moises	Mariona
Felicia	Tiago Elias	Kanjila	Nahuma
Jorge Chilulu	Kuvuka	Jonas Soma	

By 1925 sixty-five outstations of the Dôndi mission/church had been established.

Currie Institute and Means School were directly responsible for the founding of the Dôndi church and were one cause of the rapid growth of the whole church in central Angola as their graduates settled into villages of the area to work as catechists, teachers, and church elders. These statistics show the great increase in the 1920s in membership of churches served by Currie and Means:

```
1910 ............................. 625
1920 ............................. 983
1930 ............................. 8,475
```

"In spite of the extensive projection of the Dôndi mission, the Quéssua mission was by one observer considered the Mecca of Angolan Protestantism."[14] José Júlio Gonçalves, the Portuguese Catholic missiologist, thus described the importance of the Methodist mission eight miles from Malanje on the Lombe River. Quéssua corresponded to the Dôndi mission, being the training center for the Methodist church as Dôndi was for the Council of Evangelical Churches in Central Angola.

Quéssua had educational institutions for boys and girls from nursery and preprimary to secondary courses in a technical school and the William Taylor Bible School. Its Agricultural and Industrial Department, for many years under the direction of Loyd Schaad, gave much practical instruction and made a significant contribution to the economy of that area. The health services included a hospital and nurses' training school.

Government Intervention

The intimate relation between church and school was illustrated by the dual role of catechists. According to Decree 77 of December 9, 1921, no Angolan could teach or be in charge of an outstation without an official identification card, which only the regional Portuguese authority could

---

14. José Júlio Gonçalves, *Protestantism em África: Contribuição para o Estudo do Protestantismo na África Portuguesa,* Estudos de Ciências Políticas e Sociais 39 (Lisbon: Junta de Investigações do Ultramar, 1960), 2:86.

issue. The decree required that candidates for such a card be presented by the director of a mission and that they speak Portuguese. The law did not prescribe how this language ability was to be tested; that was left entirely to the discretion of the official. If relations were good between the director of the mission and the official, the cards were simply presented and the official signed them without even seeing the candidates. This was generally true with Catholic missions since their missionaries were colleagues of the officials. In dealing with some Protestant missions the authorities submitted the candidates to both written and oral tests.

Once the catechists/teachers were documented, they were responsible for the life of the church in their village and were expected also to teach reading and writing in Portuguese. By law and missionary convenience the school and church were two sides of the same community. The Umbundu term *Ndukuasikola*, literally "I belong to the school," meant "I am a Christian."

The Catholic scholar Adrian C. Edwards, comparing the Catholic and Protestant work in central Angola, wrote:

> At the local level a number of differences can be noticed, in such matters as the neater, more planned appearance of the Protestant villages; which have far more rudimentary (preprimary) schools than the Catholics. These schools are entirely financed by the Protestant villagers; among the Catholics while there is a desire for more schooling there is a lack of drive that the Protestants show. A *chefe de posto* said that the Protestants spoke Portuguese better than Catholics; and the Protestants are more "Europeanizing" in their outlook.[15]

In 1941, when the Missionary Statute entrusted the education of Africans entirely to the Catholic church, there were only seven thousand Catholic students in Angola. If the statute had been enforced strictly, Protestant schools would have been closed and Catholic schools would have received government support to provide education for the African population of Angola. However, neither happened. On February 6, 1950, ten years after the concordat and Missionary Statute, the Portuguese government issued a law (Portaria 7.079) instituting a new system of education for Africans, Rudimentary Education.

Although Decree 77 in 1921 had asserted the government's authority over all education and established Portuguese as the medium of instruction, it did not define the curriculum nor provide the bureaucratic machinery for its supervision. Twenty-nine years later Rudimentary Education gave detailed instructions as to what should be taught, when, by

---

15. Adrian C. Edwards, *The Ovimbundu under Two Sovereignties* (London: Oxford University Press, 1962), 31.

whom, and under what conditions. Portaria 7.079 was a partial implementation of the Missionary Statute of 1941. Again, if it had been rigidly enforced, it would have outlawed all Protestant schools and forced all African children to attend Catholic schools. No one expected the law to be enforced, however, least of all the Catholic church, which was charged with the administration of the schools. Father Silva Rego, the missiologist of the Overseas Colonial Institute in Lisbon, complained of the impossible task given to the church:

> Rudimentary Education is entrusted ... to the Catholic missions. The state freed itself of this education and requires that the Catholic missions undertake it, but, and this is important, the state does not give the necessary resources to make it possible.[16]

Although the government support for Catholic schools was admittedly inadequate, the new law did establish a normal school to prepare teachers to administer the Rudimentary curriculum. The Teófilo Duarte Normal School, located at Cuima near Nova Lisboa/Huambo, was supported financially by the state and entrusted to the Holy Ghost Fathers. To enter the school the student was required to have passed the official Portuguese examination for primary school (*segundo grau*) and be a Roman Catholic. Attempts were made to allow Protestant students to study there or to authorize Currie Institute to teach the same course, but the government refused all such overtures.

The normal course was three years, and upon receiving the diploma the graduates were placed as teachers in a Catholic mission school with their salaries paid by the Department of Education. In 1954 the Cuima Normal School had 153 students. From 1952 through 1966 this school graduated 592 teachers, a tremendous boost for Catholic education in Angola.

The government continued to invest money in normal schools administered by the Catholic church and placed special emphasis on teacher training for women until there was one female normal school in each diocese. The following statistics of students in mission schools indicate the impetus given to Catholic schools:

	Catholic	Protestant	Total
1954	28,275	12,227	40,502
1961	47,955	18,199	66,154

The main effect of the 1950 educational legislation, however, was not to increase the school population, but rather to establish the machinery by which more pupils could be officially registered with the education

---

16. Silva Rego, *Alguns Problemas Sociologico-Missionários de África Negra*, Estudos de Ciências Políticas e Sociais 32 (Lisbon: Junta de Investigações do Ultramar, 1960), 104–5.

department. Until 1950 only a small group of elite who had mastered enough of the national language to attempt an examination along with the Portuguese children of town and city achieved some official educational standing. Now under Rudimentary Education the youngsters beginning their ABCs in a rural school could be registered and examined at the end of the year by a jury of government examiners.

The main goal of Rudimentary Education as conceptualized by the educational authorities was:

> to contribute to the elevation of the native masses by means of the first level of instruction regarding the realities of the life of the people who are underdeveloped without alienating them from their class, their traditional hierarchy, or physical labor.[17]

To this end agricultural work and manual arts were emphasized in the syllabus. More popularly the Portuguese said that this was to avoid the creation of *calcinhas* (short-pants), a colonial pejorative referring to young men who felt estranged from their traditional culture, but were not accepted into Portuguese society.

Ironically, the effect of Rudimentary Education was the opposite of what its creators intended. The demand to register all pupils with the government education office required parents and teachers to spend extravagant amounts of time and money to acquire the necessary documentation, and the official juries gave almost exclusive attention to the pupil's knowledge of Portuguese. The successful students were those who mastered Portuguese and the maze of bureaucratic requirements. Only the failures were not alienated from "their class, their traditional hierarchy, or physical labor."

The general effect of governmental action on the Protestant community from 1921 to 1961 was to impede the development of mass education. We noted that one mission agency (ABCFM) reported 12,596 pupils in one area of Angola in 1920. This was 369 more than were officially registered in 1954 in all the Protestant schools in Angola. By continuously increasing requirements and inspections concerned with documents and statistics, the government crippled the movement for mass education, which had a good start in the early 1900s.

In contrast the governmental action increased the number of students and raised the level of education on Catholic missions. The problem of documentation was not so severe for them since the baptismal certificate of the Catholic church was accepted as a legal document that could substitute for the birth certificate from the civil register. The government increased its general subsidy to Catholic schools and, most

---

17. *Estatuto do Ensino Rudimentar* (Luanda, Serviços de Instrução).

importantly, provided normal schools to train teachers, who were then paid them from government funds.

Protestant Educational Initiatives

Angolans increasingly sought better educational opportunities, and the Protestant community responded positively in several ways: individual teachers opened private schools, and the Methodist and Congregational missions received government permission for secondary school courses in Quéssua and Dôndi. Rural life and domestic schools were also established.

Six teachers who had worked in Bailundo, Dôndi, and Elende schools established their own private schools: Eduardo Daniel Ecundi at Manico, Pedro Paulo at Bonga, Benjamin Cachiungo in Caala, Diamantino Stover Malaquias in Mungo, André Eiúba at Cutato, and Tavares Jamba in Cachilengue. Although the physical facilities of these private schools did not match mission station schools, they did compare favorably with most schools in pastoral centers. Pupils were attracted for several reasons: proximity to home village, lower fees, a willingness to accept students who had problems with which others schools would not deal, and especially respect for the ability of the teacher.

The Methodist and ABCFM/Canadian boards discussed the possibility of opening a joint secondary school, but these plans were not realized. After much difficult negotiation with the education department in Luanda, two courses were authorized: in Quéssua for the Methodist area and in Dôndi for central Angola.

The Colégio do Quéssua began to function in 1954 with fifteen students in the second year of liceu, eleven of whom were teachers in Quéssua primary schools. Edwin LeMaster was the missionary who succeeded in carrying out the Methodist church's decision to establish a combination high school and normal school in Quéssua.[18]

In Dôndi a technical school was opened in 1953 with Dr. Gladwyn M. Childs giving the missionary leadership. In the Portuguese educational system secondary and higher education followed two tracks, technical and classical. At the conclusion of primary education students chose the track they would follow, *escola tecnica* or *liceu*. The *liceu* had more prestige and the church wanted to receive authorization for that course. However, the government would grant a license only for a technical school. Some educators contended that the technical course was not only more

---

18. Emílio J. M. de Carvalho, *Ouço os Passos de Milhares* (São Paulo, Brazil: Imprensa Metodista, 1978), 181–83.

practical, but pedagogically sounder since it was a new course using modern textbooks and advanced teaching methods.

The opening of these secondary courses increased the influence and prestige of Quéssua and Dôndi, not only for their respective denominational regions, but in the whole of Angola.

In chapter 3 we noted the importance of catechists in the growth of the church and the problems in their training and support. One suggestion to meet these problems issued in a new type of school: the Rural Life School in the Dôndi missions.

Carl and Lois Dille of the ABCFM analyzed these problems:

> The custom of choosing as catechist some spiritually strong person in the village was good in the sense of emphasizing spiritual qualities in a leader, but many men so chosen had little formal education. They had difficulty in reading religious literature available. They were unable to get government identity cards as catechists. Also they seemed to have difficulty in relating to the better educated young people in the village.[19]

The Dilles envisioned a special school for rural catechists, and during a furlough in the United States shared this dream with Mr. and Mrs. Percy Foor of Everett, Pennsylvania. The Foors had some tithe money available, which they gave to the Dilles for such a school. On their return to Angola the Dilles built a school at Elende mission, calling the building *O Dízimo*, The Tithe, as an ever visible lesson in stewardship.

> Since village catechists were unpaid leaders we taught agriculture, carpentry, masonry, and tailoring as a means of self-support of future leaders. Portuguese was taught as a means toward a government *bilhete* as a catechist, and to help the men in representing their village before local government officials. Bible, Christian Education, worship leadership, general science and agriculture were taught in the classroom. Daily worship services were led by both students and faculty. Both Lois and I taught, along with African leaders. Mornings were given over to classroom studies, afternoons to carpentry, masonry, tailoring, gardening, and field work. It was a two year course.[20]

Similar schools were started at two other stations in central Angola.

More girls than boys were being left out of the educational mainstream, which presented a special problem as they reached marriageable age. The young men who had educational opportunities were looking

---

19. Personal letter from Drs. Carl and Lois Dille.
20. Ibid.

for young women with some preparation for homemaking and companionship. Therefore, many Protestant missions began programs that included domestic schools.

The first stage in the program was a dry-season (May to September) camp for girls aged twelve through sixteen who had not attended school. During the four to six weeks at camp the girls were given an intensive course in learning to read, using Laubach[21] material as well as a variety of activities such as Bible study, worship, singing, cooking, agriculture, sewing, and knitting. Girls who could pass a reading test were eligible for admission to a domestic school on the mission station in the fall. For students who were persistent, a three-year course was available to give women rudimentary training in the three Rs, Bible, home care, handiwork, and agriculture.

Each rural life school became a little Currie Institute and each domestic school a little Means School as the quality and scope of the courses increased. Yet "little" was not the right word for domestic schools that together regularly had six times the number of students at Means, which was about three hundred girls. Two outstanding Angolan professional church workers directed domestic schools: Delina Abias Satatu at Bailundo and Emi Hama at Chissamba.

Catholic Urban Schools

The two Catholic women's missionary orders with the most sisters in Angola provided elite schools for white girls in the main urban centers. In 1957 a total of 160 sisters of St. Joseph of Cluny — 109 Europeans and 51 Angolans — worked in Angola, while 87 sisters of St. Dorothy (Dorotéias) served there. The sisters of St. Joseph participated in a great variety of services while the St. Dorothy sisters were more specialized. The first rule of the Dorothean constitution orders that "the Institute of St. Dorothy ... has as its purpose the greater glory of God, through sanctification of its members, the eternal salvation of the neighbor, and in a special way, the *complete instruction and education of youth.*"[22]

---

21. Frank C. Laubach was an ABCFM missionary in the Philippines where he developed a literacy method popularly known as "Each one teach one." It was based on the use of charts and booklets that related the figure of some easily recognized object to a letter in the language spoken by the students. After completing his work in the Philippines, Dr. Laubach dedicated himself to promoting this method which was adopted by governments and churches in scores of nations.

22. Maria de Conceição Tavares Lourenço de Silva, *As Missões Católicas Femininas*, Estudos de Ciências Políticas e Sociais 37 (Lisbon: Junta de Investigações do Ultramar, 1960), 22.

Delina Abias Satatu, Director of Domestic Schools in Bailundo

With this special purpose all eighty-seven of the St. Dorothy sisters were teaching in four schools:

Sá da Bandeira (Lubango)	— boarding school	39 sisters
Benguela	— boarding school	22 sisters
Lobito	— day school	10 sisters
Moçâmedes	— boarding school	16 sisters

The students in these schools were exclusively white with an occasional exception of a mestiza or two.

The four urban schools run by the St. Joseph of Cluny sisters were also for girls:

Luanda	38 sisters
Nova Lisboa/Huambo	16 sisters
Silva Porto/Cuíto	13 sisters
Malanje	?

The Colégio de São José in Luanda sat proudly on a bluff of the central city overlooking the beautiful harbor. This prize property had been expropriated by the city from the Methodist mission across the street to give to the Catholic church for the school. In 1956 it had 400 students of whom 120 were boarding students. They were studying in primary and secondary classes and earned very good results in official examinations.

A team from the Center for Political and Social Studies, a Portuguese government board for overseas studies, visited Catholic missions in Angola and Mozambique in 1959 to study the women's missions and the role they play in the development of the African women. From the perspective of their study, in spite of the beautiful setting and excellent academic results, the investigators commented:

> Nevertheless, it is necessary to say that the Sisters and students live at a considerable psychological distance from the natives... who today comprise approximately three-quarters of the total population of Luanda, verifying that the St. Paul's mission [for Africans] and St. Joseph's school, both directed by the sisters of St. Joseph of Cluny and separated by only a few kilometers are not exactly in communication.[23]

The school of the St. Joseph of Cluny sisters in Malanje, Colégio Missionário de Nossa Senhora de Fátima, was following the same pattern as that in Luanda. As Malanje was a town, there was a much smaller white population, but only 3 percent of the students were black and 5 percent mestiza.

The investigating team judged the Colégio Paula Frassinetti in Sá da Bandeira to have the highest standards and most complete program, but concluded:

> Anyway, it is truly a pity that a certain number of black girls cannot participate without payment not only in the instruction, but in the education in a school such as this. Such an experience would show them better, without doubt, the virtues of the colonizing spirit and the ideal of complete unity which characterizes the Portuguese performance Overseas.[24]

The separation of white and black students in separate schools by Catholic missionaries came from at least two causes: first, the sisters, "preoccupied to maintain a certain level in the school, did not particularly encourage contact with natives";[25] and second, the cost of attending these eight Catholic girls' schools in the cities was beyond the means of most Angolan families. In one school the room and board for a month was $30, which did not include tuition. Considering that at that period (1958–60) an Angolan urban male might earn only $50 per month, the expense of these schools was beyond the reach of most, including most Portuguese as well.

Archbishop Manuel Nunes Gabriel defended the church against charges of elitism and racism in the Catholic urban schools.

---

23. Ibid., 24.
24. Ibid., 27.
25. Ibid., 28.

The cause, however, of this apparent segregation should be sought in areas other than any racial prejudice, which would be entirely contrary to Christian doctrine and the concerns of those who came to preach in Angola. We do not deny that in one or another case, certain responsible persons may have let themselves be influenced too much by the mentality of certain layers of the society less inclined to see their sons and daughters sitting at the same desks with boys and girls of a different color. But such exceptions do not allow us to make a generalization.[26]

He then goes on to blame the government for not giving adequate support to Catholic secondary schools, thus requiring them to charge high fees.

Catholic women missionaries were particularly concerned with the problem of educating mestiza girls, and with government aid special institutions were established for them. In Nova Sintra/Catabola the Institute of Social Assistance of Angola (IASA) built the Instituto de Artur de Paiva for mestiza girls and entrusted the operation to the sisters of St. Joseph of Cluny. Similarly, the Instituto Dom Fernanda Silva Carvalho in Huila was inaugurated in 1951 for mestizas. Most of the students were abandoned or orphaned mestizas, although a few indigent white girls were also received. In 1959 the school had five sisters and 150 pupils.

The girls, between the ages of seven and twelve years, were required to complete their primary education, which was a real achievement since some arrived at age ten without knowing their ABCs and a few could not speak Portuguese. After completing primary education they spent a year learning household care, cooking, and care of animals. In a third cycle of indefinite length, the girls learned dressmaking, knitting, and embroidery. The ideal of the sisters was to prepare a dignified future for the girls whom they educated with love. Thus they looked favorably at the opportunities the girls had for happy marriages.

Boys' House

The Boys' House of Luanda developed as the Catholic seminary of Luanda was slowly transformed into a high school and then into an asylum for orphans and abandoned boys. Father Isalino Alves Gomes began with ten boys in an annex of the Holy Ghost Fathers business office in 1942. Four years later Father Isalino had to return to Portugal because of illness, and Father Mário Alves da Silva became director of the

---

26. Manuel Nunes Gabriel, *Angola: Cinco Séculos de Cristianismo* (Queluz: Literal, 1978), 504.

Boys' House. By 1953 with the financial help of a diamond company the institution had a new building and 150 boys.

The aim of the house was to provide a refuge for homeless boys and prepare them for life. Before his death in 1967 Father Mário said that 850 boys had passed through Boys' House to become, for example, seminarians, aviators, soldiers, mechanics, and artists.

Recognizing a similar need in Nova Lisboa/Huambo, a Boys' House was established by the Catholic church in 1955 with five boys. By 1966 it had 120 boarding pupils. The aim was to make of these boys good men and good Christians. The schools had shops to teach printing, baking, milling, shoemaking, tailoring, sawing, and barbering.[27]

Catholic Seminaries

To plant the church Catholic missions identified their basic task as that of training Angolan clergy, while Protestant missions focused on translating the Scriptures into the languages of the people and teaching them to read and interpret the Bible. Therefore, the Catholics expended every effort to found and support seminaries.

As early as July 23, 1853, the Portuguese government decreed that a Catholic seminary be created in Luanda to prepare clergy for the dioceses of São Tomé, Príncipe, and Angola.[28] However, since it was impossible to implement this decree immediately because of lack of missionary personnel, in 1854 and 1855 six young men were sent to Lisbon, as had been done before, to study in the seminary at Santarem. Three of these were ordained and returned to Angola to fill important posts in the church as seminary professors and in the hierarchy of the diocese.[29]

Eight years after the initial decree, a seminary was opened in Luanda when a new bishop, Dom Manuel de Santa Rita Barros, arrived from Lisbon with some priests as professors and twelve advanced students recruited from the seminaries of Santarem and Overseas Missions at Cernache. After only four months in Angola the bishop died of yellow fever on January 3, 1862. Four seminarians died as well. Four others returned to Portugal, and of the remaining four, two were ordained. Without the support of a bishop and lacking professors, the Luanda seminary struggled to exist until 1966 when it was closed for ten years.

During that period when there was no diocesan seminary, the Holy Ghost Father Duparquet founded a seminary in the Lândana mission in Cabinda. He began teaching Latin to fifteen boys in 1875 and two years

---

27. Cândido Ferreira da Costa, *Cem Anos dos Missionários do Espírito Santo em Angola (1866–1966)* (Nova Lisboa, 1970), 278–79.
28. Ibid., 65.
29. Gabriel, *Angola*, 263.

later opened a minor seminary, where in 1892 the first seminarian was ordained.

In 1882 Bishop José Neto transferred the struggling Luanda seminary to the newly founded mission of Huila in the south of Angola, where it functioned until 1907 with students from Angola and São Tomé. Archbishop Gabriel considered those twenty-five years of the Huila seminary its most fruitful period from its establishment in 1861 to 1940. Yet during that time only six men completed the full seminary course and were ordained. This was because from the very beginning the Catholic seminaries in Angola expended most of their energies to provide general primary and secondary education. For example, in 1893 the Huila seminary had fifty "seminarians," but only three were studying "theology," which is the final three or four years that lead to ordination. Fifteen were in Latin classes, which was the academic preparation for the philosophy and theology courses, and thirty-two were in primary school.[30]

When the seminary moved back from Huila to Luanda in 1907 it developed a secondary school course as there was none in the capital. This provided a benefit for the city but caused the seminary to stray from its primary purpose. It now became known as a school for general education rather than a special institution for training the clergy.

During the republican period the seminary felt financially threatened, and in 1914 it had only one man studying for the priesthood. The first secular high school was created in Luanda in 1919 so the seminary no longer offered a high school program. This left the seminary as a primary school for children of poor families or families with domestic problems.

For ten years no men were studying for the priesthood until Dom Moisés Alves de Pinho became bishop of Angola and reopened the seminary in the 1930s. The 1939–40 academic year began with fifty students in the preparatory course, and in 1941 the philosophy course was reinstated.

The Catholic church had six seminaries in Angola in 1938–39, one major and five minor:

Caala Major Seminary	5 studying theology
	9 studying philosophy
Minor Seminaries	
Luanda	32
Lucula	33
Bângalas	48
Galangue	68
Jau	19
Total	214

---

30. Ibid., 412–13.

Students at the Catholic Seminary in Huila, 1896

Of the 200 students in minor seminaries 74 attended primary classes and 126 secondary.

The seminary in central Angola, which functioned successively in Sambo, Galangue, Nambi (near Silva Porto/Cuíto), and Caala, registered 1,276 students from 1921 to 1962 with only 3 percent being ordained. This was less than one ordination per year.[31]

Although a small percentage of the seminary students was finally ordained, all students of minor seminaries submitted themselves to a discipline that was obviously designed to prepare men for the pre-Vatican II priesthood. To be admitted boys had to have finished third class of elementary school, be practicing Catholics, and, most important, promise to pursue studies with the intention of being ordained.

Having been admitted, the students followed a strict schedule. Up at 5:45 A.M., each student said a brief prayer and did exercises. At 6 A.M. he was required to take a bath in cold water, and on the Angolan highlands the water is cold any time of the year. A student caught skipping his morning bath was whipped, lost his recess time, or had to eat breakfast on his knees.

At 6:30 A.M. the students joined in morning prayers and reading Scripture and lives of the saints. Mass was celebrated at 7 A.M. and breakfast served at 7:30 A.M. Classes began at 8 A.M., and each of the forty-five-minute sessions was followed by a fifteen-minute recess and a forty-five-minute study period. In the middle of the day students ate

31. Ferreira da Costa, *Cem Anos dos Missionários do Espírito Santo em Angola*, 241–43.

lunch in silence, preceded and followed by visits to the Holy Sacrament in the chapel.

At 6 P.M. the boys said the Rosary, and after another study hour or choral music lesson they ate dinner at 7:30 P.M. Then followed study and vespers, and they were in their beds at 9 P.M.

The schedule varied on Thursday afternoons to allow time for general clean-up and an excursion. At 6:20 P.M. on Thursdays a chapter meeting was held in which misbehavior during the past week was noted and appropriate punishment applied. Thursday supper was *com colóquio*, which meant the students could talk while eating. At most meals the boys ate in silence as someone read to them.

On Sundays the student body celebrated *Missa Rezada* (the "prayed" Mass) before breakfast and *Missa Cantada* (the "sung" Mass) at 10 A.M. Sunday dinner was also *com colóquio* followed by an outing. At 6 P.M. the boys recited *Terço*. At 6:20 P.M. there was a lesson in good manners and at 7 P.M. each student was examined by his spiritual director to ascertain his religious, moral, and academic progress.

Discipline was the key to success or even survival in the minor seminary. A system of class monitors acted as police to report any violations of the rules. Some of the most important were:

1. Punctuality.

2. Silence at all times except when conversation is specifically allowed.

3. Avoidance of special friendships, prolonged conversations between two persons, touching anyone unnecessarily, or sleeping in the same bed with another person or persons.

4. Modesty in dress.

5. No conversation with women in the seminary and no looking at women, not even your sisters or mother when on vacation.

6. Never sleep nor take a bath completely nude.

7. Avoid looking at photos of seminude women in show windows or bookstores; avoid reading novels, and going to the beach, movies, or profane theaters.

8. During vacations be submissive to the orders and decisions of the director of the Catholic mission from where you come. Attend services and help and respect the catechist.

9. During meals avoid choosing the best pieces of food for yourself, leaving the worse pieces for others.

10. Cultivate a spirit of sacrifice so that you will be a person who will sacrifice himself for others.

11. Religious discipline means:

    a. Seeking to increase your faith by reading and studying the Bible.

    b. Cultivating religion by prayer, meditation, reading the lives of the saints.

    c. Cultivating all Christian virtues, especially Love, Faith, Hope, and Charity.

    d. Never failing to do obligatory spiritual exercises such as Mass, Matins, and Vespers, the Rosary, meditation, visiting the Holy Sacrament after lunch, etc.

    e. Receiving Communion every day, whenever it is possible, according to the conscience of the student. One cannot receive Communion in mortal sin.

    f. Confessing at least once a week or as many times per week as the student feels he has fallen into mortal sin.

    g. Praying for sinners, for the conversion of heretics, apostates, and pagans, and for the souls of the dead. Praying also for the heads of the church and for the unification of all churches in all the world and for Jews, etc.

12. Respect the superior of the seminary, all professors and missionaries.

13. Avoid as much as possible attending services in non-Catholic churches as well as discussions that may be religiously destructive with missionaries and the faithful of those churches.

The punishments for violating this strict discipline ran the whole gamut from mild reprimand to permanent expulsion from the seminary. Between these extremes were the denial of certain privileges such as recess or recreation, the assignment of extra jobs, and physical punishments from kneeling on sharp rocks to whippings.

The discipline and even the punishments, however, were considered by most students a reasonable price to pay for the benefits: a secondary school education, cultural privileges such as theater, movies, and musical programs in which the students were both participants and spectators, an athletic program, trips around Angola and the camaraderie with fellow students.[32]

---

32. Personal correspondence with António Kambala.

After the concordat in 1940 each of the new dioceses felt the need of its own major seminary. Christ the King Seminary in Huambo, which grew out of the minor seminary in Galangue, became the largest. After moving the philosophy and theology students from Galangue to Ganda in 1932, they were then taken three years later to Quipeio. Dom Daniel Gomes Junqueira was named the first bishop of Nova Lisboa/Huambo in 1941, and immediately he began to build a seminary in the city so the seminarians could be near the "splendor of the worship" in the recently constructed cathedral. The new facilities were occupied in 1947.[33] This seminary prepared eighty-eighty priests for ordination: eighty-one Angolans and seven from Portugal. The missions that gave the most priests to the church through Christ the King Seminary were Bailundo (13), Ganda (13), Caconda (8), and Galangue (5). All the Catholic seminaries in Angola from 1945 to 1975 prepared 130 priests for ordination, the great majority of whom were black Angolans.

Protestant Seminaries

The Catholic church in Europe since the Council of Trent had depended on well-structured seminaries to prepare its clergy, so it began its replanting of the church in Angola in the nineteenth century with the intention of establishing similar academic institutions that would use the traditional curriculum. In contrast, all the Protestant missions in Angola came from the Free Church tradition, which depended on less formal and more diverse means of preparing its leaders.

The Baptists of Britain were considered "nonconformists" and were not allowed to study in the classical universities, but for theological reasons they would have rejected them in any case. As noted in chapter 2, William Carey, founder of the BMS, had pursued his studies at the cobbler's bench rather than at Oxford or Cambridge.

The American Congregationalists who founded Harvard and Yale to train leaders for church and state had depended on academic institutions for the theological education of their ministers. However, their missionary experience in North America, Asia, and Africa led them to be flexible in deciding the type of leadership training that suited each country and culture.

The Methodists on the frontier in America had developed a method of training lay preachers who with continuing private study and tutoring could become ordained. The Methodist church in Angola prepared a course of studies for local church leaders in 1909.[34]

---

33. Ferreira da Costa, *Cem Anos dos Missionários do Espírito Santo em Angola*, 256.
34. *Minutes of the Methodist Conference*, 1909, 67.

A four-year study course was outlined for local preachers and exhorters, including lessons in five areas: reading and writing, arithmetic, Bible, Methodist polity and doctrine, liturgy and homiletics.As the Methodist church developed and needed better trained leaders, it defined six steps on the way to ordination as a presbyter: exhorters, local preacher, substitute pastor, probationary member in the Annual Conference, permanent member, deacon, and presbyter.

To pass from one stage to another required both service and study. For example, to become a local preacher an exhorter had to give two years of service with good behavior as an exhorter, class leader, or teacher, and complete the following courses: (a) History of the Old Testament; (b) Christian Stewardship; (c) Total Abstinence (alcoholic beverages); (d) Life of Jesus; (e) Church Discipline; (f) Work of Exhorter. Before arriving at the final stage of the ministry — presbyter — the candidate usually spent at least thirteen years in service and study.

The term "pastor" was used for someone in any of the stages from local preacher to presbyter who was named by the bishop to be in charge of a local church or circuit. Only the deacons and presbyters were ordained ministers.

The questions asked of the candidates to be permanent members of the Annual Conference reveal the two most distinctive marks of Methodism: perfectionism and denominationalism:

1. Have you faith in Christ?

2. Are you going on to perfection?

3. Do you expect to be made perfect in love in this life.

4. Are you earnestly striving after it?

5. Are you resolved to devote yourself wholly to God and his work?

6. Do you know the General Rules of our church?

7. Will you keep them?

8. Have you studied the doctrines of the United Methodist Church?

9. After full examination do you believe that our Doctrines are in harmony with the Holy Scriptures?

10. Will you preach and maintain them?

11. Have you studied our form of church discipline and polity?

12. Do you approve our church government and polity?

13. Will you support and maintain them?

14. Will you diligently instruct the children in every place?

15. Will you visit from house to house?

16. Will you recommend fasting or abstinence, both by precept and example?

17. Are you determined to employ all your time in the work of God?

18. Are you in debt so as to embarrass you in your work?

19. Will you observe the following directions:

    a. Be diligent. Never be unemployed. Never be triflingly employed. Never trifle away time; neither spend any more time at any one place than is strictly necessary.

    b. Be punctual. Do everything exactly at the time. And do not mend our rules, but keep them; not for wrath, but for conscience's sake.[35]

The Methodists, being most methodical, outlined their courses at an early date, but this was the general pattern of education that all Protestant churches used for their local leaders whether they were called catechists, deacons, elders, pastors, evangelists, local preachers, or exhorters. It combined the three Rs, an understanding of the Christian faith, and the role and rules of the church, but all focused on a knowledge of and the ability to interpret the Scriptures.

This kind of teaching occurred in a great variety of forms. For example, the BMS reported in 1959 that catechists were being trained on their three stations. Students attended school each afternoon and missionaries gave them Bible teaching in the evening. At that time Kibokolo had eighteen men studying, Bembe eleven, and São Salvador five.

The need for more leaders with greater preparation impelled the various Protestant missions to organize special schools, which differed according to the traditions of the missions. The Methodist and Congregational missions expected a mature church to have ordained pastors who were trained in theological seminaries. The South Africa General Mission/Africa Evangelical Fellowship placed less emphasis on academic training and had more confidence in Bible schools as appropriate institutions for training leaders. The Swiss Mission represented a combination of the Reformed tradition, which emphasized ministerial training and ordination, with a more independent tradition coming from the experience of many of its missionaries trained in the Emmaus Bible School in Lausanne.

The Plymouth Brethren were distinctive in that they did not practice ordination and expected each local assembly of believers to be led

---

35. Draft version, *Discipline*, Africa Central Conference (1987), 224.

by several men with diverse gifts. They did not require any special academic preparation.

The Protestant missions thus founded a variety of institutions to train church leaders. The BMS began to construct a training institute at Calambata in 1954 and had twelve students in the evangelist course, but the program was interrupted by lack of teachers and the refusal of the government to legalize the property. Finally in 1958 the government gave the mission title to the land, and in 1960 the Rev. and Mrs. John Keith, Canadian Baptist missionaries, and Mr. and Mrs. Anibal Machado, Portuguese missionaries, were stationed at Calambata. However, the institute never functioned fully, because the following year the war of independence closed down all Protestant missions in that area.

At the turn of the century the Methodist church established the William Taylor Bible Institute in Quéssua. At first it required only that entering students be able to read and write for them to be prepared as catechists. As the general level of education rose the third class of primary school was required for admission. By 1937 the Bible Institute received only students who had finished primary school; the course was three years.

In 1944 in Kalukembe the Finnish missionary Matti Peltola, working with the Swiss mission, opened his living room as a classroom for the first four students of the Bible School. The two-year course for training evangelists contained two sections: general education and Bible studies.[36] Eleven years later at Pentecost 1955 a new building was dedicated for the Bible School. The course for evangelists was lengthened to three years, and a fourth year was planned for those who would enter the pastoral ministry. On the same day two new pastors were ordained: Abias Secretário and David Sandoque.

In 1937 Emil and Daisy Pearson, SAGM missionaries in Muié, initiated a Bible Training School with the Luchazi New Testament, just published in 1935, as "their only textbook." In 1948 the Bible Institute was moved to Catota, and the Pearsons were joined in teaching by their daughter, Edla.

A theological course was started at Currie Institute in Dôndi in 1935. Eight students were taking the full course: Alberto Canyanga and Victorino Chicanha from Chissamba; António Sico and Isarele Canganjo from Bailundo; Oliveira Epalanga from Lutamo; João Capuca from Chilesso; João Baptist from Camundongo; and Abraão Cachenye from Hualondo. In addition four institute students were majoring in Bible: Paulino Mutenha, André Chimuco, and Artur Mundula from Galangue and Francisco Chivanja of Sachiquela.

---

36. *J'ai ouvert une porte devant toi: Essai sur l'histoire de la Mission Philafricaine* (Lausanne: Alliance Missionnaire Évangélique, 1972), 38.

John T. and Leona Tucker taught the theological course, but as they had many other responsibilities the church looked to the time when it would have a seminary with its own staff and facilities. Finally in 1947 the mission established Emmanuel Seminary at Dôndi with Ralph and Jean Collins assigned to that work full time. It was a three-year course primarily in Umbundu with a complementary course for wives.

In 1949 a proposal was made for a united seminary to serve all the Protestant churches in Angola. After discussion by missions in Angola and their respective boards overseas, three boards agreed to support such a united seminary: the Methodists, the United Church of Canada, and ABCFM.

It was decided to use the new seminary facilities in Dôndi, which had classrooms, chapel, dormitories, and houses for students — both single and married — as well as residences for staff. The two requirements for admission were a recommendation from the home church and satisfactory completion of the first two years of secondary education or the equivalent. The course was three years and the special classes for wives were continued.

Emmanuel United Seminary opened its doors in Dôndi on October 15, 1957, with Norwegian Methodist missionary the Rev. Juel Nordby as first principal. In making a report to the Annual Conference of the Methodist church two years later he stated the purposes of the United Seminary:

> Its objective is to prepare workers for more efficient service in the future and to improve relations between the Methodists and colleagues in the churches of the south of Angola, thus making more effective our unity in Christ.[37]

Studies Abroad

The church recognized the limitations of educational opportunities within Angola and began to send students abroad in the 1940s. The ability to send students out of Angola to study depended on three main factors: the availability of students who had completed at least five years of secondary school, scholarship support for the students, and government permission to leave.

The Catholic church could meet these requirements with relative ease. The academic standards in Catholic seminaries were much higher than those in the small scattered Protestant seminaries and Bible schools. The centralized Catholic church could draw on more resources to support Angolan students and also had a variety of Catholic institutions in

---

37. *Actas*, Conferência Anual de Angola, 1959.

Rome that were organized to receive students from the whole church. The close relation between church and state also reduced the problem of official permission to leave Angola.

Alexandre de Nascimento, who was born in Malanje on March 1, 1925, did his primary education there and then was sent to the minor seminary, first located at the Bângalas mission and later in Malanje. After completing the two-year philosophy course in Luanda the church sent him to Rome in 1948. He received his licentiate at the Gregorian University and was ordained on December 20, 1952. Returning to Luanda Father Alexandre de Nascimento became professor of dogmatic theology in the diocesan seminary and would some thirty years later become Angola's first cardinal.

Another Catholic priest who was sent to Europe for further education was Manuel Franklin da Costa, native of Cabinda, where he was born on August 31, 1921. He studied in the minor seminary at the Lucala mission and then did the philosophy and theology courses in Luanda where he was ordained on January 25, 1948. After teaching at the Luanda seminary, Father Franklin was sent to Paris in 1953, where he studied a course in Gregorian Chant at the Catholic Institute and another in spirituality with the Sulpician Fathers. Upon his return to Luanda he became vice-rector of the seminary and editor of the Catholic newspaper, *O Apostolado*. The Rev. Manuel Franklin da Costa became the first bishop of Henrique de Carvalho/Saurimo in 1975.

In 1957 two more Angolan priests were sent to Rome to take advanced studies without knowing, of course, that this would be a preparation for service as bishops twenty years later. Eugénio Salessu, born in Huambo on August 27, 1923, did all his academic preparation for ordination in the seminaries of that diocese. He was consecrated presbyter in Nova Lisboa/Huambo on July 14, 1957, and went on to Rome to do his licentiate in theology. In 1977 Pope Paul VI chose Padre Eugénio to be bishop of Malanje.

Próspero da Ascensão Puaty, five years younger than Father Salessu, was born on April 10, 1928, in Imánya, Cabinda, did his ecclesiastical studies in Malanje and Luanda, and was ordained a priest on July 17, 1957. The church sent him that same year to Rome for a licentiate in canon law. On returning to Angola Padre Puaty taught in the seminary in Luanda and then in Nova Lisboa/Huambo before being named bishop of Luso/Luena in 1977.

The educational opportunities given to these four men not only prepared them personally for the responsible positions they were to hold in the Catholic church after independence, but enabled them to play significant roles in strengthening the major seminaries in Angola.

More Methodist students could meet the requirements to study abroad than students from other Protestant churches. Luanda, where the Methodist headquarters were located, had one of the two government secondary schools in Angola and the capital had several private secondary schools as well. Additionally, the Methodist mission board in New York had established a worldwide find for Crusade Scholars.

António Agostinho Neto was one of the first and certainly the most famous of the Protestant students sent out of Angola to continue his studies. His father, the Rev. Agostinho Pedro Neto, was a Methodist minister and his mother was a teacher. Born on September 17, 1922, near Luanda, Agostinho Neto had roots in the Catete people of the Kimbundu group. Though Catete was close geographically to the capital, nevertheless the people were more immersed in traditional Kimbundu culture in the early twentieth century than even the inland Ambaquistas. Soon the Catatense recognized the need for eduction in order to acquire the benefits of European culture. Neto's parents shared this enthusiasm for education, which was reinforced by the Angolan Protestant conviction that school and church were equally important institutions in the Christian community. A Methodist church report used the colorful simile, "a church without a school is like a couple without children."

Agostinho Neto began his primary education in a village school, and when his father was transferred to the Luanda church his son's high school education was facilitated. Neto went through public secondary school on a government grant for excellence in scholarship and bought books and supplies from the small wage he received working as secretary for Ralph E. Dodge, the Methodist bishop, who reported that

> even as a boy, Neto was quiet, reserved, a bit shy, but always correct and businesslike.... António always got good marks in school and progressed from one grade to the next with yearly regularity....
> The pattern of the Portuguese was to admit the African students in the same school with the Europeans, but thin them out especially in the upper grades. António was one of the few who was able to complete his education in Angola up to the university level.[38]

Neto had set medicine as his goal, but when he completed secondary school in 1944, Angola had no university or postsecondary courses. He then worked for three years in the government health service in Luanda and quietly participated in the formation of a cultural association, which was as close as an African could come to being active in politics at that time.

In 1947 the Methodist Board of Missions in New York accepted the

---

38. John Marcum, *The Angolan Revolution* (Cambridge, Mass.: MIT Press, 1969), 1:330–33.

recommendation of the Angolan Methodist church and granted a scholarship to António Agostinho Neto. Before he left Luanda to continue studies in the medical faculty of the University of Coimbra in Portugal he wrote "Farewell at the Hour of Parting":

> My Mother
>   (all black mothers
>   whose sons are gone)
> you taught me to wait and hope
> as you hoped in difficult hours
>
> But life
> killed in me that mystic hope
>
> I do not wait now
> I am he who is awaited
>
> It is I my Mother
> hope is us
> your children
> gone for a faith that sustains life.[39]

After almost thirteen years in Portugal studying medicine in the university and politics in prison, Dr. Agostinho Neto returned to Angola. Neto had barely begun his medical practice in Luanda when he was again arrested on June 8, 1960, for "subversive activities against the external security of the state."[40]

In 1960 when Agostinho Neto, a Methodist scholarship student, was going home to Angola on his way to being its first president, another Methodist Crusade Scholar, Emílio de Carvalho, arrived home in Luanda on his way to being the first Angolan Methodist bishop.

The Methodist church recognized the special abilities of the Carvalho family. In 1953 Pastor Júlio Miguel de Carvalho and his sister, Eva de Carvalho, received scholarships to study in Brazil, and the next year Pastor Júlio's son, Emílio, followed them. The father and son studied in the Methodist theological seminary in São Paulo, and Eva de Carvalho attended the Methodist Institute in the same city. In the 1950s, when few Angolans had the opportunity to study abroad, the Carvalho family had three members studying in Brazil at the same time.

The Protestant community in central Angola hoped that some day the Institute at Dôndi might become a university, but it had not progressed very far toward that goal by 1950. Consequently in the 1950s

---

39. Agostinho Neto, *Sacred Hope*, trans. Marga Holness (Dar es Salaam: Tanzania Publishing House, 1974), 1.
40. Ibid., xv.

the church requested the ABCFM to grant scholarships for Angolans to study in Portugal.

In 1950 the Rev. Jessé C. Chipenda attended the World Conference of Christian Education in Toronto and while visiting Congregational churches in the United States he received small personal gifts. Upon his return to Angola he decided the best use for that money would be to send his oldest son, José, to Lisbon to study. Some missionaries thought Pastor Jessé was being too aggressive by not having José do the seminary course first in Dôndi and then wait for the church to recommend him for further study. Pastor Jessé wisely recognized that if he did not use the money immediately to send José, it would be used for any number of worthy projects at home. In 1951 José sailed for Lisbon, fully expecting that he would receive a scholarship from the ABCFM to study at the Presbyterian seminary in Carcavelos. The plan worked, and José Belo Chipenda returned to Lobito in 1955 to replace his father as pastor of the Lobito church. He possessed at that time the best training of any Angolan Protestant minister.

After José Chipenda had opened the door for students from central Angola, the church proposed several other candidates during the 1950s. José Liahuka, son of the Rev. Paulino Ngonga Liahuka of Elende, was the first Umbundu to study medicine. He was a good student at the University of Lisbon, but when the colonial war broke out in Angola in 1961 he fled from the Portuguese political police just before completing his medical course. He was able to finish at Louvainium University in Leopoldville/Kinshasa, be he could not return to Angola to practice.

João Gomes, a white Angolan, was sent to Lisbon by the church in central Angola to study at the Institute of Fine Arts with a scholarship from the ABCFM. He returned to Angola and taught for many years in the Technical Institute in Dôndi.

The church sent four more students to Portugal in 1958: Rubem Sanjovo, Jonas Savimbi, Jorge Valentim, and Jerónimo Wanga. They began their postsecondary courses in Lisbon, but all fled from Portugal when the war of independence broke out.

Of those four students the one whose name is best known thirty years later is Jonas Savimbi. Frequently he is erroneously described as the son of a Protestant pastor, which is understandable since so many of the young elite in the colonial era came from the homes of clergy. Jonas's father, Lote Malheiro Savimbi, was not a pastor, but he was a very active and effective lay leader of the church in central Angola. When Lote Malheiro was graduated in 1921 from Currie Institute, he was expected to accept a job back in his home church, Chilesso, but instead he went to work for the Benguela railroad.

The church and mission considered that taking such a secular, "worldly" job was not only a waste of talent and training, but a sure road to perdition. Lote Malheiro Savimbi proved the church and mission wrong on all counts. As a railroad worker he probably founded more churches than most pastors. Wherever he was stationed along the rail line he gathered a few believers together and started a congregation, which generally grew because of his faithful witness and enthusiasm. He was transferred frequently because Catholic priests did not appreciate having such a fervent Evangelical in their parishes.

Jonas Savimbi inherited from his father at least three characteristics: a sense of community, which had its roots in the Umbundu culture and was strengthened by commitment to the Christian church, an independent spirit, which moved him to try new paths, and an inner strength, which allowed him to survive severe trials.

Jonas had his early education in rural schools of the Chilesso mission, and then in 1951, at age seventeen, he entered Currie Institute at Dôndi, where his father had been graduated thirty years earlier. After completing the institute in 1954 Savimbi went to Silva Porto/Cuíto to continue his secondary education at a school administered by the Marist Brothers. This was one sign that Savimbi had inherited the independent spirit of his father, for the Protestant and Catholic communities were divided and on many occasions were in competition, if not in open conflict. For a promising Protestant student to go to a Catholic school was not easily accepted by the Protestants. However, the Protestant church-mission gave him a scholarship to complete the sixth year of secondary school in Sá da Bandeira/Lubango. In 1958 Savimbi went to Lisbon with the other mission scholarship students to complete his *liceu* course and enter university.

Political ferment was strong in Lisbon among overseas students in spite of a vigilant and violent political police (PIDE). Jonas came under official scrutiny when he was invited by his school to speak at a patriotic rally and his speech was judged lacking in Portuguese patriotic fervor. Savimbi decided in 1959 to flee to Switzerland to continue his studies, first in Fribourg and then in Lausanne. He entered the medical course, which had been his aspiration for years, but in 1962 he changed to the Institute of Political and Social Sciences of the Law Faculty in Lausanne.

Conclusion

Angolans living in the most populous parts of the country during the colonial period hungered and thirsted for education. In these circumstances the school became the main means of planting the church and promoting its growth.

As that period came to an end some Protestant seminarians were discussing the revolutions sweeping Africa and wondering how the winds of change would affect the church. One young man asserted, "If it no longer runs the schools, the church will disappear." This young man perceived well the importance of the school in the planting and growth of the church, but he did not see the future clearly.

Chapter 6

The Healing Ministry of the Church

Bantu and biblical cultures shared a common worldview that saw the visible world as part of a whole containing also an invisible world of ancestors, spirits, and mysterious powers. Personal and social health and welfare depended on good relations with the whole of reality — visible and invisible.

The word "salvation" comes from the Latin *salus*, health, and in Jesus' ministry salvation and health were intimately related. A paralyzed man was brought to Jesus. "Son, your sins are forgiven," Jesus said to him.

> Now some of the scribes were sitting there, questioning in their hearts, "Why does this fellow speak in this way? It is blasphemy! Who can forgive sins but God alone?" At once Jesus perceived in his spirit that they were discussing these questions among themselves; and he said to them, "Why do you raise such questions in your hearts? Which is easier, to say to the paralytic, 'Your sins are forgiven,' or to say 'Stand up and take your mat and walk'? But so that you may know that the Son of man has authority on earth to forgive sins" — he said to the paralytic — "I say to you, stand up, take your mat and go to you home." (Mark 2:5–11)

This was not an isolated incident in Jesus' ministry. More than a third of the eighty-nine chapters in the four Gospels contain accounts of Jesus' healings, referring explicitly or implicitly to both sin and disease, faith and health.

Jesus healed and also sent his disciples out to "preach the kingdom of God and to heal" (Luke 9:2). It is not surprising therefore that Jesus' disciples who were sent to Angola not only preached the Reign of God, but carried out the ministry of healing.

Healing was as important in African ideology and practice as it was to the Christian faith. Thus this ministry provided a point of contact for the church with Angolans, producing both positive and negative results. Positively, medical work became "the feeder of the evangelistic work, as many who came under the Christian influence would never have heard the gospel message, or had given any heed to it, but for the necessity of seeking physical relief."[1]

The healing ministry allowed the lame to walk, the blind to see, and sufferers to be relieved of their pain. Christian healing was also popular among Angolans, because it recognized the whole person, the importance of social relations, and the two dimensions of the worlds in which they lived. Christian healing was second only to the schools as an instrument of evangelization, and theologically perhaps more important. The healing ministry was the most explicit demonstration that the church also lived in two worlds. The visible world was evident in the physical exams, the variety of medicines and surgery. The invisible world was recognized as the daily hospital schedule began with prayers, Scripture, and hymns referring to the kingdom of God. Surgeons also frequently preceded their interventions with prayer.

Mission hospitals were especially appreciated, because they were built with provisions for the presence of family helpers who accompanied the patients. This was necessary economically, but it also recognized that separating the patients from their families was sufficient to make them ill, or at least to impede their recovery.

The similar Bantu and biblical worldviews and the close relationship between the spiritual and physical in both provided a point of contact between the Christian message and the Angolans' search for health, but also caused a conflict between the missionaries and traditional healers. The control of the healing process is "important . . . in shaping ideology. The power to name an illness, identify the causes, is also the power to say which elements in the experience of life lead to suffering."[2]

The fact that in African cultures generally the material and the spiritual cannot be separated or easily distinguished gives Westerners problems in finding the proper terms for the persons who deal with illness and healing in African cultures: witch doctor, magician (black and white magic), sorcerer, healer, diviner, and fetishist. The most popular term in English for the person who uses traditional means to heal has been "witch doctor." This term recognizes that such persons have

---

1. Report of the West Central African Mission — ABCFM, ABC 15:1, vol. 18, no. 56.
2. Steven Feierman, "Struggles for Control: The Social Roots of Health and Healing in Modern Africa," *African Studies Review* 28, nos. 2/3 (June–September 1985): 75.

learned certain methods to overcome illnesses, but also that they use means that are generally considered magical or superstitious from the perspective of Western science. Early missionaries reported that at first people were fearful of Western medicine and of reprisals threatened by witch doctors. Dr. W. S. Gilchrist stressed that the marvels of surgery were a great weapon in combatting "black magic."[3]

An eerie tale from Chissamba gives an example of black magic:

A young man attended school here for a season, but wearying of the discipline of spirit required he reverted to the world. Shortly after, he became ill and consulted the witch doctor. His case proved obstinate and he spent all his goats and pigs and suffered many things of many physicians but was healed of none. The climax came when it was revealed to him that nothing but partaking of human blood and flesh would avail. A corpse was disinterred and the most revolting rites and ceremonies observed. The skull became his drinking cup and the mortifying flesh his food. Perhaps it was this which brought him to himself. At any rate there came to him the prompting, *Natuka, ngenda ku Tate*, "I will arise and go to my Father." He brought his many charms and the drinking cup and his wasted body to the Mission and begged to be received. He recovered and is now a member of a Chissamba outstation.[4]

In her book *Missionary Doctor* Dr. Mary Cushman stated that witch doctors knew much about medicine, and many people were cured. Some witch doctors removed cataracts successfully and were inoculating for smallpox before Jenner began vaccination in Europe. When examining pupils in the mission school Dr. Cushman noted some with scars on their wrists showing they had been inoculated. However, witchcraft was used to cover failures. People were obliged to pacify the evil spirits with gifts before a cure could be effected. Dr. Cushman told how witch doctors could be hired to poison enemies or they could punish any offense with just the degree of pain, disability or lingering illness considered deserved. She felt at first that Christian witch doctors would be a great help with their knowledge of native medicine, but finally realized this was impossible because "The witch doctors belong to a cult. Any betrayal of its secrets would be instantly fatal to him."[5]

Protestant missions sent out medical missionaries in the early nineteenth century primarily to serve the missionary community. For exam-

---

3. W. S. Gilchrist, *Seven Years of Leper Work in Angola* (Bela Vista, Angola: Dôndi Press, 1938), 8.

4. Elizabeth Logan Ennis, *The Hope of Glory: An Account of the Work of the West Central Africa Mission of the American Board for the Year 1916–1917* (Kamundongo: Sarah H. Bates Memorial Press, n.d.), 34.

5. Mary Floyd Cushman, M.D., *Missionary Doctor: The Story of Twenty Years in Africa* (London: Harper and Brothers, 1944), 56–57, 63–64.

ple, in 1816 the ABCFM sent to Ceylon two young men trained both in theology and medicine. They were told that "strictly speaking you are not missionaries." The Catholics held a similar view, stating that the physicians were "mere lay members of a missionary staff." While the debate continued in board rooms over whether this was a legitimate aspect of mission work, doctors and nurses continued to serve in increasing numbers, and by the end of the century most mission organizations recognized that medical personnel were valued members of the missionary team. Among lay supporters at home "no missionary activity has provoked less controversy or raised fewer objections ... than has the work of medical missions; they provide the point at which interest and support have been secured from many who have been far from a Christian understanding of the significance of world evangelism."[6]

The ministry of healing was in fact an integral part of the mission of those who came to plant the church in Angola. In 1878 H. E. Crudgington, who had studied medicine at Leeds Infirmary, was sent to São Salvador by the BMS. The sisters of St. Joseph of Cluny arrived at the Catholic mission of Lândana in Cabinda in 1883 to assist in evangelization, education, and health. The pioneer party of missionaries who came to Angola with Bishop William Taylor in 1885 included two medical doctors, William H. Summers and Mary Myers Davenport, but neither performed medical work in Angola. The latter died in 1887 in Dondo. Dr. Gertrude Jacobs Cotton, an ABCFM missionary, arrived in Benguela on her way to Bailundo in October 1889. The next year a Plymouth Brethren missionary, Dr. Walter Fisher, participated in the opening of Christian work among the Luena-speaking people.

The report of expenses of the Bailundo mission in 1890 listed the medical costs as the largest item in their modest budget:

medical	$50
tribute to local chiefs	35
evangelistic	25
educational	25
repairs	25
industrial	10
miscellaneous	15
Total	$183[7]

Not all those who were ministers of healing were physicians or specialists in the field. Many like Brother Gervásio Dantas of the Congregation of the Holy Ghost combined healing with other ministries. He

---

6. Guy E. Alling, "The Evolving Role of Medical Care as a Legitimate Aspect of Mission Work (1810–1900)," *Whole Earth Newsletter* (UCBWM) 5, no. 2 (1975).

7. ABC 15.1, vol. 9, no. 134.

worked for sixty years (1889–1949) in Cabinda as gardener, bookbinder, teacher, and nurse.

The church's ministry of healing began in most cases as a kind of first aid in treating tropical ulcers, fevers, intestinal parasites, and malnutrition. Walter T. Currie, who engaged in such healing practices while founding the Chissamba mission in 1888, came to recognize that more was needed. He was convinced that a strong, intelligent Christian faith could not be developed in the people without the help of a wisely conducted medical department seeking to heal bodily ills in the hope of "strengthening their faith in God and destroying their confidence in idle, foolish superstitions."[8]

"A wisely conducted medical department" meant a hospital, and although Currie spent half his first furlough studying at the Medical Training School in New York, he and the mission society knew that they needed a thoroughly trained medical person to meet the needs. So in 1899 the Canadian Congregational Mission Society appointed Alfred Yale Massey, M.D., and in July of that year he sailed with two missionary colleagues from Montreal. At the end of three months they arrived in Chissamba amid the firing of guns and blowing of horns. Among those who welcomed them was the chief of Chiyuka, who presented the new missionaries with an ox. From other villages old men came with their presents of corn, and according to Angolan etiquette it was necessary to give small gifts in return.

One of Dr. Massey's first duties was to superintend the building of the hospital. Instead of one large building, the customs of the people made it necessary to have several smaller buildings. The patients came with their retinue, the size depending on their wealth and social standing. They may have had anywhere from three to ten or more followers, consisting of spouses, children, and slaves. They brought their pots and food and came to stay with the patient. The slaves or family members did the cooking and looked after the patient generally, some sleeping in the room with him or her. If there had been only one large ward for twenty patients, where would all the families have stayed?

It was therefore decided to construct three central buildings, one for the dispensary and waiting rooms, another for the operating room, and a third, at the rear, for the kitchen. These three central buildings formed an open court. The central buildings were surrounded by eight cottages, each about sixteen by thirty-two feet, with two small wards and storerooms in each. The storerooms were also used for cooking. Each of the eight cottages cost about $200; individuals or Sunday school classes in Canada made special offerings to cover the cost.

The Protestant hospitals received no government subsidies for build-

---

8. John T. Tucker, *Drums in the Darkness* (New York: George H. Doran Co., 1927), 82.

ing or expenses. In fact, they paid duties on imported medicines and property taxes on the buildings.

Dr. Massey's first official report showed twenty-five to fifty daily consultations, with seventy-eight on the busiest day. Many patients came from long distances and all had to bring a letter from the village chief, which helped avoid conflicts between the mission and chiefs and healers.

In 1901 smallpox raged through the Chissamba area, but Dr. Massey had only enough vaccine for one village near the mission. When many people died in neighboring villages, but none who had been vaccinated became ill, the missionaries' "magic" gained new respect.

Dr. Massey himself became ill with fever in 1903 and early the next year had to return to Canada. This left Miss Helen Melville, a Canadian nurse, in charge of the medical work. In 1907 a young couple, both of whom were doctors, Libbie and William Cammack, arrived in Chissamba.

After that first mission hospital in Chissamba the ABCFM- Canadian mission built others at Camundongo, Dôndi, Elende, Galangue, Chilesso, and Bailundo. These seven hospitals formed the major health-care network on the Benguela highlands during the colonial period, providing medical and surgical services, nurses training, a series of village dispensaries, midwives, and public health programs.

Church Health Facilities

Three BMS doctors served briefly in the 1880s and 1890s: Sidney Comber, William Seright, and Sidney Webb. In 1907 Dr. Mercier Gamble was appointed to São Salvador and Nurse Alys Bell in 1909.

The BMS built its first hospital in San Salvador in 1913. Robert Arthington, who gave the challenge contributions to both the BMS and ABCFM to begin work in Angola, also made a gift to BMS with which a prefabricated hospital was built in the United Kingdom and sent out to Angola. This was a wooden frame building with walls of galvanized iron sheets and corrugated iron roof. This original hospital had one surgical and one medical ward for men and one general and one maternity ward for women, giving a total bed capacity of about forty. Temporary additions built of old roofing sheets and mud blocks with sleeping mats on the floor between the beds provided a total capacity of about eighty patients.

Each of the other two BMS stations, Kibokolo and Bembe, had a dispensary in charge of a missionary nursing sister and gave much the same service as the main hospital except for surgery.

In 1923 Methodist bishop Johnson appointed Dr. Alexander H. Kemp to medical work in Angola. At the same time the conference adopted a statement of policy calling for maintenance at each of the mission's main stations of a medical staff, a hospital, nurses' training, and instruction in health care. The first steps toward realization of these goals had already been taken. John Wengatz distributed medicine to the sick as he went about his evangelistic and supervisory activities in the Quiongua district.

When small pox, fever, pneumonia, and bubonic plague were rampant in 1921, Marie E. Lindquist, a Methodist nurse from Sweden, established a clinic in Luanda. In her first year, receiving patients at the clinic as well as visiting outlying villages, she gave some two thousand medical treatments. At the same time Alice K. S. Ekstromer, another Swedish nurse, began a similar work at Quiongua. Mrs. Eddie E. Edling, who came to Quéssua with her husband in 1921, soon began clinical treatments and visiting nurse work in villages. In 1923, following a year in which she gave twelve thousand treatments, she transferred her medical work from her kitchen and back porch to a three-room infirmary.

When Dr. Kemp arrived in Angola he settled first in Quiongua, but soon moved to Quéssua, where he worked for the next twenty-nine years. There he built a hospital with a central building and more than a dozen two-bed houses for patients. Dr. Kemp, like other Christian medical workers in Angola, saw his professional tasks as part of his wider evangelical mission and in picturesque language said: "When we 'carve our initials' upon the outward parts of our patients, we aim to carve the Cross of Jesus upon their hearts."[9]

The Seventh-Day Adventist Doctrinal Statement gives the basis for that church's emphasis on health:

> That believers should recognize their bodies as the temple of the Holy Spirit, and that therefore they should clothe them in neat, modest, dignified apparel. Further, that in eating and drinking and in their entire course of conduct they should shape their lives as becometh followers of the meek and lowly Master. Thus the followers of Christ will be led to abstain from all intoxicating drinks, tobacco and other narcotics, and to avoid every body and soul-defiling habit and practice.

As part of their emphasis on health, the SDAs give a central place to their hospitals, as shown by the prominence of the Bongo hospital in their work. Dr. A. N. Tonge from Loma Linda, California, began the

---

9. J. Tremayne Copplestone, *Twentieth Century Perspectives: The Methodist Episcopal Church 1896–1939* (New York: United Methodist Church Board of Global Ministries, 1973), 933.

Bongo hospital in 1926 and worked there for four years. In 1931 Dr. and Mrs. Roy B. Parsons, who replaced him, built Bongo into one of the most popular medical centers in the country. Protestant missionary doctors were restricted to practicing on "natives" unless they had repeated their medical course and a special tropical medicine course in Lisbon. In that case they could treat anyone. Dr. Parsons was one of the few missionary doctors who fulfilled the requirements for such a license, and he developed a larger Portuguese clientele than any other Protestant missionary doctor. People came from all over Angola and Dr. Parsons was not only allowed to receive them, but also to charge them the standard fee for medical services. This gave the Bongo hospital a greater income, which it needed, since it, like all Protestant institutions, received no government subsidies. The Bongo hospital was one of the most influential factors in SDA church growth in Angola.

During his thirty-seven years in Angola Dr. Parsons performed more than fifteen thousand operations in addition to all the necessary medical work. Most of the time he was the only physician-surgeon at Bongo.

A contemporary of Dr. Parsons of Bongo was Dr. Aaron McMillan, a black doctor from Omaha, Nebraska, who with his wife, Wilena, was appointed in 1929 by the ABCFM to join the staff of the Galangue mission. He too took the necessary courses in Lisbon to receive a license to practice without restrictions in Angola. Taking advantage of this opportunity Dr. McMillan opened an office in Nova Lisboa/Huambo on the Benguela Railway line, where he gave consultations regularly. Persons needing surgery or inpatient treatment were invited to travel to Galangue, about sixty-five miles south of the railway over rutted dirt roads. And travel they did.

With the income from his European practice Dr. McMillan built a two-story hospital in Galangue. It was a rather crude facility by North American or European standards, but an impressive structure considering it was the only medical institution at that time from there to the southern border of Angola.

During his fifteen years in Galangue Dr. McMillan never had a missionary nurse to assist him, training his own nurses from among the local people. His wisdom in choosing candidates for nurses' training and his skill in teaching them is shown by the fact that twenty years after he departed some of these nurses were administering the Galangue hospital; and even when there was no resident doctor, patients came from miles away to be treated by the nurses trained by Dr. McMillan: João Cornélio, Faustino Muteka, Valerio Capamba and his wife, Julia, Luís Miguel Capusso, Isaias Molossongue, and others.

Mary Floyd Cushman, M.D., was the woman missionary doctor with the longest term of service during the colonial period. This American physician-surgeon was fifty-one-years old when she applied to the

ABCFM and was accepted for the Chilesso mission near Andulo. Without stopping to study Portuguese in Lisbon, Dr. Cushman went directly to work at Chilesso, arriving in November 1922. Mr. and Mrs. Neipp, Swiss missionaries who had transferred from the Philafrican mission to the ABCFM and were working in Chilesso, prepared an unoccupied residence as a dispensary and apartment for the doctor. A room beside the dispensary was the operating room in which Dr. Cushman placed a used Navy operating table she had brought from Portsmouth, New Hampshire.

One night soon after she arrived the doctor heard cries of the approaching hammock carriers. She went immediately to the dispensary and found a woman barely able to speak, her pulse gone and her breath coming in feeble gasps. A quick examination discovered a ruptured tubal pregnancy with severe internal hemorrhaging. The doctor said to herself, "God help me! I'll try to save her."[10]

She had two inexperienced helpers: Sapunga, who became her most faithful assistant, handed her the instruments, and Chief Konjamba, who had learned a little about anesthetics, administered the chloroform as the doctor gave instructions. The doctor prepared the saline and started it flowing to keep the patient alive. The operation began at 3 A.M. in the feeble light of a kerosene lantern. Deftly Dr. Cushman found the ruptured blood vessels and tied them off. The tube and contents were removed and the operation completed. The patient survived and her recovery was satisfactory.

The second largest Protestant health network was established by the Swiss mission under the leadership of Dr. Rodolphe Bréchet and his wife, Anny. Although two doctors had been members of the pioneer party that founded the Kalukembe mission in 1897, when they arrived in May 1943 they found only a small nine-by-twelve-foot building, a missionary nurse, Miss E. Burkhardt, and an African aide, Salomão Francisco. Nine days after their arrival Mrs. Bréchet gave birth to their first child, Anne-Lise.

Construction began immediately, following the pattern that Dr. Bréchet had seen in the Belgian Congo/Zaire and also on brief visits to other Protestant hospitals in central Angola. Several buildings were laid out on a campus providing space for patients and their helpers and service areas for pharmacy, classroom, laundry, storerooms, kitchen, and private rooms. This central complex provided at the initial stage for seventy-five beds. Separated by a curtain of trees was an outpatient village that provided about seventy huts for helpers. On the other side of the hospital was the village for tuberculosis patients, the embryo of a future sanatorium. Across a small valley was a line of houses for nurses'

---

10. Cushman, *Missionary Doctor,* 26.

residences. Up a hill and through some woods was the leprosarium with some sixty huts and small houses grouped about three central buildings: an infirmary, a chapel, and a warehouse.

In July 1947 at the fiftieth anniversary of the Kalukembe mission a Portuguese official inaugurated the new, enlarged hospital. For the rest of the colonial period the medical work at Kalukembe continued to develop by improving and increasing the physical plant, adding missionary personnel, and training Angolan nurses, aides, and laboratory technicians. By 1953 the medical work was directed by a medical commission, a majority of whose members were Angolans. Dr. Bréchet not only supervised the building and organization of the medical complex in Kalukembe, but regularly visited the satellite missions of Ebanga and Sussangue.

The Plymouth Brethren built two hospitals, one at Boma near Luso/ Luena and the other at Mt. Esperança near Coemba. Dr. Leslie Bier was director of the Boma hospital for thirty-five years from 1932 to 1966. Dr. Ross Woodward built the Mt. Esperança hospital.

The center of medical work of the SAGM was located at Catota, where under the direction of Dr. Alex Henderson a hospital was built after World War II.

Nurses' Training

Every doctor trained helpers for the ministry of healing. They might have started simply cleaning up the dispensary and utensils and then proceeded to learn various procedures such as sterilization, giving injections, dressing wounds, etc. Many became skilled and reliable even though they had no formal lessons; all their training was practical.

The story of Dr. Mary Cushman at Chilesso and her assistant, Sapunga, illustrates how helpers were chosen and trained at many missions. In 1922 as a young lad of fourteen Sapunga moved from a village school to study at the mission when Dr. Cushman arrived. At her first clinic Sapunga was one of the first patients, with a leg wound. Schoolboys went to classes a half day, and the other was spent in some work. Older boys learned carpentry, masonry, and sewing, but younger ones worked in the fields, cultivating beans and corn for the school. In the field a boy had accidentally hit Sapunga with a hoe and the wound became infected and needed treatment. As Sapunga came regularly to the clinic the doctor put him to work helping others. His fingers were gentle and patients liked to have his help. Sapunga became more and more useful as he began to help in the operating room and learned even to do simple operations.

Dr. Cushman also trained others: Kisiko, who worked with women;

Julio Kanualuku, who treated ulcer patients; and Estevão Chitumba, who was especially good at ear, nose, and throat complications, preparing patients for operations and giving anesthetics.

In addition to the individual practical training given at each mission hospital the Medical Association of Protestant Missions of Angola planned a course of medical education for assistants at Dôndi mission. Various doctors and nurses gave lessons and students visited the other hospitals to receive varied practical experience. The depression in the 1930s and then World War II reduced the number of medical missionaries so that the ambitious program of nurses' training planned by the Medical Association was never fully realized.

The two nursing schools that trained the largest number were at Dôndi and Kalukembe.

The original plan for Dôndi was to be a station for central training institutions. The boys' school, Currie Institute, was inaugurated in 1914, and Means School for Girls in 1916. To care for the health needs of students and provide training in health sciences it was planned that a teaching hospital would also be a part of the complex.

Dr. Robert George Moffat worked at Dôndi beginning in 1926, and in 1933 Dr. Veazie Markham arrived and directed the construction of the first major block of the hospital. In the post–World War II period, 1947–1956, the nurses' training program developed in breadth and depth under the direction of Dr. William Sidney Gilchrist.

In Kalukembe shortly after the Bréchets arrived a nursing school was begun with a two-year course and a third year of practical work. In 1943 the Kalukembe hospital had only two Angolan aides. Ten years later twenty Angolan nurses and technicians were working alongside the missionary staff.

Although the primary aim of mission nurses' training was to provide personnel for mission hospitals and village dispensaries, some graduates took jobs in cities or on plantations where they generally could earn more money.

At first the scholastic level of nurses' training was very low; in fact, it was required only that students could read and write. However, as the general level of instruction rose, the academic level of nursing instruction rose also. For the ministry of healing, honesty, dedication, and a loving spirit were as important as technical knowledge.

Leprosy

The Gospel of Luke records that Jesus sent out his disciples to preach the Reign of God and to heal. Matthew is more specific: "Heal the sick, raise the dead, cleanse lepers, cast out demons" (10:8). The Protestant

churches during the colonial period responded especially to the injunc-
tion to "cleanse lepers." The precise meaning of leprosy in the Bible is in
dispute since it is a vague, comprehensive term including several skin
conditions. Whether it included what is now popularly called leprosy,
but technically classified as Hansen's disease, is not known.

Leprosy, as described by medical science, is a chronic and contagious
disease that demands long periods of treatment. It was common practice
on Protestant missions to construct leper camps in which patients could
live at least until they had established the routine of their treatments,
and in more severe or advanced cases they stayed for years.

The main treatment for leprosy patients was chaumoogra oil until 1947, when a sulfone drug, diasone, came into regular use. In 1952
another advance was made, and sulfetrone was substituted for diasone in subcutaneous injections. Shortly thereafter dapsone became the
preferred drug for most cases of leprosy.

Leprosy patients commonly had other complaints, such as conjunc-
tivitis, malaria, and rheumatism, which were also treated. Medical care
was not sufficient to "cleanse lepers." Physical and occupational ther-
apy were also necessary as the disease causes members to stiffen and
become immobile if they do not exercise. Consequently each mission
leprosarium provided handicrafts as well as plots of ground for gardens
or fields.

A leper camp was not a hospital but a community in which residents were able to satisfy their physical, economic, social, and spiritual
needs. Even a foot race was part of the treatment at Camundongo when
Dr. W. S. Gilchrist was in charge of medical work in the 1930s. The
doctor's letter home to Canada describes the event:

> But now what? "This crazy white doctor wants the men to run —
> to take part in such childish amusements." Yes, that's the idea!
> Come on, now! . . . What shouting and laughing! Some find it hard
> to shout for their vocal cords are "asleep," "their voice is asleep"
> as the Umbundu has it. The larynx has been attacked by the dread
> disease. Some find it hard to laugh for there are thickened nodules
> of leprous tissues about their eyes and mouth.
>
> "No, no, Master Doctor, *Hameko, Hameko* ("Not I, not I"). Look,
> how can I run? I have no toes!"
>
> That sounds like a good excuse to the others, for there are many
> who have some deformity and they take up the strain, "Look at the
> ulcer on my foot! How can I run?"
>
> Here's another problem that my early training did not fit me to
> meet. How many toes do you need to run? Well, I strike an arbi-
> trary figure of fifty percent, and soon all who have sound feet and
> most of those who have but half a set of toes are lined up for the

race.... And here they come stamping, stumbling, laughing down the road.... The crowd roars and we are all lost in a cloud of dust as the winners cross the finish line! Yes, it was a great day.[11]

Protestant missions united in an effort to obey Jesus' mandate to "cleanse lepers" in 1950 when through the Angola Evangelical Alliance they established the Kavangu Leprosarium south of Bela Vista/Kachiungu. Missionary doctors and nurses from several Protestant agencies assisted in the founding and administration of that central institution for Angola.

Catholic Health Services

During most of the colonial period Catholic ministries of healing centered in small mission dispensaries and in collaboration with the government health services. Missionary sisters served in government hospitals, usually as supervisors. This was true especially in the central hospital in Luanda and the regional hospitals in Benguela, Nova Lisboa/Huambo, Silva Porto/Cuíto, and Sá da Bandeira/Lubango.

In 1936 a decree (No. 27:294) authorized the government to requisition Catholic missionary nurses from the headquarters of Catholic missions to work in its state health services. Such nurses would be considered as special personnel with the same salary (440 angolares per month = $17.60 U.S.) and working conditions, including food, as other employees.

The number of Catholic missionary nurses was many times greater than the number of Protestant missionary nurses, and the number of Catholic health centers (dispensaries, nurseries, maternity centers, and clinics) was greater than the number of Protestant facilities. The number of treatments given in the Catholic institutions was also greater than that in Protestant health centers. However, the relatively large Protestant hospitals served by doctors who spent more than twenty years in Angola gave the Protestant health ministries an excellent reputation and prompted some criticism of the Catholic services even by Catholics.

Father J. Alves Correia, a Spiritan leader who made an analysis of "Medical Action in the Colonies and that of the Christian Missionaries" in 1945 commented:

Instead of real hospitals, as the principal Protestant missions have (everyone in the South of Angola knows the "Lord of Fatima

---

11. Frank E. Archibald, *Salute to Sid: The Story of Dr. Sidney Gilchrist* (Windsor, Nova Scotia: Lancelot Press, 1970), 44–45.

of Angola" as the grateful public christened an American missionary physician and surgeon) we are content, until now, with dispensaries.[12]

The "Lord of Fatima" was Dr. Walter Strangway, the director of the hospital at the Chissamba mission near Nova Sintra/Catabola in Bié. He combined an exceptional surgical ability with administrative skill and a charming manner, attracting patients of all races and classes from all over Angola. His wife, Alice Strangway, made a distinguished contribution to the hospital, developing and directing an efficient laboratory, not only to do routine analyses, but to do research in such important diseases as sickle-cell anemia and scurvy.

In the 1950s the Catholic church decided to establish its own hospitals as well as to continue to furnish personnel to the government health services. This two-pronged approach was shown in the diocese of Sá da Bandeira in 1958 when five sisters of the Congregation of the Holy Ghost arrived to take charge of nursing services at the regional government hospital in the city, and a new building for outpatients and a small leprosarium were opened at the Chiulo mission in the extreme southwest corner of Angola. The latter mission was staffed by Irish doctors and nurses of the Medical Missionaries of Mary.

The Congregation of the Most Holy Redeemer entered Angola in 1954, and under the leadership of the Rev. Manuel Garcia established the Vouga mission in 1957. After building a boys' boarding school and missionary residences, he began the construction of a large hospital in 1959. It included three pavilions with space for four hundred beds. The Vouga Missionary Hospital, which was the best equipped in Angola, was built with financing by the Banco de Providência, a government bank, a grant from the Angolan government, private contributions, subscriptions, and lotteries. Father Manuel Garcia also visited Portugal to raise money to equip the hospital.

The original staff of the Vouga hospital included a Redemptorist priest, who was also a doctor, a doctor and his wife, who was an analyst, and a missionary nurse. The couple was touted as the "first lay missionaries in Portugal."[13]

Public Health and Community Development

Health is more than dealing with disease. The World Health Organization defines health as "a state of complete physical, mental, and social

12. J. Alves Correia, "Acção Médica nas Colónias e a dos missionários cristãos," *Portugal em África* 2 (1945): 283.

13. *Além-Mar: Revista dos Missionários Combonianos* 5, no. 62 (November 1961).

well-being." The healing ministry of the church cannot be confined to the white smocks of doctors and nurses. It has been estimated that 70 percent of the disease in Angola could have been prevented by observing a few principles of public health, such as providing a source of clean water, using soap, removing the breeding places of the mosquito, using latrines, and maintaining a balanced diet. It could be argued that the church's most effective healing ministry was not exercised in hospitals, but rather in the educational, social and community development programs promoted by the missions.

The basic unit in this public health effort was the Christian village. As families adhered to either a Catholic or Protestant mission they formed a new village with the school/chapel as its center and the catechist as the recognized leader. Each village community became a new creation in which a different way of life was taught.

Both Catholic and Protestant observers noted a contrast between the two types of Christian villages. Not only could they be distinguished by the wooden cross atop the Catholic school, but the orderliness, cleanliness, presence of fruit trees, and general prosperity of Protestant villages distinguished them from the average Catholic community.

This distinction was based on the different educational strategies noted in chapter 5. The Catholic church emphasized the training of clergy and used the traditional catechetical teaching by rote for the majority of lay people. The Protestant churches stressed the teaching of reading and writing to each person, so he or she could read the Bible. This ability also made the Protestant community more capable of assimilating the teachings of public health, agriculture, and child care.

A Catholic lay observer in central Angola, António Kambala, argued that these were signs of a fundamental difference in orientation between the Catholic and Protestant communities. The Catholic church focused its attention on the spiritual life of its people while the Protestant community had a more holistic view of the gospel:

> The Protestant missionary was not concerned only with the soul and the spiritual life of the Christian. He was equally concerned with the physical life, housing, health, and general well-being of the Christians.... A Protestant village was clean with some houses plastered and white-washed. In those villages an irrigation ditch brought water to gardens, sugar cane, and fruit trees such as papaya, orange, and banana, etc.
>
> The Protestant man dressed well, ate well, had a clean house and more money than the Catholic. The Protestant was more social than the Catholic as well as being more political and revolutionary than the Catholic. To combat this style of the Protestants the Catholic missionaries and catechists told their faithful that the

Protestants were heretics and very materialistic. They taught that the Protestants would not go to heaven, because they did not believe in Christian truths and did not practice the Christian virtues of Faith, Hope, and Charity, and that in their worship they only sang choruses.[14]

A Portuguese Catholic observer who agreed with this description of the contrast between Catholic and Protestant communities in Angola was José Júlio Gonçalves, a missiologist at the Junta de Investigações do Ultramar in Lisbon. He used one hundred pages in his book *Protestantismo em África* to describe the effective methods of evangelization employed by the Protestant community. His list of twenty-one Protestant methods of propagating the faith could be combined into five main headings: education, health, communication, community development, and Africanization.[15]

Gonçalves reluctantly praised the educational program of the Protestants, for he preferred that Angolans be educated by government and Catholic schools. He recognized the efficacy of Protestant schools and was amazed at the low fees charged in them even though they did not receive any government subsidy. He did not understand the well-organized support given by the Angolan Protestant communities to their schools.

This Portuguese Catholic analyst considered the health ministries one of the most effective means that the Protestants used to "seduce the native populations." He recognized not only the skill and dedication of medical missionaries, but the strong influence of the Protestant catechist-nurses in the villages.

Communications were also being used effectively by Protestant missions in Angola. Gonçalves collected many books, pamphlets, and leaflets produced in the missions. He noted that they included not only religious and academic booklets, but many practical publications on health, nutrition, agriculture, and domestic science.

Many effective means of community education that Gonçalves found Protestants using in Angola were simply the adaptation of African culture to the mission of propagating the gospel and promoting the healing ministry. Angolans had a special talent for singing so that was made central in any kind of meeting. African leaders were equipped as catechists, teachers, nurses, and pastors, and they were more effective than foreign personnel with superior academic training. African games were adapted for educational purposes. The important role given to vil-

---

14. António Kambala, unpublished manuscript.

15. José Júlio Gonçalves, *Protestantismo em África, Contribuição para o Estudo do Protestantismo na África Portuguesa*, vol. 2 (Lisbon: Junta de Investigações do Ultramar, 1960).

lage elders in Protestant churches took advantage of prestige that they had in traditional society.

Gonçalves ostensibly was describing the Protestant community, but at the same time he was criticizing Catholics for not giving more attention to village schools, neglecting the health ministry, being slow in employing new technologies of communication, ignoring the needs of community development, and failing to Africanize the Catholic community.

Community development is a large umbrella covering a variety of services commonly offered in Protestant missions: agriculture, public health, trades, and domestic arts. Such services were not only offered academically in the classroom, but in such programs as *Melhoramento do Povo* (People's Development) in which several villages gathered for a period to learn, for example, how to grow vegetables, dig latrines, make adobe and floor tiles, and care for babies, by participating in programs to benefit their own homes and villages.

The People's Development program centered in the Dôndi mission near Bela Vista/Kachiungo dates its birth from 1953, but similar efforts had been made sporadically for many years. In the 1930s the Rev. Lauretta Dibble and the Rev. and Mrs. Kenneth Prior did village visitation in which they used their various talents as minister, agriculturalist, nurse, and group leader to present the gospel in its wholeness.

In 1953 the Rev. Merrill Ferguson of the Camundongo church invited Dr. Allen Knight, an agriculturalist, Dr. W. S. Gilchrist, a physician-surgeon, and the Rev. Marcolino Samacuva, an Angolan pastor, to work for one week in a Camundongo village. A protected spring was constructed using two sacks of cement, stone and sand, and bambu pipe. Sekulu Jimi took change of making tiles with very simple equipment and an outdoor oven. It was during this one-week project that soybeans were toasted on the top of a two-hundred-liter drum and pounded into meal in a mortar. Three parts of corn meal were mixed with one part of toasted soy meal to feed babies lacking protein.

As this program developed the village projects expanded to four weeks and included teaching the people to dig latrines for their houses, select seed corn, and use flails for threshing beans and corn. The introduction of soy beans involved the teaching of the processes of inoculation, planting, harvesting, toasting, and milling. In some places in central Angola soy beans were known as "Protestant beans" since the Protestant missions had done so much to promote their cultivation and consumption.

From the beginning Angolan staff was involved in leadership in these projects. André Euba, professor at Currie Institute, and João Cunanga, nurse at the Dôndi Hospital, visited villages six months in advance of the projects to assess the potential for community effort, to talk to the local Portuguese authorities, and to bring back samples of clay from different sites to be made into roof and floor tiles.

Five projects were conducted in each of the dry seasons from 1955 to 1960. One project under the leadership of Pastor Feliciano Nunda and his wife, Befilia, in the center of Sapessi in the Chilesso area produced twenty-five-thousand roof tiles and five thousand floor tiles in the four-week period. Sufficient floor tiles were subsequently made for seven villages within a thirty-mile radius of Sapessi.

Conclusion

As we have noted, the word "salvation" comes from the Latin *salus*, health, and in Jesus' ministry salvation and health were intimately related. Evidently this truth of Jesus' ministry has been acted out by the church in Angola for in reviewing a century of work by the Congregation of the Holy Ghost an observer wrote: "All missions provide medical help, some on a larger, some on a smaller scale, but the Angolans would not believe that a missionary did not know how to treat them and they know that he or she seeks to cure them of their illnesses."[16]

---

16. Cândido Ferreira da Costa, *Cem Anos dos Missionários do Espírito Santo em Angola, 1866–1966* (Nova Lisboa, 1970), 263.

Chapter 7

The Organization
of the Church

Each missionary agency or parent church planted a seed that contained
its own ecclesiastical, doctrinal, and cultural genes, but the Angolan soil
affected the plants that grew out of the seeds. The parent bodies covered
a broad spectrum of ecclesiastical structures, from the highly centralized
Roman Catholic church to the zealously independent assemblies of the
Plymouth Brethren.

Decentralized					*Centralized*		
Plymouth Brethren	SAGM	Swiss	BMS	ABCFM Canadian	Methodist	SDA	Roman Catholic

Ecclesiastical structures of Parent Bodies

In this chapter we will discuss briefly the polity of each sending community and the structures of the churches that grew out of the Angolan
soil.

The Catholic Church

The Catholic church centered its organization in the pope, who was considered to be the successor of Peter (Matt. 16:18) by orders of Jesus Christ.
Thus his jurisdiction was received immediately from God upon his election and acceptance. The Roman pontiff authorized the consecration of
bishops, who formed the episcopal college under and with the pope,
the bishop of Rome.

Over a period of five centuries the worldwide organization of the Catholic church slowly embraced Angola. As the first step Pope Calixtus III in 1456 entrusted to the Supreme Order of Christ, with its headquarters in Tomar, Portugal, the spiritual authority over all the overseas territories already discovered or to be discovered by the Portuguese.

In 1514 at the request of King Manuel I of Portugal, Pope Leo X created the diocese of Funchal, on the island of Madeira, and transferred to it all spiritual jurisdiction previously exercised overseas by the Order of Christ. This included all the African coast from Morocco south to the Cape of Good Hope.

As Portugal continued its discoveries in Africa, King John III (1521–57) petitioned the Supreme Pontiff to create new dioceses, and the diocese of Funchal was divided. When Paul III created the diocese of São Tomé in 1534, it included the islands of São Tomé and Príncipe, other islands of the Gulf of Guinea, and all the coast of Africa from Sierra Leone to the Cape of Good Hope. So the territory to become Angola belonged to this new diocese. The first bishop of São Tomé to visit the Congo was Dom Gaspar Cão, who stayed there three months, confirming believers and ordaining priests.[1]

The first diocese with its seat in Angola was created in 1596 by Pope Clement VIII at the capital of the kingdom of the Kongo, São Salvador, as he subdivided the diocese of São Tomé and created the diocese of the Congo, giving it the territories of the kingdoms of the Congo and Angola. Thus after more than a century of the church's presence in Angola it was organizationally complete, with the creation of a diocese that belonged to the *Padroado* of the king of Portugal.

The diocese is the basic administrative unit in the Catholic church, for it is the territory over which the bishop exercises his spiritual jurisdiction. The bishops are considered the heirs of the apostles, who were given the authority to confirm church members and to hand on the priesthood by performing ordinations. It is also through the diocesan bishops that the authority of the papal government is transmitted to the people, since the bishop is appointed by the Holy See, usually after a local nomination.

A diocese may have a curia to assist the bishop in dealing with local affairs. In 1943, for example, the archdiocese of Luanda had a curia of the archbishop Dom Moisés Alves de Pinho, Monsignor Manuel Alves da Cunha, vicar general, and four other men who had secretarial responsibilities. The title "monsignor" is a papal honor conferred upon a diocesan priest, and "vicar general" is a priest chosen by the bishop as his immediate assistant who shares the jurisdictional powers of the bishop.

---

1. Manuel Nunes Gabriel, *Angola: Cinco Séculos de Cristianismo* (Queluz: Literal, 1978), 81–83

The newly created dioceses of Nova Lisboa and Silva Porto at that time had curias with only two men plus the bishops, Dom Daniel Gomes Junqueira and Dom António Ildefonso dos Santos Silva respectively.

From 1879 until 1940 the Catholic church in Angola was organized in two structural forms: the diocese of Angola and Congo under the *Padroado*, and the apostolic prefectures of the Congo and Cimbebasia (later called Cubango) directly under the Vatican. The evangelization of the prefectures was entrusted to the Congregation of the Holy Ghost.

In 1940 the prefectures were abolished and the Vatican created the archdiocese of Luanda and the suffragan dioceses of Nova Lisboa and Silva Porto. The next dioceses to be created were Sá da Bandeira (1955) and Malanje (1957).

This very brief review of the organization of the Catholic church in Angola reveals a fundamental characteristic of its ecclesiastical structure that it shares with other "established" churches such as the Church of England and the Lutheran churches in the Scandinavian countries. From the time of Pope Calixtus III in 1456 the Catholic church claimed to have "spiritual authority" over all of Angola, which at that time was simply described as "all the overseas territories already discovered or to be discovered by the Portuguese."

At the end of the colonial period in 1960 this same spiritual authority, which had been entrusted to the Supreme Order of Christ with headquarters in Tomar, Portugal, was exercised organizationally through the ecclesiastical province of Luanda, which embraced the archdiocese of Luanda and the dioceses of Nova Lisboa, Silva Porto, Sá da Bandeira, and Malanje. In turn these dioceses had given authority to 51 parishes and 119 missions.

According to Roman Catholic canon law, the one, holy, catholic, and apostolic church is located and active in the diocese or local church.[2]

Until almost the end of the colonial period the Angolan bishops were integrated into the assembly of Portuguese bishops, and the Metropolitan from Portugal attended some of their meetings. In 1957 the Holy See decided that the bishops of Angola and Mozambique should constitute an episcopal conference over which the archbishop-cardinal of Lourenço Marques, Dom Teodósio Clemente de Gouveia, would preside, but only two meetings were held of this conference.

The Seventh-Day Adventists

The Seventh-Day Adventists share with the Roman Catholics the extreme right end of the structural spectrum of the church in Angola for it

---

2. *Código de Direito Canónico* (Braga, 1984), no. 369.

was organized not as a series of separate national or regional churches, but as one worldwide, unified, international church,using one church manual and operating by one general policy.[3] It functioned on a hierarchical ladder with five steps: local church, local conference, union conference, division, and general conference. The General Conference of Seventh-Day Adventists has its headquarters at 6840 Eastern Avenue, N.W., Washington, DC 20012.

In 1961 the eight SDA missions in Angola formed the Angola Union belonging to the Euro-African Division, which was responsible to the General Conference.

The Methodist Church

Structurally the Methodist church bore two similarities to the Catholic church: it was episcopal and subject to direction from an international ecclesiastical organization. However the differences between the Methodist and Catholic structures were more important than their similarities. The Catholic church chose its bishops from the top, believing that they were the successors of the apostles, and so they alone had the authority to choose new bishops. The Methodist bishops were elected by conferences composed of an equal number of lay and clergy delegates. The Methodist church had what it called a "moderate episcopacy" and was "persuaded that the uninterrupted succession of bishops from the Apostles could be proved neither from scripture nor antiquity."[4]

The structure of the worldwide Methodist church was determined by the Book of Discipline. In the preface to the 1956 edition of the Discipline in Portuguese, Bishop Nowell S. Booth and Bishop Ralph E. Dodge wrote:

This Book of Discipline furnishes the direction that our churches need. It was prepared through a careful study of the commission of the Central Conference of Africa. It maintains and reaffirms the Discipline of the church as a collection of laws and decrees marvelously adapted to the peoples of Africa. It also furnishes directions for the adjustments and arrangements proper for the special needs of this area. This book is clearly and truly the Discipline of the Methodist church and expresses the unity of this church everywhere, but at the same time, it is adapted to the exist-

---

3. *Seventh-Day Adventist Encyclopedia*, rev. ed. (Washington, D.C.: Review and Herald Publication Association, 1976), 493.
4. H. Shelton Smith et al., eds., *American Christianity: An Historical Interpretation with Representative Documents*, vol. 1, *1907–1920* (New York: Charles Scribner's Sons, 1960), 457.

ing conditions in the missionary field and is thus an African edition of the Discipline.

The chart below illustrates the structure of the worldwide Methodist church and the location of the Methodist church in Angola within that structure.

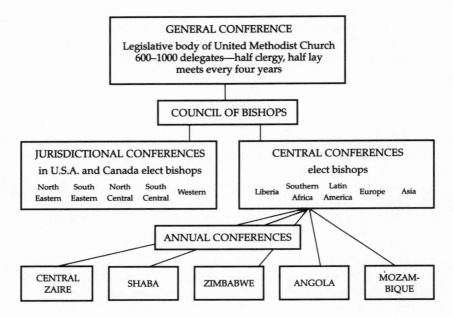

It took years for the Methodist church in Angola to become a full partner in the worldwide Methodist church. From 1885 through 1896 Angola was a district in the Annual Conference of Liberia. This conference included all work in Africa south of the Sahara and soon proved too extensive.

From 1902 through 1919 the Angolan Methodist church functioned as a part of the Missionary Conference of West Central Africa. The next step was the formation in 1920 of the Missionary Conference of Angola, which continued through 1938. In 1939 the Angolan Methodist church satisfied the denominational requirements and became the Provisional Annual Conference of Angola.

The Annual Conference is the fundamental body of the Methodist church, and after sixty-three years the Methodists in Angola became full partners in the denominational structure with the formation of the Annual Conference of Angola in 1948. The next year it had its first Angolan secretary, J. J. Cristiano, and ever since then secretaries have been Angolan.

In 1951 Filipe de Freitas was appointed assistant district superintendent for the Quéssua District, and by 1956 all the district superintendents were Angolans.

District	1956	1960
Cuanza North	Sebastião Sousa e Santos	Raymond Noah
Dembos	Guilherme Pereira Ingles	Guilherme P. Ingles
Luanda	Raimundo Sousa e Santos	Alexandre Rosa Tavares
Malanje	Manuel Francisco Abrigada	Raimundo Sousa e Santos
Quela	Paulo António de Brito	Júlio João Miguel

So after seventy-one years all appointments to ministerial leadership in districts, parishes, and circuits were Angolans.

The Methodist church was hierarchical at the local level as it was in its international and national structure, built up from class to congregation to pastoral charge or circuit. One of the unique features of Methodism was the class.

The centrality of the school in the Christian communities in Angola made it easy to assume that "class" was an academic term. That was not true in Methodism. Rather in John Wesley's use of the word it came from the Latin *classis*, the six divisions or orders of the Roman people under the legislation of Servius Tullius. Wesley, the founder of Methodism, divided the Methodist Society in London into classes and appointed a leader for each class. Attendance at the class meeting soon became the test of membership in the Methodist movement.

The first Methodist missionaries to Angola had inherited the tradition of the class meeting. For Bishop William Taylor, Amos Withey, William Dodson, and Robert Shields the class meeting was a vital tool.

The 1956 edition of the Methodist Discipline of the Central African Conference defined the purposes of the class in this way:

Para. 131

1. To establish a system of pastoral supervision which makes available to each member the total program of the church: spiritual, evangelistic, educational, social and financial.

2. To promote and support social contacts and worship and to communicate the plans of the church that the Grace of God may be attracted to it: and that the classes may be a means to develop on the part of each member loyalty to the activities of the church.

Para. 132

1. The principal objective of the distribution of the members into classes, is, besides the guarantee of the necessary pastoral supervision, to assure that each member prays and serves in order to carry forward the constructive program of the church.

2. The classes when possible will be composed of 20 church members together with the members of their families, and the class

leader should give a report to each Trimestral Conference on the attendance and activities of the class members.

3. Each class leader should inform himself of the spiritual state of each member of his class, not only to know if he is cooperating in the work of the church, but also to know if he is growing in the knowledge and love of God.

Para. 135

The class leader should follow a course of study and reading to prepare himself for his service.

Baptist Churches

The Baptist churches in the British Isles were a product of the independent, or separatist, church movement of the seventeenth century, which sought to reform the established Anglican church by returning to New Testament beliefs and practices. They emphasized two ecclesiastical features — the gathered community and believers' baptism — that tended to place authority in the local congregation, but still allowed for the formation of Baptist unions and associations. These structures became tools for expanding the work in Britain and forums for discussing theological and disciplinary queries and establishing a "Baptist viewpoint."

The BMS, which had as its object "the diffusion of the knowledge of the religion of Jesus Christ throughout the whole world beyond the British Isles," could be expected to see its mission from the "Baptist viewpoint," which included gathered communities and believers' baptism.

In Angola the BMS functioned as part of the Congo Mission, which had been one field since the first missionaries arrived in the Congo basin in 1878 before the boundaries were drawn establishing separate French, Belgian, and Portuguese colonies. The Congo Mission was governed by the Field Council, which divided the basin into four regions: Upper Congo, Middle Congo, Lower Congo, and Angola. The council, with two full-time officers, secretary and treasurer, met annually and had its offices in Leopoldville/Kinshasa.

The BMS missionaries from the three Angolan stations, São Salvador, Bembe, and Kibokolo, had their own council and met annually for business and fellowship. Alongside the mission organization was the church structure. The founding of the church in São Salvador on December 4, 1887, was recorded under the title, "Baptist Church — São Salvador, In connection with the Baptist Missionary Society, London." "In connection" did not refer to the kind of relationship in a "connectional" church in which all the parts are related organically, as in the Catholic, Methodist, or Seventh-Day Adventist structures. The relationship between the São Salvador church and the BMS mission might more properly have been described as "in association."

In the beginning the São Salvador Baptist Church was one congregation on the mission station, but the church grew by the creation of new Christian communities in surrounding villages. It was generally agreed that seven or more baptized adults could form a congregation. Since these congregations had their legal identity through their relationship with the São Salvador mission, they were not considered separate churches.

Ideally a congregation or Christian village had two leaders: a catechist who was responsible for the religious instruction and organization and a deacon who was the spiritual counselor and local pastor.

As the number of local congregations increased to ten, they were linked together in a circuit, whose boundaries were determined primarily by geography.

The third level of ecclesiastical structure was the church — which corresponded to the station in the mission organization. The area served by the BMS mission in Angola had three churches: São Salvador, Bembe, and Kibokolo. Each church had its own secretary-treasurer and finance committee, who were responsible to the monthly church meeting. They kept the church membership rolls and the financial accounts, which were audited by a missionary.

The Baptists had no general rules comparable to the Methodist Discipline, so this ecclesiastical structure developed gradually to meet the needs of the growing Christian community.

All the Protestant missions believed in the church as a "gathered community," but those who practiced exclusively "believers' baptism" found that the Angolan traditional kinship relations made the establishment of separate, gathered, believer communities very difficult. Even when separate Protestant communities were built across a river or on the other side of the hill from Roman Catholic or traditional villages, they were not composed solely of believers. Generally in Europe and North America "gathered communities" were not residential as they were in Africa.

Council of Evangelical Churches of Central Angola (CIEAC)

The church structure developed by the ABCFM and CCFMS in central Angola was very similar to that of the churches planted by the BMS among the Kikongo. In 1960 eight churches in central Angola belonged to the Council of Evangelical Churches of Central Angola: Bailundo, Camundongo, Chilesso, Chissamba, Coast, Dôndi, Elende, and Galangue.

The ecclesiastical organization in central Angola followed closely the pattern of Umbundu social structure. The mission station assumed the functions of the *ombala*, the king's village, and during the colonial period the missionary was the king. Dependent on the mission stations were the outstations similar to the *atumbu*, where chiefs ruled. As the work developed and some leaders were ordained, these outstations became pastoral centers. The other Christian villages, as in the traditional Umbundu villages, were ruled by elders. After 1921 the government required that one person in each Christian village have a catechist card. Another level of the hierarchy was created as pastoral areas were subdivided and deacons were given responsibilities to help the church in the local congregations and to assist the pastors in their duties.

Such a hierarchical structure was not brought by the missionaries from Canada and the United States, for they came mostly from Congregational churches whose major characteristic was the autonomy of each local congregation. Nor did the structure follow some plan that missionaries and Angolan leaders developed consciously. It was simply the organization that grew as the church developed within Angolan society. The free rein given to the church by the missionaries is illustrated by the practice of Walter Currie, the pioneer Canadian missionary in Chissamba, who did not attend the business meetings of the nascent Chissamba church unless he was invited.

The missionaries had an organization provided for them when the ABCFM voted in 1879 to form the West Central Africa Mission (WCAM). They had to meet annually to formulate requests for financial subsidies and personnel from the ABCFM and to deal with matters pertaining to the placement of personnel and planning new work.

According to classical congregational polity, each village congregation could have been considered a church. However the small size of most villages and the lack of trained leaders made the pastorate a more logical candidate for the ecclesiastical status of "church." The pastorate had an ordained clergyman with authority to administer the sacraments so it could legitimately be considered a church. Yet the importance of the mission station in the process of the planting of the church and the government requirement that all official business go through recognized mission organizations distorted the congregational polity to which the missionaries were accustomed, and the churches of central Angola developed a hierarchical system that served their interests.

As the churches developed around the mission stations, which were quite separated and isolated by poor transportation and communications, there was little interchurch fellowship or cooperation. In 1911 a deputation sent by the ABCFM to Angola noted that the isolation of the individual mission stations was detrimental to the health and progress of the churches. In the same year the WCAM proposed that there be a council or association of churches "to promote fellowship among the churches and mutual helpfulness in Christian life, work, discipline, etc." According to the proposal the delegates to the association of churches would be the missionary director of each mission, the active pastor or chief elder of each church, and delegates elected annually by the local churches. The missionaries who made the proposal — Wesley M. Stover, T. W. Woodside, and Merlin W. Ennis — were not suggesting a connectional church in which the association would have binding legislative authority as in the Methodist conferences. Rather, the powers of the association would be purely advisory. The proposal was approved by the missionaries, and the churches were requested to send delegates to the 1913 Annual Meeting of the WCAM. The delegates gathered at the Chilesso mission at the same time as the missionaries met in the WCAM and formed the *Ohongele Yakongelo Umbundu*, the Association of Umbundu Churches.

The association was primarily composed of the churches founded by the ABCFM and CCFMS, but some representatives also participated from churches planted by the SAGM and CMML. As the local churches multiplied and the number of members increased, the association meetings expanded dramatically. In 1922, thirteen hundred delegates attended the meeting.[5]

These meetings provided good fellowship, stimulating Christian worship and the discussion of the churches' common disciplinary problems, but did not produce an ecclesiastical structure. In 1928 the joint meeting of the ABCFM and the United Church of Canada missionaries agreed that "a meeting be called at Bailundo immediately following the mid-year meeting of the Board of Trustees for the purpose of organizing a responsible ecclesiastical body among the native churches: such a meeting to be attended by the missionary in charge of evangelistic work at the various stations of both missions and also three native leaders from each church."[6]

In reporting this action to the mission office in Boston, G. M. Childs, the missionary secretary, commented that this was "the most important decision of the meeting. [It] grew out of a discussion as to the possibility of ordaining ministers and we realize that we have no body compe-

---

    5. ABC 5:1, vol. 21, no. 4.
    6. ABC 15:1, vol. 21, no. 134. In 1925 the Methodist, Presbyterian, and Congregational churches in Canada merged to form the United Church of Canada, which established its own mission society. Prior to that time Canadian Congregational missionaries had been sent to Angola through the ABCFM and were members of the WCAM. From this date the United Church of Canada sent its own missionaries directly to Angola and formed their own organization on the field, parallel to the WCAM of the ABCFM.

tent to do that at present. While there are organizations of the several churches, more or less functioning, as between them no permanent organization exists. We hope that the February meeting at Bailundo may register real progress in the Native Church."[7]

In 1931 the Native Church Council, *Onjango Yakulu*, was organized as an ecclesiastical body. It followed the path of the Baptists in the north, where the mission and church formed parallel structures. The mission societies in the United States and Canada noted with approval the establishment of the African Advisory council and in 1947 recommended that the council have representation on the Board of Managers, which administered the central mission institutions at Dôndi.

In 1952 the Joint Angola Consultative Committee for Africa meeting in Boston voted to record its appreciation of the steps which have been taken in further cooperation with the African church by the presence of nine Africans as voting members of the Board of Managers.

So the parallel lines of mission and church were converging with mission society approval. "This is all pointing the way toward the eventual amalgamation of Mission Council with the Church Council. The process is long and difficult, but the result is greatly to be desired."

The 1950s saw the church and mission move steadily toward this desired amalgamation. In 1950 four delegates of the Umbundu Church Council: Jessé Chipenda, Paulino Ngonga, Enoque Gomes, and Frederico Mussili presented three recommendations to the mission council:

1. that stations take more care that the Third Class material be covered for candidates to Currie Institute;

2. that plans be made for a pastors' retirement fund; and

3. that the theological seminary consider starting a course for church workers in addition to the present one for pastors.

In 1951 the Umbundu Church Council and the Mission Council worshipped jointly while the meetings were held simultaneously but separately. The next year the meetings of the two councils overlapped, and in 1954 they held the first fully joint meeting. Finally in 1956 they drafted a constitution for the "Council of Evangelical Churches in Central Angola," which not only changed the organization, policies, and procedures of church and mission, but provided for the first time a written guide for eight churches and three mission organizations in central Angola.

---

7. Ibid., no. 137.

Pastor Jessé Chiula Chipenda

Ordination of Pastor Herlander Felizardo in Lobito

The first name proposed for this new organization was "The Church of Christ in Central Angola." Through the Aliança Evangélica de Angola all missionary agencies working in Angola had agreed to the common name of the Church of Christ in Angola to avoid the use of divisive denominational titles. However, differing ecclesiastical traditions made it impossible to define whether the Church of Christ referred to local congregations or to the whole body of believers in Angola. The choice of name for the organization being formed in 1956–57 in central Angola was not decided theologically, but rather on the basis of four practical considerations:

1. The organization was not to be a church, but a council of churches.

2. It was hoped that other mission/churches working in central Angola that had had relations with the Church Council would find the title of the new organization simple and not a barrier to continued association.

3. The name adopted, Council of Evangelical Churches in Central Angola, was more suitable for public relations. The Portuguese Roman Catholic background made "Evangelical Churches" more understandable for those outside the fold than "Church of Christ."

4. The term "Central Angola" was used to indicate a general area without defining strictly geographical limits. The previous church council was designated as "Umbundu," which indicated the area served and language used. In the new organization some "Umbundu churches" were not immediately included and Portuguese became the official language.

Article 2 of the constitution defined the purposes of the council:

1. To work for the coming of the Kingdom of God proclaiming Jesus Christ as Savior and Lord, in word and deed.

2. To develop the Church of Christ in Central Angola, co-ordinating the work of the churches and evangelical missions in the same.

3. To strengthen relations with the Church of Christ in all Angola, and through the Angola Evangelical Alliance with evangelical churches throughout the world.

Article 2 did not produce great discussion, which revealed the theological inarticulateness of the Christian community in central Angola. The first paragraph reflected the basic evangelical purpose that had always motivated the mission and, in the first phrase, also expressed the influence of liberal theology. The second and third paragraphs maintained the line between a covenantal and connectional ecclesiology.

The delegates to the annual General Assembly of the CIEAC would be four from each church plus one additional delegate for each two thousand communicant members. The central institutions, Currie Institute, Means School, the seminary, the hospital, the center of literature, and the press, also had representation.

No quotas were established, but it was provided that "in the choice of delegates each member [church] will take into consideration the proportion of pastors and laymen, women and men, teachers, nurses, etc. so that all the branches of the work of the church may be represented" (art. 4, para. 8).

An executive committee composed of the president, vice-president, general-secretary, treasurer, corresponding secretary, minutes secretary, and three members-at-large would meet four times a year. The general-secretary was the administrative officer of the council.

The general assembly elected permanent committees, such as evangelism, education, health, literature, people's development, agriculture, technical assistance, finances, construction, and missions. The last provision for a "missionary committee" was the most radical aspect of the document. Whereas the missionaries had been organized to handle monies that came from abroad, place missionary personnel, set policy, and in general be responsible for the missions and related church organizations, the new constitution gave those responsibilities to the Council of Evangelical Churches, CIEAC.

This action was taken none too soon. With the outbreak of the colonial war in 1961 and the reduced number of Protestant missionaries and government restrictions on their movements, it was necessary that the churches assume responsibility for their own life and activities.

The first general-secretary elected by the council was the Rev. Jessé Chiula Chipenda.

The constitution was adopted by the General Assembly at the Dôndi mission on March 19, 1956.

The Evangelical Church of the Philafrican Mission

The synod founded by delegates from Kalukembe, Ebanga, and Sussangue who met in 1945 adopted statutes, Ovisila Viakongelo Omissão Evangélica Filafricana, which outlined in thirty-two articles the organization, beliefs and practices of the Evangelical Church of the Philafrican Mission.

The first article declared that the church belonged to the union, *kohongele*, of evangelical churches of Angola. This was simply an affirmation of intention and commitment for there was no organizational expression of the "union of evangelical churches," and in 1945 the

Aliança Evangélica de Angola was a missionary rather than a church organization.

The church based its teaching on the Bible and on the conviction that there was no salvation except that which was given by Jesus, the only Son of God who died on the cross for sinful humanity.

The local church was defined in the statutes as a congregation of at least forty communicant members that was able to support a pastor and elected a council composed of the pastor, secretary, treasurer, and four elders. Smaller congregations were led by catechists who should hold official identity cards. Evangelists were superintendents of catechists in newly formed village congregations. All church workers volunteered their services except pastors, evangelists, and catechists, who received small salaries. Elders might receive gifts if there were a surplus in the church treasury.

The synod was composed of the Philafrican missionaries, pastors, evangelists, and church delegates. Delegates were chosen on the basis of the membership of the churches, with one delegate from each church plus one more for each sixty members. The president of the Philafrican missionaries presided over the synod.

Plymouth Brethren

The Christian Missions in Many Lands (CMML) work in Angola was the result of one branch of the Plymouth Brethren movement in Europe and North America. The movement had been divided since its beginning in the early nineteenth century between "open" and "exclusive" Brethren.

"Open" meant an assembly of believers, congregational in character, but above all independent. "Exclusive" designated a kind of federation of assemblies, which an outsider might call a "denomination." That word was, however, utterly rejected by the Brethren, who referred to a "circle of fellowship," which meant that the members of the circle acted in harmony. Discipline exercised in one assembly was ratified by the others of the circle; preachers approved by one were similarly accepted by the others.

Since all the Brethren missionaries in Angola were commended by "open" assemblies, we will examine how that pattern of church organization was reproduced in Angolan soil.

Among the truths that the Brethren believed that they had recovered was the doctrine of the church in its three aspects: (1) the local assembly of all believers in a city (Acts 8:1, 13:1; 1 Cor. 1:2), (2) the Body of Christ, or the Universal Church of God on earth of which Christ is the head in heaven (Col. 2:12; Acts 20:28), and (3) its complete and future aspect as a "glorious church" (Eph. 5:25–27) embracing all believers from Pentecost to the Rapture.[8] The church therefore had no structure on earth except the local assembly. According to Brethren all other forms of association, such as councils or synods, were unscriptural. The local assembly was the church, capable of performing all church functions and directly responsible to its Lord.

The Brethren recognized three aspects of the Christian ministry as diagrammed below:

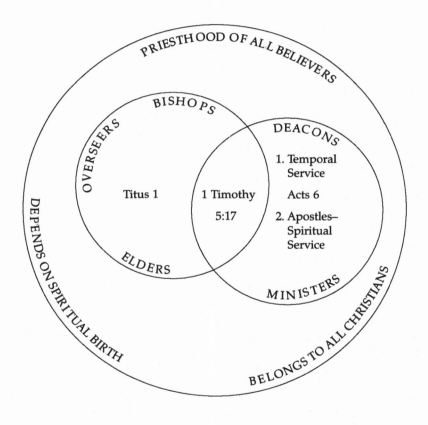

The emphasis was placed on the plurality of ministers. The ministry was dependent on gifts from the risen Lord (Eph. 4:11–12) and the Scriptures stressed the variety and distribution of gifts among the saints (1 Cor. 12). The affirmation of the plurality of gifts and ministries led to a sharp criticism of a one-man ministry.

---

8. Charles S. Howard, "The Local Church," *Letters of Interest* 29, no. 112 (January 1964): 13.

First we would say that a "minister" such as we see in the churches of Christendom has no counterpart in the New Testament. By this we mean a man who has the title "Reverend" and who, to all intents and purposes, is the sole spiritual leader of a congregation. He is a man who has graduated from a theological school and has been ordained by the laying on of someone's hands. He does the preaching, the praying and the visitation, and is looked up to as the sole leader. This is the view of Christendom in general and we realize that many born-again, godly men included in the system are serving God in good conscience. However this fact does not minimize the truth that the system is completely unscriptural.[9]

Such a criticism, made in Great Britain, was not applicable in Angola for there in all Protestant communities lay leaders preached, prayed, and visited.

In Angolan traditional society kings and chiefs occupied positions of authority on various levels of the political ladder, but still most important decisions were made by a small group of elders. In the Protestant communities also small groups of elders exercised most authority even though the government required that one person have a catechist's card in each village, which made him legally the responsible person.

The Brethren pattern of a multiple ministry shared by elders, deacons, catechists, and other ministers was in harmony with traditional practice. Bishop Sundkler in his study of the Christian ministry in Africa noted "the lack of differentiation between pastor, catechist, and ordinary laymen."[10]

Favoring the multiple-ministry pattern of the Brethren also was the fact that very few Angolan Protestant pastors in the colonial period worked full-time in their ministry. They supported themselves and their families primarily by farming, and their modest salaries were not sufficient to raise them above the economic level of other subsistence farmers. The Angolan soil during the colonial period was very different from the social scene of the United Kingdom a century earlier. John Nelson Darby wished to separate himself from a corrupt church to pursue what he considered a purer and more scriptural Christian way. For the Brethren missionaries on the vast bushland plateaus of Africa, dealing with pagan African chiefs and exploiting white colonialists, the sharp religious separations of the homeland dimmed and they found the strength and joy of Christian fellowship with their colleagues of other ecclesiastical traditions. Henry A. Nevinson, a journalist who vis-

---

9. Ibid., no. 3, 10.
10. Bengt Sundkler, *The Christian Ministry in Africa* (Uppsala: Swedish Institute of Missionary Research, 1960), 53.

ited Angola in 1904, was amazed to find that missionaries in Angola acted "almost like followers of Christ":

> There are two other notable orders at work in Angola — the American mission (Congregationalist) under the "American Board" and the English Mission (Plymouth Brethren) under divine direction only.... All are on terms of singular friendship, helping one another in every possible way, almost like followers of Christ. Of all the sects that I have ever known, these are the only two that I have heard pray for each other, and that without condemnation — I mean they pray in a different spirit from the Anglican prayer for Jews, Turks, infidels and heretics.[11]

Such a spirit of cooperation led Brethren missionaries to take a leadership role in the Missionary Conference, which became the Aliança Evangélica de Angola in 1934. Although neither the Brethren missions nor assemblies became official members of the AEA, they gave both moral and financial support. The confidence established between Brethren missionaries and their colleagues of other boards and societies was reflected in an article in *Echoes Quarterly Review* by two of Britain's leading Brethren: "We thank God that the Gospel in its fullness is preached by the great majority of the brethren and sisters in the missionary societies."[12]

The first factor that altered the extreme independency that was typical of the Brethren movement in North America and Europe as it bore fruit in the soil of Angola was the mutual confidence and harmony established with other Protestant groups.

The second factor curbing independency was the mission station pattern of operation in Africa. Brethren missions did not differ markedly from other Protestant missions as they became centers of an everexpanding community both on the station and in surrounding villages. C. Donald Cole, one of the most articulate Brethren missionaries in Angola, described the difficulty of transplanting independent assemblies to Africa:

> As for Angola, the [Brethren] missionaries all represent "open" assemblies. Yet for years the set-up seemed to approximate the exclusive way of doing things. There is the mother-church at the mission surrounded by the satellite churches. These are independent in theory, though in practice they were subordinate to the mother church.... Since coming, I have striven to cut the umbili-

---

11. Henry W. Nevinson, *A Modern Slavery* (London: Harper and Brothers, 1906), 140.
12. A. Pulleng and W. T. Stunt, "Angola," *Echoes Quarterly Review* 10, no. 4 (October–December 1958): 2.

cal cord, making them independent in practice as well as theory. But it's not easily done.[13]

The mission station was not only the center of a community that created ecclesiastical ties; it was the summit of a hierarchy. In the colonial situation the white man had power and authority. He lived and operated from the mission station. The missionary might enjoy using his power, or he might have had a distinct distaste for his position; however, it did not depend primarily upon his taste. In the colonial situation he was an authority. Dan Crawford, who spent twenty-two consecutive years in Central Africa as a Brethren missionary, wrote: "Many a little Protestant Pope in the lonely bush is forced by his self-imposed isolation to be prophet, priest and king rolled into one — really a very big duck he — in his own private pond."[14]

Conclusion

The spectrum of Protestant church organizations in Angola was broad, reaching from the Methodist Episcopal system, an integral part of the world Methodist Episcopal Church, to the individual assemblies of the Plymouth Brethren. However, there was a unity among the Protestant communities that was not always visible, but nevertheless real.

The general-secretary of the Aliança Evangélica de Angola expressed this reality in the opening session of the Aliança annual meeting in Huambo in 1960. He entitled the presentation, "The Church of Christ in Angola," contending that such a church existed in Angola and then describing briefly the signs of this united church. The doctrinal sign was the unanimity of beliefs that the Bible was the source of all teaching and action. Hermeneutically the unity was heard in simple, biblical, exhortative, and moralistic sermons that were preached all across Angola — the only difference being the regional language. The sacramental unity was a reality in the observance of the Lord's Supper and even in baptism, which was practiced in both infant and believers' forms, for in most cases a communicant member of a church who had been baptized as an infant was received by a church that practiced believers' baptism with a simple letter of recommendation.

Liturgically the church praised the Lord with congregational and choral singing and spontaneous prayers. The ethical standards of the church were also quite uniform as the discipline fell most heavily on

---

13. Personal letter from C. Donald Cole, Missão de Chilonda, Angola, November 19, 1964.

14. D. Crawford, _Thinking Black: Twenty-two Years without a Break in the Long Grass of Central Africa_ (London: Morgan & Scott, 1914), 324–25.

sexual irregularities, the abuse of alcoholic beverages, and the practice of magic and divination. Even in the area of ecclesiastical organization, whose variety we have described in this chapter, we can discover an underlying unity. The African social structure and the mission station pattern imposed a hierarchical form of church polity even in mission communities that believed in a congregational system.

Protestant unity owed as much to the common opposition from Portuguese colonialism as to any other factor.

Chapter 8

The Church at Worship

God is spirit, and those who worship him must worship in spirit and in truth. (John 4:24)

I have held out my hands to you [in prayer]. And he who holds out his hands dies not.[1]

The church is the community of God's people. Worship is the dialogue in which God is revealed in Jesus Christ and the people respond to God's initiative.

An Angolan catechist arguing the superiority of Catholicism to Protestantism began by saying that the Protestants had no sacraments. Protestants would have disputed his statement, but the catechist did recognize an important difference between Catholic and Protestant worship. Catholic worship centered in the sacraments and their liturgy while the main medium of Protestant dialogue with God was the Bible — its reading and interpretation.

Dom Moisés Alves de Pinho, bishop of Angola and Congo, began his first communication to parish priests and missionaries in issue no. 1 of the *Boletim da Diocese*, extolling the liturgy:

The holy liturgy, being the most excellent fount to which the priest should resort to feed himself and the souls entrusted to his zeal, with an enlightened, solid, and practical piety, capable of exercising the most holy influence in the daily thread of life, it seemed necessary, beloved cooperators, to indicate with precision and clarity those among the sacred functions which by law, by our

---

1. Aylward Shorter, *Prayer in the Religious Traditions of Africa* (New York: Oxford University Press, 1975), 51.

determination or by that of our venerable antecessors, should be considered by all as rigorously obligatory.[2]

Bishop Moisés then gave very precise directions for blessing water for the baptismal fount, for the services of Maundy Thursday and Good Friday, the Exposition of Forty Days, the Month of the Rosary, the Novena of Pentecost, the Blessing of the Most Holy Sacrament, and other liturgical acts.

The Seven Sacraments

Catholic worship through the centuries has organized the essential moments of dialogue between God and God's people into seven sacraments: outward signs of inward grace ordained by Jesus Christ. The seven moments, some unique in a lifetime, others occurring perhaps every day, correspond in a spiritual order to a natural life on earth. Baptism with water is the rebirth when Christians become "children of God" (1 John 3:1), and even "partakers of the divine nature" (1 Pet. 1:4). Confirmation is the moment in which the Christian faces the responsibilities of Christian living in an adult world and when it is plain that a grace over and above being "children of God" is required. The third sacrament,the Eucharist, is not for a particular moment in a lifetime. It is concerned with the daily sanctification of Christians and their spiritual health by an increase in knowing Christ through Communion. The sacrament of penance exists to restore Christians from their sickness of sin to their proper state of grace or friendship with God.

In the Christian life there are two moments when a Christian may be called by God to enter upon a particular vocation. In either case it is a task that is essential to the Christian body as a whole, when a special strength is required: the grace of the sacrament of holy orders, by which the continuation of the sacramental life of the church is assured; and the grace of the sacrament of matrimony, by which the propagation of the Christian people is continued in the world. Finally there is the sacrament of anointing, when the Christian faces the danger of death by sickness and needs the strength of God's friendship in this crisis. Both Catholic and Protestant communities recognized and celebrated these moments of intimate dialogue between God and God's people, observing them in some form of worship. While the Catholic church defined all seven as sacraments, the Protestant churches in Angola differed in their definition and practice.

---

2. *Boletim da Diocese de Angola e Congo* (Luanda) 1, no. 1 (January–February 1935): 2.

Baptism

No one is born a Christian. The New Testament uses several metaphors to indicate how a person becomes a Christian. The Apostle Paul described becoming a Christian as being united with Jesus Christ (Rom. 6:3–5; Col. 2:12). Baptism joins the candidates in the mystery of the death and resurrection of Jesus in which they participate by this sacrament.

A second New Testament figure of speech, closely related to the first, sees baptism as incorporation into the church, Christ's body (1 Cor. 12:13). Jesus' conversation with Nicodemus describes the initiation into the Christian life as the new birth (John 3:5). A fourth New Testament metaphor sees initiation in the Christian life as forgiveness, or washing away of sins (Acts 2:38; 22:16; 1 Cor. 6:11; Heb. 10:22; 1 Pet. 3:21). A final figure, which is less exclusively tied to baptism, is receiving the Holy Spirit (Acts 2:38; Matt. 3:16).

Since New Testament times baptism has passed through various stages. Until the fifth century baptism was administered predominantly to adults in two parts: the entrance into the water and a profession of faith. Beginning in the sixth century candidates for baptism were more frequently children. This raised the serious question as to the validity of baptism for someone who could not respond to questions of faith. St. Augustine (354–430 C.E.) gave an answer to the question:

> Mother Church loans to the infants the feet of others so that they can come, the heart of others so they can believe, the tongue of others that they may affirm their faith. The one who carries the child responds: the child is cured by the word of another, just as he was wounded by the act of another. Do you believe in Jesus Christ? That is the question; he responds: he believes.[3]

However, the change in circumstances soon led to the change in liturgy and the subject was reduced to a passive role.

Baptism by immersion was normal in the Catholic church until the fourteenth century, when it was substituted by infusion (pouring).

The initiatory sacrament in Angola at the beginning of the colonial period returned to the apostolic practice of baptizing mainly adults, but as the number of adult married Christians increased, so did the number of infant baptisms. By the end of the colonial period baptisms in the Catholic church were about equally divided between adults and infants.[4]

Among the liturgical practices that Bishop Moisés Alves de Pinho said should be considered "rigorously obligatory" was the blessing of

---

3. A. G. Martimort, *A Igreja em Oração: Introdução á Liturgia* (Singeverga: Ora & Labora; Tournai: Desclee & Cie, 1965), 602.

4. *Boletim Eclesiástico* 20, nos. 111–14 (January–December 1960): 58.

the baptismal water at the Easter vigil. The exact words of the sacramental formula were also essential: "_____, I baptize thee in the name of the Father, Son and Holy Spirit," and they were accompanied by the gesture of pouring the water or immersing.

The Protestant churches in Angola all practiced baptism and used the same words and gestures, but there were some significant differences from Catholic practice.

The care with which each liturgical act was performed was essential to Catholic worship because of its doctrine *ex opere operato* "in virtue of the action itself." According to Catholic doctrine the liturgy was the exercise of the priesthood of Jesus Christ. The sacraments possessed an objective virtue by which souls become participants in the divine life of Jesus Christ. The efficacy of the sacraments was therefore not dependent on the virtue of the persons involved but on that of Jesus Christ. The only condition put upon such a saving power was that the participants did not place a positive obstacle and that the forms recognized by the Catholic church be respected.

Three of the Protestant churches — Methodist, Church of the North of Angola, and the Council of Evangelical Churches of Central Angola — celebrated baptism and Communion, or Lord's Supper, as sacraments. All other Protestant churches also observed baptism and the Lord's Supper, but called them "ordinances" to show they considered them to have originated by orders of Jesus Christ. They avoided the term "sacrament," which those churches thought too closely associated with the Roman Catholic church.

Actually the division among the Protestant churches was not only over terminology. The same churches that used the word "sacrament" also followed the practice of infant baptism while the other churches practiced only believers' baptism. The Church of Southwest Angola explained this position:

> Baptism is administered to all who accept Jesus as Savior and Lord and only to those. It is a public testimony of faith of the believer in the Lord Jesus Christ and of his submission to Him and signifies his death to sin and his passage to a a new life. Thus infant baptism is excluded.[5]

All Christians in Angola could have agreed with the scriptural affirmation that there is "One Lord, One Faith, One Baptism" (Eph. 4:5) but there the agreement would end. Which is the one baptism? The Catholic church had established its rules, which "should be considered rigorously obligatory by all." During the colonial period the Catholic church did recognize some cases of Protestant baptism as valid; in other cases the

---

5. *Estatutos da Igreja Evangélica do Sudoeste de Angola*, Art. 24.

priest prefaced a second baptismal service with the phrase, "If [name] has not been validly baptized..."; and in still other cases Protestants were simply rebaptized. The action of the Catholic church was determined by the priests' confidence as to whether the first baptism was performed with the required words, gestures, and intentions, or not.

The churches that practiced believers' baptism also had to make decisions as to whether a person initiated into a Christian community by infant baptism should be received without a personal declaration of faith and immersion. In some cases the person was received simply by a letter of recommendation, and in other cases rebaptism was required. The Seventh-Day Adventists did not require the rebaptism of persons who came to them from other religious communities in which they were baptized by immersion and had led a "coherent Christian life according to the light they had," but their manual counselled that "rebaptism would be desirable."

Among Christians who used believers' baptism the practice of infant dedication became common. For example, the church of Southwest Angola included in its Ecclesiastical Acts the presentation of children: "Sons and daughters of believers, members in full communion, may be presented to the Lord in the presence of the community."

Confirmation

In the Catholic church the initiation into the Christian life included three sacraments: baptism, confirmation, and the Eucharist. The Protestant churches did not recognize confirmation as a sacrament, but those who practiced infant baptism did celebrate the act in which a person on reaching the age of discretion ratified and confirmed the solemn promise and vow that were made in his name at baptism. This distinction illustrates the difference between the Catholic and Protestant views of sacraments. Catholic confirmation was the sign/act by which God strengthened the candidate by bestowing the Holy Spirit. Protestant confirmation was the ceremony in which candidates confirmed promises made for them.

The Catholic sacrament of confirmation was presided over by the bishop, who used two gestures: the laying on of hands and anointing with chrism, the holy oil. The sacrament of confirmation was not essential for salvation, but it empowered the baptized Christian to meet the trials of adult life. Confirmation could not be repeated, just as our growing up cannot be repeated. At baptism the Christian becomes a friend of God and confirmation produced a "firm friend."

In a missionary territory such as Angola during the colonial period the processes of catechesis and confirmation were at times confused.

Strictly speaking, confirmation must follow baptism for it is the process of strengthening a relationship already established. Yet because of the importance of catechetical teaching many catechism classes combined both baptized and nonbaptized persons. The baptized were preparing to be confirmed and the nonbaptized were studying the same catechism to prepare for baptism.

Eucharist

The Eucharist, or Lord's Supper, was the most characteristic form of Christian worship. Yet it would be difficult for a person ignorant of Christian tradition to believe that from the simple Jewish passover meal of Jesus with his twelve disciples in the upper room could have come such a broad spectrum of worship services as Angolans have experienced every Sunday.

For example, at one extreme a Catholic bishop wearing a miter and colorful robes entered a majestic cathedral accompanied by priests, deacons, a subdeacon carrying the processional silver cross, acolytes with lighted candles, and the vase with incense while hundreds of the faithful showed respect by standing reverently. They then sat or kneeled according to the rubrics until the supreme moment of the consecration of the bread and wine; these were transubstantiated into the body and blood of Christ as the priest said, *"Hoc est enim corpus meum. Hic est enim calix sanguinis mei."*

At the other extreme in a small Protestant chapel in a remote village a score of faithful Angolans were seated quietly. The center of attention was an ordinary unfinished table with a white cloth, a plate of bread, and one or more cups of wine. Behind the table were seated two lay elders and in front were the brothers and sisters listening for the same familiar words: *"Tambuli, li, ombolo eyi etimba liange,"* "Take, eat, this is my body."

The popular name of this sacrament, the Mass (*missa* in Portuguese), came from *mitto* meaning "dismissal." In the period of the formation of Catholic liturgy this service had two transition points at which the phrase *Ite missa est* was used: the first to dismiss the catechumens after the liturgy of the word and before the Eucharist itself and the second to invite the faithful to move from the Eucharist to Communion.

The Mass was divided into two parts, the liturgy of the word and the liturgy of the Eucharist, and each of these had two divisions. In the liturgy of the word after the entrance of the priest and assistants, the priest recited, in the name of the assembly, prayers of pardon, praise, and petition — all in Latin (before the liturgical reform of Vatican II). Then God spoke to the people, as the priest read passages from the Old and New Testaments, also in Latin. The only part of the Mass that was in the language of the people was the homily.

In the beginning of his reign as prelate of Angola Bishop Moisés Alves de Pinho urged the priests to give special attention to preaching, which he described as "the most serious, the first and greatest duty of the shepherd of souls . . . and therefore it is also the preferred work of the missionary."[6]

Dom Moisés used considerable space in his bulletin during its first few years to provide sermon outlines and content especially for teaching-sermons on the catechism and creed.

Concluding the liturgy of the word the congregation responded to God's word with the creed and prayer, thus ending the first major section of the Mass.

The liturgy of the Eucharist began as the priest prepared the gifts of bread and wine, which would be consecrated during the eucharistic prayer. This began with the Preface (*Vere dignum et justum est . . .*) according to the Canon. It was composed of various parts, including prayers for the church, for the living, and for those who have passed into eternity. The priest asked God to accept the offering — his and the church's — and by the repetition of the words of institution the gifts of bread and wine were transformed into the body and blood of Christ. Since the Lord commanded, "Do this in memory of me," the Memorial Prayer followed, which called to mind his death, resurrection, and ascension. The succeeding prayers petitioned the Holy Spirit to gather the people and then to unite them with the saints in heaven.

This series of prayers united the offering of the people and of the whole creation with Christ to the Father and the congregation responded, "Amen."

During the first part of the liturgy of the Eucharist the people offered the bread and wine and gave themselves to God. In the second part, Communion, God gave himself to the people. This began with the Lord's Prayer, which had a special meaning in preparation for Communion since it referred to the "daily bread," "forgiveness," and "deliverance from evil."

The Rite of Peace followed the Lord's Prayer and then the priest took Communion in two species, bread and wine. As the faithful came forward they received Communion only in the form of the host, the consecrated altar bread.

With the Prayer of Thanksgiving and Blessing the people were sent back to their daily lives to live and witness to the life of God in them.

In Angola Mass was celebrated daily in the large churches at the

---

6. *Boletim da Diocese de Angola e Congo* (Luanda) 1, no. 1 (January–February 1935): 11–12.

Catholic mission centers for the students and the resident nonordained missionaries. On Sundays and Holy Days the liturgy of the Eucharist was celebrated for the larger assemblies who came from the surrounding villages. In central Angola the First Friday of the month, dedicated to the Sacred Heart of Jesus, was the most popular time for the celebration of the Mass on the mission stations.

As the missionary priests visited the villages in their districts at least once a year, they celebrated Mass on those occasions in the small chapels.

The Protestant Communion service in structure was not significantly different from the Catholic Mass, but in style and substance it contrasted sharply with the Catholic sacrament of the Eucharist.

The Protestant guide for worship was the Bible, and in the case of Communion this meant that the principal passages orienting the service were 1 Corinthians 11: 23–29, Matthew 26:17–29, Mark 14:12–25, and Luke 22:7–23.

Among the Protestant communities in Angola the Plymouth Brethren took this sacrament most seriously, even though they did not use the words "sacrament" or "Eucharist," but "ordinance," "Lord's Supper," or "Lord's Table." The Brethren believed that according to Scripture a group of believers as disciples of Christ could "break bread" as the Lord ordered, remembering the Lord's death.

An incident in the life of Anthony Norris Groves, one of the founders of the movement of Brethren, illustrates two principles that have influenced the style of worship that they brought to Angola. Groves was a dentist in Plymouth, England, a member of the Church of England, and a very devout Christian. He wished to go abroad as a missionary and at first thought to prepare himself for ordination in that church through the Church Missionary Society (CMS). In contact with other persons of the Brethren movement with whom he met to break bread he came to the conclusion that it was not necessary to be ordained in order to be a missionary or to celebrate the Lord's Supper. He offered himself to the CMS, but when they informed him that he could not celebrate the Lord's Supper even if there were not an ordained minister available, he did not go to the mission field as an Anglican but went as a simple "brother."

This episode in the life of one of the founders of the Brethren revealed two of their characteristic beliefs: the importance of celebrating the Lord's Supper every Sunday, and the rejection of the ordained ministry in favor of a "plural ministry" in which the spiritual gifts were ministered by lay elders.

From the complex liturgy of the Catholic church to the simple service of the Brethren the central worship experience of Angolan Christians drew its inspiration from the Last Supper of Jesus with his disciples.

The Methodist church gave instructions to its ministers for celebrating Holy Communion:

1. The Lord's Supper is a sacrament instituted by Our Lord Jesus Christ and as such is not only a sign of love among Christians, but is a sign of our communion with Christ and participation in His death and resurrection for our redemption and a perpetual Memorial of His vicarious sacrifice.

2. The Holy Supper is served to all communicants in both elements, bread and wine, symbols of the body and blood of Our Lord Jesus Christ.

3. Before the celebration of the Lord's Supper the communicants should be exhorted to examine themselves and rededicate their lives to the Lord's service and to the love of neighbor. This intention should be shown by an offering for the relief of the needy. However, it should be clarified in the exhortation that the offering is not a payment to participate in the Supper or that it is possible in any way to pay for the grace and mercy of God.

4. The Lord's Supper can be celebrated in any place, although the natural place is in the House of the Lord which is consecrated to serve as a center for the church's worship.

5. No minister should celebrate the Lord's Supper unless there are at least one or two other persons present.

6. In case the Lord's Supper is requested by a sick or dying person the family, if Christian, should be invited to participate.

7. The minister should show an attitude of reverence and adoration during the Act and should expect the same from the congregation. Reverence and an attitude of adoration are vital to the service of the Lord's Supper. At the same time they are the means of perfecting the spirituality of the communicants.

8. Any table may be used for the celebration of the Lord's Supper, being covered with a clean cloth, preferably white. If flowers, candles or a cross are used, they are simply to beautify and create an atmosphere of adoration and dignity.

9. The minister should prepare beforehand the elements of the Lord's Supper and place them on the table covering them with a clean white cloth, and after the celebration cover again the remaining elements.

10. If the consecrated elements are finished before all have communed the minister will consecrate more, repeating the prayer of consecration.

11. The elements that are left should not be kept. Immediately after the benediction, the minister may invite communicants to eat and drink reverently the remaining elements.

12. If time is short, the Rite may be abbreviated, but the prayer of consecration and the words of the Lord at the distribution of the elements must never be eliminated.

These instructions were specifically for the Methodist church, but they represent the spirit and practice common in most Protestant communities.

The Communion service in Protestant churches was either an integral part of the Sunday morning worship or a separate service. The communicant members of the Brethren assemblies gathered early every Sunday morning to "break bread." Later in the morning they were joined by catechumens and "hearers" for a preaching service. In other Protestant communities the nonmembers were dismissed after the regular morning service, and the communicants stayed or returned in the afternoon for the Lord's Supper.

The order and content of the Protestant Communion was not set rigorously as was the Catholic Mass. The contrast was noted especially in the prayers that were canonical formulas in the Catholic service.

Each Protestant community developed its own traditions for celebrating the sacrament of Communion, but they all allowed for considerable flexibility. As in other services the prayers were mainly spontaneous, *ad libitum*, with the exception of the Lord's Prayer. However, the Communion was one of the few occasions when some Protestant communities used prescribed prayers. The Rev. Archibald Patterson, an Anglican, brought to Angola the Portuguese translation of the Book of Common Prayer, which included the Communion Service with "the prayer of humble access":

> We do not presume to come to this thy Table, o merciful Lord, trusting in our own righteousness, but in thy manifold and great mercies. We are not worthy so much as to gather up the crumbs under they Table. But thou art the same Lord, whose property is always to have mercy. Grant us therefore, gracious Lord, so to partake of these elements that by faith we might appropriate the merits of the passion and death of thy dear Son Jesus Christ, and that our sinful souls and bodies may be purified by his most precious blood, and that we may evermore dwell in him, and he in us. Amen.

The Catholic church observed strict regulations concerning the bread and wine used in the Eucharist. As noted in the organization of the first Protestant congregation in São Salvador (see p. 40) they used kwanga instead of the white man's bread. "Since then bread has become a part of the native food so we use it at the Lord's Table." In central Angola many churches made the drink for Communion from such wild plants as *olohengo*, wild plum, amora mulberry, and *groselha*. In urban areas where fruits were not readily available, soda pop has been used.

The sacrament of Eucharist, or Communion, reveals even in small details the difference between the Catholic *ex opere operato* "in virtue of the action itself" and the Protestant *ex opere operantis* "in virtue of the agent's acting." In the Catholic liturgy of the Eucharist every word, gesture, and physical arrangement was mandated by canon law so that the "action" would be correct. In the Protestant service the focus was on the "agent" or more exactly on the participants. For example, the Methodist church viewed the presence of candles on the Communion table as suitable if it enhanced the beauty of the service to "create an atmosphere of adoration and dignity," for "reverence and an attitude of adoration are vital to the service of the Lord's Supper." At the same time they were means of perfecting *the spirituality of the communicants*, which was the most important element in the service.

A Catholic priest asked the bishop if it would be permitted to use tallow candles in the Mass and other sacred functions. The bishop answered that the rubrics prescribed candles made of pure wax. However, it was admitted that if it were difficult to obtain pure wax candles they could have a mixture, but that during the paschal cycle the candles must be at least 75 percent pure wax and in other periods of the year between 40 and 50 percent wax.[7]

The Seventh-Day Adventists included footwashing according to the description in John 13 into their regular quarterly observance of the Lord's Supper. During this act the men and women were separated in different rooms, or if such were not available, a curtain was hung to divide the sanctuary or hall in which the service was being held. After the footwashing the brothers and sisters were reunited for the Lord's Supper. They used unleavened bread and unfermented grape juice. The bread was distributed among the members, who held it until all were served, and then all partook together. The same was true of the cups of "wine."

The substantial differences in Catholic and Protestant understandings of the Eucharist revolved around the phrases "sacrifice" and "real presence." The church recognized that "Christ was offered once to bear

---

7. *Boletim da Diocese de Angola and Congo de Angola e Congo* (Luanda) 3, no. 15 (May–June 1937): 82.

the sins of many" (Heb. 9:28), but the churches differed in the way in which this sacrifice became effective. The Catholic church affirms:

At the Last Supper, on the night on which he was being betrayed, he willed to leave to his beloved bride the church a visible sacrifice such as the nature of man requires.... He therefore offered his body and blood to God the Father under the appearances of bread and wine, and under the symbols of the same delivered them to be taken by the apostles . . . and to them and to their successors in the priesthood he gave command to offer, with the words "Do this in remembrance of me" (Trent, Sess. 22: D 938); and again the singleness and total efficacy of the sacrifice of the Cross is repeated.[8]

The Discipline of the Africa Central Conference of the United Methodist Church states a Protestant position on the relation between the sacrifice of Christ and the Mass:

The offering of Christ, once made, is that perfect redemption, propitiation, and satisfaction for all sins of the world, both original and actual; and there is none other satisfaction for sin but that alone. Wherefore the sacrifice of masses, in which it is commonly said that the priest doth offer Christ for the quick and the dead, to have remission of pain or guilt, is a blasphemous fable and dangerous deceit. (Article XX)

The discussion over the "real presence" has centered on the technical term "transubstantiation," which means that the substance of the bread and the wine has been changed into the body and blood of Christ, but the appearance or "accidents" continues to be that of bread and wine. Transubstantiation as an "article of faith" was reaffirmed at the Council of Trent in 1551, which meant that the Catholic church considered it a human statement that was recognized by faith as corresponding to the revealed reality already expressed in Scripture by "This is my body" and lying within the tradition of the church, which preserved that revelation. The true presence of Christ in the Eucharist is according to Catholic teaching a reality and not a subjective impression dependent upon the faith of the recipient, so that unbelievers receiving the sacrament receive the body of Christ, whether they believe this or not.

The Methodist Discipline, a representative Protestant statement, charges that:

Transubstantiation, or the change of the substance of bread and wine in the Supper of the Lord, cannot be proved by Holy Writ, but is repugnant to the plain words of Scripture, overthroweth

---

8. Sebastian Bullough, *Roman Catholicism* (Baltimore: Penguin Books, 1963), 64.

the nature of a sacrament, and hath given occasion to many superstitions. The body of Christ is given, taken, and eaten in the
Supper, only after a heavenly and spiritual manner. And the means
whereby the body of Christ is received and eaten in the Supper is
faith. (Article XVIII)

Of all the Catholic sacraments the Eucharist was the one that was
most visibly reformed by Vatican II, as we shall see in chapter 11.

Penance

The Catholic sacrament of penance was very popular in Angola. Although the rules required that a practicing Catholic must observe the
sacrament at least once a year, most Angolan Catholics sought to go to
confession every time they had the opportunity to receive Communion.

The church in Angola grew so rapidly and the number of priests was
so limited that when thousands of faithful flowed to the mission stations
for Mass on the first Friday of the month the priest spent all day Thursday in the confessional. The crowds were so great that the confessions
had to be very brief and quite formal, but to fulfil the requirements of
the sacrament of penance there had to be contrition, confession, and
satisfaction on the part of the penitent and absolution pronounced by
the priest.

Protestants in Angola did not practice the sacrament of penance, but
confession of sin, repentance, and forgiveness of sins were so central
to the gospel that the Protestant community made many occasions to
experience this dimension of the Christian life.

The Litany of Confession in the hymnbook of the Council of Evangelical Churches of Central Angola, which was used regularly in public
worship by a majority of Umbundu Protestants, contained the following
passages:

LEADER: Though your sins are like scarlet, they shall be as white as
            snow; though they are red like crimson they shall become
            like wool (Isa. 1:18b). . . . If we walk in the light as he is in the
            light we have fellowship with one another, and the blood of
            Jesus his Son cleanses us from all sin (1 John 1:7).

PEOPLE: If we say we have no sin, we deceive ourselves, and the truth
            is not in us. If we confess our sins, he is faithful and just, and
            will forgive our sins and cleanse us from all unrighteousness
            (1 John 1:8–9).

LEADER: He who conceals his transgressions will not prosper, but he
            who confesses and forsakes them will obtain mercy (Prov.

28:13). Let us confess our sins for Blessed is he whose transgression is forgiven, whose sin is covered (Ps. 32:1).

PEOPLE: I acknowledged my sin to thee, and I did not hide my iniquity; I said, "I will confess my transgressions to the Lord"; then thou didst forgive the guilt of my sin (Ps. 32:5).

LEADER: I know the plans I have for you, says the Lord, plans for welfare and not for evil, to give you a future and a hope. Then you will call upon me ... and seek me and find me; when you seek me with all your heart (Jer. 29:11, 12a, 13). Let us test and examine our ways and return to the Lord (Lam. 3:40).

PEOPLE: Have mercy upon me, O God, according to thy steadfast love; according to thy abundant mercy blot out my transgressions.... Create in me a clean heart, O God, and put a new and right spirit within me (Ps. 51:1, 10).

LEADER: For our sake he made him to be sin who knew no sin, so that in him we might become the righteousness of God (1 Cor. 5:21). So you also must consider yourselves dead to sin and alive to God in Christ Jesus (Rom. 6:11).

PEOPLE: In him we have redemption through his blood, the forgiveness of our trespasses, according to the riches of his grace ... (Eph. 1:7).

LEADER AND PEOPLE:
Thanks be to God for his inexpressible gift! (2 Cor. 9:15).

The Protestant manner of dealing with sin was a return to the practice of Christians in the first centuries when they confessed before the congregation of believers and were publicly reprimanded or barred from Communion for a stipulated period or until true repentance was shown. The elders in each Protestant congregation had as their first responsibilities the leading of worship and teaching catechumens, but as demanding in time and energy was the maintaining of discipline in the community. This involved not only listening to voluntary confessions, but more frequently hearing charges by one member against another and judging the case to assess blame and decide what disciplinary action should be taken.

In the church during the first centuries three sins were considered most serious: idolatry, adultery, and murder. In the Protestant communities in Angola during the colonial period the first two were the most common objects of discipline. Idolatry in the Angolan context referred to magic and witchcraft.

In 1947 the church in Southwest Angola formulated rules for discipline in their community in which sins were divided into two classes.

The most serious, such as adultery, polygamy, magic, and divination, required excommunication for at least a year. When transgressors had confessed before the elders and shown true repentance, they would be allowed to confess before the church and be received into fellowship again. The second class of sins included drunkenness, drumming, stealing, lying, missing worship, failing to give offerings, domestic disturbances, slander, fear of magic, working on Sunday, indecency, and smoking.

According to Philafrican rules all punishments were to be verbal and not corporal nor by the application of fines; the last two sanctions could be applied only by political authorities. They were however applied within the Catholic community.

The scale of punishments administered by the Kalukembe church followed these steps:

1. to reprimand before the council of elders,

2. to reprimand before the congregation — but not during a worship service,

3. to excommunicate and remove from any responsibilities or offices in the church for a limited time, and

4. to expel from the church indefinitely.

The excommunicated person (*u wa kapiwa ponele*) was still considered a Christian and could continue to contribute financially to the church. Those expelled from the church were no longer called Christians and their contribution was not accepted. However someone expelled from the church might be urged to reenter the catechism class.

The purpose of the rules was twofold: that the sinner might confess and thus return to the fellowship of believers, and that the evil committed not spread.

The most detailed record of discipline in the Protestant community is contained in the minutes of the monthly meetings of the São Salvador church from 1887 to 1960. Practically every meeting included a discussion of some item of church discipline. Members were accused of violating one or another commandment and if the person was found guilty an appropriate punishment was prescribed. The most common violations were for practicing magic or witchcraft, adultery, drunkenness, stealing, and negligence of Christian responsibilities such as attendance at worship or not contributing to the support of the church.

According to the Methodist Discipline the class leader, a layman, had the responsibility for visiting each member of his class regularly "to see how he is prospering in his soul, ... to counsel, reprove, comfort and exhort as the occasion requires." The Discipline included detailed instruction for the conduct of church members under the General Rules (nos. 95–98) and also under Chapter II, Special Counsels: Christian Marriage, Recreations, Temperance and Abstinence, Christian Stewardship, Possessions, Personality, and Prayer.

The chief difference between Catholic penance and Protestant Discipline was that penance was private and depended on the priest; Protestant Discipline was public and mainly directed by lay leaders, a clear example of the belief in the priesthood of all believers.

Ordination

Baptism, confirmation, penance, and the Eucharist all depended on the action of the priest in the Catholic church. Therefore the sixth sacrament, holy orders, could be considered first in importance. By it certain men were empowered to perform the sacraments, the efficacious signs of Christ's life in the church on earth, and to wield the jurisdiction of Christ within that society.

The ordination service was one of the greatest celebrations in the Catholic church during the colonial era. Its importance depended on a series of facts. First, the Catholic church gave priority to the preparation of the clergy so when one young man out of hundreds had finished the long and laborious journey through primary school and minor and major seminaries, it was seen as the fulfillment of the main purpose of the missionary endeavor. Second, the bishop had to preside, which gave luster to the occasion. As the number of bishops increased they were all invited to participate, and a large number of priests also were invited. It was common to combine an ordination with a retreat of clergy in the same place so the number of clerical participants would be greater. Third, a young man in the course of his academic and ecclesiastical preparations became well-known in the Catholic community, at least in his diocese, so not only family, but many friends attended.

Holy orders in the Catholic church included two levels: the minor orders and the major. The four minor orders were porter, who looked after the building; lector, who read to the people; exorcist, whose task was to keep good order in the congregation; and finally the acolyte, who was to serve at the altar.

The ceremonies conferring these holy orders were dramatic, including actions and gestures related to their functions in the liturgy. The first step in entering holy orders was to submit to the ceremony of tonsure, in which a ring was shaved from the crown of the head, signifying the total severance from the attractions of this world and dedication to God. This was followed by the placing of a surplice on the candidate, signifying the creation of a new man.

The three major orders were subdeacon, deacon, and presbyter. The subdeaconate was preparation for the entrance into the priesthood. In taking this step the candidate promised to be celibate and had a year to meditate on this promise before he became a deacon and finally entered the priesthood. According to Catholic doctrine there is no other Christian priesthood but the one priesthood of Christ, which the priest shares in a special way. This is what makes him a man apart, something different from what he was before. The sacrament of order made him something that cannot be unmade.

Since this was such a permanent and sacred step the church performed the ordination of deacons only with great caution. In the service the bishop enquired of the rector of the seminary if the candidate was worthy of receiving the order of deacon. The prelate then explained the seriousness of the step he was taking in which he would have to be chaste and celibate all his life and invited the assembly to be witness to the promises made by the candidate. The candidate then took one step forward, and the bishop repeated his admonishment, and the man took a second step. The bishop repeated his words with a more serious tone and the candidate took a third step. The bishop then placed his hands on the head of the candidate; the other priests did not participate in the imposition of hands because the deacon was not being ordained into the priesthood, but to serve the bishop.

Usually after a year as deacon the candidate was ready to be ordained to the priesthood as presbyter. In this ceremony also the bishop asked the superior of the seminary if the candidate was worthy and requested the intervention of the congregation as witnesses. Again the bishop repeated his admonitions three times as the candidate took three steps forward. The essential rite in the ordination of the priest was the silent imposition of the hands by the bishop. Further rites were the "handing of the instruments," a chalice and paten with the phrase "Receive the power to offer the sacrifice..."; the anointing of the hands; and then the formal commission of the bishop, "Receive the Holy Spirit" with the power to forgive sins.

Holy orders reached its climax with the consecration of the bishop, who possessed the fulness of the priesthood according to Catholic teaching. He was consecrated on a Sunday in the presence of the people, priests, and neighboring bishops. The bishops imposed their hands on the candidate while "All keep silence, praying in their hearts that the Holy Spirit might descend." Then the consecrating bishop gave the prayer of blessing while he placed his hand on the one being consecrated. In this prayer he asked God to pour his Spirit, given through Jesus Christ to his Apostles, and then enumerated the functions of the bishop: to feed the holy flock, exercise the supreme priesthood serving God night and day, offering the gifts of the holy church, forgiving sins, distributing offices, and exercising the power to "bind" and "loosen" that was given to the Apostles (Matt. 16:19). After the prayer of consecration the new bishop, received the kiss of peace and greetings. Then the deacons presented the oblation to the bishop, who imposed his hands with the whole *presbyterium* and repeated the eucharistic prayer.

The first bishop in modern times to be ordained in Angola was Dom Daniel Junqueira, who was named to be the first bishop of Nova Lisboa/Huambo. He was consecrated in the cathedral of Luanda on June 1, 1941, with Dom Moisés Alves de Pinho, metropolitan archbishop, presiding. Two French Spiritans participated as co-consecrators: Paul Biechy and Henrique Friteau, apostolic vicars respectively of Brazzaville and Loango (Ponte Negra).

All Protestant churches in Angola except the Plymouth Brethren ordained ministers. Ordination ceremonies were joyous and meaningful occasions for those communities, but the meaning was not the same as in the Catholic church. The Protestants taught the priesthood of all believers; therefore the community had the authority and responsibility of carrying on the dialogue with God that is worship. However, following the biblical example, the Protestant communities selected and ordained some members to exercise certain functions in the name of the community.

One of the special features of many Protestant ordinations was the candidates' statements of faith and Christian experience and the questioning by church members. The statement and questioning of a candidate could occupy most of Saturday and the ordination was celebrated on Sunday morning. The newly ordained minister then presided at Communion on Sunday afternoon.

The Protestant churches also had ceremonies for the dedication of other workers such as catechists, deacons, deaconesses, and evangelists.

Plymouth Brethren, without using the terminology or forms of ordination, still recognized certain men as leaders chosen by God: elders or presbyters, who gave spiritual leadership (1 Tim. 3:1–7; Eph. 4:11; Acts 20:17); deacons who worked with the material goods of the assembly (1 Tim. 3:8–13; Eph. 4:11; Acts 6:1–8); teachers who instructed and exhorted the believers (Eph. 4:11; Acts 13:1); preachers and evangelists, who preached the gospel (Eph. 4:11; Acts 21:8; 2 Tim. 4:5).

Matrimony

Matrimony, the sixth of the seven Catholic sacraments, could be discussed as appropriately in a chapter on church and society as in one on the church at worship. The structure of the family was so central to Angolan society that matrimony was much more than a sacramental or liturgical matter. In fact the very sacrament had always been distinguished from the other six by certain features.

According to Christian belief matrimony was not initiated by Jesus or by the church, but at the creation God said in the garden of Eden:

> It is not good that man should be alone, I will make him a helper fit for him. . . . So the Lord caused a deep sleep to fall upon the man, and while he slept took one of his ribs . . . and the rib . . . he made into a woman and brought her to man. Then the man said, "This at last is bone of my bones and flesh of my flesh." . . . Therefore a man leaves his father and his mother and cleaves to his wife and they become one flesh. (Gen. 2:18, 21–24)

This original matrimony, termed "natural" in Catholic writing, was recognized as a universal fact of human life and fully valid independent of the sacrament. Matrimony, as a sacrament, consisted in the very act in which the bride and groom promised to be husband and wife. The other sacraments were created by the church and depended for their validity on the action of the church and the authority of the priest. Even when marriage was performed in the church it was not the priest who was the minister, but rather the man and the woman who gave their consent to unite in marriage. However this principle was compromised in the colonial period by the practice of the priest saying *Ego conjungo vos in matrimonium:* "I join you in matrimony."

In colonial Angola the church not only encountered "natural" marriage, but also "tribal." This was the principal point of social contact between Bantu and biblical cultures and raised serious questions about the proper application of the sacrament of matrimony. The church considered the consent of the partners to be the essence of marriage, but in tribal marriage the will and consent of the families took precedence over the consent of the partners. The exchange of the dowry or bride-price given by the groom to the bride's family also clouded the process of consent because the fulfillment of the dowry agreement was the decisive act in the alliance rather than the consent of the partners.

During the early part of the colonial period (1870–1940) mixed marriages between baptized and nonbaptized mates were common and allowed many appeals to what was called the "Pauline privilege." This referred to an ecclesiastical provision based on chapter 7 of Paul's first letter to the Corinthians, which said in part: "If the unbelieving partner desires to separate, let it be so; in such a case the brother or sister is not bound. For God has called us to peace" (vs. 15).

The following example shows some of the complexities in applying the sacrament of marriage in Angola. Ticio married Ticia "naturally" or "traditionally," and later after catechetical instruction Ticio was baptized. Ticia, who was sickly, separated from her husband and when questioned responded that she did not intend to be baptized nor to return to her husband. Ticio was about to marry a Christian woman when Ticia fell gravely ill and was baptized *in articulo mortis* by a catechist. She recovered, but continued to refuse to join her husband. The priest reported that he feared that Ticio, who had shown himself an excellent Christian, was anxious for a solution to his problem.

The answer from the bishop was as complex as the situation. The case was considered worthy of a detailed answer because of Ticio's situation by which he was impeded, without any fault of his own, from having a Christian marriage. The following assumptions were drawn from the consultation:

1. that Ticio and Ticia's traditional marriage was valid, i.e., according to common use in their region there was no doubt that both parties had given their free consent;

2. that the baptism administered by the catechist *in articulo mortis* was valid; and

3. that the marriage was not consummated after the baptism of Ticia.

Based on these assumptions it was concluded that the traditional marriage of Ticio and Ticia became a sacrament from the moment that Ticia received baptism, independently of any renewal of consent to marriage.

It was also clear from that moment that the possibility of invoking the "Pauline privilege" ceased, since the essential condition had disappeared — that one spouse not be baptized. But the Supreme Pontiff can dissolve the marriage bond *ratum et non consummatum* if there is "just cause" (Canon Law 1119).

This was a truly sacramental marriage, but one that was not consummated after it became sacramental. The bishop, considering that there was a "just cause" believed that the Holy See would not refuse to give a favorable response to the request for dissolution. Therefore the consultant should seek instructions from the diocesan curia to prepare the process, which would show:

1. that one of the spouses remained unfaithful during the whole period of the marriage,

2. the nonconsummation of the marriage after the baptism of the unfaithful partner,

3. the impossibility of reestablishing married life, and

4. that the eventual concession of dissolution would not result in scandal as would happen if the concession were confused with divorce, which is always opposed by the church.[9]

Particularly to be noted is the assertion by the bishop that the moment the nonbaptized wife received baptism, even *in articulo mortis*, the marriage became a sacrament. There was no ceremony, no priest or blessing by the church, but the "natural" marriage became automatically sacramental.

The church opposed polygamy and divorce, which were permitted in traditional marriage, yet found it difficult to apply the sacrament of matrimony without condoning some kind of separation, even though it might not be called divorce.

Since the Council of Trent (1545–63) the Catholic church has condemned polygamy: "If anyone shall say that it is lawful for a Christian to have more wives than one, and that this is not forbidden by Divine law, let him be anathema." Father Lecomte, the pioneer Spiritan missionary, translated the church's rule into the language of the people in his *Cartilha da Doutrina Cristã: nda ngo kovasendiyu, olohwela viatete ovyo lika vyochili.* "Even among natives the first marriage is the true one."[10]

In the sixteenth century the Catholic church issued three Apostolic Constitutions dealing with polygamy: *Altitudo, Romani Pontificis,* and *Populis.* Together they were known as the Petrine Privilege. According to these rules, which were adopted at the request of missionaries, a polygamous man could repudiate his wives, keeping only the one who would be baptized on the same day as her husband, whether she was the first one or not.

The application of the sacrament of matrimony by the Catholic church became much simpler as the community of Christian families grew. The increase of canonical marriages reflected both the change in Angolan social structure and the more frequent use of the liturgy of matrimony.

Year	Canonical marriages
1929	2,195
1934	4,252
1937	4,491
1940	5,043[11]

When "natural" marriages became "canonical" by the baptism of the two partners, an annotation was made in the baptismal registers of the

9. *Boletim da Diocese de Angola e Congo* (Luanda) 2, no. 7 (January–February 1936): 291–93.

10. Francisco Valente, *A problemática do matrimónio triba* (Lisbon: Instituto de Investigação Científica Tropical, 1985), 150.

11. Manuel Nunes Gabriel, *Angola: Cinco Séculos de Cristianismo,* 378.

missions. When two Catholics indicated their intention to marry, a legal process was prescribed since the canonical marriage was also recognized by the state as a valid civil marriage. In such cases the priest was responsible for fulfilling both ecclesiastical and governmental requirements. It was common in the more populous areas of central Angola, where the Catholic community was largest, that several couples were married in the same service, frequently on the Saturday following the First Friday when the people came to the mission for Communion. The sacrament of matrimony could be celebrated with the full Mass or only with Communion.

Protestant churches celebrated the rite of marriage, but it was not considered a sacrament nor were Protestant marriages recognized civilly.

The Methodist church gave the following guidance regarding Christian marriage:

1. It is our opinion that a true marriage is both a human and a divine institution. It is the function of the state to determine the reasons for which a legal divorce may be granted. It is the function of the church to determine the rules that the ministers must take into account in the celebration of the marriage of divorced persons who are members of the church. In cases in which a marriage is authorized by the church instead of the state it is the function of the church to determine also the reasons for which the marriage may be dissolved. The fact that the couple does not have children is not a sufficient reason to dissolve a marriage.

2. No minister may solemnize the marriage of a divorced person whose wife or husband is still living and has not married again; but this rule does not apply (1) to a person, who, when it has been proven by competent witnesses, has no blame in the causes that led to the divorce and these causes were adultery or other immoral condition, such as having suffered mental or physical cruelty or threats against one's life, which reasons would invalidate the marriage vows; nor (2) to divorced persons who wish to remarry their former mates.

3. A divorced person who seeks membership in our church, who shows a spirit of repentance, and who responds satisfactorily to questions directed to candidates may be received as a member.[12]

The Brethren Catechism in Portuguese and Quioco produced in the Boma mission, Luso, in 1957, gives a most succinct view of marriage:

---

12. *Doutrinas e Disciplina da Igreja Metodista*, 1956, 60–61.

1. Who confirmed the law of matrimony?

   Our Lord Jesus Christ confirmed it according to the acts and laws of God in the beginning. Genesis 2:18; Matthew 19:4–6.

2. What is marriage?

   Marriage is when a man and a woman, leaving their parents, promise before God to live together in love until death. Ephesians 5:31; Genesis 2:24; 1 Corinthians 7:39.

3. If a couple makes their vows before God can they later separate?

   Never. Because they are considered by God to be one flesh, and the promise is for all of life. Matthew 19:5–6; 1 Corinthians 7:39.

4. After marriage to whom does the woman belong?

   She belongs to her husband and not to her parents. Genesis 2:24; Matthew 19:5; Ephesians 5:31.

5. Does the Word of God permit a believer to marry a divorced person?

   It is not permitted because such a person belongs to someone else and whoever does it commits adultery. Romans 7:2; 1 Corinthians 6:16; Matthew 19:9.

6. Is it permitted for a believer to marry a nonbeliever?

   It is not permitted a child of God to marry a child of Satan. 1 Corinthians 7:39; 2 Corinthians 6:14–17.

The Angola Evangelical Alliance in 1935 drew up "Provisional Recommendations concerning Christian Marriage among Angolan Natives." It proposed that the catechist or someone chosen by the church be the intermediary between the families of the man and woman and that he keep a record of the first declarations of intent to marry and the consent of both parties and both families. After at least six months the same intermediary would convoke the couple and their families to testify that their desires and consent had not changed and then a date would be set for the wedding.

The proposal assumed that the groom would give presents to the bride and her family through proper channels, but stipulated that neither should request anything from the groom.

The information would then be given to the minister, who would verify that everything was in order and the final arrangements would be made for the wedding ceremony.

This document ended with five brief recommendations:

1. That in the wedding feast the couple should not spend beyond their means;

2. That when a couple preparing to marry (or even when they are not) breaks the Seventh Commandment they should be obliged to marry, but not in a Christian wedding. If they do not accept, they should be excluded from the church.

3. If a man or woman separates from his/her spouse he/she cannot remarry while the spouse is living.

4. A couple that marries religiously after the woman is pregnant — as soon as the church knows about this sin — should place them under discipline.

5. The church should not unite in marriage a widow or widower until a year has passed after the death of the spouse.

Since these were only recommendations and the alliance had no authority to enforce such suggestions, the value of this document is only as an indication of the orientation of the missionaries of the various Protestant groups in Angola at that time.

The Protestants had no canon law to help them resolve the complicated cases of marriage and even when they sought light from the Bible the teachings were not clear. T. Ernest Wilson recalled a conference of Brethren where polygamy was being discussed. Some missionaries argued that it was unreasonable to expect a higher standard from "primitive Africans," than from Abraham, Jacob, or David, who were polygamists. Others cited the statement in 1 Timothy 3:2, "Now a bishop must be above reproach, the husband of one wife," and assumed that an ordinary church member might be a polygamist, but an elder must be the husband of one wife.

After considerable discussion a much-respected Angolan elder named Sawimbu quietly rose and said:

Brothers, I think you have all forgotten what the Lord Jesus said about this matter. He said in Matthew 19: "From the beginning, He made them male and female, and for this cause shall a man leave his father and his mother and shall cleave unto his wife: and they two shall be one flesh." Brothers, if one is thirsty and desires a drink of clear pure water, he does not go away downstream where the water has been befouled by men and by the feet of animals, but rather to the head of the stream, where it comes bubbling out of the source. I would suggest that in deciding this matter, we should not go to Abraham or Jacob or David, but right back to the fountainhead.[13]

That settled the argument for the occasion; and generally the Protestant community accepted monogamy as the rule, but the application of the rule was knotty.

Anointing

The last sacrament in the Catholic church is anointing, which is based on a passage in the Epistle of St. James 5:14–15:

> Is any among you sick? Let him call for the elders of the church, and let them pray over him, anointing him with oil in the name of the Lord; and the prayer of faith will save the sick man, and the Lord will raise him up; and if he has committed sins, he will be forgiven.

The Catholic sacraments are the means of grace available to the faithful from baptism at birth to anointing at death. This passage from James's epistle concludes with the promise of forgiveness, which in the Catholic faith is received through the sacrament of penance. Therefore depending on the physical and mental state of the patient the priest may hear his confession and absolve him. Even if the sacrament of penance is not performed, the priest still may invite the patient and others present to recognize their sins and God's forgiveness.

The oil used for anointing the sick was olive oil according to James, and it was blessed by the bishop on Maundy Thursday. The oil was applied at least on the head and hands, but at times it was applied to the eyes, ears, nostrils, lips, hands, and feet representing all the senses. The anointing of the body in this way represented the various channels by which temptation to sin comes to us and the sanctification of these channels.

Traditionally Communion was also offered to the dying. This had the special name of Viaticum, from the Latin word meaning provisions for a journey. Communion for a moribund person was considered the food for the journey to Christ. It strengthened the person for the last struggle against evil and was medicine for the body and the soul.

The Protestants celebrated the sacraments of baptism and Eucharist and observed rites that corresponded to confirmation, confession, matrimony, and ordination. Except for those of the Anglican tradition they

---

13. T. Ernest Wilson, *Angola Beloved* (Neptune, N.J.: Loizeaux Brothers, 1967), 73.

did not have a rite for the unction of the moribund. Although the Protestants did not relate the passage in James specifically to the moribund, they did pray for the sick both publicly and privately.

Sacramentals

To see the church at worship only through the sacraments is fairer to the Catholic community than to the Protestant, but even to the former it is a very incomplete picture of the worship life of the church during the colonial period. Both communities were scattered in relatively small villages in rural areas and seldom saw their priests or ordained ministers, who had authority to celebrate the sacraments. Their regular worship was led by catechists or other lay leaders in small stick-and-mud chapels or schools. Such services and private spiritual exercises were known as "sacramentals" among Catholics. An active Catholic village had services daily in the morning and evening. Morning prayers were brief, using the formulas provided in the catechism that had been memorized by all. Then a song or chorus would be sung. Evening prayers were longer and included some teaching materials. The catechist would give a homily based on the catechism or some teaching material provided by the mission. On a pleasant night the congregation would go outside and the catechist would lead in the repetition of parts of the catechism that all had memorized. Special sessions were held for persons preparing for baptism, confirmation, or marriage. Memorization was the principal method used by the catechists. This was appropriate since Catholic religious education was based on "Official and Obligatory Texts of Common Formulas of Prayers and Primary Elements of Christian Doctrine." A document with that title was published in the *Boletim Eclesiástico de Angola e S. Tomé*, giving thirty-two official formulas for use in all of Portugal, e.g., the Sign of the Cross, the Apostles' Creed, the Lord's Prayer, the Ave Maria, the Act of Faith, the Confession, the Ten Commandments, the Beatitudes, the Fruits of the Spirit, etc.[14]

The Protestant churches also used the traditional catechetical method of questions and answers, but efforts were made to encourage catechumens to respond in their own words. The Council of Evangelical Churches of Central Angola departed radically from the traditional method by publishing in 1960 *A Nossa Fé*, written by the Rev. Frederico Mussili and Dr. Lois Dille. It followed the same outline as other catechisms: God, Man, the Bible, Sin, Forgiveness, the Ten Commandments, the Life of Jesus, etc., but this one-hundred-page booklet in Portuguese and Umbundu gave brief statements of Christian doctrines

---

14. *Boletim Eclesiástico de Angola* 1, no. 6 (42) (November–December 1941): 199–204.

with biblical references and at the end of each chapter included a few questions to be answered in the students' own words. Also included was a list of Scripture passages which the catechumens were encouraged to memorize.

The contrast in catechetical methods between Catholics and Protestants was accentuated in the two styles of worship. Catholic worship was characterized by strictly defined liturgy and sacraments prescribed by the hierarchy while Protestant worship was distinguished by its spontaneity and focus on the Bible as the guiding authority.

Protestants carried their Bibles and hymn books to each service. As we saw in chapter 2, an essential element in the planting of the church by Protestant missions was the translation of the Scriptures into the languages of the people. The only community to have the whole Bible in its own language during the colonial era was the Kikongo. The New Testament had been completed in 1893 and the Bible in five volumes in 1916. The one-volume edition was circulated in 1926. W. Holman Bentley, J. H. Weeks, and Nlemvo, an Angolan, were the principal translators of the Kikongo Bible.

The New Testament in Kimbundu was completed in 1922 after work by Heli Chatelain, J. D. Cordeiro de Matta, and Herbert Cookman Withey. The Umbundu New Testament was completed by Wesley M. Stover in 1897, and after much revision and the publication of individual books the diglot version with Umbundu and Portuguese was published in 1927.

In the same year several Brethren workers — F. Olford, H. W. Griffiths, M. B. MacJannet, Manuel, Kapoko, and Kapitau — finished the Kioko New Testament, which was published in diglot with Portuguese. The Psalter was similarly issued in a diglot edition in 1927. The Brethren also worked on the translation of the Scriptures into Lunda, and in 1929 the New Testament was published in that language.

South Africa General Mission workers at Muié translated portions of Scripture into Mbunda, and the whole New Testament translated by Emil Pearson into Luchazi was published in 1935.

The government requirement that nothing be published in an Angolan language without a parallel version in Portuguese made the publication of the Bible very expensive. The British and Foreign Bible Society in London printed the Bible for the churches in Angola at a reduced cost so it was possible to sell them at a very modest price. In the early 1930s the Bible Society reported that it had distributed the following Scriptures: 45,000 in Kikongo, 8,000 in Kioko, and 70,000 in Umbundu. Such a wide circulation would not have been possible without the subsidy of the Bible Society. This is a considerable number when it is recognized that at the same time the total of Protestant members and catechumens in Angola was only 46,871.

The Portuguese translation of the Bible used in all the diglot editions was that of João Ferreira de Almeida (1628–91), a Portuguese who was raised in the home of an uncle who was a Catholic priest in Mangualde, Portugal. At age thirteen João went to Holland and from there to Java. Batavia, the capital of the island of Java, had a Dutch Reformed mission where the young man found a leaflet in Spanish on the difference between Reformed and Roman Christianity. The lad was converted to Protestantism, and having a passion for languages he translated a summary of the Gospels and Epistles from Spanish into Portuguese. He was later ordained as a minister of the Dutch Reformed Church, but worked mainly with Portuguese-speaking congregations in Indonesia and Ceylon. After learning Greek and Hebrew João Ferreira de Almeida finished a translation of the New Testament from the original languages into Portuguese in 1677. At his death at age sixty-three he was still working on the translation of the Old Testament. Two contrasting honors have been paid to João Ferreira de Almeida: he was burned in effigy by the Inquisition in Goa, and his translation of the Bible in Portuguese is being used by thousands of Christians in Angola and throughout the Portuguese speaking world three hundred years after his death.[15]

The standard work on Catholic liturgy in Portuguese, edited by A. G. Martimort, notes that at the beginning of the church in the first and second centuries there was no other liturgical book except the Bible (p. 40). The Protestant churches in Angola during the colonial period likewise used the New Testament and Psalms as the main resource for their worship services. Passages of Scripture were used as invocations at the beginning of the service. Psalms were read responsively as prayer-litanies. Texts were chosen by the preacher as the foundation of his sermon.

Worship based on the Bible was possible because the ability to read was considered essential for church membership. Exception was made for persons who because of age or poor eyesight were unable to learn, but generally part of the examination of catechumens included the requirement of reading a portion of Scripture.

The placing of the Bible in the hands of the people and allowing ill-trained persons to interpret the Scripture was criticized by the Catholic church. However the Protestants lived with the Bible. In the village schools or on mission stations the curriculum always included Bible study. As early as 1900 W. M. Stover of the Bailundo mission had prepared lessons on Old Testament stories and words of Jesus in Umbundu. In 1929 an edition of thirty thousand copies of Old Testament stories by E. L. Ennis was printed at the Dôndi mission. Sunday schools also con-

---

15. John T. Tucker, *Heróis da Cruz* (Lisbon: Junta Presbiteriana de Cooperação em Portugal, 1957), 9–20.

centrated on Bible teaching and lessons covering the whole Bible were published in 1917–18. All this reading and study did not provide a sophisticated knowledge of the Scriptures, but for Angola Protestants the Bible was not a collection of historical documents; it was their story.

The term "Celebration of the Word" came into the Christian vocabulary after Vatican II, but it described Protestant worship from the planting of the church in Angola all through the colonial era. The Word was in the hands of the people and they carried it faithfully to every service. At a brief morning or evening service there might not be a sermon, but there was always some reading from the Bible.

Congregational Singing

A second book that was the constant companion of Angolan Protestants was the hymnal. The Gospels of Matthew and Mark report that after the Last Supper Jesus and his disciples sang a hymn and went out to the Mount of Olives (Matt. 26:30; Mark 14:26). The first characteristic of Protestant worship was that it was based on the Scriptures. Also distinguishing Protestant worship was the centrality of music in the form of congregational and choral singing. In 1893 a hymn book was produced on the mission press at Camundongo. An edition of thirty thousand copies of hymnals in Umbundu and Portuguese, compiled by H. A. Neipp and W. E. Roberts, was published in Lisbon in 1923. In 1930 the mission press in Malanje printed a collection of gospel songs in Kimbundu and Portuguese.

Just as the Catholic leaders criticized the Protestants for placing the Scriptures in the hands of the common people and allowing them to interpret it freely, they also considered the free hymn singing to be less responsible and appropriate for worship than the regulated use of chants and other traditional Catholic music.

This difference of opinion regarding the proper type of church music was not peculiar to Angola or to the rivalry between Protestants and Catholics. Some of the most heated disputes in church history have been over the music used in worship. One school promoted the exclusive use of Psalms and criticized the use of nonscriptural hymns. Other disputes centered on the music. Ambrose, bishop of Milan (373–97) introduced antiphonal singing of his new metrical hymns by the congregation. The Gregorian chant, or plainsong, became popular in the sixth century and was the most acceptable worship music in the Catholic church in Angola during the colonial period. In 1903 Pope Pius X issued *Motu proprio* restoring the purity of the plainsong and enjoining its use in the whole Catholic church. Whatever the theological, poetic, or musical values of Protestant hymnody in Angola it was concluded from a study made in the 1940s in central Angola to have been one of the most influential factors in the conversion of Angolans to the Protestant Christian faith.

Hymns were a medium of Christian doctrine, an inspiration for Christian living, an effective means for the people's participation in public worship, and an expression of social solidarity especially in Africa. South of the Sahara African culture was oral, so music was used as a tool in all areas of life to facilitate memory. African music was also "liturgical" in the origin Greek meaning of the word, "public work."

Bantu languages themselves are musical since they are tonal. Each syllable has a tone, an intensity, and a duration so that words can be translated into musical notes. The richness of African music consists more in the human voice than in musical instruments. The most common instruments are various types of drums, which accentuate the rhythm of the music, although wind and stringed instruments are also used. Drumming was prohibited in most churches during the colonial period, because it was associated with pagan religious practices. However the Baptist church in the north of Angola used drums to accompany their hymn singing.

The Protestant community in Angola inherited indirectly Martin Luther's work "in freeing the hymn from its shackling Latinity, and developing a vernacular hymnody more on the lines of German folk song."[16]

But it inherited the bulk of its hymns directly from British hymnody, which was developed in the eighteenth century by Isaac Watts (1674–1748), John Wesley (1703–91), Charles Wesley (1707–88), and other poets and musicians, and increased greatly in the nineteenth century by Bishop Reginald Heber (1783–1826), Thomas Kelly (1769–1854), Joseph Scriven (1820–86), and others.

Protestant revivalism in North America also contributed greatly to hymnody in Angola. The task of translating the words of the hymns from English to the Angolan languages fell to the missionaries who knew English and were anxious to provide music for worship services. During the colonial period only a few hymns were composed by Angolan Christians. The names of two should be recorded. Nekaka wrote both words and music of several Kikongo hymns, and Maveka Mutemba of Chissamba should be mentioned for his composition of the favorite Umbundu hymn *Osoma Yenda Hu*.

Father Lecomte and other Catholic missionaries produced some hymns and choruses for use outside the liturgy, but they used principally tunes modified from plainsong and known as French church melodies.

---

16. Louise F. Benson, *The Hymnody of the Christian Church* (Richmond: John Knox Press, 1956), 75.

Personal Devotions

Catholic teaching and practice distinguish between liturgical prayer and private prayer. Private prayer is used by individuals who approach God with words and gestures dictated by their own needs and aspirations. A liturgical prayer, whether spoken by an individual or a group, is a prayer of the whole family of God in Christ; it is also called an "official" prayer and is subject to the strict rules of the church.

The *Boletim Eclesiástico* of November–December 1941 gave the official and obligatory texts of the common formulas for prayers and for the primary elements of Christian doctrine. The included the Sign of the Cross, the Apostles' Creed, the Lord's Prayer, the Gloria Patri, the Hail Mary, the Act of Faith, the Act of Hope, the Act of Contrition, etc. These were provided because some minor variations had crept into the catechisms and other devotional booklets in use in Angola. It was recognized by the bishops that it might be difficult for some who had learned incorrect formulas to change, but they would be amply rewarded because of the advantage of uniformity, "being applicable here the word of St. Ignatius, the martyr, that *there is no good superior to unity.*"

Forms for morning and evening prayers were included in the Catholic catechisms. Portuguese and the local language were used in the daily services in villages, which were conducted by catechists or could be used individually or in families.

The Rosary, the most popular formula of personal Catholic devotion, is a series of meditations on the great events of redemption. They number fifteen and are divided into three groups of five: the joyful mysteries begin with the annunciation and include the birth of Christ, the five sorrowful mysteries are concerned with Christ's passion, and the five glorious mysteries focus on the resurrection. During the consideration of each mystery the Our Father is recited, then the Hail Mary ten times: "Hail, Mary, full of grace, the Lord is with thee; blessed art thou among women, and blessed is the fruit of thy womb, Jesus [Luke 1:28, 42]. Holy Mary, mother of God, pray for us sinners now and at the hour of our death. Amen." Each series of ten Hail Marys is followed by: "Glory to the Father and to the Son and to the Holy Spirit, as it was in the beginning, is now and ever shall be. Amen."

Protestant public worship was much freer than Catholic and this was true also of private devotions. Memorized prayers, except the Lord's Prayer, were not encouraged in the Protestant community. Spontaneous prayers could be said individually or by any person in family prayers. Emphasis was given also to individual or family Bible reading. The selection of passages could be made personally, but the Scripture Union, an international association that promoted daily Bible reading, had a committee in Portugal that worked with churches in Angola to produce the yearly calendar of readings and the commentaries in both Portuguese and Umbundu.

Movements of the Apostolate

In addition to the liturgy of the church and private prayers the Catholic church had various organizations or movements to promote personal piety and to enlist the laity in the apostolate. The most common of these organisms in Angola were the Conference of St. Vincent de Paul, Catholic Action, the Legion of Mary, and the Apostolate of Prayer.

The *Boletim Eclesiástico* published in each issue the General Intentions of the Apostolate of Prayer for the following months. For example the "intention" for May 1935 was "Veneration of Most Holy Mary" and for June, "Frequent Attendance at Holy Mass." The intention was then followed by a page or two of heavy theological reflections on the theme, evidently written for the priests, who were then to interpret them in more accessible language to the faithful.

At the end of 1934 there were groups of the Apostolate of Prayer at six Catholic missions with 549 leaders and 15,470 members or "associates." At each mission the groups had an annual festival and observed the Holy Hour and Mass on the first Friday of the month.

The Legion of Mary is a relatively recent Catholic organization, founded in Dublin, Ireland, on September 7, 1921, by Frank Duff. As the name suggests the Legion is organized according to the model of the ancient Roman army and uses military terminology. Mary is the general and her image is always at the center of the table about which the legionnaires gather for their weekly meeting, called the Praesidium. In a "supernatural atmosphere of prayer, piety, and a gentle fraternal spirit" each member accepts a special responsibility for the week and reports on the duty he performed during the previous week.[17] Under the direction of Mary they carry on the war against the world and the powers of evil, exercising the apostolate in such practical ways as visitation in homes, hospitals, or prisons, teaching catechism, "always being a live mirror of the solicitude and virtue of Mary."

The Legion of Mary was introduced in Angola on October 28, 1961, by Padre Henrique Verdijk at the Seminary of St. Joseph in Malanje. After eighteen months there were already nine thousand members "in all the dioceses laboring for God and for the salvation of souls."[18]

---

17. *Manual Oficial da Legio de Maria,* 5th ed. (Dublin: Concilium Legionis Mariae, 1977), 45.

18. *Além-Mar: Revista dos Missionários Combonianos,* May 1963.

Conclusion

Organizationally the church in Angola covered a broad spectrum from the highly centralized and authoritarian Roman Catholic church to the decentralized and spontaneous Brethren and Pentecostal assemblies.

In its liturgical and devotional life the church in Angola stretched across a similarly broad continuum. The Roman Catholic church at one extreme provided strict formulas for its congregational worship and for private devotions while some Baptist churches did not even use the Lord's Prayer in their corporate worship for fear that it might become "vain repetition."

The whole church in Angola at prayer would be strengthened if it were able to take advantage of both the rich treasury of prayers, litanies, and liturgies, of which the church is heir and at the same time have the liberty given by the Holy Spirit to enter into spontaneous intercourse with the Lord of the church.

Chapter 9

Church and State

During the colonial period the church in Angola occupied two contrasting positions in relation to the Portuguese state: the Catholic church was allied by treaty and tradition with the colonial regime while the Protestant churches were tolerated, but never officially recognized by the state.

Church-State Alliance

The close alliance between the Catholic church and the Portuguese state gave the church political strength, but weakened it spiritually. By contrast, the Protestant community suffered political disadvantages, but benefited spiritually.

The Catholic-Portuguese pact dates back to 1455 when Pope Nicholas V published the bull *Romanus Pontifex* establishing the *Padroado*, or "patronage," which gave the Portuguese monarch considerable authority over the choice of ecclesiastical personnel and the formation of districts and institutions within Portuguese territory. In compensation, the state promised to assume responsibility for the support of the church and its institutions. The collaboration between church and state continued during the fifteenth century, and in order to settle conflicts between Spain and Portugal arising from Columbus's first voyages, Pope Alexander VI in 1493 set up a line of demarcation from pole to pole one hundred leagues west of the Cape Verde islands. Spain was given exclusive rights to the regions west of the line in return for converting the heathen. Portuguese expeditions were to keep to the east. King John II of Portugal was dissatisfied because Portugal's rights were not specifically affirmed and the Portuguese would not have sufficient sea room for the African

239

voyages. Meeting in Tordesillas in northwestern Spain, Spanish and Portuguese ambassadors reaffirmed the papal division, but the line was moved to 370 leagues west of the Cape Verde islands. Papal sanction of the change was finally given in 1506.

This was the period in which Portugal was attempting to plant the church in Angola, and both the Catholic church and the Portuguese state assumed that they had divine right and obligation for the evangelization and colonization of Africa as a joint venture.

The world changed in the succeeding four centuries, but many Portuguese Catholics tried to carry their medieval worldview into the twentieth century. The Protestant Reformation had divided Western Christendom so the Catholic church no longer had a monopoly. In 1622 Pope Gregory XV founded the Sacred Congregation for the Propagation of the Faith for the spreading of the Catholic faith, which decreased the role of the "Christian states" in the propagation of the faith. The political revolutions in England (1688) and in its colonies (1776), in France (1789), and in central Europe (1848) produced secular states that no longer assumed the mission of the church, although they were willing to use the church and its missions to establish political control as the British, French, Germans, and Belgians did in Africa.

Christendom had disintegrated by the time the church was planted and replanted in Angola in the last quarter of the nineteenth century, but the Western nations had replaced the religious and ecclesiastical unity with the vaguer notion of "civilization." The West African Conference (1884–85), which clarified the status of international trade on the Congo and defined conditions under which future territorial annexations in Africa might be recognized, also provided that the signators: "shall, without distinction of creed or nation, protect and favour all religious, scientific, or charitable institutions, and undertakings created and organized for the above ends, or which aim at instructing the native and bringing home to them the blessings of civilization."

Church and African States

In the early part of the colonial period in Angola the "state" in the term "church and state" referred not only to the Portuguese state, but also to the Angolan kingdoms and chiefdoms.

The most powerful of the Angolan kingdoms in the latter half of the nineteenth century was the kingdom of the Kongo. The first planting of the church in Angola was done by the Portuguese explorers at the end of the fifteenth century in the capital of the kingdom of the Kongo, Mbanza Kongo, which was renamed São Salvador. Nzinga Mbemba, who became king in 1506 and was baptized Afonso, began his frequent correspondence with King Manuel I of Portugal (1495–1521) with the salutation "Most high and powerful prince and king, my brother."[1] This brotherhood was based not only on the fact that each was a monarch, but that they both claimed to be Christian monarchs.

Although the church as a vital Christian community expired in the kingdom of the Kongo during the following three centuries, enough of the tradition remained that the king of the Kongo, writing to the governor-general of Angola, signed his letter in July 1880, "D. Pedro V, Catholic king of the Kongo."[2] Later the same year the governor-general wrote to the king of the Kongo to express his opposition to the Protestant mission, established two years earlier in São Salvador, by saying: "the teaching of the Protestant doctrine cannot be allowed by us who profess the Roman Apostolic Catholic religion which is also yours and that of the good people of the Kongo."[3] Yet the same Catholic king, Dom Pedro V, not only had welcomed the BMS missionaries, but had chided them for not starting immediately to hold Protestant services in his court (see above, p. 38). It was not uncommon for Angolan chiefs and kings to welcome both Catholic and Protestant missions to their territories.

The relations between Angolan rulers and missions were subject to variation and seeming inconsistency. For example King Ekwikwi II of Bailundo had constrained the first missionaries on the Benguela highland to stay in his territory in 1881 rather than to proceed to Bié, which was their intended destination. Two years later, however, he expelled them. This change in attitude by the king is usually attributed to the mestizo trader, Eduardo Braga, and his alleged economic motives. But the official correspondence between the Portuguese overseas office in Lisbon and the governor-general in Luanda indicates that the Portuguese government worked covertly through Braga in order to have the Bailundo Protestant mission closed.[4] The American Board missionaries Stover and Fay returned to Boston when they were expelled from Bailundo. Whether American pressure had any effect is difficult to determine, but, whatever the reason, the mission was reopened and King Ekwikwi apologized.

The most violent opposition to Catholic missions by Angolan rulers was in the south, where kings and people were most aggressive in the defense of their territory. One of the Kwanyama kings was more civilized in his defensive strategy than many nations are today. Recognizing that the Kwanyama kingdom was threatened by both Germans and Portuguese, King Iulo sent a message to the governor of Damaraland

1. Basil Davidson, *The African Slave Trade* (London: Little and Brown, 1961), 122.
2. António Brásio, *Spiritana Monumenta Histórica*, 2: 439.
3. Ibid., 445–47.
4. Ibid., 3:223–25.

saying, "It is useless to kill a lot of people: choose one of your men and I will go and meet you with one of mine and he who wins will be the ruler." It was noted that Iulo was a good shot and so was bold to make this challenge.[5] Later Kwanyama chiefs were not so civilized.

As Kwanyama raiding bands attacked the Catholic missions in the south of Angola, the Catholic missionaries requested arms to defend themselves. In 1894 Father Ernest Lecomte reported that the Portuguese government had given the Cassinga mission twenty excellent rifles and two thousand shells.[6] However, this isolated case of providing arms to one mission did not satisfy the need that the Catholic missionaries felt for military protection. A royal commissioner concurred in this view after a visit to Moçâmedes with Father Antunes in 1896. In communicating to the overseas minister regarding the establishment of a Catholic mission in the Kwanyama area he reported that "practice has shown that missions in the bush cannot be maintained without the protection of military posts nearby."[7]

The Established Church

The symbiotic relation between the Catholic church and Portuguese state was expressed in many ways during the period of the planting of the church in Angola. Father António Brásio compiled and edited more than seven hundred documents exchanged between the Portuguese state and the Catholic church from 1868 to 1903 pertaining to the relations between church and state. These letters, reports, and decrees reflected a variety of views and opinions, but they all accepted the principle that by tradition and treaty the Catholic church was the official church in all Portuguese territory.

In 1890 the overseas minister presented two proposals to the national legislature in Lisbon:

1. All Catholic missions founded in the Portuguese overseas territory are considered Portuguese missions.

2. The government will make a contract with these missions, represented by their legal agent, in which they undertake to recognize the sovereignty of Portugal, to respect the national flag, to teach the Portuguese language, to support the practices and customs of Portugal, and to do everything possible to consolidate its domination.[8]

---

5. Ibid., 4:406.
6. Ibid., 4:232–33.
7. Ibid., 4:395–97.
8. Ibid., 4:328–29.

The Portuguese recognition of the Catholic church was motivated by a conviction that the state had a religious responsibility. Commenting on the creation of the Malanje Catholic mission, the overseas minister stated that "there is imposed on the government the strict duty to care as much as possible for the evangelization of these people."[9]

During the early colonial period another motivation weighed heavily in Portugal's recognition and support of the Catholic church. The Congress of Berlin had required that a colonial nation must prove "effective occupation" of any territory that it claimed as a colony. Father José Maria Antunes (1856–1928), the most active Portuguese missionary in southern Angola from 1881 to 1904, analyzed how Portugal could best satisfy this requirement of the Congress of Berlin. He described four methods of occupation:

1. Commercial factories: possible along the coast and as far east as Bié, but that would leave half of Angola unoccupied.

2. Military occupation: this would be a decisive method but very expensive and would not contribute to the "civilizing" of the populations.

3. European colonization: this is only possible in a few healthful parts of Angola.

4. Missionary occupation: this is the best method and it is practical as proven by the fact that in thirteen years fifteen mission have already been founded.[10]

This argument was made not only by missionaries; the governor-general had written to the overseas minister that a mission led by Portuguese, combining the love of religion and of the nation, would facilitate the control and conquest of the barbarous peoples better than one or more battalions.

Civil and ecclesiastical leaders used these arguments to achieve greater material support for Catholic missions. They succeeded in persuading the government to cede large areas of land to the Catholic church, to provide free passage for missionaries to and from Angola, to exempt baggage and freight from the payment of customs duties, and to budget substantial amounts each year for the payment of mission personnel, for construction, and for programs. The Portuguese state was never able to satisfy all the requests of the Catholic church for support from national and colonial budgets, but church and state created an Associação de Obras Católicas Coloniais to raise additional funds in Portugal "for the propagation of the Catholic faith in the vast regions

9. Ibid., 4:736.
10. Ibid., 4:251–61.

of the overseas belonging to the royal patronate."[11] Internally the jurisdictional dispute between the diocese of Angola and the Congo and the prefectures of Congo and Cimbebasia/Cubango caused some friction. Also the church had not succeeded in stimulating vocations and preparing Angolan candidates for the priesthood in order to supply its own clergy.

Republicanism

The Catholic hierarchy in Portugal and the Congregation of the Holy Ghost with its motherhouse in France were well aware that liberal and republican forces were threatening the Catholic church in Europe with serious consequences for its work in Africa. In 1870 France declared itself a republic. Spain followed in 1873–74. Republicanism in Portugal grew in the latter half of the nineteenth century, and it opposed the monarch, the church, and the oligarchic groups that controlled Portugal. In 1905 the French government decreed the separation of church and state. The pope refused to accept this unilateral action, and the work of the Congregation of the Holy Ghost was restricted in France.

The rise of republicanism in Portugal encouraged a liberal and republican movement among both Europeans and *assimilados* in Angola. In 1890–92 some European commercial leaders plotted to create an Angolan republic and to end control from Lisbon, but the plot failed to gather strength. Republicanism also took root in the urban *assimilado* community, which was composed of both mestizos and Africans who had adopted the Portuguese language and culture. The *assimilados* provided most of the skilled workers in Angola in the nineteenth century and increasingly supplied the colonial civil service, army, and police. The church also depended upon *assimilados* for its clergy. African priests were in the majority until the regeneration of Portuguese colonialism after 1875.

José de Fontes Pereira (1823–91), a mestizo lawyer and writer, espoused an Angolan brand of republicanism. "He conceived of a unified Angola under an expanded Portuguese domain in which 'civilized' Angolans would eventually dominate society."[12] Like most of his fellow Angolan republicans, Fontes Pereira generally accepted Portugal as a colonizer. However, in his last writings he suggested that Angola should be colonized by Britain or another colonial power better prepared than Portugal to "civilize" Angolans. Although Fontes Pereira was a devout

11. Ibid., 4:272.
12. Douglas L. Wheeler and René Pélissier, *Angola* (New York: Praeger Publishers, 1971), 100.

Catholic who attacked anticlericalism, he saw in the Protestant missions a new means for the advancement of Angolan *assimilados* and for the more rapid assimilation into civilization of the masses of Angolans.

Heli Chatelain, who was a member of Bishop Taylor's first contingent of Methodist missionaries to Luanda in 1885 and later founded the Philafrican Mission, became American consul in Luanda and reported to the United States government on efforts by *assimilados* and Europeans to sever ties with Portugal and seek some other colonial connection.

In spite of republican victories in France and agitation in Portugal and Angola, many people in Angola were surprised to hear of the proclamation of the republic on October 5, 1910, in Lisbon. The Catholic church in Angola was very anxious to know what the end of the monarchy would mean in Portugal and what its repercussions would be in the colonies. Its worst fears seemed justified as it learned that all religious houses had been banned.

Father José Maria Antunes, the representative of the Holy Ghost Fathers in Portugal, explained to the republican government the grave problems that the closing of the seminaries would cause the Catholic missions in Angola: there would be no more Portuguese missionaries, but Portugal would be forced by international treaties to accept foreign missionaries. Father Antunes reinforced his argument by warning that the foreign Protestant missionaries would be able to take over.

The Portuguese episcopal conference formulated a pastoral letter protesting the suppression of religious vows, the abolition of Catholic holidays, the expulsion of religious orders, the law of divorce, the projected extinction of the faculty of theology, the prohibition of teaching religion in the schools, etc. The government prohibited the reading of the pastoral letter in the churches, but some clergy refused to obey the prohibition. The bishop of Porto was charged with inciting his parishes to disobedience and was deposed in 1911. By mid-1912 no Catholic prelate in Portugal was residing in his own diocese. Pope Pius X issued the bull *Jamdudum in Lusitania*, which the government refused to have published and distributed in Portugal; relations were severed with the Vatican.

The Law of Separation

The republican government was not disposed to respond favorably to the Catholic church's complaints and on April 20, 1911, published the Law of Separation, which the church considered an attack on religious liberty. This Law of Separation was applied to the colonies on November 22, 1913, indicating that the state would recognize the existing Catholic missions. It guaranteed the salaries and other benefits that had been legally provided for their personnel, but the state would not support additional religious services.[13]

The second article of the Law of Separation of Church and State in Overseas Portugal read:

> From the publication of the present decree ... the Roman Catholic Apostolic religion will no longer be the religion of the state and all churches and religious confessions are equally authorized as legitimate private associations as long as they do not offend public morals nor the principles of Portuguese political law.

Article Four was more threatening to the Catholic missions in Angola, for it declared that as of July 1, 1911, all subsidies for religious services would be eliminated from the budgets of the state, local governments, or any public establishments.

The seventh article abolished the distinction between Catholics and non-Catholics regarding the use of civil registers. This was hailed by the Protestants, who had been at a considerable disadvantage because births, baptisms, and marriages could be registered legally in Catholic missions or parishes, but not by the Protestant missions or churches. However this article never passed from decree into practice.

The Portuguese in Angola who were concentrated in Luanda protested the separation of church and state. On June 10, 1914, 118 residents of Luanda signed a petition to the governor-general of Angola:

> The population of Luanda meeting and considering that the separation of the church from the state in Angola will not contribute to the expansion of religious ideas, but will have as inevitable consequence the disappearance of the national clergy in order, according to international treaties, to give place to foreign clergy, who, as everyone knows, will limit themselves to the work of denationalizing the Angolans.
>
> Considering that the national clergy has been, here, the only agency conscious of the light of science;
>
> Considering that it has been the best collaborator in the work of the pacification of the province;
>
> Considering that the Seminary-High School of Luanda, in preparing students in higher education, has followed an orientation that was not Jesuitical and in all respects was praiseworthy, which can be attested by all civil teachers and also by all the students who have studied there;
>
> Considering that the schools can continue functioning perfectly, as till now, with only the supervision of the state;

---

13. Manuel Nunes Gabriel, *Angola: Cinco Séculos de Cristianismo*, 333–34.

Considering that the establishments run by the clergy are the most economical, due to the small salaries the personnel receive; And considering principally that we do not see how the state will replace the establishments that will be so sorely missed;

Request your Excellency to telegraph the minister of Colonies requesting the suspension of the Law of Separation and petition your Excellency to concern yourself with this subject which is of such importance of the highest interests of the Province.[14]

The petition was not approved by the governor-general, who argued that the state would care for the schools in the province as it judged most convenient for the interests, development, and promotion of education. The governor-general did, however, transmit a copy of the petition to the minister of colonies in Lisbon.

It is difficult to assess the effectiveness of these various protests by the church in Portugal and Angola, but the political climate did begin to change in Portugal, attenuating the restrictions against Catholic personnel and institutions. When Bernardino Machado became president of the ministry in 1914, he sought an understanding between church and state. To take advantage of the political shift, Catholics campaigned and elected a few representatives to parliament in 1915. Beginning in 1916 some religious orders returned to Portugal — the first being the sisters of St. Dorothy. The reconciliation between church and state proceeded as more conservative governments came to power in 1917, and in 1918 diplomatic relations were reestablished with the Vatican.

The End of the Republic

In the early 1920s political instability in Portugal produced scores of changes in government — seven in 1920 alone. Power shifted back and forth between right and left, tending more and more to the right, until on May 28, 1926, General Gomes da Costa, a hero of World War I, revolted in Braga and began a march to Lisbon. The army supported the general, and on May 30 the republican government resigned and was replaced by a fascist government, which was to hold power forty-eight years until another military coup on April 25, 1974.

In less than five months after the "28 de Maio," the new minister of colonies, João Belo, published a new missionary law, with the collaboration of the prelates of Angola and Mozambique as well as the representatives of the various Catholic missionary institutes.

The statute opened with a history of Catholic missions in the colonies in the modern period, which noted the decrease in missions in

---

14. Brásio, *Spiritana Monumenta Histórica*, 5:298–301.

Angola during the republican period from 1910 to 1926. It recorded that in 1919 of the thirty parishes in Angola only a few were functioning and of the four missions with secular personnel two were closed and the other two were also threatened with closure. Of the twenty-four Holy Ghost missions two had been closed and the rest had reduced personnel. The greatest reduction in missionary personnel came among the secular clergy. Of the forty-nine secular priests serving in Angola in 1911 only twenty-nine were still there in 1914. The parishes inland from Luanda were almost all vacant. The number of missionary sisters was also seriously reduced during the republic period from sixty-six to thirty-three.

The introduction to the missionary law of 1926 failed, however, to report that during the republican period seven new Catholic missions were founded. Among the Ganguelas the Cuchi mission was established in 1912. In the extreme south the "martyr-mission" of Mupa, which had been built in 1913, was resettled in 1923. The Malanje mission founded the Mussuco station among the Bângalas in the Cassange basin in 1913. The greatest growth in Catholic mission stations during the republican period was in the Huambo area. In 1910 a mission was established in what was to be the city of Nova Lisboa, and then it was moved to Cuando in 1911. To the south of Cuando the Sambo mission was established in 1912, and further south and west the Galangue mission in 1922.

A secondary effect of the legal action separating church and state were some attacks on Catholic missions by Portuguese residents in Angola who expressed by direct action the republican spirit of anti-clericalism and nationalism. In Bailundo some Portuguese threatened the Catholic mission and succeeded in closing it briefly. Anticlerical traders wrote insulting letters to Father Manuel Braz, director of the Cachingues mission in Bié. The most serious incident was in the Cuchi mission, where a military patrol arrested the director, Father August Muller, and took him under military escort to Lubango.[15]

Portuguese-Protestant Clashes

The republican period in Portugal coincided with the resurgence of nationalism in Europe at the end of World War I, which united liberals and conservatives in a common desire to nationalize their colonies. One result of this Portuguese nationalism was Decree 77, ordered by Norton de Matos, the high commissioner of the Republic in Angola. The decree showed its republican flavor by affirming the guarantee of liberty to all

15. Gabriel, *Angola: Cinco Séculos de Cristianismo*, 350.

forms of worship and making no mention of special provisions for the Catholic church. It was seen as a threat to the Protestant missions because of the provision (Art. 3:1) that "the use of the native languages in written form or of any other language besides the Portuguese, by means of pamphlets, papers, leaflets, or whatever kind of manuscripts, is forbidden in the religious teaching of the missions, in their schools, or in whatever relations with the Natives." This hit the Protestant missions particularly because of the great emphasis they placed on reading and writing in the vernacular.

The next paragraph of the decree softened the prohibition by allowing that the Portuguese text "may be accompanied by a parallel version in the native language. The use of the native languages in any form are only "allowed transitorily and while the knowledge of the Portuguese language is not general among the Natives" (Art. 3:3).

During the republican period church-state clashes occurred between the colonial government and Protestant missions in north and central sections of Angola. In the north the Portuguese were pressing to occupy the kingdom of the Kongo, where even twenty-five years after the treaty of 1885 they only controlled the enclave of Cabinda, a strip along the Atlantic coast, and an area around the capital, São Salvador.

The Kongo people resisted Portuguese efforts to collect taxes and to send workers to the cocoa plantations of São Tomé. This resistance broke into open warfare in the Great Revolt (1913–15) under the direction of Tulante Álvaro Buta, a chief of the region of Madimba.[16]

The BMS missionaries of São Salvador, Kibokolo, and Bembe were accused of instigating the revolt, and such accusations seemed to be confirmed by actions that Protestants took: when the Portuguese military officer ordered the population of São Salvador to gather in the fort, the Catholics obeyed and the Protestants refused; and Buta requested that the BMS missionary Rev. J. Bowskill be the mediator. In the course of the revolt Rev. Bowskill was arrested and imprisoned.

It did not escape the notice of the Portuguese that an international boycott of São Tomé cocoa had been organized by the English chocolate manufacturers Cadbury, Fry, and Rowntree.

And the cocoa of São Tomé was cultivated with Angolan workers recruited in the Portuguese Congo where there existed three English missions: in São Salvador, Kibokolo, and Mabaya (Bembe). . . . All these circumstances led to the creation of a bad atmosphere around the Protestant missions, and especially São Salvador, which is accused of influencing the revolt. In addition, at the time,

---

16. René Pélissier, *História das Campanhas de Angola: Resistência e Revoltas (1845–1941)* (Lisbon: Editorial Estampa, 1986), 286–315.

there were rumors that England and Germany were negotiating the partition of Portuguese overseas territories.[17]

Professor E. A. Ross of the University of Wisconsin visited central Angola in 1924, mostly under the guidance of Protestant missionaries, and delivered his "Report on Employment of Native Labor in Portuguese Africa" to the Temporary Slavery Commission of the League of Nations in 1925. The missionaries had received Ross as an academic doing research and were surprised when he presented the report to the League of Nations.

John T. Tucker, who was the most prominent Protestant missionary in governmental relations during the colonial period, felt the impact of the Ross Report even though he was not in Angola during Ross's visit. Dr. Tucker wrote:

> An article in the *Manchester Guardian* brought the news of the Report to Angola, and the storm broke with terrific vehemence. Newspapers shouted, not to say, bawled. Individuals were definitely insulting. Night after night men came out from Bela Vista and fired off guns between our house and Figueiredo's.... Figueiredo [a Portuguese professor at Currie Institute] had to leave the Colony or risk a nervous breakdown on the part of his wife.[18]

Several Protestant missionaries suffered abuse because of the Ross Report, simply described specific cases of forced labor in central Angola, but it was the Angolans related to those missions who suffered most. T. Ernest Wilson, a Brethren missionary, described an incident in the Chitutu mission, which gives an example of the repercussions of the Ross Report on church-state relations:

> One evening a large party of Ovimbundu, in charge of native soldiers, passed by our house and made their camp on the other side of the hill. I was surprised to see that each man carried a New Testament and hymnbook in Umbundu. In the evening they sang and prayed around the campfires. They had come from Bailundu... and were on their way to the newly discovered diamond fields in the Lunda district in northeast Angola. Most of them were intelligent men, of a superior type who could read and write, and nearly all were professing Christians. They told me that a Dr. Ross, a professor of sociology from America, had visited their mission at Bailundu, and later had made a report to the League of Nations in Geneva about unsatisfactory labor conditions in Angola

---

17. Major Hélio Esteves Felgas, *História do Congo Português* (Carmona, 1958), 166.

18. John T. Tucker, *A Tucker Treasury: Reminiscences and Stories of Angola, 1883–1958*, selected and prepared by Catherine Tucker Ward (Winfield, B.C.: Wood Lake Books, 1984), 180.

and how he had seen women and children being forced to work on the roads without pay or food. In reprisal an official had recruited these men by force and they were being deported to the diamond fields. The object was to smash or seriously deplete the work at Bailundu by scattering them and sending them over 800 miles away from home. That night I read with them the passages in the Acts which describe the persecution which arose after the death of Stephen, and how the scattering of the disciples resulted in the gospel spreading to other places. We had a happy time of fellowship around the fires and the next day they moved on.[19]

Hopes were raised among Protestants by the Law of Separation. The day after Angola established its law in 1914 allowing non-Roman Catholic bodies to build churches, the Hartzell Methodist Church was begun in Luanda. Six years later Angola Methodism had thirteen hundred members.

In 1922 a representative group of Protestant missionaries gathered in Dôndi to discuss an appropriate response to the provisions of Decree 77, particularly the provisions restricting the use of the vernaculars. They formed a loose association called the Missionary Conference of Angola with the Rev. A. W. Bailey of the SAGM as president and the Rev. J. T. Tucker of the Canadian Congregational mission as secretary. J. T. Tucker and F. T. Lane of the Plymouth Brethren went to Luanda to discuss the decree with the high commissioner, Norton de Matos. He refused to amend the order and responded, "No, that decree is your Magna Carta; it gives you formal recognition, and you have all sorts of privileges under it."[20]

Norton de Matos received a copy of the by-laws of the newly formed Missionary Conference, and he expressed his wish that the Protestant work "prosper but that we must integrate it into the Portuguese framework for the development of Angola."[21]

In 1934 the Missionary Conference meeting with the presence of the Rev. Eduardo Moreira, a respected Protestant leader from Portugal, decided that the missions needed a more efficient representation before the Portuguese, which would require a secretary with permanent residence in Luanda. The name was also changed to Aliança Evangélica de Angola (AEA, Angola Protestant Alliance) to follow the example of the Aliança Evangélica Portuguesa, which had its headquarters in Lisbon. The Rev. Eduardo Moreira was invited to become the first secretary of the Aliança, but he declined.

---

19. T. Ernest Wilson, *Angola Beloved* (Neptune, N.J.: Loizeaux Brothers, 1967), 128–29.
20. Tucker, *Treasury,* 178.
21. Ibid.

The Rev. John T. Tucker, who had been part-time secretary of the organization since its founding in 1922, became its first full-time, resident secretary in 1949; he was called to Lisbon in 1950 to be general secretary of the Aliança Evangélica Portuguesa and to teach at the Presbyterian Seminary. The Rev. James Russell, a BMS missionary replaced Dr. Tucker as general secretary of the AEA in Luanda.

As the Protestant churches became more distinct from their mission organizations the Aliança altered its constitution to indicate that its first purpose was to represent "the churches" and then the missions. However when the colonial period came to an end in 1961, the Aliança was still primarily a mission organization, even though it attempted to represent the interests and concerns of the churches. This swing from mission to church was barely perceived within the Protestant community. The Aliança with its missionary officers was seen as a mission organization, and it was never recognized by the Portuguese government as a legal body.

Concordat and Missionary Accord

Portugal celebrated the 800th anniversary of its independence in 1940 in the midst of World War II (in which it maintained its neutrality). One of the first acts of these celebrations was the signing on May 7 in Rome of a concordat and the Missionary Accord. These formalized the church-state relationship that had already been traced by the Missionary Act of 1926. By the concordat the Portuguese state recognized the Catholic church as an institution to further its national and colonial aims in the overseas territories, and it was promised a favored position in relation to all other churches and guaranteed financial support.

As important as the specific provisions of the treaties were the interpretations by the leaders of the church and state who would administer them. On May 10 Cardinal Cerejeira, the patriarch of Lisbon, gave an address on national radio in which he affirmed that the concordat reintegrated Portugal into the springs of its spiritual life and that the Missionary Accord consecrated its missionary vocation.[22]

In both ways the nation inwardly restored and renewed itself and launched overseas the Portuguese and Christian conquest of souls. Cardinal Cerejeira denied that the concordat restored either the regal control that asphyxiates the church with a protective embrace or the Jacobinism that persecutes the church. The concordat did not create a state church, according to the cardinal, although it did recognize that it is the church of the great majority of the nation. (This was not true,

---

22. Brásio, *Spiritana Monumenta Histórica*, 5:688ff.

if by the nation was meant not only continental Portugal, but all the overseas territories.) Speaking to the Portuguese nation, the cardinal also denied that the concordat would result in a financial burden on the nation, affirming that "the church in Portugal will continue to live exclusively on the spontaneous generosity of the faithful." He went on to condemn the Law of Separation, which he considered a "law of oppression." Finally Cardinal Cerejeira identified the common mission of the church and state saying, "The New State [the Salazar regime] faced loyally and forcefully the Portuguese reality of the Catholic Church."[23] In his brief comments on the Missionary Accord he assured the national audience that this agreement was a historical document in the Christian occupation of the colonies "to spread the Faith and the Empire."[24]

A fortnight later President Salazar spoke to the National Assembly on the two documents, analyzing the relation between church and state. He recognized that kings and bishops, state and curia, had fought at times in Portugal, but never the nation and the church. He then reduced the accords to three fundamental questions: religious liberty, the missionary organization of the Portuguese overseas territories, and the guarantee of the Oriental Patronate.

Salazar contended that the only conditions placed on religious liberty were "the higher requirements of national interest and public order, the guarantee of patriotic education for the clergy, and the selection of the highest ecclesiastical authorities in collaboration with the state." The president still referred to the "conditional" religious liberty as separation of church and state.

The second problem that Salazar addressed in his National Assembly speech was that of the religious organization of the overseas territories. He saw the Missionary Accord as the completion of the goal of the Colonial Act, which was to nationalize the missionary work so that it might be definitely integrated into Portugal's colonial action. After condemning the Law of Separation, Salazar claimed that in the formulation of the concordat and Missionary Accord they had their eyes fixed on the "aggrandizement and consolidation of the Empire."[25]

The third problem — the Oriental Patronate — was solved to the satisfaction of Salazar, although he recognized that the continued use of the phrase was more an echo of past glory than of current power or influence.

Salazar concluded his speech to the National Assembly with a very revealing vision of his basic belief in the relationship between church and state. "We return with the force and vigor of a reborn state to one

---

23. Ibid., 5:694.
24. Quotation from Camões, *As Lusíadas* I.2.
25. Brásio, *Spiritana Monumenta Histórica*, 5:703.

of the greatest springs of our national life and, without abandoning our contemporary period with its material progress and the victories of civilization, we are in the upper spheres of spirituality — the same as eight centuries ago."[26]

Salazar wished Portugal to return to the unity of Christendom, which was characteristic of the Middle Ages. He refused to admit that the church had lost its political power and that the state had been secularized. What is so striking about this twentieth-century politician, who dictated the fortunes of Portugal for forty-two years, was not his illusion that he was still living in the twelfth century, but his ability to keep his nation behind the rest of Europe for almost half of the twentieth century.

Protestant Handicaps

The relationship between the Portuguese state and the Protestant church/missions had no tradition such as the Portuguese-Catholic history. The Catholic church in Portugal had not experienced a reformation as it had in Germany, Switzerland, France, and England. The very small Protestant groups in Portugal in the early colonial period were transplants from Great Britain: Lusitanian (Anglican), Plymouth Brethren, Methodist, and Presbyterian. Local government officials and Catholic clerics sporadically impeded the work of the tiny congregations, but the national government had little occasion to notice the Protestants and tolerated their existence.

At the end of the nineteenth century the first Protestant missionaries from Great Britain, the United States, Canada, and Switzerland applied in Lisbon for permission to work in Angola just when the European nations were setting rules for the occupation of African territories, so Portugal had to face a new question of church and state. How should the state deal with religious organizations that from the Catholic point of view could not be considered churches?

The first Protestant missionaries received oral assurances of freedom of religion from Portuguese officials. Bagster and Sanders (ABCFM) were received by a counselor of the king of Portugal, who bade them good speed in their undertaking.[27] Bishop William Taylor reported that "the King of Portugal . . . bade me welcome to work under the flag of Portugal. I asked no favors of his royal majesty, but nevertheless was favored by his good will in all our subsequent intercourse with his Angolan government officials from the Governor-General down."[28]

---

26. Ibid., 5:705.
27. Tucker, *Angola: Land of the Blacksmith Prince*, 170.
28. *William Taylor of California: An Autobiography* (London, 1897), 396.

International treaties also gave some security to the Protestant missions. The Berlin Act (February 26, 1885) provided that "freedom of conscience and religious toleration are expressly guaranteed to the natives, no less than to subjects and to foreigners.... The free and public exercise of all forms of divine worship and the right to build edifices for religious purposes and to organize religious mission belonging to all creeds shall not be limited or fettered in any way whatsoever." The Berlin Act was supported and in some ways elaborated and extended by the Anglo-Portuguese Treaty (June 11, 1891), the Treaty of St. Germain (September 10, 1919), various decrees of the republic, and the Colonial Act of 1930. These guarantees of religious liberty, which were unequivocal in their written form, were frequently ignored or in practice repudiated under the legal provision that "it ... behooves the government of the Province as a right of sovereignty to regulate and oversee the action of missions of religious propaganda, so as to ensure security and public order and to guarantee the maintenance of the precepts of the Portuguese constitutional law" (Decree 77).

Crises such as the Buta Revolt in the north and the Ross Report in central Angola inflamed the relations between the Protestants and the Portuguese, but more important were the legal disabilities under which the Protestant churches operated their day-to-day business.

In comparison with the Catholic sociopolitical position in Angola the Protestants suffered several handicaps: (1) no legal recognition; (2) strained relations with local government officials; and (3) no financial subsidies for health, education, and welfare programs required by law.

De facto recognition was given to the Protestant missions so that they were required to make reports to government departments concerning their activities. However, this did not imply de jure recognition, so that when the Protestant missions sought to legalize the land that they had acquired for their use they usually resorted to the expediency of registering land or property in the name of individual missionaries. For example, the land in the city of São Salvador was ceded by Portaria No. 521 of September 25, 1890, to the Rev. Thomas Lewis. This produced problems and extra expenses, for when the missionary left Angola or died the property had to be transferred to another missionary. Even though it was acknowledged that no sale or change in the use of the property was involved, a transfer tax had to be paid. So the Protestant missions, which were not recognized as legal entities, still had to pay taxes on their properties, which legally they could not own. The Catholic church was exempt from all taxes.

For Angolan Protestants the most vexing result of this situation was the nonrecognition of baptism and marriage certificates. To be registered in school a birth certificate was required. Catholic baptisms were valid birth certificates; Protestant baptismal certificates were not recognized.

Protestant students had to request birth certificates at the civil registry, which was usually at a considerable distance from home or mission. The birth had to be registered and then a certificate had to be requested. Each part of the process was expensive in time and money, requiring not only the payment of legal stamps and fees, but frequently involved a twenty-to-fifty-mile walk to the nearest civil registry and an indefinite wait until the functionary had time or disposition to attend the petitioner.

It is impossible to determine how many students and their parents found it advantageous to be Catholic rather than Protestant because of the facility in entering school in a Catholic mission.

"For the effects of canonical marriage between natives, the Catholic parishes and missions are considered delegacies of the Civil Registry."[29] Protestant couples could be married by traditional customs and/or religious ceremony, but they were not legally married unless they had a canonical or civil wedding. To be married civilly required that the couple become assimilated, which was a very difficult process. Less than 1 percent of the Angolan population became legally assimilated during the colonial period.

Another privilege of the Catholic church was the recognition of their catechists as functionaries, which meant that they did not have to pay the regular native tax nor were they subject to contract labor. However some Protestant leaders considered this an advantage, since the Protestant catechists thus shared the common lot of other church members.

In most cases personal relations between Portuguese local officials — *chefe de posto, administrador* — and Protestant missionaries were good and at times very friendly. However there was a constant pressure on Portuguese officials to favor Catholic missions. For example the governor-general of Angola issued a dispatch in 1946 reminding Portuguese officials that Catholic missions were "instruments of civilization and national influence" with the right to protection and help from the state and that the missionary effort would be reduced if the natives recognized that the officials were not collaborating actively with the Catholic missions. A note to this dispatch warned Portuguese officials against neglecting Catholic missions and giving preference to Protestant missions.[30]

All through the colonial period the relations between church and state in Angola were colored by the zeal — at times xenophobic — of Portuguese nationalism. As we have seen in chapters 2 and 3 the preponderance of foreigners among the Catholic missionaries was a source of tension within the Portuguese Catholic community. However, even for-

---

29. Brásio, *Spiritana Monumenta Histórica*, 5:852.
30. Ibid., 5:862–64.

eign Catholic missionaries used Portuguese nationalism to strengthen the Catholic cause and attack the Protestants.

The Alsatian Catholic missionary Monsignor Alfredo Keiling (1868–1937) described the politico-religious conflict in Angola in terms of nationalism:

> The battle in which the Catholic and Protestant missions are engaged is more than a battle of religious creeds, it is more than a battle of dogmas, it is more than a battle of theological principles: it is a battle of nationalities. In Angola, either Catholicism will win, which has always marched in Portuguese lands carrying the flag of the five shields [Portuguese flag], or Protestantism will triumph... and the result — go ask the spirits of Mandume [the Kwanyama king], go investigate the history of all the revolts of the blacks which have taken place in Angola and Mozambique.[31]

In the public debate over the denationalizing influence of the Protestant missions much of the anti-Protestant argument was based on the false assumption that the churches supporting the missions in Angola were state churches. Not only Catholics but many Angolan Protestants mistakenly assumed that Protestant missionary funds came at least in part from the governments of the United States, Britain, Canada, and Switzerland. England does have its established Church of England, but it has never had a mission in Angola. The Scandinavian and German Lutheran churches also receive government funds, but the few Scandinavian or German Protestant missionaries in Angola were from the Methodist church, which is a "free church."

The popular view in the Portuguese community was expressed by the Lisbon daily *O Século* of June 13, 1954, "The foreign missions... especially the American missions are swimming in money." What created this impression? Perhaps the primary factor was the creation of "central mission stations" by the various Protestant mission agencies. Since the government did not permit the multiplication of mission stations, as happened with the Catholic missions, central institutions were created to serve the churches in wider areas. Quéssua (United Methodist Church), Dôndi (United Church of Christ/United Church of Canada), Caluquembe (Philafrican Mission), Boma (Plymouth Brethren), and Bongo (Seventh-Day Adventist) were impressive concentrations of educational, health, and ecclesiastical institutions, with their respective personnel. However these were only 5 out of 58 Protestant stations in contrast to 119 Catholic missions.

Whatever the relative resources were before the concordat and Missionary Accord, afterward the Catholic missions moved ahead steadily

---

31. Monsignor Alfred Keiling, *Quarenta Anos de África* (n.p., 1934), 189.

with the increase in government subsidies from $199,273 in 1940 to $283,032 in 1945, $359,000 in 1950, $718,356 in 1955, and $1,129,027 in 1960.[32]

Conclusion

In the colonial period (1866–1960) Portugal established military and political control over its largest and potentially richest colony, Angola. The Portuguese state expressed itself ambivalently in relation to the church in Angola: it supported and used the Catholic church to strengthen its control and restricted Protestant action, which was considered a threat to Portuguese sovereignty.

By the end of this period the church, in its various forms, had learned the art of survival in a very political ambience. This experience stood the church in good stead as it entered the period of transition in which political activity and military conflict did not allow the church to confine itself to ecclesiastical concerns.

The political education that the church received during the colonial period was even more valuable after independence when it faced, not a state that professed Christianity, but atheism.

---

32. Eduardo dos Santos, *L'état portugais et le problème missionnaire* (Lisbon: Junta de Investigações do Ultramar, 1964), 112–19.

PART II

THE TRANSITION
FROM COLONY
TO INDEPENDENT STATE
1961–1974

Chapter 10

The Church
in the Midst of War

In his definitive study, *The Angolan Revolution*, John Marcum calls 1961 "The Year of Rebellion" — the year that marked the end of the colonial period in Angola.[1]

It could be argued that the colonial period ended prior to 1961. In 1955 Portugal was admitted to the United Nations, and the UN Charter obligated Portugal to lead its subject peoples to independence and thus to terminate its colonial empire. Although Portugal did not recognize the authority of the UN to intervene in what it claimed to be its internal affairs and the UN had no power to enforce its resolution, it could be contended that once Portugal's anachronistic colonial system was exposed, it would crumble.

In 1955–56 a "king palaver" between the Bakongo and the Portuguese government shook the north of Angola and led to the arrest of several prominent Protestant Bakongo. The conflict was precipitated by the death of King Pedro VII on April 17, 1955. A group of Bakongo royalists resident in the Belgian Congo, led by Eduardo Pinock, urged the choice of a stronger king and proposed a Protestant, Manuel Kiditu. The local Portuguese administrator, prodded by the Catholic clergy, vetoed Kiditu and "gave his nod instead to a promisingly weak nonentity, one António José da Gama."[2] He was elected by an assemblage of elders of the royal Kivuzi clan, which was being guided by the Portuguese authorities.

---

1. *The Angolan Revolution* (Cambridge, Mass.: MIT Press, 1969), 1:121.
2. Ibid., 1:56.

Having lost the first battle, the Protestant monarchists organized public support for the appointment of Protestant advisors: Eduardo Pinock as first counselor, Manuel Kiditu as second counselor, and Borralho Lulendo as secretary. In spite of the strenuous opposition of the local Catholic mission, the new king, Dom António III, succumbed to the popular pressure and named the three Protestant advisors.

The conflict between the Bakongo and the Portuguese government climaxed in December 1955 when Eduardo Pinock delivered a "destitution proclamation,"[3] hoping to evict Dom António III from the Kongo throne. In response the government arrested many Africans, the most prominent being Norman Ambrósio Luyanzi, the eighty-three-year-old secretary of the local Baptist church, Rosa Ginga, a seventy-two-year-old businessman, Manuel Kiditu, the unsuccessful aspirant to the throne, and two younger political leaders, Liboro Nefwane and Figueira Lello. This incident showed that Kikongo nationalism was ready to confront the Portuguese government and was considered by Clifford Parsons, an astute missionary observer, as "the final breach between the Africans and the Government."[4]

Urban Ferment

The kingdom of the Kongo provided one focus for Angolan nationalist sentiment and action. Luanda, with its mixed population of Europeans, mestizos, and Africans, was the center of political ferment more influenced by foreign ideology. In the late 1940s the Portuguese Communist Party was active in Luanda, and there was a discernible Marxist influence within the city's young intellectual movements. The Angolan Communist Party (PCA) was born in October 1955, and in early 1956 the Party of the Struggle of the Africans of Angola (PLUA) was created as a nationalist front party, "which adopted an action program similar to that of the PCA. Toward the end of 1956 the young Marxists of the PCA, the leaders of PLUA, and other patriots founded the Movimento Popular de Libertação de Angola (MPLA, the People's Movement for the Liberation of Angola).[5]

In 1957 the Portuguese political police (PIDE) was established in Angola, and it began immediately to move against anyone suspected of anticolonial sympathies. It arrested five men in Lobito who were associated with the Angolan Cultural Organization (Organização Cultural dos Angolanos). Júlio António Afonso was head teacher in the Protes-

---

3. Ibid., Appendix C, 5:339–40.
4. *Angola: A Symposium, Views of a Revolt* (London, Oxford University Press, 1962), 58.
5. Marcum, *The Angolan Revolution*, 1:26–30.

tant school in Lobito, and Isaas Canutula de Almeida was secretary of the Lobito Protestant mission. Tomás de Cunha and Lourenço João Sequeira from the Methodist church in Malanje worked as nurses for the Lobito Port Authority, and Alfredo Benga was a civil service employee. Their crime was to have contacted Africans from independent nations such as Ghana and Liberia.

The signs of the end of colonialism increased in the 1950s. In 1958 the Union of the People of Northern Angola (União das Populações do Norte de Angola, UPNA), a Kongo nationalist organization, sent Holden Roberto to participate in the All-Africa Peoples' Conference in Accra, Ghana. In the course of his preconference contacts he realized that his organization was being criticized as a "tribal anachronism," so he changed the name to the Union of the People of Angola (União da Populações de Angola, UPA), which called for the national liberation of all Angola. So at the end of 1958 an Angolan nationalist movement entered the international forum of African nationalism.

On Easter Sunday, March 29, 1959, PIDE conducted a massive arrest of suspected subversives in Luanda. In July more arrests were made and on December 21, 1959, a Luanda newspaper published three lists with the names of fifty-five persons indicted for subversive activities. The first list was composed of twelve mulattoes and three Africans — reportedly all Catholics.[6] The second list totalled seven and was made up of one mulatto, one African, and five Europeans, including a female physician who had worked at the Methodist clinic in Luanda, Dr. Maria Julieta Guimarães Gandra. The third, or African list, included only two mulattos and one European. Thirteen of the fifty-five were Luanda Protestants, and twelve resided abroad. These indictments led to a "trial of fifty" in 1960, which was a public acknowledgment of the breadth and depth of anticolonial movements. In another wave fifty-two more persons were arrested in June 1960, including Father Joaquim Pinto de Andrade and Dr. Agostinho Neto.

ACOA Visit

Frank C. Montero and William X. Scheinman, directors of the American Committee on Africa (ACOA) with headquarters in New York City, visited Angola for five days in February 1960. They drove from Leopoldville to Luanda, meeting the BMS missionary David Grenfell in São Salvador. He gave them the name of the Rev. James Russell, the general secretary of the Aliança Evangélica de Angola in Luanda. When the two American visitors arrived in the capital, they sought out Mr. Russell and asked him

---

6. Ibid., 1:33.

to help them make contacts with Angolans and interpret for them. They expressed interest in the fifty-seven persons held for periods of up to a year to be tried for subversive activities and indicated that they intended to raise funds in the United States to aid the families of the prisoners and to secure legal counsel. With some misgivings Russell arranged for the Americans to meet two Angolans in the Aliança residence and interpreted for them. Russell also served as intermediary to help Montero and Scheinman contact Father Joaquim Pinto de Andrade, chancellor of the archdiocese of Luanda, from whom they received confidential government documents. Father Joaquim was the older brother of Mário Pinto de Andrade, who was one of the most prominent Angolan nationalist leaders. He was the first president of the Conference of Nationalist Organizations of Portuguese Colonies (Conferência da Organizaçães Nacionalistas das Colónias Portughesas, CONCP) and for a time acting president of MPLA.

When the ACOA representatives returned to New York, they gave interviews to the press, and the March 8 issue of the *Christian Science Monitor* and the *New York Times* each carried the story. The latter reported:

> The United States is being advised to support African nationalism in Portuguese territories "before it is too late." The advice comes from two members of the executive board of the American Committee on Africa who have just returned from a trip to Angola. . . . They brought back with them evidence of a suppressed nationalist movement and a forecast of trouble to come when the neighboring Belgian Congo gets its independence June 30. . . .
>
> Messrs. Montero and Scheinman said that they based their warning that it might become too late for the United States to support nationalism in Angola on documented evidence of military skirmishes that have taken place already in the southern part of Angola on the border of South West Africa, on military preparations on the Congo border, and on unverified reports of Soviet radio and even arms penetration.

A fortnight later Portugal denied the statements of Montero and Scheinman, claiming that the secret "military documents" that they produced as evidence of an African nationalist uprising in Angola were imaginary operation orders for a military exercise.

Whatever the truth or falsehood of Montero and Scheinman's revelations, they resulted in the expulsion of the Rev. James Russell from Angola in March 1960 and gave PIDE another excuse to arrest Father Joaquim Pinto de Andrade on June 25, 1960.

Father Pinto de Andrade reported the words of the director of PIDE after a week of interrogation:

I have given your declaration to the Governor General [then Silva Tavares]. We have concluded that there is no reason for you to be kept in prison. You could be immediately released. However your presence in this city is dangerous. There are hotheads who wish to organize demonstrations to free you, and you would be received as a hero and a martyr. Now we do not wish to make either a hero or a martyr. It has therefore been decided that you will leave immediately by military plane for Lisbon, where you will stay at liberty for three or four months — time to calm down the wave of indignation aroused by your arrest. Then you will be able to return to Luanda.[7]

Father Joaquim Pinto de Andrade was deported on July 1, 1960, and kept in solitary confinement at the Aljube political prison in Portugal until November 1960, when he was sent to the island of Príncipe on the equator. There he was kept under house arrest until he was brought back to solitary confinement in Lisbon in March 1961. He spent the next ten years in Portugal between periods of solitary confinement in prisons and under house arrest in various parts of the country. In 1971 he was brought to trial in Lisbon with nine other Angolans accused of "subversive activity."

The Angolan nationalist movement was stimulated psychologically, politically, and logistically when Belgium granted independence to the Congo on June 30, 1960. This affected especially the area along the Congo border. Angolan peasants in the Cassange basin killed their own livestock in November and December 1960 in revolt against the Portuguese government's forcing them to grow cotton and sell it at a low price. Then they abandoned their fields and refused to pay taxes. This rebellion carried over to the new year, and Portugal responded with its first air attacks on Angolan villages.

The air strike coincided with attacks organized by MPLA on February 4, 1961, in Luanda. One to two hundred Africans armed with knives and clubs attacked two prisons and a police station with the hope of freeing political prisoners. Agostinho Neto explained the significance of the attacks: "The operation was not, in fact, a success, because the prisoners were not freed, but from that moment the people became conscious of the imperative to fight, and the Portuguese had to face an unexpected situation, a prelude to the difficulties in which they would find themselves in order to maintain their domination."[8] The MPLA took the date of February 4 as the official beginning of the war of liberation, and when

---

7. A. F. Santos Neves, *Quo Vadis, Angola?* (Angola: Editorial Colóquios, 1974), 214.
8. *Libertação Nacional: Textos e documentos do MPLA sobre a revolução angolana* (Angola: Edições Maria da Fonte, 1974), 33.

it came to power in 1975 it named the airport in Luanda and several other institutions and places after that date.

Ides of March

It was, however, on the ides of March 1961 that the world became aware of the war against Portuguese colonialism. On that date Angolan mobs attacked about thirty small towns, administrative posts, and coffee plantations in two separate areas of northwest Angola. The first was along the Congo-Angolan border near São Salvador. The second was the Dembos area within seventy-five miles of Luanda.

How may people did the rebels kill on March 15? Holden Roberto, the president of UPA, which claimed to have ordered the attacks, was quoted in the March 20, 1961, *New York Times* as deploring the "extreme violence" of the African attacks on Portuguese settlers. John Marcum, after studying the diverse estimates of the number of victims, concluded that perhaps 250 Portuguese civilians were killed during the first few days of the uprising, a figure which may have been closer to 750 by the end of three months. These unexpected and ferocious attacks shook Portuguese colonialism, but even more shattering was the Portuguese retaliation, which was estimated to have killed 20,000 Angolans.[9]

The epicenter of the earthquake that shook all Angola on March 15 was in the districts of Zaire and Uige, where the Protestant church had its densest population. It is therefore easy to understand why the church in that area suffered the first repercussions from the quake. The rebellion in this region of strong Protestant influence confirmed the long-standing suspicions of the Portuguese that the Protestant missions were subversive. The governor of the Uige district in the Portuguese Congo, Major Rebocho Vaz, in his report on the causes of the rebellion said:

> One of the fundamental causes is the missionary program of the various Protestant sects, which functioned simultaneously as a front for Communist ideas and international doctrines and which aimed basically to separate us from the indigenous population so that the countries they represent can gain new markets for their products or obtain raw materials.[10]

Another bit of evidence that the Portuguese authorities saw as confirmation that the Protestants were supporting the revolt was the fact that most of the Protestants fled from São Salvador to the Congo when the

---

9. Marcum, *The Angolan Revolution*, 1:142–43.
10. Thomas M. Okuma, *United Church Herald*, June 14, 1962, 8.

war broke out. By August 1961 only 171 Protestant refugees remained at the Protestant mission station, while 1,500 African Catholics sought refuge in the Catholic mission of São Salvador. Flight from the scene was interpreted by the government as proof of guilt.

Consequences for the Missions

São Salvador, the first Protestant mission founded in Angola, was one of the first to be closed in 1961. On the limited mission area in the center of São Salvador were a church, school, dormitories, hospital, and residences, all of which were turned over to the Portuguese military command by government decrees dated July 12 and October 9, 1961.

The BMS Quibocolo mission, fifteen miles from the Congo border, was ordered closed by the government, although the Zombos had not participated in the March revolt. The missionaries pled with the authorities to allow them to stay at the mission, but the government did not give permission so the missionaries were forced to leave. Immediately the frightened Zombo population fled across the border into the Congo, and the mission was destroyed. The Bembe mission was evacuated in March 1961 with the population of the town of Bembe. The newest BMS mission at Calambata was also closed in March 1961. No personnel of the BMS churches or missions suffered any injury from the rebels, but after the people departed the buildings were ransacked.

The four mission stations that had been founded by Matthew Z. Stober and then after his death were "inherited" by the Canadian Baptist Foreign Missionary Society (CBFMS) were affected by the "happenings" according to their location. The mission in the city of Cabinda was prospering in 1961 mainly due to the arrival of young Canadian missionaries in 1958, and it did not suffer directly from the March 1961 attacks. The Mboca mission was surrounded by rebels and was abandoned by mission personnel and local population. The Quimpondo mission in Santo António do Zaire was affected by the military activities, but because of the presence of a medical missionary, Dr. Walter Johnson, its health services continued and even increased. The Ambrizete mission was evacuated by orders of the authorities in March 1961. At the end of 1962 the Canadian Baptist Foreign Mission Society ordered the withdrawal of all their personnel, forcing the missionaries to leave Cabinda and Quimpondo.

Following the outbreak of violence in Angola Ambassador Adlai Stevenson of the United States criticized Portugal's colonial policy in the United Nations. This triggered a demonstration by a Portuguese mob in Luanda, which dumped the car of the U.S. consul into Luanda Bay. The Methodist mission about a mile up the hill from the U.S. consulate was known as the "American Mission," so the mob surged up the hill and stoned the Methodist church and its administrative building. A Luanda daily paper featured pictures of the church with its broken windows and accompanied them with an editorial that explained that this violence was simply caused by the pain of the brutal killings in the north of Angola on March 15. The newspaper story implied that the Methodist church was responsible for the revolt in the north of Angola and so the mob was justified in stoning the mission.

In his annual report of August 17, 1961, the general secretary of the Angola Evangelical Alliance disclosed that the number of Protestant missionaries in Angola had declined from 256 on January 1, 1961, to 167 on August 1 — a reduction of 34.7 percent. This decrease was due to several factors: six missions in the north were closed (Uige, Bembe, Quibocolo, Mboca, Salazar, and Ambrizete), the UCBWM– United Church of Canada mission in central Angola withdrew mothers and children, and reentry visas were refused to missionaries who were on furlough.

Six Protestant missionaries were expelled from Angola, accused of collaborating with the rebels. The first was Archibald Patterson, popularly called Mfumu Patty, founder and head of the North Angola Mission, who was ordered to leave Quicaia, the station six miles from Uige, immediately after the attacks in that district. Patterson was not even aware of what had happened in the district when a military escort came to take him to the airport to force him to fly to Luanda. As soon as he departed, the mission was pillaged by local Portuguese. This was a shock to Mr. and Mrs. Patterson, and they were still confused as to what had happened as they continued their journey from Luanda to England. They were in their late sixties at the time.

The leaders of the church that Patterson had founded were not so fortunate. Some of the pastors, including João Gonçalves, António Duarte, and Pedro Banza, were killed. Others died in the bush, including Timóteo Malanda. The largest number of leaders succeeded in escaping to the Congo where they spent many years in exile: Manuel Coxo, Pedro Dambi, Alexandre Kiduati, Manuel de Conceição, and Daniel Geto. In the villages around Uige, where some of the Protestant community remained, they still did not feel free to continue their religious activities, while the Catholic church constructed new chapels under the protection of the Portuguese authorities.

The most dramatic expulsion of Protestant missionaries occurred in the Methodist community. Four men, Marion Washington Way Junior, Wendel Lee Golden, Frederick Charles Brancel, and Ernest Edwin LeMaster, were arrested. After being held in prison in Luanda they were sent to Lisbon, where they were released. The official communiqué of the minister of foreign affairs acknowledged that the arrests of the missionaries would not be understood by some sectors of the Methodist church, but

> overriding reasons of national security made the measure impera-
> tive. In fact documentation and testimony collected by Portuguese
> authorities did not leave the least doubt of the connivance of these
> missionaries with groups of terrorists, their participation in meet-
> ings of a political character, their instigation of acts contrary to
> national sovereignty, their implication in the publication and cir-
> culation of subversive pamphlets and their help in recruiting of
> individuals to join the terrorist movement.[11]

Such documentation and testimony were never produced, nor were the four Methodist missionaries charged with any specific crimes.

In a separate action in July 1961 PIDE arrested another Methodist missionary, Raymond Noah. This was a unique case in which the
police charged a missionary with a specific crime to which the missionary confessed. Three Methodist students were fearful of being detained
by Portuguese authorities so they left Luanda for Lisbon, ostensibly to
study there. However, when they arrived in Kano they disembarked
and sought political asylum from the Nigerian authorities. They were
placed back on the same plane and arrested in Lisbon. Under interrogation they asserted that Raymond Noah had encouraged their attempted
escape. Noah admitted that he had helped the students arrange papers
and passage for their unsuccessful flight. He was then expelled from
Angola.

Dr. Rodger Shields, the BMS medical missionary at the São Salvador
mission, was arrested and held for two weeks for leaving the perimeter
that the authorities had drawn around the town to stop any contact between the residents and the nationalists. The doctor had gone to find a
mentally ill woman who had wandered away from the town. Shields
was not actually ordered out of Angola when he was released from
prison, but he soon departed since his movements were so restricted.

Retaliation against Angolans

The retaliation of the Portuguese against the Angolans was much more
unrestrained and violent than the assault on the Protestant missions and
missionaries. The Portuguese military and civilians bombed villages, set
fire to the bush to flush out Angolans in hiding, shot anyone who fled,
and sought especially the educated Angolans whom the Portuguese
assumed must have been responsible for the revolt.

---

11. *Boletim Geral do Ultramar* 37, no. 432–38 (July–December 1961): 279.

Richard Beeston of the British newspaper *Daily Telegraph* was the only foreign correspondent in Angola for some weeks; correspondents of other papers were excluded on the grounds of "biased reporting." During his time in Angola, under restriction of the censor, Mr. Beeston's dispatches had seemed slanted in favor of the Portuguese. On his return to London, however, he wrote:

A widespread persecution of educated and semi-educated Africans has been ruthlessly carried out since the uprising in March by the PIDE — Portugal's secret police. As soon as it was realised that most of the ringleaders of the revolt were from the small minority of mission-trained Africans who could read and write, all educated Africans and *assimilados* immediately became PIDE's top suspects.[12]

As the Baptist missions were closed and the Portuguese retaliation struck the north of Angola, the people fled across the border into Zaire, which was still called Congo-Leopoldville. The São Salvador mission was only thirty-one miles from the border, Quibocolo twelve miles, and Bembe eighty-five miles. So the vast majority of the Baptists in Angola were within eighty-five miles of the Congo border, still a long walk, and most of the people who fled had to spend considerable time hiding or fleeing Portuguese troops before they succeeded in reaching the frontier.

The wave of refugees began in March. It was estimated that by June 100,000 had crossed the border, and by the end of 1961 the estimate reached 160,000. The two northern districts — Zaire and Uige — had a total population of 503,216, according to the 1960 census. By 1966 it was calculated that the Lower Congo had received 400,000 Angolans.

This flood of refugees was not only facilitated by the proximity of the border and stimulated by the counterterrorism of the Portuguese, but was encouraged by the establishment of a reception center and a network of social services in the Congo. David and Margaret Grenfell, experienced BMS missionaries from Quibocolo, worked for five years at Kibentele (named after the pioneer BMS missionary W. Holman Bentley). The Grenfells registered thousands of Angolans as they arrived ragged, exhausted, and hungry after days, months, and even years in the bush of northern Angola. Most Angolans presented a card that they had received from the nationalist organization, the União das Populações de Angola (UPA) to prove that they were "legitimate" refugees. Having qualified, the Angolans were given a ration card, which entitled them to receive food and clothing and at times seed, a hoe, and a pot to cook in.

---

12. Len Addicott, *Cry Angola* (London: SCM Press, 1962), 36.

The Grenfells were not alone in providing this service to refugees. In fact in 1966 forty-eight ex-Angolan Protestant missionaries or personnel who had intended to go to Angola provided emergency relief, health, agricultural, educational, and religious services in the Lower Congo. Nor were they all from the BMS. In 1966 in addition to the seventeen BMS missionaries there were fifteen Canadian Baptists, nine American Methodists, and seven United Church of Canada missionaries. These Angolan missionaries were not only sustained by their respective mission agencies, but were supported by personnel and material aids from a vast network that included the Mennonite Central Committee, the Congo Protestant Relief Agency, the Baptist World Alliance, the Society of Friends, the World Council of Churches, Church World Service, the Bible Societies, Scripture Gift Mission, Oxfam, United Nations High Commissioner for Refugees, UNESCO, War on Want (British), Heifer Project, Bread for the World (German), Agency for International Development/USA, and governmental relief and development programs of Canada, Sweden, the Netherlands, and others nations.

Rosário Neto, minister of information of GRAE, wrote to a Catholic priest in Angola in December 1969:

> The religious missions that assist the refugees with food, clothing, and medicine are all English or American Protestants and act throughout the Congo. They built schools and churches; they opened hospitals and social centers for the education of young girls; they promoted their former pastors to superintendents and provided scholarships for the students. On the other hand, the Catholics are like sheep without a shepherd, left to themselves in conditions that verge on despair.[13]

During the nine years that Kibentele served as the chief reception center for Angolan refugees in the Lower Congo it is estimated that 200,000 were registered and received some aid there.[14] Still not all the relief agencies concentrated their efforts in Kibentele. Many other centers also rendered valuable service. Songololo was a center for food distribution and medical aid. Sona Pango was the base for a mobile medical team, baby welfare clinic, and satellite dispensaries. An African trained nurse was in charge of each dispensary, giving treatment and screening patients so the most urgent and complicated cases could be seen by the visiting doctor. The central Protestant hospital at Kimpese provided medical services, and the small hospital of the sugar company at Moerbeke gave emergency care to Angolan refugees. The Sona

---

13. A. F. Santos Neves, *Quo Vadis, Angola?* 226.

14. F. James Grenfell, "Angola Today," *Missionary Herald: The Magazine of the Baptist Missionary Society* (London), April 1978.

Mbata secondary school agreed to allot 120 of its 360 places to Angolan refugees. In 1966 a new institution (CEDECO) was established under the leadership of Dr. Allen T. Knight, formerly of the Dôndi mission, on 430 acres at Kimpese to provide agricultural training programs for local Congolese and Angolan refugees. These institutions and programs served the Angolan refugees as they arrived and were getting settled in the early 1960s. In the later 1960s the Angolans dominated the region. They produced the greater part of vegetables, fruit, and livestock and marketed them in the Lower Congo and in Kinshasa. The primary school statistics of the Kibentele district showed the dominance of the Angolans, in that area. Out of 8,512 students, 6,943 were Angolans, and only 1,569 were Congolese.

The refugees found a welcome in the Lower Congo, being met by missionaries who spoke Kikongo and who were supported by organizations that could provide at least a minimum of material aid. The Protestant churches in the Lower Congo were also of the same tradition as those in northern Angola, the largest in both cases being Baptist. The church in Songololo, Luku, and Sona Mpangu area of the Lower Congo was planted by the American Baptist Foreign Mission Society, and since Congolese independence on June 30, 1960, it had been led by African pastors. It was known as ADEBCO. This Congolese church agreed that the Angolan Christians should appoint one of their own people to help integrate the Angolan Christians into the local churches. They chose Gabriel António, who had been a church secretary of the Bembe district in Angola. Most of the Angolan refugees in that area were from Bembe and São Salvador. In his 1966 report Gabriel António recorded visiting 97 villages in which he found 2,697 Angolan church members in good standing. In the same villages he registered 65 Angolans working as evangelists. The majority of these leaders were Baptists, but some were Methodists or from the North Angola Mission.

In the Kibentele area where the church had been planted by the BMS no Angolan was doing the visitation work. The Église Baptista Bas-Fleuve (EBBF) reported 3,970 members — 1,232 Congolese and 2,739 Angolans. This count of Angolans was judged very low by David Grenfell, who calculated that the church secretary included only those who had paid their church dues of $3.50 per year, which was very difficult for many of the refugees.

In 1968 the Angolan Baptists formed the Association of Baptist Churches in Exile (ACEBA) and elected its first secretary, the Rev. Ntoni Daniel Nzinga. The church in exile provided training for the future leaders by sending forty-five young men to Bible school or theological seminary in Zaire, and some went abroad for further study.

One of the many Angolan Baptists who took advantage of his exile to prepare himself for service in the church was the Rev. João Makondekwa. In 1958 he had been sent by the Quibocolo church to the theological seminary in Dôndi. He fled from Angola in September 1961, and seven months later after many vicissitudes reached the United Kingdom, where he was received as a student by Spurgeon College in England. Completing his theological course, he did specialization in pedagogy in Belgium and then went to Kimpese, Zaire, as the director of studies at the Institut Pedagogique Évangélique (IPE). After the independence of Angola he became secretary of the Bible Society in Luanda.

The refugees in the Lower Congo continued to anticipate their return to Angola. In 1964 when Angolans were still leaving their homes in large numbers, some of the Zombo church leaders in Leopoldville opened a fund for rebuilding the Quibocolo church, which had been razed. "Imperturbably they were convinced that God was preparing for their return in His own time."[15]

The Catholic Church in the Portuguese Congo

As the Protestant church in the Congo and Zaire districts of Angola was served predominantly by Baptist missionaries (BMS and CBFMS), the Catholic church during the colonial war was served in that region by Capuchins. This order of friars (Ordo Fratrum Minorum Capuccinorum, O.F.M. Cap.), which was a reforming offshoot of the Franciscans, was constituted as an independent order in 1619. They worked in northern Angola from 1645 until 1834, when Catholic orders were expelled from Portugal.

The Capuchins returned to Angola in 1948, and by 1961 they had assumed responsibility for most of the Catholic mission stations in the Congo and Zaire districts. On their arrival in 1948 they founded the missions of Camabatela and Damba. They then received responsibility for São Salvador, Maquela do Zombo, and Sanza Pombo and established three new mission stations: Quiculungo in Cuanza North, Cangola, Bembe, and Quimbele in the Congo.

The ides of March hit the Capuchins with full force. Several of the Catholic missions in the north had to be abandoned in the first shock of the March 15 quake. Bembe, Sanza Pombo, Quimbele, and Cangola were so violently attacked that all personnel fled. On March 15 Father Lázaro de Sarcedo (Angelo Graciani) was killed in the village of Pangala in the area of Buela. With him was killed Professor Tibúrcio of the São Salvador mission school and the headman of the village. The catechist who was with them fled to the Congo. On April 21 another Capuchin missionary

---

15. *Missionary Herald* (BMS), June 1964, 86.

was fatally shot in Damba, one of the Portuguese towns most frequently attacked by the Angolans in March and April 1961. Father Pedro João de Trieste (Francesco Filippi) had been a missionary in Damba for six years, so he must have been well known by the local population, rousing suspicions that the killing was not accidental. A third Capuchin, Father Felisberto de Travettore, was killed in a military plane that crashed near Negage on August 5, 1961.

In the north of Angola in 1961 both Catholic and Protestant missions were closed, but for different reasons. The Protestant missions were considered sympathetic, or even allied, with the Angolans so the Portuguese government ordered their closure. The Catholic missions were attacked or at least threatened by the Angolans so some were temporarily abandoned, such as Bembe, Sanza Pombo, Quimbele, and Cangola.

As the Portuguese government regained military control of the north, the Catholic church reopened its missions and established the new mission of Samba Caju, which was separated from the Quiculungo mission area. In 1967 the Catholic church erected the new diocese of Carmona-São Salvador and then founded three new missions: Negage, Buengas, and Bungo. The new diocese covered an area of over 38,000 square miles, and included a population of 400,000. The Catholic church estimated that half of that population was over the border during the transition period (1961–74) and that 80,000 of those remaining were Catholics.

The first bishop of Carmona-São Salvador was Dom Francisco de Mata Mourisca, who was born in Portugal in 1928. After studying and making his religious profession in the order of Capuchins, he was ordained in Oporto in 1952. He taught in seminaries of his order and became the provincial of the Capuchins in Portugal. Dom Francisco was ordained bishop in Oporto on April 30, 1967, and took possession of the diocese on July 30.

The War in Luanda, Cuanza North, and Malanje

The first attacks of the war of independence centered in the northern districts of Zaire and Uige, but they also spread to the second tier of districts: Luanda, Cuanza North, and Malanje. However, the effects on the people of the two areas differed. In the extreme north the proximity of the border made it possible for at least half the population to flee into what was then the Congo-Leopoldville. For geographic reasons the Angolans in the second tier of districts found escape much more difficult. The Angolan population, and particularly the small educated elite and the Protestants, were threatened because of the larger concentration of whites in these three districts. According to the 1960 census the northern districts of Zaire and Uige had 6,849 whites, while the districts of Luanda, Cuanza North, and Malanje had 71,530 whites. This meant that the African population was not only subject to retaliation by the military and paramilitary forces, but the white civilian population was larger so could more effectively vent its wrath on the African population.

The Methodist church, the largest Protestant community in this area, suffered greatly. The leadership personnel of the Luanda Methodist church decreased from 155 to 10 — pastors from 88 to 4 and teachers from 67 to 6 — during the first few months of the war. In August 1961 it was impossible to ascertain how many of those workers were killed, how many were hiding in the Angolan bush, and how many had succeeded in fleeing to the Congo. After the war it was verified that the following Methodist leaders had been killed:

Churches	Workers
	Dembos and Nambuangongo Area
Piri	Rev. Guilherme Pereira Inglês,
	Supt. and daughter Juliana Inglês
	Rev. Cristóvão Miguel da Silva
	Profs.: Geraldo Silveira and António
	Class leaders: António Sebastião,
	Cassule João Caetano, and Gomes Mukaji
Kaxexe-Bula Atumba	Rev. Sebastião João Rodrigues,
	former missionary to São Tomé
Kiaji	Pastor António de Almeida
Kazuuangongo	Pastor Domingos Germano
Kipaulo	Pastor Manuel Andre da Silva
Kakulo ka Henda	Pastor Fualo Domingos
Mukiamakakulo-Lombiji	Rev. Moises Domingo Cafala
Ngombe-a-Mukiama	Lima and Graça, daughters of the
	Rev. Santos Paulo da Costa Matoso
Mukondo	Lila Gregório Webba, wife of Rev. Julião Webba
Kizele Nambuangongo	Pastor Manuel Maria de Almeida Bucharte
Ngumbe de Nzombo Makando	Pastor Manuel da Silva Izata
	Pastor Conceição Bernardo Agostinho,
	Evangelist of Annual Conference
	Caxito Area
Dande	Rev. Manuel Miguel de Morais was
	imprisoned and killed in the
	S. Pedro da Barra prison in Luanda.
	Golungo Alto Area
Kiluanji	Rev. Domingo João de Almeida
	Class Leaders: Baptista Mateus,
	Manuel Lourenço Luís Kilamba,
	Mateus Ado and Uabinga Segundo
Muenembala	Pastor Pedro de Sousa Liberto
Kikulungo	Pastor António Pereira Santana
	Class Leader: Carlos de Almeida

Churches	Workers
	Libolo Area
Calulo	Rev. Jacinto João Matias de Almeida
Kandemba	Pastor António Manuel Luís
Munenga	Pastor Diogo Jerónimo
Bango-Anga	Exhorter: Sebastião de Vasconcelos
	Cambambe-Dondo Area
Caxissa	Pastor João Maria de Almeida Bucharte
Kassoalala	Class leaders: Domingo António e
	Mário Lumbongo
	Malanje Area
Nova Gaia	Pastor Francisco Mendes da Conceição e Silva
Muquixi	Joaquim Ramos Duarte, lay leader of
	Annual Conference
Mussolo	Manuel Morais, evangelist and teacher
Mulo-Xa Muteba	Cassanje, exhorter and candidate
	for Bible School in Quéssua
	Icolo e Bengo Area
Kakulo Kazongo	Class leader: António Vicente[16]

In September 1961 the Portuguese government took direct action against the top leaders of the Methodist church in Luanda, imprisoning the Rev. Júlio João Miguel and his three sons: Rev. Emílio Miguel de Carvalho, João Miguel de Carvalho, and Roberto de Carvalho.

In addition to Father Joaquim de Andrade several other prominent Catholic clergymen were imprisoned and sent in exile to Portugal. Monsignor Manuel Mendes das Neves was dean of the cathedral and vicar general of the archdiocese of Luanda when he was arrested in 1961. He was accused of hiding arms, which were to be used by the "terrorists." He died in 1966 in the Jesuit novitiate in Braga, where he was held under house arrest.

Father Alfredo Osório, superior of the Pius X mission, was arrested and held under house arrest in the Spiritan Seminary in Viana do Castelo.

Father Gaspar Domingos, parish priest of Muxima, a Marian sanctuary in northern Angola, was in solitary confinement and suffered torture in Angola and then was held under house arrest in Lisbon.

Father Martinho, a priest in the neighborhood of Samba in Luanda, was beaten and spent six months in prison in Angola. Then he was sent to Braga, Portugal, where he was held under surveillance in the Franciscan monastery.

The professor of dogmatic theology at the major seminary in Luanda, Father Alexandre do Nascimento, was also arrested and forced

---

16. Emílio J. M. de Carvalho, *Ouço os Passos de Milhares* (São Paulo, Brazil: Imprensa Metodista, 1978), 199–201.

to live in exile in Portugal. Another seminary professor, Father José Vicente, who had studied at the Gregorian University in Rome, was sent to Portugal in exile where he lived in the Church of the Magdalen in Lisbon.

Finally Father Lino Guimarães of the Quibala mission was arrested on Maundy Thursday, 1961, and after being tortured was sent to Lisbon and lived there with the Capuchin Fathers under police surveillance.

These examples of the arrest of Catholic priests illustrate the ambivalent position of the Catholic church, which had many priests and lay people who sympathized with the liberation struggle; the government still had confidence in the hierarchy, however, so these offenders could be kept safely in Catholic houses or monasteries.

Another incident showing a similar ambivalence was the reception by Pope Paul VI on July 1, 1970, of the three leaders of nationalist movements in Guinea, Angola, and Mozambique: Amilcar Cabral, Agostinho Neto, and Marcelino dos Santos. The Portuguese government presented a protest to the Vatican and called its ambassador back to Lisbon. The subsequent statements by the Vatican were vague.

Church and War in Central Angola

The Portuguese claimed that the terrorism in the north was caused by external forces that subverted Angola from across the Congo border. To support this argument and also to divide the Angolans, the Portuguese government spoke and wrote frequently of "the loyal Bailundos." They used this term to refer to the Umbundu, the largest ethnolinguistic group in Angola, and more vaguely to include all the peoples of central and southern Angola.

However, as noted above, PIDE had arrested several Angolans in Lobito in 1957 for suspected subversive activities, and as soon as the earthquake shook the north on March 15 Portuguese police and administrative officials attacked centers of "terrorism." One of the earliest and most dramatic attacks was that directed at the Protestant community in the Bocoio-Balombo area some hundred miles inland from Lobito. Just before dawn on Easter Sunday the police entered the principal Protestant villages and arrested the leaders. They were taken to the prison in Lobito and subjected to interrogation and torture.

What had aroused the suspicions of the Portuguese authorities? The interrogations of the prisoners taken to Lobito indicated that the activities of Júlio Cacunda, the son of Pastor Gaspar Vanhale of the Balombo center of the Elende church, had attracted their attention. After completing the Dôndi Institute, Júlio was hired to teach in the Protestant elementary school in Lobito in 1959. Before finishing his first academic year he was inducted into the Portuguese army in 1960. He is alleged to have promoted political activity among African soldiers and used his contacts with other graduates of the Currie Institute in Dôndi to form clandestine political groups at Nova Lisboa, Lobito, Luanda, Sá da Bandeira, and a number of smaller centers in the Bailundo area. Júlio was supposed to have distributed leaflets calling for rebellion against whites, one of which read:

> Freedom is coming. Now the time has come. Show yourselves so that we can save our country from the whites. Freedom! On the 2nd of April wherever you see a white man, kill him.
>
> Eyovo lu Viali. Kaliye otembo ya pitila. Limalehe oco tu popele ofeka yetu kovindele. Eyovo! Eteke lia vali ka sai ya kupupu apa posi wa muili ocindele pondi.[17]

Two principal Protestant centers served the Bocoio/Monte Belo area: Caluvango, belonging to the Lobito church, and Essoquela of the Ebanga church. These centers, only ten miles apart, were a product of the tension between the "American" and "Swiss" missions in central Angola. Pastor Jessé Chipenda, the founder of the Lobito church, began the evangelization of the Bocoio area. A few Cisanji who inhabited that area were converted, but most of those who joined the church in Bocoio were Umbundu who resided in Lobito and had fields and family in the Bocoio area or Umbundu from the interior who had sought land in that sparsely populated region. Jessé and Teresa Chipenda developed a prosperous farm at Kanyala on the southern edge of the Bocoio area to grow food for their family in Lobito and to provide a retirement home for themselves.

In 1949 the Lobito church sent teachers to four centers in the Bocoio area to establish schools, which, as we have seen, had proven to be the most effective method of evangelization. Of the four, Caluvango, north of Monte Belo, became the pastoral center related to the Lobito church, and the Rev. Antonino Cavita Ngola was chosen to be pastor.

The Ebanga mission sent catechists across the Mepo mountains to the northwest into the Kanyala area. Patients who had been treated in the Ebanga or the Caluquembe hospitals returned to the Bocoio area and requested teachers from the Swiss mission. The Ebanga church established the pastoral center of Essoquela and placed the Rev. João Moko to minister in the Bocoio area. On Easter Sunday in 1961 instead of celebrating the resurrection of their Lord, the pastors and local leaders of both Caluvango and Essoquela were arrested and the Protestant church was paralyzed in the whole Bocoio area. The Essoquela center was revived

---

17. Marcum, *The Angolan Revolution*, 1:155; Luciano Kasoma, "The Outbreak of the Angolan Revolution in the South," Lincoln University, unpublished typescript, 1965.

beginning in the fall of 1962 when the young pastor Alfredo Cambonde was placed there. He worked for seven years and with a nurse, Marcos, and a teacher led the people in rebuilding the center spiritually and physically.

The police raid on the church in the Bocoio area fit into a pattern that appeared in police and civilian retaliatory measures in other places in central and southern Angola. The raids were precipitated by the discovery of an alleged plot against the Portuguese. The most imaginative of the plots was that supposedly planned in Sá da Bandeira for June 10, 1961, which is a Portuguese national holiday. All African gasoline pump attendants were to spray the streets with gasoline fifteen minutes before the start of the day's festive parade. When the parade began, the attendants were to light a match to the gasoline. The governor of the district, merchants, and soldiers would be burned to death and the plotters would then seize the city. This plot like others in central and southern Angola did not materialize, but it served as a pretext for a series of arrests.

The peculiar feature of the alleged Bocoio plot was that it had supposedly been created and organized within the network of the Protestant church. Without doubt the Protestant community provided one of the best networks for the spread of anti-Portuguese propaganda and for the organization of Angolan nationalist associations and activities. This network had several advantages. First, the Protestant emphasis on schools had created an educational elite that had completed elementary school so they could read and write and had a certain social prestige. Second, the Protestant church was led mostly by lay men and women and functioned as a representative democracy. The people had experience in organizing and administering schools, clinics, and village development programs as well as the ecclesiastical structure. Third, the anti-Protestant attitude and actions of the Portuguese officials disposed the Protestant community to be anti-Portuguese and anticolonial. Fourth, the mission was a slight shield or buffer for the church since the Portuguese officials dealt with the church only indirectly through the mission. Fifth, the relative independence of the church from the missionaries and mission structures allowed the church leaders to communicate among themselves and to plan and organize without the missionaries participating or even being aware of what was happening.

The three Protestant communities in which these advantages were most pronounced were the Baptist, the Methodist, and the United Church in central Angola. Since most of the BMS stations in the north were closed, the missionaries had departed, and a majority of the population had fled in 1961, the Methodist and United Church networks were the two most available to Angolan nationalists. The Plymouth Brethren, Swiss mission, and SAGM privately had anti-Portuguese feelings before

1961, mostly because of the close tie between Portugal and the Roman Catholic church, but they were less politically activist than the Methodist or United Church missions. Because their churches were smaller in both number and organization, they did not provide such useful networks.

The Church's Responses

The verbal responses of the church to the March 15 rebellion were varied. In their pastoral letter of April 15, 1961, the bishops of the Catholic church expressed a spirit of conciliation by deploring the killings and terrorism of March 15 but also criticized the violent retaliation.[18] The letter lamented the lack of charity between the races and affirmed that the authorities must regard the just aspirations of the people if peace was to be established.

The Angolan elite of the Catholic hierarchy were in prison for suspected subversive activities: Father Joaquim Pinto de Andrade, Monsignor Canon Manuel Mendes das Neves, vicar general of Luanda, Father Nascimento, editor of *O Apostolado*, and Father Manuel Franklin, secretary of the archbishop of Luanda. Through these well-known African priests the Catholic church identified with the nationalist aspirations of the Angolan peoples. However since the Portuguese government and the Catholic hierarchy concerted to keep the dissident priests out of sight, the Catholic church continued visibly identified with the Portuguese colonial rulers.

The Portuguese confidence in the Catholic hierarchy was reflected in the report of a council on countersubversion in the Huila district of Angola:

> We believe that the bishops of Angola have manifested very well their patriotism and their dynamic will for the expansion of the Catholic faith among the masses with the accent on civilizing in the constructive sense of Portugalization.[19]

The same council gave a a negative evaluation of the influence of the Protestant missions:

> In meetings of the District Council we have often spoken about the pernicious influence which the Protestant missions exercise through individuals who made harmful statements and propaganda. These are foreign agents who exert influence over the na-

---

18. Addicott, *Cry Angola*, 122–23.
19. *Angola: Secret Government Documents on Counter-Subversion*, trans. and ed. Caroline Reuver-Cohen and William Jerman (Rome: IDOC, 1974), 119.

tive masses. They generate admiration and enthusiasm for certain anti-Portuguese ideologies and movements. They surreptitiously undermine the idea of Portuguese citizenship. They create mentalities in the service of ideas inimical to Portugal. At best they limit themselves to propagating a religious ideology not in conformity with our tradition. They neutralize our efforts for Portugalization and occupy key positions which make it easy for them to implant ideas contrary to our interests.[20]

The Protestant missions were well aware of the Portuguese criticism of their influence, but continued to work within the constraints set upon them by the government. They seldom confronted the authorities with the serious questions of religious liberty and political independence. For example in the reports that the government required annually of each Protestant mission, the missionary directors pointed especially to the work of the schools that taught Portuguese, the health services, and the good character and citizenship produced by the Christian faith. Infrequently a report did discuss some of the problems, such as the report of the Dôndi mission for 1965. The final section of the report, which was entitled "Results and Benefits of the Work of the Year," said in part:

We have used this section of the General Report to explain the problems which impede the more effective action of the mission. These problems are well known: (1) the lack of missionary personnel, (2) restrictions on the movement of missionaries, (3) lack of legal recognition of Protestant organizations, (4) impediments to the registry of students, (5) difficulty of Protestant students to be admitted to official courses for rural teachers, (6) the placement of government schools beside Protestant schools, although there are many areas without any school, (7) lack of mutual trust between missions and authorities, (8) lack of authorization for church meetings, etc. We have created among us Protestants an inferiority complex if not paranoia or a spirit of martyrdom. This should not be. If it is true that all the problems we usually mention are real and important, it is also true that all have their positive aspects. Or, to speak more biblical and Christian language, " . . . for the sake of Christ, then, I am content with weaknesses, insults, hardships, persecution, and calamities; for when I am weak, then I am strong" (2 Cor. 12:10).

The lack of missionary personnel has led local leaders of the church to assume much more responsibility. The harassment of missionaries when they need to travel binds them to the peo-

---

20. Ibid., 115.

ple who know the same harassment constantly. The separation of church and state in schools, hospitals, etc. produces a stronger church and more responsible people. (Many Roman Catholics know that their "privileges" have damaged the spiritual and even the material life of that church.)

Therefore to conclude these observations, sincerely we give thanks to God not only for the privilege which we have to continue to witness to Christ — preaching, teaching, and healing in this Province — but we are grateful too for the impediments and difficulties, trusting that even in these the Spirit of God may work to accomplish His Will.

Further Government Restrictions

To regulate church meetings the government in 1963 invoked decree No. 22,468 of April 11, 1933. This stated first that all citizens were guaranteed the right of assembly, but then added that meetings called for the purposes of political or social "propaganda" must receive authorization from the civil authorities. The only exceptions were worship services or scientific, literary, or cultural lectures. The government ruled that meetings such as the Protestant Congress, the Annual Meeting of the Aliança Evangélica de Angola, the general assembly of the Council of Protestant Churches of Central Angola, and the annual meeting of the Methodist church were not exempt from the restrictions of decree No. 22468. On the basis of reports from past meetings of these organizations the government concluded that the meetings included "social and political propaganda." In justifying its response to the Aliança the government claimed that in past meetings the participants not only discussed the internal business of missions and churches, but spoke of the low prices of some local products and contended that profits stayed in the hands of middlemen — "the white traders." The government had received information that opinions of "heavy political content" were expressed.

In this exchange of communications between the government and the Aliança, the Aliança recognized that it was difficult to distinguish sharply between worship services and meetings for general discussion. At times business meetings followed directly after worship services and the whole congregation would participate, or at least be present. The Aliança assured the government that officials would always be welcome at such services and meetings. If they knew more about the nature and scope of Protestant work there would be more opportunities for cooperation. The Aliança communication noted that the governor-general had recently proclaimed a social policy with two fundamental objectives: to better the conditions of rural and urban populations, and to accelerate the process of development of all the inhabitants of the province in the benefits of civilization. A great part of the work of the Protestant church-missions coincided exactly with these objectives.

This exposition by the general secretary of the Aliança did not convince the government. It continued to refuse permission for area or regional meetings. When the government refused permission for the Annual Meeting of the Aliança it did not refer to decree No. 22468, but the official gave a more basic reason: "I do not authorize the meeting because the Aliança Evangélica de Angola does not have legal existence."

The most aggravating restriction placed on the Protestant missionaries was the order given in June 1963 that required them to receive permission from the PIDE in Luanda to travel outside their local administrative areas. This order applied only to foreign Protestant missionaries, not to other foreigners, nor to other missionaries. The director of PIDE agreed to interpret the order liberally, but admitted that for the missionaries outside of the larger urban centers, it would take a month to receive a travel permit. Actually bureaucratic delays were common, and although very few requests were directly refused, not infrequently the permission arrived only after the date of the trip had passed. The restriction was particularly serious because to carry on established programs with a diminishing number of missionaries required a more mobile personnel.

The authorities also prohibited the Protestant radio programs that were being broadcast from several cities in Angola and impeded the shipment of literature from the press in Dôndi.

The Caponte Controversy, Lobito

The war of independence was not a struggle between black and white, but it did exacerbate the already poor race relations in Angola. This racial tension existed in the church also. For example the dominantly Portuguese congregation of Caponte in Lobito came into conflict with the African congregations that composed the coast church. The Caponte congregation, which had been organized in 1950, using funds contributed by the mission as well as monies that members raised locally, constructed a modern building for a Portuguese-language congregation. The author served the congregation as pastor from its inception until 1960, when he was transferred from Lobito to the Bunjei mission station. To replace him as pastor of the Caponte congregation the coast church called Herlander Felizardo, a Portuguese Baptist student who finished his theological course at the Presbyterian seminary in Carcavelos, Portugal. He was ordained by the coast church in 1960 and shortly thereafter began to lead the congregation to change its doctrine and practice according to the pattern of Baptist churches in Portugal. Felizardo prepared a simple catechism for the preparation of candidates for membership in the Caponte congregation, which required believers' baptism by immersion. The congregation also left the fellowship of the coast church, which was part of the Council of Evangelical Churches in Central Angola (CIEAC) with headquarters in Dôndi, and they joined the Angolan Baptist Convention.

Most of the congregation supported Pastor Felizardo, with the notable exception of Francisco de Figueiredo and his family. Figueiredo, a leading layman in the Caponte congregation and also an officer in the coast church, appealed to the CIEAC to resolve the conflict so that the congregation would continue as a part of the coast church and the council. Or, if the congregation insisted on its exclusive Baptist orientation, then it would be required to leave the building to a congregation that was in harmony with the coast church. No compromise was found and the congregation changed its name to the Evangelical Baptist Church of Lobito. CIEAC and the UCBWM intervened to try to resolve the conflict, but the Portuguese members maintained control of the Caponte property, having the leverage of a "white" congregation in conflict with a predominantly "black" church. The Baptist congregation returned the building to the coast church only after April 25, 1974, when it was clear that Portuguese colonialism had lost its authority.

The War Comes to Central Angola

In the first two or three years of the war of liberation the Protestant churches of central and southern Angola did not suffer as severely as those of the northern regions since the armed conflict was more distant. The situation changed, however, in the mid-1960s. The MPLA and GRAE moved to begin military operations in eastern and southern Angola. Even more important for the churches in that part of Angola was the formation of a third Angolan nationalist movement UNITA, the União Nacional de Independência Total de Angola.

On September 21, 1965, Jonas Malheiro Savimbi wrote from Dar es Salaam to the missionaries of the United Church Board for World Ministries in New York. After thanking them for the scholarship that allowed him to complete his course in political and legal sciences at the University of Lausanne, Savimbi gave his political analysis of the problem of Angola. The first principle was that the struggle must be fought from inside Angola: "Only the Angolan people within the country is capable of freeing itself from foreign domination."

Savimbi's second assumption was that the struggle must be democratic and national in order to include all Angolans: "The social reality of our country is today reflected with cruel tangibility in the existing political parties. The MPLA only includes representatives of the Kimbundu except for Daniel Chipenda. GRAE only contains Kikongos except for Rosário Neto and Gourgel. These two parties together still leave outside the political struggle more than half the population."

In pleading for the unity of all Angolans Savimbi affirmed that the struggle was not ideological because it could not exclude anybody. It had to unite all. Political and economic theories that are based on atheistic attitudes are not in line with African belief. Africans believe in a higher Being, whatever that Being's name may be or whatever the place that Being is worshipped. There is an ancestral force that transcends humankind. All alienation from this profoundly popular feeling will tend to divide the forces that could openly show themselves against colonial domination. It is vital to avoid a direct or indirect confrontation of the great powers on Angolan soil.

Savimbi continued his letter naming his "companions in the struggle": Dr. José Liahuca, Alexander Magno, and Marcolino Nyani in Brazzaville; Jerónimo Wanga, Ruben Sanjovo, and Victor Afonso in Europe; and Jorge Valentin on the International Student Committee. All these men had been scholarship students of the Protestant church in central Angola or were leaders in that church. Therefore the church felt the impact when Savimbi hiked into Angola in March 1966 and gathered sixty-seven supporters in Muangai in the lightly populated savanna of Moxico district about 250 miles from the Zambian border to formally organize UNITA. The political organizing was accompanied by small guerrilla attacks — the most effective being sabotage of the Benguela railway near the Congolese border. This echoed down the rail line, which runs through the populous highlands of the Bié and Huambo districts, and prompted the government to launch a more systematic campaign to control nationalistic activities in central and southern Angola.

In a letter dated June 9, 1967, a missionary wrote from central Angola to the UCBWM and the United Church of Canada stating that things had "blown wide open" and documenting this with a list of events during January–May 1967.

In January police and military patrols wandered around the missions at night, at times just instilling fear by the presence of the Jeeps and the bright lights and at other times questioning and threatening students. On January 18 a meeting was held on the mission at which the administrator's representative informed everyone that:

1. There were to be no guests in any of the villages unless the host and soba first presented them at the administration; if they disregarded this order they might as well burn their villages to the ground, for this is what would happen to them.

2. Everyone was to turn in his guns to the administration. (This meant that even the hunters with their old shotguns lost their livelihood. Of course, this and all these rules applied to Africans only. Whites could still roam around with guns.)

3. No one was to leave the mission area without a travel permit. Previously, in theory, those with identity cards were exempt. Now everyone (Africans that is) had to spend hours, sometimes days, waiting at the administration to receive a permit for any trip whatsoever.

In February the army and police continued to roam about the mission and villages, terrifying the people by their presence. On March 23, Maundy Thursday, in a predawn raid, a large army patrol rounded up everyone in one of the pastoral centers and checked for identity cards and tax receipts, arresting those men who could not produce them. On March 27, Easter Monday, the director of the mission learned about the incident and found one of the church teachers who had been held incommunicado and fed only once a day since March 23. His "crime" was not being able to show his identity card (which was at another administration for renewal). Through the director's testimony the teacher was eventually released.

On April 27 some ten or twelve midwives from two pastorates were arrested. One of them, while in a Catholic village, had made some remark to the effect that "we are now one faith." A white trader hearing about this went to the police, whereupon the women were arrested. They were beaten with a *palmatória*, questioned, and released after five days.

In May the government sent several officials to the Bailundo Protestant mission to inform it that the dry season courses for catechists and other church leaders could not be held. The request for permission for nine courses had been submitted to the administration in December 1966. No answer had been received so the courses were begun and the officials arrived in the midst of the sixth — the women's school. The local officials, the PIDE, and the governor of the district all refused to give any reason for the cancellation. In May the harassment intensified, especially in the pastoral centers. Leaders' meetings were prohibited and the Week of Prayer lessons were confiscated.

Protestant Leaders Arrested

This localized harassment in central Angola was complemented by a systematic campaign to remove the top echelon of Protestant church leaders. In 1967 the Rev. Frederico Mussili, pastor in Nova Lisboa, the Rev. Eurico Sangueve, pastoral superintendent of the Bailundo church, Domingo Catanha, head teacher in Bailundo, and the Rev. Henrique Daniel Etaungo, director of the student hostel in Nova Lisboa, were all arrested. This campaign reached its climax with the arrest in June 1968 of the Rev. Jessé Chiula Chipenda, the general secretary of the Church Council of Central Angola. When he was picked up at the Dôndi mission, he was informed that he would not need a jacket or coat, although it was in the cold season, because he was being taken to the local government administrative office in Bela Vista, three miles from his home. Instead he was driven four hundred miles to Luanda, the capital of Angola. After some weeks women relatives in Luanda inquired for Pastor Jessé at the PIDE prison, and they were informed that he was in the mental hospital. In their fight against communism the Portuguese had adopted certain Soviet tactics. Mrs. Teresa Chipenda went from Bela Vista to Luanda to visit her husband, but when she arrived the guards informed her that Pastor Jessé did not wish to see her.

The author was shown the police file of Pastor Jessé in October 1968. In Portuguese practice no charges were made against the prisoner. He was simply "invited" to confess, and the confession was facilitated by questions put by an interrogator. The answers were then copied and transcribed into an orderly confession, which the prisoner was then again invited to sign. Pastor Jessé's confession covered some twenty typewritten pages. It reviewed his career in the mission school and his work as catechist and pastor. At each stage he mentioned the missionaries with whom he was associated and declared that they were primarily dedicated to the propagation of anti-Portuguese political ideas. Pastor Jessé's confession explained that in recent years, with the steady decrease in missionary staff, the Angolan pastors had inherited the missionaries' role of propagators of subversive political views.

After the author finished reading the confession, he said to the two police agents who were present at the reading, "Either Pastor Jessé is crazy, or I am. I have known him for twenty years, and although I recognize his signature, he would not have made such a 'confession' in his right mind." As the author left the police office, one of the agents said, "You will be happy to know that the Rev. Chipenda was moved from the mental hospital back to the prison." The police thus made the more significant confession that Pastor Jessé's statements were made and signed while he was mentally confused or under the influence of drugs or torture.

In November 1968 Jessé Chipenda was moved from the prison in Luanda to the concentration camp or "recuperation center" of São Nicolau near Moçâmedes. Mrs. Chipenda went with two other wives to be with their husbands, but she was refused permission to join her husband because the authorities claimed that prisoners could only receive family after an initial "orientation period," which Pastor Jessé had not completed. Teresa Chipenda returned to Bela Vista and never again saw her husband.

Family and friends sent greetings and gifts to Jessé Chipenda for Christmas 1968. He acknowledged their receipt with the following letter:

Dear Friends,

This letter has the purpose of thanking you for the Christmas presents. We were also happy with the precious greetings.

My health is pretty good; just my swollen feet which are not fully recovered, but I am not worried about this.

I consider my coming here as a blessing from God. If I had continued always at Dôndi, I would never have had the privilege of contacting Christians from all parts of Angola. Here there are Christians from Cabinda in the north to the Cuanhama country in the south, and from the Atlantic ocean on the west to Dilolo on the frontier in the east. Here God is worshipped by all the tribes. Here one can appreciate better the extent of the church in Angola.

Morning prayers are held in the barracks daily at 5:30 A.M. We recite a Bible verse, sing a hymn and finish in prayer. Mondays and Thursdays after supper we have services of worship with preaching. Saturday afternoons we have a prayer service. Sunday morning we have Holy Communion and in the afternoon a big outdoor service of worship.

We held the Week of Prayer January 2–9. During this week many who had left the church were received again into the fellowship. We used the theme of the Prodigal Son.

Here neither Bible nor hymn book enters, but God performs miracles even today.

It is by the will of God that I am here. In spite of my weak health I am immensely joyful through my communion with God. Here I "enlarge the place of my tent" (Isaiah 54:2).

Faith, confidence and hope in God dissolve all bitternesses of the present life.

Your brother in Christ,
Jessé Chipenda

No member of Pastor Jessé's family was with him when he died in the prison camp on October 24, 1969; he passed away in the arms of his brother in Christ and dear friend, the Rev. Frederico Mussili.

Foreign Reactions to the War

The church in Angola had shared the colony's isolation except for the contacts maintained by foreign missionaries and the few Africans who had opportunities for study outside of Angola. The churches in North America and Europe were aware of the conditions that led to the war of independence, but generally had followed the missionaries' and Africans' advice to avoid public criticism of Portuguese colonialism for fear of jeopardizing the churches' work in Angola. However the earthquake of 1961 broke the wall of self-imposed censorship by churches outside of Angola, and they began publicly to condemn Portuguese colonialism by passing resolutions, publicizing colonial oppression, lobbying governments to withdraw military and economic aid for Portugal, and participating in boycotts of foreign companies doing business in Angola.

Since the first Angolan church struck by the war in 1961 was the Baptists in the north, their sister churches in Great Britain were the first to enter the public arena against Portuguese colonialism. Missionaries of the BMS inspired the Baptist Union of Great Britain and Ireland to start a public protest against British support of Portugal. The protest climaxed in a petition with 37,524 signatures, presented to the House of Commons on July 5, 1961, which viewed "with grave concern the continuing harsh and oppressive policy of the government of the Republic of Portugal toward many of its subjects in its African territory of Angola," then humbly prayed "that no military supplies should be allowed to be sent from the United Kingdom of Great Britain and Northern Ireland to the Republic of Portugal and its overseas territories in Africa . . . while such repressive policy is continued."[21]

Such protests, which were joined by liberation support groups and Portuguese opposition groups in London, did not weaken the centuries-old Anglo-Portuguese alliance. After supporting the 1961–62 United Nations resolutions critical of Portuguese colonial rule of Angola, Great Britain either abstained or opposed subsequent resolutions designed to put pressure on Portugal to free its African colonies. Britain also supplied frigates for the Portuguese navy, light aircraft for the air force, and jeeps to the army. Both Great Britain and the United States required assurances from Portugal that military assistance would be used only to meet Portugal's NATO obligations.

---

21. Addicott, *Cry Angola!*, 101, 144, and *Angola: A Symposium*, 58–79.

The American Methodist Church was aroused against Portuguese colonialism by the expulsion of its missionaries from Angola, especially when they began visiting the local churches in the United States to tell the story of their arrest and the sufferings of the Methodist Church in Angola. Wider publicity was given by succeeding issues of the *Christian Century*. On November 15, 1961, George Daniels of the Methodist mission board wrote an article entitled "Agony in Angola: Portugal's brutal oppression of the people of Angola proceeds apace; thousands have been killed, thousands more fled." The next week Ralph E. Dodge,the former Methodist bishop of Angola, entitled an article, "Angola and Protestant Conscience: The indictment against the Salazar regime in the Angola crisis: brutal treatment of Africans, intimidation, terrorism, religious discrimination and lack of forthrightness in official dealings."

Several Methodist agencies responded to the reports of the liberation struggle in Angola and other territories by expressing their condemnation of white-minority oppression in Southern Africa and support for movements for basic human rights and fundamental freedoms. A comprehensive program was adopted at the annual meeting of the board of missions in January 1968:

> Christians in liberated societies are called by Christ to be the voice of the voiceless, to cry for justice for the black people in Southern Africa. . . . Politically it will mean speaking to the governments in Southern Africa and supporting those who oppose the present policy of minority domination; it will mean supporting African movements outside Southern Africa which seek to change the present political situation.

This action was backed up by a determination to use resources to assist in the improvement of the conditions of human life, particularly among those who have been oppressed for racial reasons, and a three-year program with funding of $600,000 was set up. This money was to be used to aid those working for social change both inside and outside of Southern Africa.

The UCBWM and UCC Act

The United Church Board for World Ministries on May 1, 1962, adopted a resolution that supported the World Council of Churches, appealing "to the government of Portugal in the name of humanity and of all that the Christian conscience cherishes, to bring to an end promptly and without delay the continuing tragedy in Angola; and believing that the fate of Angola is of international import we urge Portugal to take immediate steps so that the legitimate rights and political aspirations of the indigenous African people of Angola may be met expeditiously."

The United Church of Christ (USA) through its Eighth General Synod in 1971 proposed that the various denominational agencies and boards:

1 Urge the U.S. government and her NATO allies:

   (a) to refrain from any sales of arms to South Africa and Portugal,

   (b) to end those military, diplomatic and economic practices and policies which support minority rule and colonialism; and

   (c) to seek new ways to press for racial justice

2. Discourage United States tourism in Portugal and the Republic of South Africa;

3. Examine the role which U.S. corporations play in Southern Africa in maintaining the status quo ... ;

4. Support the humanitarian programs of Southern African liberation organizations through the World Council of Churches;

5. Educate themselves:

   (a) about the situation in Southern Africa, the serious implications of the situation and the extent to which the United States is involved;

   (b) by holding seminars, conferences and educational workshops on this issue.

In August 1972 the General Council, the highest policy-making body of the United Church of Canada, resolved:

Whereas Portugal, while receiving support from NATO, continues to oppress her indigenous peoples contrary to the principles of the United Nations Declaration of Human Rights; and

Whereas Canada has supported those United Nations resolutions which have consistently condemned Portugal's colonial practices which bar progress toward independence for Angola, Mozambique and Guinea-Bissau;

BE IT RESOLVED that this General Council:

   1. Urge the Canadian government through NATO to discontinue assistance to Portugal until Portugal has given independence to her African territories; and

2. Continue to give humanitarian aid and succour through the World Council of Churches or other international agencies to the African people in these territories in their struggle for liberation.

These ecclesiastical resolutions by North American Protestant churches were directed primarily at influencing the actions of the United States and Canadian governments. In fact the U.S. strengthened its ties with Portugal in December 1971 by renewing the agreement for American use of the Lages air base in the Azores. The new accord and the closer relations between the United States and Portugal were given greater visibility by the meeting at the Azores base between President Richard Nixon, Prime Minister Marcelo Caetano, and President Pompidou of France.

The churches outside of Angola also attempted to put pressure on international corporations to diminish their support of Portuguese colonialism. The most publicized example in the United States was the boycott of the Gulf Oil Corporation promoted by the United Church of Christ. The boycott was not initiated by one of the national agencies of that denomination; rather, the Ohio Conference in June 1970 passed a resolution calling attention to the desperate plight of the people of Angola, Mozambique, and Guinea-Bissau and the major role of Gulf Oil in supporting their suppression. The resolution urged that members of its constituent churches discontinue the use of Gulf products, that conference delegates and church members turn in Gulf credit cards, that UCC members owning Gulf stock use their voting power to develop humane policies in the company's African operations, and that Gulf be asked to withdraw immediately from "any operation in Africa which contributes to the suppression and suffering of people." This resolution carried with a standing vote of 223 for, 84 against, and 78 abstaining.

On July 27, 1970, R. B. Dorsey, president of the Gulf Oil Corporation, responded to the resolution in these words: "Our attorneys have been asked to determine what legal action should be taken to obtain redress for the damages done to the Gulf Oil Corporation and to the reputation of its principal officers by the dissemination of the defamatory document."

Immediately this church resolution became news. The *New York Times*, the *Washington Post*, and other newspapers carried articles and commentaries on Gulf Oil's activities in Angola and the church's criticisms of such activities. The *1971 Yearbook of the Encyclopaedia Britannica* described the resolution and Gulf's reaction to it. If Gulf Oil had not responded by threatening legal action, the resolution passed by a state ecclesiastical body would have been ignored by the general public and buried in the minutes of the meeting. However, Gulf's initial response and its continuing readiness to debate the issue in any forum provided the churches with a platform for educating the American public about the war and the church in Angola.

The result of this pressure on Gulf Oil was no more effective than the lobbying effort to change United States policy in support of Portugal. The only practical value of these efforts was to demonstrate solidarity with the Angolan people and to inform North Americans concerning the struggle there.

Other Foreign Reactions

A week before the National Assembly elections in November 1965, from which all opposition candidates had withdrawn their names, a group of one hundred prominent Portuguese Roman Catholics issued a "testimonial" denouncing the government for "systematically offending and violating" Catholic values. On the eve of the election a counterstatement, apparently drafted in great haste, was issued by 327 progovernment Catholics, who described signers of the "testimonial" as being "chained to Moscow."[22]

A third kind of pressure that churches outside Angola created to oppose Portuguese colonialism was to support the Angolan liberation movements. This was done most regularly through the Programme to Combat Racism of the World Council of Churches (WCC). In 1969 the WCC responded to the Angolan nationalist movements' requests for assistance by establishing the Special Fund of the Programme to Combat Racism. From 1970 through 1974 the program made grants totaling $1,050,000 (U.S.) "to organizations of oppressed racial groups or organizations supporting victims of racial injustice whose purposes are inconsistent with the general purposes of the World Council of Churches." Of the total of $656,000 that was granted to Southern African liberation movements, the Angolan movements received $176,000: MPLA, $78,000; FNLA, $60,000; and UNITA, $37,000.[23]

Conclusion

This chapter has described an ambivalence within the Catholic church as regards its relationship to the Angolan nationalist movements and may have given the impression that the Protestant communities were

---

22. *Ecumenical Press Service*, no. 40, November 11, 1965.
23. Elisabeth Adler, *A Small Beginning: An Assessment of the First Five Years of the Programme to Combat Racism* (Geneva: World Council of Churches, 1974), 15–17, 92–95.

solid in their support of these movements. This was not true. The Protestants also represented contrasting positions. Missionaries of the Swiss mission, SAGM, and Plymouth Brethren expressed support for the Portuguese "powers that be" (Rom. 13:1). Dr. Bréchet advised the Portuguese authorities that his mission was not sympathetic with the actions of the WCC. Emil Pearson (SAGM) was quoted in a Luanda paper as supportive of Portuguese colonialism, and David Long of the Plymouth Brethren gave an interview to a Canadian newspaper praising Portuguese colonialism and condemning the actions of the Angolan rebels.

The ambiguities and contradictions that appeared in the church in Angola under the stress of the colonial war appear in other shapes in the reforms that were being proposed and effected during this same period of transition (1961–74). They are the subject of the next chapter.

Chapter 11

The Church and Reform

My love for an institution is in proportion to my desire to reform it.

— John Stuart Mill

Angola moved from colonialism to independence on two tracks — revolution and reform — and the church played roles on each. On the revolutionary track the church contributed to the revolutionary spirit, helped prepare the leaders of the liberation movements, and was one of the principal victims of the Portuguese government's counter-revolutionary violence. The church also played a role in the reform movement that changed Angola during the transition period from 1961 to 1974.

The earthquake of March 15, 1961, not only shocked the Portuguese government into sending troops to Angola to establish military control over the colony; it also awoke the Portuguese to the three basic complaints of the Angolans: their lack of citizenship, their frustrated educational aspirations, and the oppression of forced labor.

Citizenship Reform

Whites were citizens automatically, but blacks had to prove that they were "civilized" by passing an examination and were thus worthy to be classed as Portuguese citizens. Portugal claimed to have dominated Angola for almost five centuries, but in the 1950s only thirty thousand Angolans were "assimilated," or holders of Portuguese citizenship. Such meager results made a mockery of Portugal's alleged "civilizing mission." If less than 1 percent of the Angolans became citizens in five centuries, how long would it take for all 4.5 million Angolans to achieve this status? Since a white skin was automatic proof of being "civilized" and a black skin a mark of not being civilized until contrary evidence was presented, cultural and racial distinctions coincided in 99.3 percent of the cases.

In just less than six months after March 15, 1961, the Portuguese government revoked the Statute of Natives (Estatuto dos Indígenas, Decreto-Lei 39.666, May 20, 1954), thus abolishing legally the distinction between civilized and noncivilized, or native. This reform made available to all Angolans the identity card that had formerly been the sign of citizenship and therefore restricted to whites and assimilated blacks.

Most rural Angolans found the reform more bother than benefit. The government sent teams of functionaries into remote areas to take pictures, collect fingerprints,and register the vital statistics necessary for the new identity cards. People were expected to pay for these services in time and money, and when they finally received the card, it guaranteed no new privilege. In fact in some cases it laid new burdens on them. For example, the special head tax levied on natives was abolished, which meant that every male had to pay a general minimum tax (Imposto Geral Mínimo), which doubled the tax for former natives from $5 to $10.

Angolans had complained that they were not citizens, but the reform did not satisfy them because what they sought was not Portuguese citizenship, but to be citizens of their own country, Angola.

The churches inherited several roles of the Angolan traditional society: selection of leaders, legitimization of social behavior, implementation of discipline and strengthening of social cohesion. Since the churches served them in these ways, Angolan Christians gave loyalty to their Catholic and Protestant communities. The Portuguese claimed that membership in the Catholic community was a sign of being a Portuguese citizen, but in practice Angolan Catholics were still "natives" and not "citizens." Angolan Protestants expressed even stronger loyalty to their Christian community because they were not only classed as "natives," but as natives belonging to a foreign community.

Educational Reform

The church and missions whetted the appetite of Angolans for education, but could not satisfy it. The state subsidized the Catholic schools, but not sufficiently to provide schools for even a significant minority of Angolan children. It not only refused to subsidize Protestant schools, but in fact hindered their growth by bureaucratic requirements.

The Portuguese responded to the March 15 explosion by a reform of the educational system that recognized the school as a weapon in the struggle between Portuguese and Angolan nationalism. Believing that the weapon should be in the hands of the government, the Portuguese moved in 1961 to assume direct responsibility for the education of the total Angolan population instead of leaving African education to a patchwork of church educational networks. To accomplish this reform the first task was to train more teachers for rural schools. In 1962 vacation courses of two and a half months were established to train *monitores* (practice teachers to teach the first year of the rural education course). The next year the government repeated the first-year course and added a second-year course in seven centers with 791 students. By 1965 each of the fourteen administrative districts had courses for *monitores* with a total of 2,413 students. Since these students became teachers on government salary after completing the first two-and-a-half-month course, this new program almost doubled the number of teachers in Angola in the first five years.

To prepare primary teachers with more adequate training the government established two new levels of normal schools: *escolas de habilitação* and *escolas de magistério*. The former received students who had completed primary school and gave them a four-year program that included community development courses as well as secondary school material and pedagogy. The six *escolas de habilitação* established by 1965 were administered by the Catholic church and had 649 students. Both these new courses gave the Catholic schools a greater advantage over Protestant schools. Catholic and non-Catholic students were admitted to the monitor courses, but with rare exceptions the government paid the salaries only of teachers who taught in Catholic or government schools. To add to the disadvantageous position of the Protestant schools, new government schools with *monitores* were opened near established Protestant schools. Since the government schools were free, this attracted students away from the Protestant schools.

The educational reforms shifted the balance decisively in favor of Catholic missions, putting the Protestant schools in a much inferior position. The general secretary of the Angola Evangelical Alliance visited fifteen Catholic missions in 1964, and he wrote in his report:

> The Protestant missions have the reputation of having more interest in eduction. Now the Catholic missions have surpassed us in all fields of education. With government subsidies they have thousands of students in the Rural Education program. Many teachers are being trained in the Teachers' Training School in Cuima to teach in primary schools in the villages. The minor seminary in Quipeio has 250 students and Jau has 100, all doing their first five years of secondary school. The new Holy Ghost Fathers' school in Nova Lisboa will be the largest private secondary school in

Angola. The most important new fact in the educational field is the establishment of four Teacher Training Schools for girls with large government subsidies. I have never seen such luxurious installations anyplace in Angola as in the school in the Catholic mission of Bela Vista. The contrast in personnel between this school and its neighbor — Means School at Dôndi — is striking. In addition to the Angolan staffs at each school the Catholic school has 13 nuns as teachers. Means School has one missionary teacher.[1]

But the Catholic church also felt that it suffered as a result of the government's educational reforms. Bishop Ribeiro de Santana, writing in 1966, complained of unfair competition from state schools and *monitores*.[2] He cited as proof the comparative amounts spent on instruction by the state in 1961 through the state schools and through the diocese of Sá da Bandeira. The government expended $133,000 on education in the district of Huila and only $10,800 through the diocese of Sá da Bandeira.

The educational reform was qualitative as well as quantitative. Until 1961 all primary textbooks came from Portugal and described exclusively European geography and customs. Parrot pedagogy prevailed. Some educators had been preparing new curriculum and texts, but they did not receive official support until March 1961, when the government finally recognized that new materials with illustrations and vocabulary from the daily life of the students were essential if mass education was to succeed. The new books still looked at Angola through Portuguese eyes, but some effort was made at least to look at Angola. Prewar books were exclusively Portuguese; the reformed books were colonial Angolan.

To cap the educational reform the government established the University of General Studies in 1963 with three campuses: Luanda with the faculties of arts and medicine, Sá da Bandeira with the faculty of education, and Nova Lisboa with agronomy and veterinary science. In 1963 the three campuses had 314 students; by 1966 they almost doubled the number to 600, practically all whites.

The effects of the educational reforms continued on into the 1970s as shown by the official statistics for 1970–72:

TEACHERS		1970	1971	1972
Elementary		8,714	10,065	11,979
Secondary		3,505	3,707	3,834
University		213	280	329
	Total	12,432	14,050	16,142

1. General Secretary of the Aliança Evangélica de Angola, *Carta Circular*, no. 10.
2. *Portugal em África*, nos. 133–34 (January–April 1966).

STUDENTS		1970	1971	1972
Elementary		395,293	443,552	496,217
Secondary		49,298	56,977	66,319
University		1,780	2,332	2,668
Technical		6,440	8,242	8,525
	Total	452,813	511,103	573,729

The Portuguese reformed the educational system in Angola on the assumption that it would be a significant part of a counterinsurgency program. Since Africans complained of not having access to education, the provision of schools, teachers, and new books, according to the Portuguese analysis, should have produced loyalty to Portugal. The experience in Angola, however, would seem to support those who contend that social and economic improvements may be more subversive than supportive of the established regime. Rather than satisfying the population's expectations and desires, the government's efforts, which the people never judged to be sufficient, exacerbated the frustrations and further alienated the people.

Abolition of Contract Labor

The third reform that the revolution forced on the government was the abolition of the contract labor system. The economy of Angola during the colonial period had been based on cheap labor on coffee and sugar plantations, in diamond mines, and in fisheries. Unless Angolans were assimilated or had a regular Portuguese employer to sign a work card, they were subject to forced labor, more euphemistically called "contract" labor. The larger industries reported regularly to the government in Luanda the number of workers needed. The total of "hands" requested was divided among the administrative districts and then subdivided until the African *regedores*, who had become the lackeys of the local Portuguese administrators, were ordered to bring in their quotas of men for contract. If a man had not paid his tax, he was on the top of the list of those to be "contracted." The *regedor* then consulted the village elders to discover those men who should be sent to work. If he did not find enough men by this process, the *regedor* was subject to beatings at the *posto* and perhaps also a fine. The Portuguese administrator's next recourse was to send out his African policemen (the *cipaios*) to capture men.

The word "contract" was a misnomer when it referred to the relation between the African workers and their white employers. However, the colonial government took very seriously its contract with the major employers of Angola to provide the number of workers they required. The recruiting fee that employers paid to the administrative services in many cases was equal to or exceeded the cash payment to the worker for eighteen months' labor. The Portuguese administrator had a stake in providing his quota of laborers. Aside from showing his efficiency as an official, he received a per capita bonus. The regional government doctor gave a superficial physical examination to each worker, for which he and his nurse received their per capita allowances. The men were then shipped to the coffee plantations in the north, the sugar plantations or fisheries at the coast, or the diamond mines in the interior. They were separated from their families for one to three years.

The contract laborers were exploited all along the way, and the system not only produced suffering in Angola, but protests from anti-colonialists outside of Angola who were offended by the injustice of the system. In many cases, however, the contract laborers fared little worse than their brothers or cousins who worked as volunteers for a white boss. The scandal was not so much the disadvantage of the contract workers in relation to the volunteers, but the contrast between the miserable wage of the contract workers in relation to the profits of the diamond company and the coffee and sugar plantations.

The explosion of March 15, 1961, moved the Portuguese government to abolish the contract labor system so laborers were no longer recruited forcibly through administrative officers. Rather the government licensed private labor recruiters who went into the villages to enlist men to work in the larger industries. Since the recruiters were denied the use of the coercive machinery of the administrative system, they frequently gave some small amount of money as bait to the man or his family. The competition for labor caused by the growing economy and the conscription of young men into the army improved wages and working conditions during the transition period.

The Reforms of Vatican II

The reforms of citizenship, education, and labor did not resolve the basic conflict between the Portuguese and Angolans. The Portuguese dictator Salazar had said that there were no Angolans, only Portuguese living in Angola. All Portuguese reforms were enacted with the hope of strengthening Portugal's hold on its colonies. Any move to weaken or subvert Portuguese sovereignty in Angola, Mozambique, or Guinea was treasonable and so worthy of the supreme penalty. In fact such subversion was not only treasonable, but sacrilegious. Portugal felt that it had a sacred mission to uphold the Christian faith in Africa. According to the foreign minister, Dr. Alberto Franco Nogueira, anything that weakened Portugal's control was a blow to the Christian faith. Christianity, seen through Portuguese myopia, was inextricably joined to Western European civilization.

Portugal's rulers were not only unwilling or unable to recognize the winds of change that were blowing away the political system of colonialism, but were ignorant of the equally forceful winds of change that were blowing through the Roman Catholic church. The man in the Catholic church who responded most dramatically to the winds of change was Angelo Roncalli, the popular patriarch of Venice who succeeded Pope Pius XII as Pope John XXIII. On January 25, 1959, shortly after his election, Pope John addressed seventeen cardinals gathered in the Abbey of St. Paul's Outside the Walls, reviewed the religious situation of Rome and the world, and then announced his intention of holding a diocesan synod for the city and an ecumenical council for the universal church. In his conception the council was not only to restore the church's energies and seek the forms best adapted to its present-day needs, but also to invite the separated brethren of East and West to join in the search for reunion. In subsequent messages and addresses Pope John often expressed the hope that the council would be a new Pentecost and a means of spiritual renewal for the church as well as an evident sign of its internal unity. The Italian word *aggiornamento* (updating) used by Pope John came to characterize his view of the council throughout the world.

Return to the Bible

The reforms of the council were to be applied to the whole Catholic church, but they seemed to be especially pertinent to the church in Angola. First, the daily enthronement of the Bible at the beginning of each conciliar meeting was more than liturgical ornamentalism. It signaled a restoration of sacred Scripture to the center of Catholic faith and spirituality. In Angola the Bible had been at the center of the Protestant community, but was neglected and at times banned in the Catholic community.

Two conciliar documents especially urged the church to read the Sacred Scriptures more assiduously. On November 18, 1965, Pope Paul VI promulgated the Dogmatic Constitution on Divine Revelation, which urged "earnestly and specifically... all the Christian faithful, too, especially religious, to learn by frequent reading of the divine Scriptures the 'excelling knowledge of Jesus Christ (Phil. 3:8)' for ignorance of the Scriptures is ignorance of Christ" (no. 25). Considering the importance of the liturgy in the Catholic church, perhaps the most important decision taken by the council in relation to the Bible was the norm established concerning the place of the Holy Scriptures in the liturgy:

Sacred Scripture is of paramount importance in the celebration of the liturgy. For it is from Scripture that lessons are read and explained in the homily, and psalms are sung; the prayers, collects, and liturgical songs are scriptural in their inspiration, and it is from Scripture that actions and signs derive their meaning. Thus if the restoration, progress, and adaptation of the sacred liturgy are to be achieved, it is necessary to promote that warm and living love for Scripture to which the venerable tradition of both Eastern and Western rites gives testimony. (Dogmatic Constitution on Divine Revelation, no. 24)

Specifically in reference to the Eucharist the same document directed:

So that the sacrifice of the Mass . . . can achieve its pastoral effects to the fullest . . . the treasures of the Bible are to be opened up more lavishly, so the richer fare may be provided for the faithful at the table of God's Word. In this way a more representative portion of the Holy Scriptures will be read to the people over a set cycle of years. (Nos. 49, 51)

Encouraged by the atmosphere created by the council two Angolan priests in the diocese of Nova Lisboa, Francisco Viti and Eugénio Salessu, translated *A Harmony of the Holy Gospels into Umbundu*, and it was printed in Rome in an edition of ten thousand.

The People of God

Next, Vatican II made the "people of God" the fundamental category of theological and pastoral self-understanding. This concept was developed most fully in the Dogmatic Constitution on the Church (*Lumen Gentium*) and the Decree on the Apostolate of the Laity (*Apostolicam Actuositatem*).

The former, after describing "The Mystery of the Church" in the first chapter, explains the meaning of "the people of God" in the second. Paragraph 10 defines the "common priesthood":

Christ the Lord, High Priest taken from among men (Heb. 5:1–5) made a kingdom and priests to God his Father (Apoc. 1:6; 5:9–10) out of this new people.

The baptized, by regeneration and the anointing of the Holy Spirit, are consecrated into a spiritual house and a holy priesthood. Thus through all those works befitting Christian men they can offer spiritual sacrifices and proclaim the power of Him who has called them out of darkness in His marvelous light (1 Pet. 2:4–10). Therefore, all the disciples of Christ, persevering in prayer and praising God (Acts 2:42–47) should present themselves as living sacrifices holy and pleasing to God (Rom. 12:1). Everywhere on earth they must bear witness to Christ and give an answer to those who seek an account of the hope of eternal life which is in them (1 Pet. 3:15).

Though they differ from one another in essence and not only in degree, the common priesthood of the faithful and the ministerial or hierarchical priesthood are nonetheless interrelated. Each of them in its own special way is a participation in the priesthood of Christ.

Perhaps for Angola the most significant practical action by the council to make real the term "people of God" was the first document, the Constitution on the Sacred Liturgy, in which the people were exhorted to participate in the liturgy "knowingly, actively and fruitfully" (no. 11).

In several Catholic missions, even before Vatican II, priests were preparing the people and encouraging them to participate more actively in the reading of the Scriptures, singing parts of the services and allowing them to express the exuberance of their faith. With the publication of the conciliar documents such participation was not only approved, but promoted.

Another provision of the Constitution on the Sacred Liturgy that gave reality and meaning to the phrase "people of God" was paragraph 36.3:

Since the use of the mother tongue, whether in the Mass, the administration of the sacraments, or other parts of the liturgy, may frequently be of great advantage to the people, the limits of its employment may be extended. This extension will apply in the first place to the readings and directives, and to some of the chants, according to the regulations on this matter to be laid down separately in subsequent chapters.

Obviously the use of the languages of the people not only stimulated greater participation in the liturgy, but also allowed the creation of a new sense of community for the "people of God."

Vatican II also emphasized that the church is indeed the "people of God" by recognizing a larger role for the laity. This was made most explicit in the basic document on the church, *Lumen Gentium*, in its chapters on the laity and the call of the whole church to holiness.

The Decree on the Apostolate of the Laity defined in greater detail the various responsibilities to which the laity was called and in chapter 6 described the necessity for and means to use the formation for the apostolate.

This too had very practical results in Angola in the recognition of programs for the preparation of catechists, like that in Ganda under the leadership of the Congregation of the Missionaries of Our Lady of LaSalette. It stimulated similar programs in Malanje and in Sanza Pombo in the diocese of Uige.

> The initiation of these schools and the conciliar doctrine diversified the functions of the catechists and created a new role: the chief catechist or general catechist or evangelist, according to the location. They became the coordinators and animators of the local catechists (village catechists).[3]

The Church in the Modern World

A third reform propagated by Vatican II concerned the view of the church in the world defined in *Gaudium et Spes*. This pastoral constitution reunited faith with action and ended the preconciliar attitude that reigned in Angola, assuming that Catholic Action was valid only as "pre-evangelization":

> The good news of Christ constantly renews the life and culture of fallen man. It combats and removes the errors and evils resulting from the sinful allurements which are a perpetual threat. It never ceases to purify and elevate the morality of peoples. By riches coming from above, it makes fruitful, as it were from within, the spiritual qualities and gifts of every people and of every age. It strengthens, perfects, and restores them in Christ. (No. 58)

Ten years after the promulgation of the Pastoral Constitution on the Church in the Modern World, a pastoral letter of the Angolan Episcopal Conference still used the term "pre-evangelization" to describe the activities of assistance and development that had engaged so much of the energies and resources of the church during the colonial period. It is too much to expect that one conciliar document would resolve the tension between the religious and the secular or between evangelization and social action. In fact that is not the aim of this document or of the church. It is out of that tension that evangelization is brought face to face with the reality of those who are to hear the gospel, and from this same tension the modern world is challenged to believe that there is good news.

Ecumenism

During the colonial period the Catholics and Protestants lived and labored in separate worlds. A spirit of competition at times motivated the missionaries of both communities, but direct conflicts were rare. The

---

3. Augusto Farias, "Catequistas em Angola," *Boa Nova*, no. 728 (May 1987): 20–31.

council's Decree on Ecumenism began with words that emanated from neither the Catholic nor Protestant communities of Angola. It was a challenge not only to the parochialism of Catholics and Protestants, but also to that of each separate Protestant mission:

> Promoting the restoration of unity among all Christians is one of the chief concerns of the Second Sacred Ecumenical Synod of the Vatican. The Church established by Christ the Lord is, indeed, one and unique. Yet may Christian communions present themselves to men as the true heritage of Jesus Christ. To be sure, all proclaim themselves to be disciples of the Lord, but their convictions clash and their paths diverge, as though Christ Himself were divided (1 Cor. 1:13). Without doubt, the discord openly contradicts the will of Christ, provides a stumbling block to the world, and inflicts damage on the most holy cause of proclaiming the good news to every creature. (No. 1)

The decree was promulgated on November 21, 1964, and a year and a half later, on July 13, 1966, in Luanda the Catholic archbishop, Manuel Nunes Gabriel, the Methodist bishop, Harry P. Andreassen, and the bishop of the Lusitanian Evangelical Apostolic Catholic Church of Portugal, Luís César Rodrigues Pereira, participated in a paraliturgy. In his words of welcome Archbishop Manuel remarked:

> That which a few years ago seemed an unrealizable dream, we see transformed into a consoling reality in our day: Christians of various confessions and religious denominations who have met together to make common prayers for the unity of the Holy Church.[4]

From the homily of Bishop Luís Pereira the Catholic newspaper in Luanda chose a phrase for a headline: "We have already gone so far that we cannot stop," and in his sermon Bishop Pereira added, "and much less can we turn back." Following the homily Bishop Andreassen led the congregation in prayer and then all joined in the Lord's Prayer.

The encounter of three bishops in the capital gave legitimacy to the ecumenical meetings that were being held in many places throughout Angola. However, the picture of these three white bishops — two Portuguese and one Norwegian — on the front page of *O Apostolado* made visible the fact that during the period of transition the Angolans were still not in positions of top leadership in the church.

---

4. *O Apostolado* 31, no. 2235 (July 16, 1966).

An interchurch service in Luanda in 1966: Dom Manuel Nunes Gabriel,
Dom Luís César Rodrigues Pereira, Bishop of the Lusitanian Church in Portugal,
and Bishop Harry P. Andreassen of the United Methodist Church

Angola's Bishops Call for Renewal

The Catholic bishops of Angola, all Portuguese, attended the Second
Vatican Council, and shortly after it concluded on December 8, 1965,
they signed a pastoral letter on February 9, 1966, giving a brief resumé
of the official conclusions of the council. They reported that the central
theme of the sessions was the church, and they called *Lumen Gentium*
the basic document of the council. After mentioning the other conciliar
documents, the bishops exhorted the faithful to use the period of jubilee
declared by Pope Paul VI from the beginning of the year until Pentecost
on May 29

> to prepare themselves for the renewal of their individual, domes-
> tic, public, and social Christian life which was the supreme object

The Catholic bishops of Angola in 1963: Dom Manuel Pires (Silva Porto),
Dom Daniel Gomes Junqueira (Nova Lisboa), Dom Pompeu Seabra (Malanje),
Dom Moisés Alves de Pinho (Luanda), Dom Manuel Nunes Gabriel (Luanda),
and Dom Altino Ribeiro de Santana (Sá da Bandeira)

of the Council. We appeal to our priests and to all other responsible leaders of cultural and apostolic organizations in our dioceses to organize study sessions, meetings, and conferences so that all may hear the authentic voice of the Council.

The circulation of the pastoral letter and the sessions organized in response as well as the mass media gave Angolans some information about the council, but the greatest impact of the council was produced by three priests who arrived from Portugal at the beginning of 1966. Jorge Sanches, António Fernando Santos Neves, and Waldo García had been on the faculty of the Holy Ghost Seminary in Carcavelos, a suburb of Lisbon. They transmitted effectively to the church in Angola the message of Vatican II, because they were personally enthusiastic about it; and they were placed at the largest seminary in Angola — Christ the King in Nova Lisboa. They revamped the curriculum of the seminary and organized "Pastoral Colloquies" in Nova Lisboa, Lobito, and Luanda, which had as their main topics such subjects as Pastoral Ecclesiology, Biblical Renewal, Liturgical Renewal, Pastoral Renewal, and the Task of the Laity in Postconciliar ecclesiology. Each colloquy closed by approving a series of recommendations that were very radical in the Angolan Catholic context, for example, new translations of the Bible, the Missal, and the ritual in African languages, preparation of a hymn book based on the biblical-liturgical renewal, and a new catechism.

A third initiative taken by Fernando Santos Neves, Jorge Sanches, and Waldo García was to propose the formation of a Catholic Superior Institute, which was in fact canonically established by Daniel Gomes Junqueira, bishop of Nova Lisboa, on June 16, 1966. In the document publishing this act Bishop Daniel stated:

1. One of the first and most specific intentions of the Second Vatican Council was to make Christianity present to the contemporary world as the last document, the Constitution on the Church in the Modern World, declares.

2. Among the necessary presences of Christianity, the presence of the polydimensional universe of culture is the most fundamental because the universe of culture conditions all human activities. If this is valid for all times, it is especially true in Angola today.

3. Therefore in order to give Christian animation to culture at the superior or university level;

    In gratitude for the twenty-fifth anniversary of our episcopacy and for the centenary of the arrival of the missionaries of the Holy Ghost Congregation to this land of Angola;

As the fruit of the First Pastoral Colloquium on the Conciliar Renewal and Modernization of the Church in Angola realized in Nova Lisboa from April 12 to 15, 1966;

We have considered it proper to erect canonically the Catholic Superior Institute.

Signed — Daniel Gomes Junqueira
Bishop of Nova Lisboa[5]

In retrospect it is difficult to understand how conservative Bishop Daniel Junqueira was persuaded to create officially an institution that proposed to take the most radical elements of the Second Vatican Council and apply them to the church in Angola. Even more incredible and bizarre was the inaugural address, "The Fact and Task of the Catholic Superior Institute," given by the Rev. Antonio Fernando Santos Neves on October 25, 1966, to inaugurate the academic activities of the institute. With the governor of the district, the magistrate, the military commander, and the bishop seated on the dais, Santos Neves began: "It may come as a surprise to some, but Angola is in Africa." This struck at the heart of the official doctrine that Angola was an integral part of Portugal. Then the young, high-strung lecturer proclaimed the end of the Constantinian era. The distinguished audience that filled the hall and the honored guests on the dais obviously did not understand that they were the Constantinians whose time was up.

The three priests were not content to proclaim the message of Vatican II through the classes of the seminary and the lectures of the pastoral colloquies or the Catholic Superior Institute. Father Santos Neves collected these lessons and lectures on ecumenism that had been given in Angola, added the speech of Pope Paul VI given to the United Nations on October 4, 1965, and had them all published in the book *Ecumenismo em Angola: do Ecumenismo Cristão ao Ecumenismo Universal* (Ecumenism in Angola: From Christian Ecumenism to Universal Ecumenism).[6]

The censorship laws in Angola required that periodicals submit all their copy to the censor prior to publication. Books were not subject to such previous approval. They could be published "freely," but as soon as they were off the press they could be confiscated by the authorities. That is what happened in the case of *Ecumenismo em Angola*. It was put on sale in a few bookstores and distributed to some friends before being banned. This led not only to the confiscation of copies that could be discovered, but also to the interrogation by PIDE of people who had acquired or distributed the book.

---

5. A. F. Santos Neves, *Quo Vadis, Angola?* (Angola: Editorial Colóquios, 1974), 182.
6. A. F. Santos Neves, *Ecumenismo em Angola: do Ecumenismo Cristão ao Ecumenismo Universal* (Nova Lisboa: Instituto Superior Católico), 1968.

By January 1968 the Portuguese authorities in Luanda were more alert to the danger of Vatican II teachings than were the civil and religious leaders who listened to Father Santos Neves in October 1966. They not only banned the book, but also cancelled the First Social Colloquy of Angola, which had been scheduled for April 1–4, 1968, in Luanda.

Since both civil and ecclesiastical authorities recognized the danger in applying the teachings of Vatican II to the Angolan situation, they collaborated in removing the three subversive priests from Angola. Father Jorge Sanches was sent to the Holy Ghost headquarters in Rome to be the representative of the Portuguese province of the congregation. Father Waldo García was returned to his homeland, Spain, and Father Santos Neves was sent to Lisbon and then proceeded privately to Paris. But the expulsion of the three priests did not silence the echoes of Vatican II in Angola. The three continued their writings and personal contacts to criticize the Catholic church in Angola as a collaborator with Portuguese colonialism.

The Two Churches of Angola

Waldo García wrote an article in *Africasia* in which he described "the Two Churches of Angola": one a martyr of Portuguese colonialism and the other a collaborator, one black and the other white, one African and the other Portuguese.[7] According to Father Waldo the division reached into the hierarchy since the only black bishop was Monsignor Muaca, who was the auxiliary of the archbishop of Luanda with little possibility of independent action.

Father Jorge Sanches wrote an analysis from Rome of the Catholic mission and Portuguese colonialism, which was published in the magazine *Spiritus*.[8] It criticized the church in the Portuguese colonies that not only served the colonial policy, but its very structures were distorted by a totalitarian and colonial regime. Father Sanches contended that the church lived in a symbiotic relationship with the Portuguese state, which alienated it from the rest of the Catholic world. He insisted that the basic evil was the alliance between church and state formalized in the concordat and Missionary Accord. When the bishops tried to defend the Catholic church in Portuguese territories by pointing to the "peace" in which the missions were able to function or to the pastoral letters that proclaimed great principles of Christian morality and social justice, they

---

7. Waldo García, "The Two Churches of Angola," *Africasia* (Paris), no. 57 (January 1972).

8. Jorge Sanches, *Spiritus*, no. 51, 370–82.

were ignoring the fundamental error, which was the compact between the church and the totalitarian colonial state.

In addition to these criticisms leveled at the church from the priests who had been expelled from Angola, Catholic voices inside Angola called for reform. Father Adalberto Postioma, an Italian priest who taught in the seminary in Luanda, proposed to include in his course in social ethics the subject of the right of peoples to independence. His ecclesiastical superior in Italy and the archbishop in Luanda decided that such teaching was inappropriate for Angola, so he was transferred to Italy in 1968.

A serious effort to reform the Catholic church from within Angola was made by twenty-two younger Holy Ghost missionaries, all Portuguese, under the leadership of Father Torres Veiga. They presented a program to the Episcopal Conference in 1970 according to which they would renounce their position as state functionaries and go into the villages to live as priests with the people. They proposed to abandon the paternalistic, clerical, and domineering character of the church:

> Paternalism destroys, it does not save. It uproots and does not permit an authentic assimilation. It gives "form," but does not form. It creates an Institution, but does not produce Communion. It achieves a substitution of myths and a sense of magic, but conversion is not accomplished. Conversion implies the perfect consciousness of oneself, of one's personal dignity, and it creates demands....
>
> What church are we who accept and cooperate in this?
>
> What does Christianity mean that does not save the people?
>
> What do all these sacraments mean that do not have saving sacramental power?
>
> What is the significance of a society of the baptized (Can we really call it church?) that allows to go to waste and to its destruction a community life as rich as this of the African peoples, which even possessed biblical roots?
>
> What value has the witness of fraternal service and of poverty of a society of the baptized that demonstrates a style of superiority — an imposing, prestigious, official society intimately associated with the powers of the world and conditioned by them?
>
> What evangelical witness of understanding and of peace can the church give, when in the face of an armed conflict that has dragged on for nine years, it does not seek publicly to enable the parties to the conflict to meet at the negotiating table?

The twenty-two young Portuguese missionaries then proposed the formation of missions different from the traditional ones, as an experiment with the following characteristics: they would be (1) fraternal communities living in poverty from the fruit of their labor; (2) without subsidies of any type; (3) without legal recognition, that is, they would not be parishes and they would not have the canonical attributes of traditional parishes or missions; (4) they would not administer baptism or marriage; they would not contribute to the aid of parishes or missions, except sporadically or through the medium of missionaries as volunteers.

The Episcopal Conference responded to Father Jose Veiga in terms that Veiga described as being a "no that is a yes, and a yes that is a no." The gospel orders that our speech be simply "Yes" or "No" (Matt. 5:37).[9]

The bishops acknowledged that there were "some deficiencies" that the church should consider and remedy, but that the bishops had been attempting to do that lately. The Episcopal Conference then affirmed that the reforms could be made through the "traditional missions." It would not be necessary to adopt the methods proposed by the young missionaries. In response to the criticism of the close relationship between colonialism and the church, the bishops reminded the young priests that there is no nation in which the church is not conditioned by the politico-social situation. The conference agreed that the missionaries might create the kind of communities that were proposed, but insisted that they be established in accord with the local prelate and that these new communities be in limited areas of "first evangelization" to avoid difficulties with existing missions.

Archbishop Manuel Nunes Gabriel, reviewing this period from the perspective of 1978, defended the attitudes and actions of the hierarchy by quoting from its pastoral letter on justice of 1972:

> The attitude of the church will always be that of stimulating the promotion of justice and of collaborating in all the works that tend toward the well-being of the peoples, independently of any political situation. The church leaves to the citizens, who are properly prepared and informed, to determine the most just decisions to make in this field.[10]

Then showing that he never accepted the criticism leveled at the church for its collaboration with the colonial regime, the archbishop praised the governors general from 1962 to 1974, who granted substantial sums of money to the dioceses for their missionary activities. He noted that in 1942, the first year after the Missionary Statute, the total state subsidy to the church was about $165,000 (U.S.). During the last years before independence the subsidy had risen to $2,100,000.[11] The archbishop con-

---

9. A. F. Santos Neves, *Quo Vadis Angola?* 246.
10. Manuel Nunes Gabriel, *Angola: Cinco Séculos de Cristianismo* (Queluz: Literal, 1978), 528.
11. Ibid.

cluded that during this transition period the "religious progress" was a "consoling reality" in spite of the dark background.

Reforms in Protestant Community

Reforms were also changing the form and spirit of the Protestant community. On January 16, 1965, the Methodist church received its first resident bishop, Harry Peter Andreassen, a Norwegian missionary who had worked in Angola since 1952. It is significant that the invitation to the consecration ceremony was sent out by "the Church of Christ in Angola (Methodist Branch)." This reflected the consensus among most of the Protestant groups that they should use a common name, "the Church of Christ in Angola." Until 1965 the comity divisions persisted so there was little overlapping on the map of the Protestant communities of Angola.

However, restrictions on the Protestant organizations and activities during the transitional period undermined the fragile unity being formed. Meetings of the three organizations that aimed to unite the Protestants — the Alliance, the Portuguese Language Congress, and the Youth Congress — were all banned from 1962 to 1973. Bishop Andreassen added to the regional isolation by dropping the name, Church of Christ in Angola, from his stationery and replacing it with the United Methodist Church. The Protestant denominations had always been divided, but the use of a common name expressed a unity of faith, hope, and love.

Not all Protestants considered "the Church of Christ in Angola" an appropriate term. Pastor António Tiago S. Pereira wrote an article in the *Baptista de Angola*, a publication of the Convenção Baptista de Angola (Angolan Baptist Convention) in which he asked, "Is it biblical to use the term 'Church of Christ in Angola'?" He answered in the negative, but his loosely reasoned argument collapsed with the last paragraph, which states: "Our churches are known as Baptist Churches by virtue of biblical baptism, which we practice and preach — the only kind in the New Testament. We like this popular name that identifies us. We will stick with it." Pastor Tiago does not even claim that the term "Baptist Church" is biblical, just that it is popular. During the transition period the Baptist churches that belonged to the Angolan Baptist Convention were Portuguese in that its pastors had come from Europe. They were located in cities and served primarily, but not exclusively, the white community.

In the Protestant community from 1961 to 1970 forces were at work to give more responsibility to Angolan leaders and to divide the Protestants regionally and denominationally. The reduction in the number of Protestant missionaries accelerated the process of devolution by which administrative control of all phases of the work passed from the hands of missionaries to those of Angolan leaders. This process was complete in the north of Angola, where all missionaries were removed whether by the action of the government or by the missionary societies, as in the case of the Canadian Baptist Foreign Mission Society.

In central Angola the war did not force the complete withdrawal of the Protestant missionaries, but the restrictions on visas reduced their number. Over the question of voluntary withdrawal the UCBWM and the United Church of Canada carried on a dialogue with their missionaries by correspondence. On November 17, 1967, the two North American boards sent a letter to their missionaries instructing them to come home on furlough according to the regular schedule, which would have meant the absence of all but one couple within a few months. The missionaries had not taken their regular furloughs after 1961, when the government refused to grant return visas. The letter precipitated a discussion among the missionaries not only regarding their permanence in Angola, but also concerning the reforms that would be advisable to meet the changing situation in Angola. The author had proposed several reforms. First, the church should adjust its organization to recognize that the centers of population had moved from the rural *olombala* (kings' villages) to the cities. Specifically this would have meant moving the office of the general secretary of the Council of Evangelical Churches of Central Angola and the United Seminary from Dôndi to Nova Lisboa/Huambo. Second, since the state would increasingly assume responsibility for the education of all its citizens, the schools would lose their role as the main instrument of evangelism and Christian education. Therefore the church should focus its resources on developing new programs of evangelism and Christian education. Third, secularism had penetrated both African traditional, magico-sacred culture and the Christian missionary culture so the cohesion of Protestant Christendom was weakening. Therefore the Protestant churches should not trust so firmly in the institutions of the mission station and the Christian village. They constituted ghettos into which the community retreated to find security in the midst of war and revolution.

This analysis of urbanization, government intervention in health-education, and the secularization of Angolan society with the respective reforms was not accepted by Protestant leaders, whether Angolans or foreigners, any more easily than the end of Constantinianism was accepted by the Catholic hierarchy. However, the discussion precipitated by the letter from the two North American boards at least raised some of the issues that the church would be facing in the next decades.

To further the discussion the boards invited two missionaries representing different positions to come to Toronto and New York for a consultation. Amy Schauffler and Lawrence W. Henderson presented their views at a joint meeting in Toronto in April 1968. Henderson repeated the analysis and suggested reforms, while Schauffler defended the majority view. The representatives of the boards were more sympathetic to Henderson's position than his missionary or Angolan colleagues had been, but in accord with their tradition of allowing the church and mission to exercise their autonomy, the board did not order the missionaries home nor demand that the church accept the reforms.

The boards sent a letter to the church with Schauffler and Henderson as they returned to Angola in which they reaffirmed their "deepest love and concern, and . . . admiration for the Christian way in which all have carried on in a most difficult time." They also expressed their hope that the way would remain open to continue the partnership "in vital programs of church growth and development, Christian education, leadership training, medical work, etc."

The board secretaries, John A. Reuling and Roy E. Webster, then commented on the roles of church and missionary in Angola:

> We urge that in spite of current difficulties and restrictions the church press forward in this process of assuming responsibility, first because the rapid decrease of missionary personnel and restrictions on missionaries' travel make it essential; secondly, and more importantly because until the final state of responsibility is assumed, all the previous progress is incomplete. The traditional role of the missionary in Angola as buffer between the church and authorities is not only imperilled by the lack of missionaries, but tends to deny the church the opportunity to assume true responsibility for its work.

The letter then made two suggestions regarding the orientation of work in Angola:

a. The church must continue to give high priority to theological education. As general educational standards are raised, standards of theological education must also rise. This priority must be expressed concretely in personnel, funds and creativity.

b. The main means of evangelization and Christian education in all of Africa during the past century has been the school. In some measure today, but overwhelmingly tomorrow, this means will not be in the hands of the church or the mission. Every church of which we know has delayed too long in instituting genuine programs of Christian education to meet the needs of its children as education by the state has increased, and many have held on to the parochial schools for far too long a time.

The board secretaries then addressed a letter to the governor-general of Angola. This was deemed advisable because he had given special permission for the missionaries to meet in February 1968 in Huambo to discuss the first board letter, had granted reentry visas to three Canadian missionaries, and special reentry visas so that Schauffler and Henderson could attend the consultation in Toronto.

The two returning missionaries presented the boards' letter in person to the governor-general on the morning they arrived in Luanda. Rebocho Vaz, the governor-general, read the Portuguese translation and reacted immediately to certain phrases. The General Statement of the Purposes of the Missionary Presence appended to the letter contained these sentences: "Yet, prophetic affirmations by the missionary, and by the church which sends him, may have political implications and be considered subversive to the government, but they are required by his Christian conscience. This is particularly true if the missionary faces a situation in which basic human rights are violated, social injustices perpetrated or tolerated and a majority of citizens is governed by an alien minority by the sole right of conquest and settlement."

The governor-general responded that the Portuguese government was working to give the Africans "something better than they are thinking of. Instead of just being offered an Angolan nationality, or a Mozambican nationality they are being given the Portuguese nationality, which is broader and more ancient than any nationality that might be created."

He then expressed his doubts about being able to arrive at a working understanding with the missions if the philosophies of the government and the missions differ so basically. Schauffler and Henderson referred to the statement from the boards: "The expatriate missionary enters a sovereign state not by right, but by sufferance of the duly constituted authority of that country. It is expected of the missionary that he will render appropriate respect and obedience to the laws of the land." The governor-general was not happy with the ambivalent position of "respect and obedience" together with "prophetic utterances" about self-determination. However, he seemed disposed to admit reluctantly that individual missionaries could make a positive contribution in Angola in spite of the boards' purposes.

Next he showed his concern about the external activities of the missions. Even though some understanding could be reached internally, the problem of the missions cooperating with anti-Portuguese organizations outside of Angola and especially in the neighboring territories was very complicated. The governor-general cited especially the activities of Mr. David Grenfell in the Congo with Angolan refugees.

Changes Forced on Protestant Missions

The discussion by church, missionaries, and government of the increasingly critical situation caused by the reduction of the number of Protestant missionaries and the restrictions of their travel did not lead to intentional reforms. Some changes, however, were inevitable. When a mission station was left without missionary personnel, an Angolan had to be named director. Lote Malheiro Savimbi, who had been the school inspector, became the director of the Chilesso mission in 1966 when the last resident missionary departed. During his many years of service on the Benguela Railway (CFB), he had learned to deal with government officials, but his job in Chilesso was made especially difficult since he was the father of Jonas Savimbi, the president of UNITA, who was considered a traitor and public enemy.

By the end of the transition period most of the mission stations on the central highlands had Angolan directors who were recognized, at least de facto, by the Portuguese authorities.

Another change was the implementation of programs to strengthen the urban churches. Ironically the person who planned and executed these programs was Amy Schauffler, who had opposed so strongly the suggestion that church institutions be moved from their original rural centers to the growing cities. In August 1970 the Rev. Miss Schauffler led the first course for urban pastors in Nova Lisboa/Huambo, which included excursions to Luanda and Sá da Bandeira.

An ecclesiastical reform adopted by the Council of Evangelical Churches in Central Angola during this period was the naming of a general pastor in each of the churches; this person would be a pastor to the pastors and assume certain administrative responsibilities. The position was to be rotated every few years so that most of the pastors would have the experience. They corresponded roughly to the Methodist district superintendents without their clearly defined responsibilities.

Two forces — urbanization and strategic hamlets — awoke the church to the realization that the Christian village could no longer be its basic unit. Military activity in some rural areas and economic development in the cities pushed and pulled the population toward urban concentrations. From 1960 to 1970 the urban population increased steadily. The cities mixed people of all regions, languages, and religions in richly blended quarters or neighborhoods (*bairros, muceques,* and *sanzalas*). The Methodist classes in Luanda and the regional church groups in Lobito sought to maintain a semblance of Protestant community in the pluralistic cities.

Strategic hamlets were not a new government tool. "Rural concentrations" had been used by the government in the north of Angola to fight against sleeping sickness (trypanosomiasis). Bakongo were forced to abandon their inaccessible villages and build houses along the main roads so nurses could inoculate the population against the disease. This system was adopted in 1961 to the pattern of strategic hamlets used against guerrilla fighters in Malaya, Philippines, and Vietnam. Military officials argued that concentrating the Angolans into larger villages alongside the roads patrolled by the military would deny the insurgents the aid and comfort they formerly received from the local populace. Civilian officials supported the plan, maintaining that strategic hamlets provided the opportunity to extend medical, educational, agricultural, and sanitary services to the people.

The strategic hamlets mixed the populations of the erstwhile Catholic, Protestant, and traditional villages, and with rare exceptions neither the people themselves nor the military and civil authorities had time or resources to construct proper residences or the various facilities for the health and welfare services that had been promised. The military and civilian officials had difficulty coordinating their plans and instructions to the people, and lack of harmony among the civilian agencies and bureaus caused considerable confusion.

The disruption of the life of the Christian villages was a serious challenge to the church. In some cases it was met positively, and the church took the mixture of population as a new opportunity for service and witness. In other cases the church became lost in the social and cultural confusion.

The reforms pressed upon the church during this transitional period moved in common directions: from paternalism to self-determination, from clericalism to lay responsibility, and from dependence to independence. The Holy Ghost missionaries criticized the paternalistic stance of the Portuguese Catholic hierarchy and urged the recognition of the church as the people of God. The reduction in numbers and restrictions on Protestant missionaries forced Angolan leaders to assume new responsibilities in all departments of church activities. Even one government program moved against paternalism and toward self-determination.

Extensão, Rural Extension

Hermann Possinger, a German agricultural engineer who had worked as a senior researcher in tropical agriculture and economy at the Institute for Economic Research, Munich, and had conducted research in Tanzania, Kenya, Uganda, Angola, Mozambique, Madagascar, South Africa, Ethiopia, and Sudan, designed the *Rural* program for Angola. After Possinger's investigation of the rural economy of Angola in 1963 and 1965–67 the Portuguese government agreed to support a pilot project of rural extension in the districts of Andulo and Nharea in central Angola. This area was chosen for several reasons: it was occupied by the energetic Umbundu people; they produced large crops of Arabic coffee, a valuable crop, and strategically it was on the left bank of the Cuanza River, which divided central Angola between the peaceful area and the part perturbed by the "terrorist movements." Possinger was able to sell this project to the government as the surest way to avoid subversion.

The government's Rural Extension program owed its short-lived success to the churches, which provided local leaders and organized communities with experience in community development projects. In all parts of Angola the Protestant missions and churches had been preparing catechists, teachers, nurses, and pastors who were doing rural extension work, although that term was not used. In the most intensive and extensive way Currie Institute and Means School in Dôndi had been training rural extension workers, who were not only trained in appropriate technology for agriculture, health, cooking, arts and crafts, etc., but were motivated and trained to motivate others.

In the 1950s the Council of Evangelical Churches of Central Angola had its own rural extension program called *Melhoramento do Povo* (People's Development). Teams of construction, agricultural, health, and religious instructors contracted with villages to build schools and clinics, make floor or roof tile for residences, dig bore-hole latrines, or undertake some other project for the good of the community. The villages had to agree to supply the labor and to provide room and board for the team of workers who would direct the project. While the villagers were gathered to work on the project, time was reserved for lessons in public health, nutrition, agriculture, Bible, and family budgeting. The program published booklets on a variety of such subjects, which were used not only during the special time of a project, but on other occasions within Protestant church programs as well as by Catholics and even by some government programs. Dr. Castillo Soares of the Department of Education made a lengthy and laudatory reference to the People's Development Program in his study on rural welfare in Angola (*Bem-Estar Rural em Angola*). It is intriguing to contemplate what might have been accomplished if the Chilesso church's 11 pastorates and 277 villages had been explicitly integrated into the Rural Extension program. Several of the government workers from Possinger on down were well disposed toward the Protestant work and would have been willing to cooperate more actively with Protestant village and area personnel. However, one of their problems was to overcome the suspicion and even hostility of other government agencies. Possinger discussed these problems in a speech delivered in Nova Lisboa in 1970:

The white population fears that the action of the extensionist in relation to the native farmer will give the African an attitude of extreme emancipation, which will in some ways hurt their business. The lower level of administrative officials fear that the nonpaternalistic activity of the Pilot Project may emancipate the populations to the point of prejudicing the type of contact which the authorities have traditionally maintained with the people.

The end of the four-year experimental period of the Rural Extension program coincided with the political independence of Angola, so we will never know what it might have accomplished in Angola had it been able to continue its ambitious plans.

The ecclesiastical and spiritual reforms of the Vatican Council and the socioeconomic reforms of the Rural Extension program were hopeful signs of a positive transition from colonialism to independence, but in neither field were the time and support sufficient to realize their potential.

Angolan Catholic Bishops

The church's transition from colonialism to independence involved in part the substitution of foreign leaders by Angolans. The first black Catholic bishop in the world was Dom Henrique, son of King Afonso of the Kongo, who was named bishop in 1520, but never exercised the functions of a bishop. Four hundred and fifty years later, in 1970, the Rev. Eduardo André Muaca was ordained bishop in the Church of St. Paul in Luanda.

He was born on October 9, 1924, in Cabinda in the village of São Miguel, which belonged to the Lucula mission. As a youngster he was orphaned and became a boarding student at the Lucula mission, where he finished his primary education and began his secondary. From Cabinda André Muaca passed to the minor seminary in Malanje and then to Luanda, where he completed philosophy and theology courses.

After ordination to the priesthood on January 18, 1953, Muaca taught in the seminary in Luanda for six years until he was placed in the Maiombe mission in Cabinda as assistant director, where he served from 1959 to 1961. In 1961 he was named canon of the archdiocese of Luanda and vice-rector of the seminary. In 1966 he was sent to Rome, where he was licensed in philosophy and for a year attended a course in pastoral theology in Madrid. Returning to Luanda he reassumed his duties as professor in the seminary and also in the Pope Pius XII Institute of Social Service.

The episcopal consecration of Eduardo André Muaca on May 31,

*Dom Eduardo André Muaca, first Angolan Catholic bishop
since Dom Henrique in the sixteenth century*

1970, was a visible step in the passage from colonialism to independence. Three years later on the death of Bishop Pompeu Seabra, Eduardo André Muaca was promoted to the position of resident bishop of Malanje to become the first Angolan Catholic bishop with full episcopal authority.

In the same year, 1970, a second Angolan was ordained bishop, Armando Amaral dos Santos. He was born on March 4, 1929, in Capeio, in the diocese of Silva Porto, of a European father and a mestizo mother. The church recognized his character and intelligence as a young lad and steered Armando to the diocesan seminary for his preparatory training. He did his philosophy and theology courses in Nova Lisboa, and after he received the order of deacon, his bishop sent him to Rome, where he was ordained a priest and was graduated in canon law.

Returning to Angola in 1960 Arnaldo Amaral dos Santos became the parish priest of General Machado (Camacupa) and director of the local Catholic school. Father Amaral was known especially for his artistic gifts expressed in music, painting, and liturgy.

The Vatican created the diocese of Benguela in 1970 and named Dom Armando Amaral dos Santos as its first bishop. He soon established himself as an independent and austere leader whom the archbishop described as at times appearing too stubborn in his ways; if he was convinced that he was right, he would not deviate from his way.[12] The church never discovered what kind of leader he would have been under political independence since Bishop Armando was killed in an automobile accident on October 13, 1973, as he was driving to the Balombo mission on a pastoral visit.

Protestant Leadership

The Methodist church also consecrated its first Angolan bishop during this period. The first resident Methodist bishop, a Norwegian, Harry P. Andreassen, had been elected by the Africa Central Conference in 1964, and he was reelected in 1968. In 1972 Emílio Júlio Miguel de Carvalho was elected as the first Angolan bishop of the Methodist church.

Bishop Emílio was born on August 3, 1933, in Pungo Andongo, the son of Pastor Júlio João Miguel and Eva Pedro de Andrade. The Carvalhos are one of the most distinguished Protestant families in Angola. Pastor Júlio went to Toronto to attend the World Council of Christian Education meeting in 1950 with pastors Jessé Chipenda and Frederico Mussili. Prior to that he served a variety of pastorates from small "bush" outstations to the largest city church.

Emílio de Carvalho had been granted his Bachelor of Divinity degree in Brazil in 1958 and then went to the United States where he received a master's degree from Garrett Seminary and Northwestern University in 1960. In the same year on June 6 he was ordained deacon by Bishop Northcott while still in the United States.

---

12. Gabriel, *Angola: Cinco Séculos de Cristianismo*, 551.

Pastor Emílio returned to Angola and was appointed minister of the Central Methodist Church in Luanda. In 1965, after several months in jail, he became a professor and principal of Emmanuel Theological Seminary in Dôndi. At the Angola Annual Conference Emílio de Carvalho was ordained elder on January 2, 1966, by Bishop H. P Andreassen. He married Marelina Stella de Jesus Figueiredo on August 6, 1966, and they have three children: Ari Cesar, Eunice Paula, and David Mauro.

After being elected bishop by the Africa Central Conference Emílio de Carvalho was consecrated by Bishop Escrivo Zunguzo of Mozambique on October 21, 1972, and assigned to the Angola area.

A second distinguished Protestant family was the Chipendas in central Angola. During the transition period (1961–74) José Chipenda was outside Angola preparing himself academically and by experience to play a leadership role in independent Angola. In 1955 when José Chipenda finished his course at the Presbyterian Theological Seminary in Carcavelos, Portugal, the mission board had suggested that if he returned to Angola to serve a few years, another scholarship could be made available. He returned to Lobito, where he was ordained in 1955, and served as pastor there in the Canata church, where his father had been pastor before him. In 1960 the opportunity came for more study, and Pastor José left Angola for the Hartford Seminary Foundation in Hartford, Connecticut. After completing that course the Chipendas went to New York City, where Pastor José finished a Bachelor of Arts at Pace College.

Two outstanding Protestant families were united in 1957 when Eva de Carvalho and José Chipenda were married in Dôndi. When the scholarship was offered to José Chipenda in 1960, it did not include Mrs. Chipenda and their two children, Selma and Gilberto. The mission board thought that the family might be separated for a year or so and then reunited. However, when the war broke out in Angola in early 1961 it was clear that the politico-military situation in Angola made Mr. Chipenda's return to Angola dangerous and Mrs. Chipenda's exit from Angola difficult. She did succeed in getting to Lisbon but was under close surveillance by the Portuguese police. Many Angolan students had fled Portugal in 1961 and 1962; those who remained were watched constantly. Finally by cooperation between the mission board and CIMADE in France, Mrs. Chipenda and her two small children were able to travel in a leaky fishing boat from southern Portugal to North Africa, where they were met and provided with air passage to the United States.

From 1966 to 1968 José Chipenda worked with college students in the United States, and in 1969 he accepted a position with the World Student Christian Federation in Nairobi, Kenya. This gave him an opportunity to visit many African nations and to become acquainted with the church in

Pastor José Belo Chipenda and his wife, Eva de Carvalho Chipenda

Africa. While in Nairobi Eva Chipenda made a significant contribution to the textile design industry.

The World Council of Churches invited José Chipenda to Geneva to serve as secretary of its Programme to Combat Racism in 1973. He traveled widely in this job until 1980, when the Chipendas returned to Angola.

Conclusion

Every phase of Angolan life changed significantly during the transition period from 1961 to 1974.

Politically the demise of Portuguese premier Antonio Salazar, who suffered a stroke on September 6, 1968, and died in July 1970, was reflected in Angola as some Portuguese and a few Africans recognized that the power of the Salazar regime was crumbling. Hope for meaningful political change was aroused.

Salazar had recognized in 1961 that a prompt military and political reaction was not sufficient to defend Angola and its other colonies. Economic development was necessary for Portugal to maintain political control. For twenty-five years Salazar had followed an economic system designed to exclude or severely limit foreign investments and to exploit the colonies for the benefit of the metropole. The colonial wars forced Salazar to change this policy, and the door was opened to foreign capital. The result was dramatic as Angola's gross internal product increased more than threefold from $850 million in 1963 to $2,800 million in 1973.[13]

The three reforms described in this chapter — citizenship for all Angolans, abolition of forced labor, and expansion of educational opportunities — combined with the crumbling of Salazar's dictatorship and general economic growth, transformed all phases of Angola's life.

The church accompanied the transition from colonialism to independence by replacing Portuguese and foreign leaders with Angolans and by participating in its *aggiornamento* (updating) stimulated by Vatican Council II.

The Angola that gained political independence in 1975 was much different from Angola in 1961, when the colonial era ended. The question facing Angola and the church in Angola at the end of 1975 was, "How many of the changes accomplished during the transition period would survive the trauma of political independence?"

---

13. United Nations A/9623, V Report of Special Committee on the Implementation of the Declaration on the Granting of Independence to Colonial Countries and Peoples (1974), October 8, 1974, 6.

PART III

INDEPENDENCE AND CIVIL WAR
1975–1991

Chapter 12

The Church Faces Independence April 25, 1974– November 11, 1975

When did the period of independence begin? The easy answer is November 11, 1975, the official date of Angola's political independence. On November 10, 1975, the Portuguese high commissioner, Admiral Leonel Cardoso, announced in a brief ceremony in Luanda that he was transferring power to the Angolan people, but not a single Angolan was present. The Portuguese flag was lowered and some two thousand Portuguese troops quietly boarded naval transports to return to Lisbon, retracing the route of Diogo Cão, who had arrived at the mouth of the Congo River almost five centuries earlier.

The Coup in Lisbon: April 25, 1974

In retrospect, however, it appears more accurate to say that the colonial era ended on April 25, 1974. On that date the Movement of the Armed Forces (MFA) in Lisbon overthrew in an almost bloodless coup d'état the police state that had ruled Portugal for forty-eight years. At twelve minutes after midnight the announcer on the Catholic radio station read the chorus of a prohibited song:

Grândola, vila morena, Terra da fraternidade
O povo é quem mais ordena, Dentro de ti ó cidade.

Grândola, dusky village, Land of Liberty
The people are the rulers, within you, O city.

At this signal, the MFA detained the commanders of the barracks and occupied the government radio-television stations without resistance. Simultaneously, the young officers took control of the national bank, the international airport, and the key highways leading to Lisbon.

At 4:20 A.M. the MFA broadcast an appeal to all inhabitants of Lisbon to stay in their houses and keep calm. Commands were given to the police, national guard, and other militarized units that were not part of the MFA to avoid any confrontation with the armed forces. The only violent confrontation on April 25 was between the MFA and the political police, the Direcção Geral de Segurança (DGS), in which five persons were killed: two DGS agents, two civilians, and one off-duty soldier.

The population of the capital did not obey the appeal, but, out of curiosity, filled the streets and soon began to show enthusiastic support for the revolutionary forces. As the coup proceeded peaceably, except for the shots exchanged around the DGS headquarters, the public gave flowers to the soldiers who patrolled the streets in their military vehicles, and a red carnation in the mouth of a rifle became the symbol of the revolution.

The Portuguese did not know just who or what the MFA was, but within twenty-four hours after the coup began, the Junta of National Salvation appeared on national TV and pledged to govern Portugal according to the program of the MFA.

On April 26 all the newspapers carried the program of the MFA. The first phrase of the document referred to the colonial situation: "Considering that after thirteen years of war in the overseas territories, the regime in power had not succeeded in defining concretely and objectively an overseas policy that would lead to peace among the Portuguese of all races and creeds."[1]

April 25 dramatically ended a political era in Portugal, but the impact on Angola was not immediately clear. The colonial regime seemed to continue as Silvino Silvério Marques, who had been a hardline colonialist governor-general from 1962 to 1966, was reinstated on June 11, 1974. Fighting between Portuguese and nationalist troops continued, although at a low level, for six months until the MPLA and the FNLA signed cease-fires in October 1974.

---

1. Otelo Saraiva de Carvalho, *Alvorada em Abril*, 2d ed. (Amadora: Livraria Bertrand, 1977), 630.

The church in Angola was more prepared for independence than other sections of the population and it recognized more promptly the significance of the change that took place on April 25, 1974.

Pastoral Note

On May 7, 1974, less than two weeks after the coup in Lisbon, the Catholic bishops of Angola issued a "pastoral note" concerning the new situation in Angola caused by the events of April 25 in Portugal. The note offered four counsels:

1. The public powers should use all their efforts to end the war, which for thirteen years has had an impact on Angola;

2. In the decisions to be taken for the political future of this land, one cannot forget the historical and social situation;

3. Experience has shown that a brusk change of institutions in general brings more damage than advantages: much good already accomplished is destroyed and existing evils are aggravated;

4. We should frankly recognize that the relations between various levels of the population do not always proceed with justice and Christian charity. We must deplore, especially in recent years, unjustifiable excesses by all parties.

Seizing the opportunity of the Holy Year that had been observed at the level of local churches under the theme of "Renovation and Reconciliation," the bishops recalled that "reconciliation was an indispensable condition for healing the wounds of the past and opening new paths to a promising life for our people."[2]

Then on June 6, 1974, the Conference of Bishops issued a communication entitled "The Christian Moment in Angola." In its first chapter, "The Church in the Present Political Conjuncture in Angola," it stated:

It is in full conformity with human nature that there should be juridico-political structures providing all citizens in an ever better fashion and without any discrimination the practical possibility of freely and actively taking part in the establishment of the juridical foundations of the political community and in the direction of public affairs, in fixing the terms of reference of the various public bodies, and in the election of political leaders. All citizens, therefore, should be mindful of the right and also the duty to use their free vote to further the common good. The church praises

---

2. *Boletim Eclesiástico de Angola e S. Tomé* 32–35 (January 1972–December 1975): 104.

and esteems the work of those who for the good of men devote themselves to the service of the state and take on the burdens of office.[3]

The bishops continued their analysis of the "Christian moment" by affirming that the church did not have any political position except the gospel, but was open to the pluralism of options proposed by its members. "Extremist parties," however, were not included in these acceptable options. More specifically the hierarchy declared that Christians could not affiliate with any party that included totalitarian, materialist, racist, tribalist, or other similar ideological principles. The bishops recognized that although the clergy could not be political leaders or militants of any party, they had the duty to promote the participation of the faithful in political life solely in the light of the gospel.

The bishops noted that each people and each country had its own characteristics, which it could not abdicate, and affirmed that the majority of Angola's population was Christian. Even the Africans who had not been touched by Christianity were declared to have a spiritual vision of life, as Pope Paul VI stated in his message directed in 1967 to the people of Africa. Therefore Angolans must be on guard against the danger of ideologies that radically confront the fundamental spiritual orientation of the peoples.

"The Construction of Peace," the second chapter of the bishops' communication, contended that a necessary foundation of peace — the right of the Angolan people to choose its own future — had been recognized by the program of the MFA. "The Guarantee of Peace" cited in the third chapter was the spirit of clemency and an avoidance of reprisals to assure peace for the future and not repeat the cycle of injustices and recriminations. The bishops recognized the importance of defining with justice the concept of "Angolan" and added that such a definition should not be by color or any arbitrary discrimination, which reason or faith condemned. All — blacks, whites, mestizos, and others — would make Angola a great people and a great nation, in which there should be a worthy place for everyone dedicated to the tasks that the construction of a new world imposed.

In the fourth chapter, "To Deserve Liberty," the basic principle is expressed that "Liberty can only be deserved through responsibility."

The pastoral letter concluded with a plea for reconciliation and pardon: "If you wish to be happy for a moment, get revenge. If you wish to be happy forever, pardon."[4]

---

3. Ibid., 105.
4. Ibid., 105–10.

The bishops who had ruled the Catholic church during the colonial and transition periods signed these documents in May and June 1974, recognizing the justice of the impending political change, but remnants of their basic conservative stance were still evident. They warned against the dangers of radical change and affirmed the necessity of pardon and reconciliation so that those who had administered colonial oppression would not be subject to revolutionary oppression. It can be recorded to the credit of the Catholic hierarchy, however, that it recognized that the Constantinian era had ended in Angola on April 25, 1974.

In September 1974 Cardinal Umberto Mozzoni was sent to Angola to study with the episcopacy the most important problems that the church was facing as the nation approached independence. One of the conclusions of the consultation was the request that the Vatican create four new dioceses.

The official response from the Vatican was not published until August 10, 1975, but it was obvious that the Catholic church was accompanying the march of the nation toward independence and that the four new dioceses would be headed by Angolan bishops.

On November 22, 1974, even before the new dioceses were created, the Rev. Zacarias Kamwenho was consecrated and named titular bishop of Tabla and auxiliary of the archbishop of Luanda.

The Episcopal Conference took another step on the way from colonialism to independence by signing a pastoral letter, "The Church and Angolan Culture," on January 10, 1975. The bishops expressed their joy at the imminent independence of Angola and communicated their decision that the church be more open to the African people by a deeper incarnation in the new society.[5]

The pastoral letter in its first section, "An Authentic Incarnation Here and Now," referred to the Dogmatic Constitution on the Church of Vatican II and affirmed that each local church — i.e., a bishop in communion with the priests — makes present and visible the universal church cooperating in the edification of the whole mystical Body of Christ. The mission of the local church cannot be different from the mission of the whole church, but it can have its own particular characteristics.

The letter affirmed that the incarnation required the church in Angola, within the limits of its competence, to be authentically African in order to serve the Africans. It would have to force itself, more than it had, to be with the people, of the people, and speak the people's language. This represented an attitude opposed to the past policy of assimilation.

The bishops stated that God requires all Angolan Christians to be authentically Angolan, as Paul VI declared that "the African, just because he becomes a Christian does not deny himself, but assumes the ancient

---

5. Ibid., 115–22.

values of his tradition."[6] The pastoral letter then indicated two ancient African values: (1) the spiritual life penetrates all authentic Africa life, as all beings and visible nature are tied to the world of the invisible and the spirit, and (2) African culture attributes great importance to the family, to paternal authority and the paradigmatic role that the institution of the family has in facing political society. We noted in chapter 1 that these were the two primary characteristic of the soil in which the church was planted a century before this pastoral letter: African life is spiritual and family-centered.

The bishops concluded by appealing to all Christians to be both children of Angola and children of the church.

New Dioceses

On August 10, 1975, three months before Angola was to celebrate its political independence from Portugal, Pope Paul VI erected four new dioceses and provided bishops so that each of the main political capitals would have its ecclesiastical head.

Henrique de Carvalho/Saurimo was separated from the diocese of Malanje and included the entire administrative district of Lunda. The diocese of Novo Redondo, to be called Ngunza (and later Sumbe), was carved out of the archdiocese of Luanda and covered the district Cuanza South plus the post of Calucinga in the district of Bié. Along the border between Angola and Namibia, the district of Cunene became the diocese of Pereira d'Eça, which adopted the traditional name of Njiva. Finally the pope created the largest geographic diocese of Serpa Pinto, or Menongue, which embraced the district of Cuando-Cubango and two areas of the district of Huila: Ganguelas and Jamba, which had been within the diocese of Sá da Bandeira.

Canon Manuel Franklin da Costa was named first bishop of the diocese of Henrique de Carvalho/Saurimo. He was born in Cabinda on August 31, 1921, the son of Joaquim da Costa and Maria Rosa Imaculadade Jesus Costa. After completing his preparatory courses in the seminaries of Lândana and Lucula and philosophy and theology in Luanda, Father Manuel Franklin da Costa was ordained in Luanda on January 25, 1948. He taught in the Luanda seminary from 1948 to 1953 and became the editor of *O Apostolado*.

The Rev. Franklin da Costa accompanied the archbishop, Dom Moisés Alves de Pinho, to Rome in 1960. On the eve of his embarkation in Lisbon for Luanda the police detained him, and he was forced to stay in Portugal until 1974. During the war years he studied in Braga in

---

6. Ibid., 118.

the faculty of philosophy and also taught there. In 1975 he returned to Braga to defend his dissertation and receive his doctorate.

Dom Franklin, as first bishop of Henrique de Carvalho/Saurimo, chose to receive episcopal consecration in his homeland, Cabinda, where his mother was living. On September 14, 1975, while the choral group of the Lucula mission performed songs in Fiote, the regional language, the apostolic delegate, Dom Giovanni de Andrea, presided at the ceremony. The delegate's homily focused particularly on the role of the bishop as the successor of the Apostles, affirming that "in the bishop . . . is Christ himself." Bishop Manuel Franklin da Costa took possession of his diocese of Saurimo on September 28, 1975.

In his address to the congregation in the cathedral of Nossa Senhora da Assunção, Archbishop Dom Manuel Nunes Gabriel noted that in September of 1975 people were asking what would be the future of the Catholic church in Angola in the face of the convulsions shaking the country. The archbishop responded that the future of the church is in the hands of its children. On them depends in great part its victory or defeat, for they are the soldiers who have the obligation to defend the fortress that the Lord has entrusted to them.

To serve the new diocese of Saurimo, which had forty thousand Catholics, the bishop was supported by only seven priests. Previously this area was served by twenty priests, one brother, and nine sisters.

The second diocese created by Pope Paul VI in 1975 was Novo Redondo, for which the Rev. Zacarias Kamwenho was nominated bishop. He was born on September 5, 1934, in the village of Chimbundo, district of Bailundo, but moved as a young boy to Nova Lisboa/Huambo, where he was baptized in the Canhe mission on January 25, 1944. Three years later Zacarias Kamwenho was sent to the minor seminary in Cala for his preparatory studies and then completed his seminary course in Christ the King Seminary in Nova Lisboa. He was ordained a priest in 1961 and sent to the Bela Vista mission. In 1969 the bishop of Nova Lisboa called him to the seminary, where he was successively professor, vice-rector, and rector. He also served as vicar general.

On August 26, 1974, Zacarias Kamwenho was named auxiliary bishop of the archdiocese of Luanda and was consecrated on November 23, 1974, in Nova Lisboa. Dom Zacarias challenged the clergy and laity gathered for his installation to pursue reconciliation among all people and to generate peace.

Pope Paul VI named the Rev. Francisco Viti as the first bishop of the third newly created diocese, Serpa Pinto/Menongue. Francis Viti was born on August 15, 1933, in Quinjenje to Bartolomeu Samukula and Catarina Tchinamwile. He studied first in the Ganda mission, then in the minor seminary of Quipeio, finishing philosophy and theology in the Christ the King Seminary in Nova Lisboa. Father Viti was ordained on July 14, 1963, and sent to the parish of Vila Nova, which lies to the east of Huambo. In 1970 he completed his licentiate in the Gregorian University in Rome as well as a pastoral course in Paris. Returning to Angola, Father Viti was named rector of Christ the King Seminary, a position he held until he was named bishop in August 1975. His episcopal consecration took place in the cathedral in Nova Lisboa on September 28, 1975.

The fourth new Angolan diocese created by the pope in August 1975 was Pereira d'Eça, or Njiva, but in this case the pontiff did not name a bishop; rather he decreed that the bishop of Sá da Bandeira, Eurico Dias Nogueira, should be responsible for the new diocese. He in turn named the Reverend Carlos Mittelberger as vicar general, governor of the bishopric of Pereira d'Eça-Njiva. In the transition to political independence the Catholic church assumed that the bishops elected to the new dioceses would be Angolan; but it surprised some people when a white Angolan, Rev. Óscar Braga, was named bishop of Benguela.

Óscar Lino Lopes Fernandes Braga, who was born on September 30, 1931, of European parents in Malanje had not followed the common path leading to ordination by entering the seminary at a young age. Rather, he finished the agriculture course in Portugal in 1953, and after completing military service returned to Angola in 1955 to become farm manager at the penal colony of Damba. There Óscar Braga exercised a fruitful lay ministry for three years. In 1958 he entered the seminary in Olivais in Portugal, where he completed philosophy and theology courses and was ordained deacon. In 1964 he returned to Angola and was ordained presbyter on July 6. Braga exercised a variety of functions in the diocese of Malanje, and in 1973 was named vicar general by Bishop Eduardo Muaca. On November 20, 1974, he was nominated to be bishop of Benguela, the diocese that had been vacant since the death of Dom Armando Amaral dos Santos in October 1973.

Some observers were not only surprised but opposed to the election of a white Angolan. Bishop Eurico Nogueira of Sá da Bandeira received a letter of protest against the nomination of Father Óscar as bishop of Benguela, which was signed by fifteen priests and laymen of his diocese. Bishop Eurico of Sá da Bandeira/Lubango answered:

Isn't the new bishop of Benguela a member *pleno jure* of the Angolan ecclesiastical community? Did he not join it by baptism (and also by birth) and above all by his sacerdotal ordination, which incarnated him in the local church? Do you think that he cannot be a leader of this church because of the color of his skin, and what is the meaning of such an attitude if not pure racism? And when it is written . . . that some white bishops can continue in Angola for the Europeans, is not this a defense of the iniquitous and anti-Christian "apartheid"?[7]

In the same communication Bishop Eurico wrote that he had already, three months previously, presented his request for resignation to the pope in order that he might be replaced by someone who could serve better as pastor in a difficult hour that required qualities he did not possess in a situation unfamiliar to him.

Nevertheless Bishop Eurico did continue at his post for two more years, and Bishop Óscar Braga took possession of the diocese of Benguela.

One of the signers of the protest letter, Father Fidel Izaguirre, a Spanish priest, concluded after further correspondence with his bishop that he should leave Angola. Father Fidel agreed with the request made by "some African bishops" that they be left alone — that foreign missionaries depart for a period of five years — so that the African bishops could organize the type of local church they needed. He also accepted the Africans' suggestion that the older and better structured communities continue to supply economic support for the church in Angola.[8]

This position was also taken by some African Protestant church leaders and was termed "moratorium." It was one of the key words in the assembly of the All Africa Conference of (Protestant) Churches held in Lusaka, Zambia, in 1974. It affected the thinking and action of conciliar churches, which were represented in Angola by the British and Canadian Baptists, the United Methodist Church, the United Church of Canada, and the UCC/USA.

In January 1975 the Episcopal Conference, changed in composition by the addition of three Angolan bishops, produced a pastoral letter, "The Church and Angolan Culture." In June 1974 the bishops were emphasizing the dangers of a radical change in institutions and orientation; now, six months later, the conference called for an authentic incarnation of the church "here and now." It would leave the almost exclusively European clothing it had worn previously and place itself on the level and at the service of the majority of the population that it served.

In May 1974 the bishops insisted that "one cannot forget the historical and social situation"; by January 1975 they affirmed that the church in Angola was "free of historical bonds that condition its action . . . and will have to be authentically African to serve the Africans."[9]

The Catholic church, after the creation of the four new dioceses, embraced the whole of the new nation and through its episcopal confer-

---

7. Ibid., 354.
8. Ibid., 358.
9. Ibid., 116–17.

ence was able to respond to independence with one voice as a national church.

The Response of the United Methodist Church to Independence

The voice of the United Methodist church, with its hierarchical structure based in Luanda and its close ties to the MPLA, was heard more widely and clearly than the voices of other Protestant communities immediately following the revolution in Portugal. At its Annual Conference held from August 12 to 18, 1974, at the Quéssua mission, the United Methodist church in Angola stated its position on the political revolution.

Like the Catholic church in its pastoral letter "The Church and the Independence of Angola," the Methodist church also gave a brief resumé of its implantation and growth in Angola. It then outlined "The Attitude of the Government toward the Missions," mentioning eight specific ways in which the Portuguese government restricted the activities of the Protestant churches and discriminated against the Protestant community. The Methodist Annual Conference argued that this oppression produced a revolt on the part of the Africans — a revolt that was at first passive and later activated by the liberation movements.

In 1961 and the following years we saw with great pain the detention and expulsion of missionaries, the destruction, stoning, and burning of churches and chapels, detainment of pastors in prison without formal charge at that time or later, followed by a hideous massacre of many innocent Angolans. Among these were included many evangelical believers specifically of the United Methodist Church in Angola. The fact of someone belonging to the Protestant church was sufficient reason for an accusation in many places.

It was verified with great sadness that the colonial government instead of recognizing the errors committed by its colonial administration thought to justify itself before international opinion by blaming the Protestant missions, alleging that they had aroused the population against the government. We wish to underline the fact that Portugal had been dominantly Catholic since the beginning of its nationhood, and the Portuguese who practiced such inhuman acts called themselves Christians. We wish to underline also that the United Methodist Church in Angola did not have then, nor does it have today, any direct responsibility in the events of 1961 as was indicated.[10]

---

10. Mimeographed declaration signed August 17, 1974, by Bishop Emílio de Carvalho.

The Methodists expressed resentment toward the Catholic church, which "did not take an unequivocal position on the suffering of the Africans of various Christian denominations in Angola nor did it even protest to the government against the unjust stance and the harsh treatment inflicted on the evangelical pastors or against the expulsion of the missionaries. If it did object, it made a very weak protest only for humanitarian reasons and not because of fraternal solidarity."

The Methodist church, with all Angolans, rejoiced at the news of the fall of the Portuguese regime in Lisbon on April 25, 1974, and acknowledged "the valuable action developed by the liberation movements."

Under the heading "The United Methodist Church of Angola and Ecumenism" the Methodist statement expressed a desire to maintain the ties that had been established through the Angola Evangelical Alliance "under a plan amplified by the present Protestant churches in Angola with the objective of a possible unification in a not too distant future.... This unification, which we foresee as an irreversible reality, will become a dynamic force both in the religious as well as in the socio-politico-cultural field." Expanding its ecumenical vision, the Methodists expressed their desire that "the relations with the Roman Catholic Church should be maintained progressively within the fraternal spirit of the World Council of Churches and the Second Vatican Council."

During the summer and fall of 1974 the impact of the Portuguese coup on Angola was yet uncertain. Whites still expected to hold on to some of their colonial privileges at the same time that blacks were feeling confident enough to challenge them. In Luanda isolated incidents flared into racial conflicts. Responding to this violence the Methodist church in August concluded its statement with an appeal:

> Deploring and repudiating vehemently the dramatic events occurring in recent days in Luanda, the United Methodist Church of Angola makes an urgent appeal to the whole population of Angola without distinction of ethnic groupings to join in a common effort to preserve calm and safeguard a climate of peace, which is necessary for all of us to construct a free, independent, and progressive Angola.[11]

On August 17, 1974, Emílio Júlio Miguel de Carvalho, Bishop, signed the statement.

---

11. Ibid.

Steps toward Independence

President António de Spínola of Portugal had proposed a referendum to allow the Angolans to vote on the question of independence — which was not at all a question for the Angolans. They all agreed that they wanted independence from Portugal, although most had no clear picture of the shape of that independence. The proposal of a referendum cast doubt on the intentions of the new Lisbon regime. The intentions became a little clearer on September 10, 1974, when Guinea-Bissau became independent from Portugal and commitments were made for Mozambique's independence.

On September 30, 1974, General António de Spínola resigned as president of Portugal, and the Lisbon government scrapped the referendum plan for Angola. This removed a major barrier to independence and within days the MPLA and FNLA signed cease-fire agreements with the Portuguese government. The Angolans then focused their attention on the three liberation movements and their leaders and asked, "How will Angolans organize themselves as a nation?"

At a summit meeting in Mombasa, Kenya, from January 2 to 5, 1975, the three movements recognized each other as independent parties with equal rights and responsibilities. All other parties were to be excluded from the negotiations. They also agreed that they were not ready to take over immediately, but that a period of transition was necessary. During the transition period the three movements would work together with Portugal to lay the basis for an independent Angolan state. According to the Mombasa agreement, every inhabitant of Angola regardless of race could become a citizen of the new country.

Ten days later, at Alvor in southern Portugal, the three movements and Portugal signed an agreement that spelled out in greater detail the general principles accepted in Mombasa and set November 11, 1975, as the date for the proclamation of independence and full sovereignty for Angola. Until that date all power would be exercised by a Portuguese high commissioner, and a transitional government was to be inaugurated January 31, 1975.

The church shared in the euphoria of all Angolans as their liberation movements were recognized as legitimate political parties and their leaders were transformed from being terrorists and bandits into national heroes.

Dr. Neto and the Bishops

On February 22, 1975, Dr. Agostinho Neto, president of the Popular Movement for the Liberation of Angola (MPLA) visited the Catholic archbishop's residence in Luanda where Dom Zacarias Kamwenho, the auxiliary bishop of Luanda, received him and other members of the Central Committee of the MPLA, affirming that the goal of liberation was shared by both political and spiritual leaders. Bishop Zacarias declared: "Christ did not come to bring anything except liberation to mankind — a liberation that is complete."

In response Dr. Neto said, in part, "We cannot ignore the religious authorities in Angola as we cannot ignore the reality that is the Catholic church here." Neto, who was to become the first president of Angola, promised:

> We will always be disposed and ready to collaborate as much as possible with the church in those problems in which our activity may be in common. As a liberation movement and a political movement naturally we have different objectives. They are different, but they have points in common.[12]

From the archbishop's residence Dr. Agostinho Neto went to the Methodist center, where he was met by Bishop Emílio Júlio Miguel de Carvalho and five ordained ministers — Júlio João Miguel, director of the mission of Luanda, Santos Matoso and Job Baltazar Diogo of the department of Bible translation, Manuel António Moniz, superintendent of the Luanda district, Rev. Gaspar de Almeida, general-director of the *Estandarte* — and Professor Nobre Dias, director of the mission schools.

Bishop Emílio greeted the visitors:

> It certainly is a great pleasure and privilege for us, principally for me, to receive here this morning Comrade President of the Popular Movement for the Liberation of Angola. The return of this great combatant to our country was long awaited by all of us who have accompanied closely the great contribution that he has made for the liberation of our country. To receive you here in the Evangelical mission of Luanda this morning is, Mr. President, to receive a son who returns home since very strong ties bind you to our church, not only in the person of your father, who during many years struggled in the ministry of our church; it is to receive a son of Angola who returns to his home.[13]

In response Dr. Agostinho Neto affirmed:

> Bishop, ministers, dear friends — for all of us, I believe, this reencounter means something. It means that we overcame certain difficulties, we ran a long race, and finally we have come together again. We returned to find an atmosphere in which we can say that

---

12. *Diário de Luanda*, February 22, 1975.
13. Ibid.

our people are winning by the force of our struggle for liberty, independence, and dignity, which were robbed from us centuries ago. We are marching toward a new stage in our life.... This visit means not only visiting old friends, but visiting the old church that I attended in my infancy. We remember past times, but it means more than this; it means that all of us in Angola desire liberty. And independently of the way of thinking of each one, we must establish a climate that favors the expression of the will of each one, whether on a political, religious, or social level. The way of thinking of each one should not divide us. We ought to be united around this ideal that is for all, to make Angola a free country and a country where all can live. Therefore, this visit, as you said, surpasses by a great measure a simple visit since I still belong to the family, but it also signifies that the MPLA advocates this liberty so that all can practice the worship that they wish.... We will defend the religious institutions so that they not be destroyed and so that all of us in Angola may feel truly free and no one constrained. The centuries of colonialism have sufficed for us to hate any type of subjection to a political, religious, or any other force that wishes to impose itself on us. It is for this liberty that the Evangelical church through its leaders and its faithful will also be capable of making a valid contribution to overcome all types of contradictions that have plagued our people during the entire colonial era.[14]

Dr. Agostinho Neto, son a of a Methodist pastor, reared in a Methodist parsonage, pupil in Methodist schools, secretary of the Methodist bishop, scholarship student of the Methodist mission, indeed was coming home when he visited the Luanda Methodist mission in February 1975. Years before, however, he had admitted to the Methodist mission that was providing his scholarship to attend medical school in Lisbon that he no longer was a believer. Still he had family and sentimental ties with the Methodist community.

Violence Escalates

The euphoria that the Angolans enjoyed with the installation of the transitional government on January 31, 1975, lasted only a few weeks. Clashes began first in Luanda between MPLA and FNLA forces on February 1, when in the MPLA-controlled Lixeira *musseque* a minor misunderstanding erupted into a shoot-out between FNLA and MPLA

---

14. Ibid.

guerrillas. Seven persons, including two officers in a Portuguese patrol who had come to restore order, were killed.[15]

Violence escalated in the capital, and at the end of March Portugal's foreign minister and the minister for overseas territories rushed from Lisbon to Luanda to bring the leaders of the movements together. The Angolan leaders and the ministers agreed to end the fighting. They also repeated the Alvor pledge to integrate the movements' military units with the Portuguese armed forces. The Portuguese ministers had hardly returned to Lisbon when conflicts broke out again in Luanda between the FNLA and the MPLA. Small clashes continued to disturb Luanda, and at the end of April another major combat between MPLA and FNLA forces shook the city. Lisbon papers estimated the casualties at more than five hundred dead and seven hundred wounded.

The efforts of the Portuguese officials to end the fratricidal struggle for power were to no avail. The violence continued, and fear increasingly replaced hope as a motivating force among the people. This fear affected the church as well as the total population. For example, Engrácia Dias Cardoso, the first elected woman treasurer of the United Methodist Church in Angola, fled from Luanda to Malanje, her home territory, when intermovement violence became severe in the capital in May 1975.

By the end of May the FNLA and the MPLA were no longer responding to local isolated incidents as they clashed, but were setting the stage for a nationwide struggle in which each was preparing itself to gain exclusive power. The FNLA received materiel from Zaire. The MPLA's aid came mostly from Eastern Europe, which presented both logistical and political problems. A communiqué of the National Commission of Defense dated April 29, 1975, prohibited the unloading of military supplies destined for MPLA from the Yugoslav ship *Postoyna*, but the commission was not able to enforce its own decrees.[16]

UNITA proposed a summit conference to avoid a direct confrontation between the MPLA and the FNLA, and the two movements agreed. However, the agreement seemed to be motivated more by a desire to gain time for the military showdown than by a commitment to the peaceful resolution of their differences.

The summit meeting of Holden Roberto, Agostinho Neto, and Jonas Savimbi in Nakuru, Kenya, from June 16 to 21, 1975, did not halt the rapid escalation of the civil war. It did, however, produce a succinct analysis of the "causes for the deterioration of the situation in Angola":

1. The introduction of great quantities of arms by the liberation movements after April 25, and especially after their move to Lu-

---

15. Lawrence W. Henderson, *Angola: Five Centuries of Conflict* (Ithaca, N.Y.: Cornell Univ. Press, 1979), 247.

16. *Diário de Noticias*, May 5, 1975.

anda. This race for arms is due to the fact that the liberation movements have maintained their mutual lack of confidence resulting from their political and ideological differences and their divergences in the past.

2. The lack of political tolerance, which manifests itself in violence in the activity of the liberation movements and their militants.

3. The existence of so-called zones of influence and of regions of supposed military superiority.

4. The arming of the civilian population.

5. Military clashes among the liberation movements and their tendency to regionalize, which, in addition to causing numerous innocent victims, aggravates the situation by tending to increase tribalism, regionalism, and racism.

6. The presence of reactionary agitation and of elements foreign to the process of decolonization.

The political leaders recognized that the assumption of "zones of influence" was one of the causes of the deterioration of the situation in Angola. The Protestant churches, which were regional, contributed to the reality and influence of the zones in spite of their pleading for national unity.

In July, the MPLA evidently decided that instead of following the agreement at Nakuru to eliminate the "zones of influence and regions of supposed military superiority," it would aggressively establish complete control of its zone — Luanda-Malanje. By the beginning of August the capital, the whole Kimbundu corridor, and the Lunda district were cleared of all FNLA military and political personnel. The only area in which the FNLA successfully resisted the MPLA was north of Luanda, where the FNLA zone dipped within a few miles of the capital.

Response of the Church to Independence

The people of central Angola responded to the news of the April 25 coup in Lisbon with scepticism and hope. They doubted that Portuguese colonialism would really change, and most Portuguese officials continued in their posts as the dry season of 1974 wore on.

On June 17, 1974, Jonas Savimbi signed a cease-fire with the Portuguese government; this changed the climate in central Angola. Since the people of this region overwhelmingly supported UNITA and its president, Jonas Savimbi, the cease-fire overcame much of their scepticism and fanned their hopes. Scores of Angolans from Benguela, Huambo, and Bié districts immediately took the train up to Luso and then traveled by car, bicycle, or foot to the UNITA headquarters. As the flow increased, thousands expressed their allegiance to UNITA and became convinced not only that Portuguese colonialism would end, but also that they might rule themselves.

On June 20, 1974, the General Synod of the Council of Evangelical Churches of Central Angola drafted a set of demands, which they had made several times in the form of requests to the colonial authorities, without any response. They petitioned that the church schools be granted official status and that they receive government subsidies, that the pedagogy course at Dôndi be authorized to train and certify teachers, and that the trades building, which had been destroyed, allegedly by arson caused by PIDE in 1968, be rebuilt and refurnished. In the field of health the church leaders demanded that the Protestant hospitals be subsidized, the Dôndi nursing course be recognized, and the admission of medical missionaries be facilitated. They continued their demands in the ecclesiastical area, soliciting that the Protestant churches be given legal recognition and that such religious rites as marriage and baptism be officially recognized.

During the public meeting when these demands were presented to Portuguese officials, the people added further demands that local Portuguese traders be disarmed, and that PIDE agents not be integrated into the armed forces but be tried, as was reportedly being done in Portugal and Mozambique. The people also wanted to see a list of Angolans who were PIDE agents.

These demands were signed for the General Synod of the Protestant Churches of Central Angola by the Rev. Ricardo Uliengue Epalanga, General Secretary, and by Eduardo Oseas Baptista Chingufo, Teacher-Director.

The new liberalism of civil and military authorities not only encouraged the Angolans to freely express their aspirations, but led them to expect that these requests would be granted. The people in Central Angola even resurrected an old hope — that the Currie Institute, which pioneered education for Angolans sixty years earlier, might now finally be on the way to becoming a university.

The unwieldy coalition government installed on January 31, 1975, inspired confidence in the Protestant community of central Angola because UNITA called some of the church's most respected educators to be secretaries of the various ministries: Teodoro Chitunda, Armindo Solunga, Benjamim Cacunda, Ribeiro Chiteculo, Enoque Oliveira, and Bencio Chissalucombe. Among the higher officials were Jaka Jammba, Cornélio Caley, Jerónimo Wanga, and Jeremias Kalandula Chitunda.

Just before the transitional government was installed in Luanda, Jonas Savimbi was enthusiastically received in Dôndi. As Agostinho

Neto was a son returning home when he visited the Methodist church in Luanda, so Jonas Savimbi made a triumphal visit to his alma mater, Currie Institute at Dôndi. Savimbi's father, Lote Malheiro Savimbi, had also been a student in one of the early classes of the institute and became, as a layman, the director of the Chilesso mission. In his remarks at his homecoming, Jonas Savimbi paid special tribute to Eduardo Daniel Ecundi, "our precursor in the fight for the independence of Angola."[17]

Savimbi's visit to Dôndi differed from Neto's visit to the Methodist church in Luanda in that Neto could only claim roots in the church. He had announced years earlier, when a medical student in Portugal, that he no longer accepted the Christian faith. In contrast Savimbi assured the cheering audience at Dôndi that he still believed in the one God who sees everything that we do. Savimbi strengthened his support in the Protestant community of central Angola by not only affirming his personal faith, but also by promising government support for educational and medical work.

The General Synod of Evangelical Churches of Central Angola held its first assembly since 1961 in February 1975, just after the inauguration of the transitional government. The meeting was highlighted by visits of the Rev. José B. Chipenda and his wife, Eva Chipenda, and the Rev. João Capuca. Capuca had fled from the Dôndi area in 1961 and been a pastor in the United Church of Zambia. The visitors stimulated their Angolan brothers and sisters to think about the role of the church in an independent country.

The delegates assumed in all their discussions that after independence the church would be able to expand greatly its total program and that the Protestant communities would have the same privileges as those previously enjoyed by the Catholics.

The Baptist Church (BMS) responded to April 25 and subsequent moves toward independence from outside Angola. Members and leaders had fled across the border into Zaire following the outbreak of the War of Independence in 1961. The 1960 population of the two northern Angolan districts of Zaire and Uige totalled 492,643. It is estimated that during the 1961–74 period 450,000 Angolan refugees were in Zaire, although not all the refugees came from those two northern districts. Many fled from Cuanza North and from Malanje, and some Ovimbundu from central Angola were working in the north in March 1961. They accompanied the other Angolans fleeing from the Portuguese reprisals for the rebel attacks.

By 1974 most of the Kikongo refugees had been in Zaire long enough to have built houses, cultivated fields, and put their children in school.

---

17. Marco Vinicios e Maria João Saldanha, *Jonas Savimbi: Um desafio à ditatura comunista em Angola* (Lisbon: Edições Armaslide, 1977), 106.

Although they expected to return to their Angolan homes, they were not ready to depart immediately because of the confused reports coming from Angola and Portugal in 1974.

Only after the establishment of the transitional government in January 1975 did the refugees flood back into Angola. Most of them found that their old villages had disappeared and their fields were overgrown. Quickly they built huts or shelters, and fields were cleared for planting. As the churches had been the cohesive force holding the refugees together as they fled, so it played the same role as the refugees returned and faced the task of rebuilding their villages.

Exactly one month before the proclamation of independence the Catholic Episcopal Conference issued another pastoral letter, "The Church and the Independence of Angola." In its introduction the bishops recognized that the nation faced independence in the midst of serious problems:

> The riches wasted, the commercial transactions suspended, the public services disorganized, the industries paralyzed, the general unemployment are the tragic result of the civil war in the midst of which we live, throwing the country into economic chaos, with the specter of hunger looming ever larger.[18]

The second section of the pastoral letter gave a brief panorama of the church in Angola, including a historical sketch and the most recent statistics of the Catholic and Protestant communities — 3,000,000 and 700,000 respectively.

The third section outlined the activities of the church in the area of human development, with some information about catechetical schools, primary and secondary education, seminaries, and health ministries. This was followed by a section, entitled "The Church at this Historical Turning Point," in which the bishops affirmed that the church is not a political society: it is the people of God marching through time to the Father's House in eternity.

> It has as its mission to communicate to men the doctrine revealed by God and contained in the Holy Scriptures and in Tradition and above all to make them participants in the liberation brought by Christ and consummated on Calvary. Although the church is not disinterested in the temporal dimension of mankind, it recognizes the state's competence and direct responsibility for the organization and conduct of the civil society....
>
> Verifying that evangelization presupposes and passes through the total liberation of man, what is important is the breaking of all the bonds that impede its full realization — ignorance, endemic

---

18. *Boletim Eclesiástico*, 131.

diseases and misery, racial segregation, economic dependence, neo-colonialism, etc. — the church does not accept violence, which places human life at risk, destroys wealth, and is the source of divisions and hate among brothers redeemed by Christ and facing the same transcendent destiny.

The bishops concluded their preindependence letter with a section entitled "Hope in the Future and Final Wishes," confident that "a great future awaits this new Nation, but it is necessary that all its sons and daughters unite their efforts."[19]

Conclusion

The church in Angola and the population as a whole faced independence with hope and anxiety. The nineteen months from April 25, 1974, to November 11, 1975, were not a transition from war to peace or from colonialism to self-government. After November 11 Angolans had to adapt to an "independence" that brought an escalation of warfare, more power and influence to foreigners, and more hunger and disease. The church had to adapt to a system that ambivalently promised religious freedom, but considered religion and the church as enemies of progress and of the best interests of the people.

---

19. Ibid., 141.

Chapter 13

Confrontations between Church and State

Communism can be outlived and out-thought by a full and adequate presentation of the Gospel.[1]

"In the name of the people of Angola, the Central Committee of the Popular Movement of the Liberation of Angola (MPLA) proclaims solemnly before Africa and the World the independence of Angola." Agostinho Neto, the president of the MPLA, thus announced the independence of Angola before thousands of cheering Angolans gathered in the largest stadium in Luanda just after midnight on November 11, 1975. Neto's forty-minute speech was punctuated by chants of "The struggle continues" and "Victory is certain." He acknowledged that the next phase of the struggle would be more arduous than the thirteen-year war against the Portuguese. Later in the day Dr. Agostinho Neto was declared president of the People's Republic of Angola.

In the same speech declaring the independence of Angola Dr. Neto stated that the People's Republic of Angola would be a lay state with complete separation between church and state, respecting all religions and protecting churches, places, and objects of worship and legally recognized institutions.

April 25, 1974, had been a pivotal date in the history of Portugal and all its colonies, but it had not been immediately known what its significance would be for Angola. Similarly, November 11, 1975, was experienced in a variety of ways in different regions of Angola. Luanda

---

1. John T. Tucker, "This Is Africa's Century," *Angola Airmail* (United Church of Canada, 1952), vii.

was the base of MPLA's support and was controlled by its military forces, reinforced by Cuban troops; therefore the population in Luanda experienced November 11, Independence Day, not only as the victory of the MPLA over the Portuguese, but also over the other two liberation movements.

In Sanza Pombo and other centers in northern Angola the people celebrated November 11 assuming that the FNLA, which was dominant among the Bakongo and still controlled the north of Angola, would be a part of the new government. Some FNLA leaders celebrated independence at Ambriz seventy-five miles north of Luanda; the celebrants did not know, however, that the FNLA forces, supported by two battalions of the Zairian army, Portuguese mercenaries, and a South African contingent, had already been defeated by the MPLA and the Cubans at the gates of Luanda near the village of Kifandongo a few hours before the declaration of independence. The uncertainty among the population of northern Angola as to the meaning of independence continued for three months, until February 19, 1976, when the *Jornal de Angola* announced the "liberation of São Salvador, the last redoubt of the FNLA in Angola.

In central Angola the celebration of independence depended on the people's political loyalties and the information they had of the military situation at that moment. In Huambo at zero hour of November 11, only two thousand people gathered in a football stadium with the sound of gunfire all around. Some of the shots were in celebration of independence and others were part of the fighting between UNITA and the FNLA. "The desultory ceremony ended as a lowly officer in the UNITA military police took the salute while the UNITA flag was raised. None of the UNITA leadership was present."[2]

Later in the day twenty thousand people gathered in the stadium to hear Jonas Savimbi announce the formation of a joint UNITA-FNLA government, which "will be provisional. It cannot be definitive. Only through general elections, when peace returns to the country, will we be able to decide definitively who will be the leaders of the nation. Anything other than this we cannot accept."[3]

The independence celebration in Bié, a center of UNITA support, was more enthusiastic, because in spite of the uncertainty of what was happening in other parts of the country they knew that Eduardo Jonatão Chingunji, director of schools at the Chissamba Protestant mission, was governor of the district, and Júlio Fausto, another Chissamba teacher, was administrator of Catabola. The Chissamba church had a

2. Fred Bridgland, *Jonas Savimbi: A Key to Africa* (Edinburgh: Mainstream Publishing Co., 1986), 133.
3. Ibid., 135.

special service on the night of November 10 to celebrate "their" independence. After the service, however, when the Angolan nurses tried to tune in on the Huambo radio station, expecting to hear celebrations, they heard only static. The people in Bié still hoped that somehow they would have a government in which UNITA would participate. It took the MPLA and Cuban troops three months to move south and take control of the cities and towns of central and southern Angola. However, in only a matter of days the MPLA government exercised its authority in Luanda to begin to reshape Angolan society according to a Marxist-Leninist model.

Most Angolans did not know what Marxist-Leninism was, but some Christian leaders had heard that it was atheistic and that Karl Marx had called religion "the opiate of the people." Yet the new constitution guaranteed freedom of religion "so long as they [the churches] comply with the state laws." Or, as was stated in the proclamation of independence, churches that are *legally recognized* will be protected. Few Angolans were aware that orthodox Communist doctrine taught that religion would disappear as all obscurantism was eliminated by the scientific teaching of dialectical materialism, which is an integral part of the creation of a socialist society. Marxist confidence in the inevitability of this process is so strong that it allows the inclusion of an article guaranteeing freedom of religion in any constitution written by a Marxist party. Yet the inconvenience of this opium is sufficient that the guarantees of religious freedom are accompanied by an educational program teaching the errors of religion and the truth of atheism.

Harassment of the Churches

Law No. 4/75 of December 9, 1975, declared the nationalization of schools. This was the first confrontation between the new government and the church. The response of the church was ambivalent. On the one hand the desire of the people for education was so great that the promise of free public schools was very appealing. However, as described in chapter 5, the school was the principal means of evangelization and Christian education.

The new government showed its intention to control all levels of education in Article 6 of Law No. 4/75: Teaching at all levels and in all institutions would depend on the general directives given by the state for education in Angola.

The same law ordered the confiscation of all centers of teaching and all goods, rights, and actions that are part of the patrimony of such centers (Art. 2).

On most mission stations the centers of teaching were used to administer primary and secondary education as well as various programs of religious education. Consequently the confiscation of these buildings not only denied the missions or churches the opportunity to administer the schools, but denied them the necessary facilities to carry on a wide range of other programs.

The sharpest confrontation between the state and a particular church was with the Jehovah's Witnesses. In June 1976 militants of the Women's Organization of Angola (OMA) protested to the prime minister, Lopo do Nascimento, demanding severe sanctions and political re-education in work camps for all who were members of Tocoism, Kimbanguism, or the Jehovah's Witnesses. They carried such banners as "CIA equals Jehovah" and "Toco equals FNLA." Although the women condemned the three religious societies, the government in succeeding months looked more sympathetically on the Kimbanguists and Tocoists, but sharpened the criticism of the Jehovah's Witnesses. The Political Bureau of the Central Committee of the MPLA-PT on March 8, 1978, declared the Jehovah's Witnesses illegal and banned in Angola.

In November 1978 the MPLA-PT published a pamphlet entitled *What Are the Jehovah's Witnesses?* in an edition of fifty thousand. It described the Jehovah's Witnesses as "a sect that is an instrument of Capitalism and Imperialism." The pamphlet found it particularly repulsive that the Witnesses refused to show respect for the official symbols of the People's Republic of Angola: the flag, the insignia, and the national anthem. It also criticized the Witnesses for refusing blood transfusions and for their conscientious objection to participation in war.

The pamphlet extended the attack beyond the Jehovah's Witnesses and gave "to the members of the party the immense task, in work places and factories, in the fields, public offices, and schools to carry on a fierce fight against all incorrect forms of thought, *especially religion* and most specifically against this repugnant sect."

Imprisonment, Kidnappings, Murders

In April and May of 1976 military activity increased in the Bié district as MPLA forces moved ahead to complete their conquest of central Angola. UNITA soldiers were withdrawing, but rear-guard forces ambushed cars that travelled the main roads. During this period both MPLA and UNITA brought wounded soldiers to the Chissamba hospital, but the UNITA soldiers never wore their uniforms. All sick or wounded were treated regardless of their political affiliations.

Harassment of the Chissamba hospital by MPLA and Cuban soldiers continued from June to October 1976, and finally on October 19 Dr. Elizabeth Bridgman and Nurse Edith Radley were arrested and taken under escort from Chissamba to Cuíto. Several months earlier the two United Church of Canada missionaries had been in the capital of Bié as guests in the home of the UNITA governor, Eduardo Jonatão, who had been director of the Chissamba schools. Arriving in Cuíto under arrest, Dr. Bridgman and Miss Radley were received in the home of Commissar Fernando Muteka. For a period Miss Radley had worked at the Bunjei Protestant mission, where the director of the hospital was Faustino Muteka, father of the commissar Fernando Muteka. The Mutekas were one of the few prominent Umbundu Protestant families who supported the MPLA before independence. In the early interparty skirmishes in Huambo one of Fernando's brothers, Fadrio, had been killed.

The relationship between religious commitment and political loyalties took many forms. One was illustrated by an incident that occurred with Faustino Muteka and his son in Bié. One night, in the fashion of Nicodemus (John 3), Mr. Muteka invited the local Protestant pastor to his residence and counselled his son, the commissar, "Politics may pull you one way or another, but remember that the pastor is your father in the faith. Listen to him."

After a few days of interrogation the two Canadian medical missionaries were flown to Luanda and incarcerated. For two months the women were held in prison incommunicado by the Angolan government, and then the Canadian government initiated inquiries as to their whereabouts. In January 1977 the Italian consul visited the women in prison, and shortly thereafter they were released and sent out of the country.

In 1976 the missionaries of the Catholic mission of Andulo were taken as prisoners to Cuíto, and after some months in prison the superior was expelled from Angola. This had been an important mission with a teachers' training school, a domestic school for girls, and a hospital-maternity ward, as well as primary and junior high schools. The Andulo mission passed through various vicissitudes and for the past few years no one has been able to live there: no missionaries, catechists, or even troops. However, some catechists in the area continue to lead the liturgy of the word for the faithful of the area and celebrate baptisms and marriages.[4]

Catholic priests and Protestant pastors were detained for brief periods or imprisoned for several years, especially in the first years after independence. Sometimes no charges were made against them, and they were held without any trial. At other times they were accused of

---

4. *Encontro*, no. 185 (January 1988): 17.

sympathy or collaboration with "the enemy," tried, and sentenced to prison. The camp at São Nicolau, which was used by the Portuguese for political prisoners during the colonial period, continued to be used after independence for political prisoners whom the MPLA government considered subversive or at least suspect.

In 1981–82 UNITA guerrilla operations became more effective, and in the mid-1980s twenty-five Catholic missionaries were kidnapped at various times. These kidnappings can be safely attributed to UNITA since the kidnappers identified themselves and either released their victims near their homes after a short time or took them to Jamba. Of those taken to Jamba, some requested to stay there and work in UNITA-controlled territory, and others were allowed to return to their homelands, which included Portugal, Italy, Spain, Brazil, the Philippines, Japan, Holland, Poland, and Uruguay.

The kidnapping that received most publicity was that of Dom Alexandre do Nascimento, archbishop of Lubango, by UNITA on October 15, 1982. He was taken to Jamba, the UNITA headquarters, and released a month later on November 16. On February 2, 1983, Dom Alexandre do Nascimento was named cardinal by Pope John Paul II, and some jokingly suggested that having been kidnapped by UNITA was one of his qualifications for the cardinalate. The government of Angola criticized the nomination of Dom Alexandre as cardinal because it was not given prior notice.[5]

The circumstances of the deaths of sixteen Catholic missionaries are more difficult to determine. Some were caught between the military forces of the civil war, and others may have been victims of personal vendettas or criminal attacks.

Father Leandro Volken, a Swiss missionary of the Congregation of Our Lady of LaSalette, was killed on January 19, 1983, as he travelled in a Forças Armadas Populares da Libertação de Angola (FAPLA) military column on the road from Benguela to Cubal. Near Caimbambo the column was ambushed by UNITA forces, and Father Leandro plus three Angolans, including the novice João Soares, were killed. The car was burned, but one sister was saved. She said later that all who were travelling in the car were saying the Rosary, meditating on the "sorrowful mysteries" as they were attacked. Father Leandro had worked in Angola since 1967 and had special responsibility for the young Angolans who wished to enter his missionary order. His death occurred as he was returning from the ordination of Father Marcial Kapingala in Catumbela on January 16.

---

5. *Encontro* (March 1983): 40.

Rhetorical Confrontation:
First Congress vs. Pastoral Letter

The sharpest rhetorical confrontation between church and state after independence reached its climax in December 1977. The MPLA held its first Congress in Luanda from December 4 to 10, and the Episcopal Conference met in Lubango at the same time.

The year 1977 was the Year of the First Congress and the preparations occupied the party all year. For weeks before the Congress the *Jornal de Angola*, the only daily paper, filled most of its pages with preparatory documents of the Congress. It explained that the MPLA had waited twenty-one years to hold its first Congress because the colonial war and then the struggle to consolidate its power after independence had made it impossible to organize a Congress with proper representation. The MPLA published the theses to be discussed at the Congress, each one outlining the movement's position on a major sector of the new nation's life: economy, industry, agriculture, education, health, etc.

The main action to be taken was the transformation of the MPLA from a movement that could include all those who wished to fight for the liberation of Angola to a Marxist-Leninist vanguard party. This raised the question, "Who could be a member of the party?" The replies to this question were rather ambiguous. Lúcio Lara, then administrative secretary of the MPLA, speaking in Luanda affirmed: "In our Movement, we have many comrades who profess different religions. These religions are not ideologically in accord with Marxism-Leninism. Still many militant comrades are religious and they continue to be good militants."[6]

A more definitive answer was given by President Agostinho Neto on May 21, 1977: "Catholics and Protestants cannot be members of the party... and perhaps fifty years from now there will be no more churches in Angola."[7]

This was the answer written into the statutes of the MPLA-Workers' Party: "Those who study and apply the principles of Marxism-Leninism" may be members of the party and since the church members do not fulfill that requirement "they cannot be in the party."

Religious persons could, however, participate in the mass organizations: UNTA (National Union of Angolan Workers), OMA (Organization of Angolan Women), and OPA (Organization of Angolan Pioneers.)

The Central Committee affirmed that "the party and the state, in the People's Republic of Angola, will not prohibit religion," which implied that the state would allow the continued existence of churches, but also

---

6. *Jornal de Angola*, February 27, 1977.
7. Ibid., May 22, 1977.

that there would be an ideological confrontation whose aim was the elimination from public life of religious manifestations and ideas.[8]

Bishop Emílio de Carvalho contended that to face this challenge:

> The work of the church was not to combat an ideology, nor to hide the difference that exists between Christianity and Marxism-Leninism, much less to minimize the consequences that such a revolutionary process could represent for the churches. The work of the church is to present the liberating *gospel* as relevant to all aspects of the life of Angolan society and as a factor of equilibrium among men and women, youth and children of our land. Thus, for the church, religion will cease to be a form of human alienation, of obscurantism, opium, or illusion, in order to become a great factor for *liberation* and of true human emancipation.
>
> The churches of Angola should be able to leave their "ghettos" and enter deeply into this multiple and liberating mission.[9]

While the party was working in Luanda in December 1977 the Episcopal Conference was formulating a pastoral letter in Lubango to be read in all Catholic churches in Angola on January 8, 1978. The Vatican Radio reported on January 21:

> The bishops in Angola have protested the frequent and lamentable violations of religious freedom in the People's Republic of Angola.... The Angolan bishops say that Catholics — half the population — suffered discrimination for their beliefs and often lost the custody of their children.[10]

The four-thousand-word letter was a rewrite and elaboration of the pastor letter that the bishops had written a year earlier. That letter did not prompt a public response from the party or the government, but this letter drew sharp reactions because of its timing in relation to the First Congress and the transformation of the movement into the Workers' Party; moreover, it had had international repercussions. Lúcio Lara, speaking in Benguela on February 4, 1978, the seventeenth anniversary of the first attacks by the MPLA on the prisons in Luanda, gave an impassioned response to the pastoral letter. (He concluded by saying that he hoped that he had spoken "without hate, calmly, and without passion.")

First he explained why this letter required a response. Other letters

---

8. Emílio J. M. de Carvalho, *A Questão Religiosa na República Popular de Angola* (Luanda, 1978), 10.

9. Ibid., 11–12.

10. Michael Wolfers and Jane Bergerol, *Angola in the Frontline* (London: Zed Books Ltd., 1983), 182.

had been published and there had been no problems since "ideological combat is ideological combat." But the other letters never offended the dignity of the leaders or the government. Lara affirmed that this letter was different. It was filled with lies: that the government violates missions and churches, that it steals children, sending them abroad without the permission of their parents, and that it is imposing a foreign philosophy.

Lara, a member of the Political Bureau of the MPLA-PT and secretary of the Central Committee, then replied to these charges. Undoubtedly missions were entered without permission because in the war missions were in many instances strategic points that were necessary for the FAPLA, the government troops, to control in order to protect the people. These were not actions taken on orders from the military or party leadership to harm the missions or churches, but in order to defeat the enemy.

Lara acknowledged that the government had sent many children abroad to study because it could not provide education for all children. Through local authorities the government and party sought to locate orphans or children whose parents could not care properly for them. Lara declared that not a single child was sent without the authorization of his or her parents.

As regards the imposition of a foreign philosophy, Lara admitted that Marx, Engels, and Lenin were not born in Angola, but then asked, "Was Christ born in Angola?"[11]

The same issue of the *Jornal de Angola* carried an editorial entitled "The Bishops and the Conspiracy." It stated:

> In the face of the shameless and fraudulent attack that the conspirators in Lubango were allowed to make, abusing the religious sentiments of part of our People and the principles of peace and tolerance of our Government, we must recall the provision in the Third Plenary Session of the Central Committee, which considered "as illegal and therefore punishable any activity which places faith or religious belief in opposition to the revolutionary transformation of society." These were the objectives of the meeting in Lubango. We call the attention of the People and the Authorities to this, certain that religious convictions should not be confused with opportunistic manipulation and the service of interests foreign to the struggle of the Angolan people for complete and solid freedom.[12]

---

11. *Jornal de Angola*, February 5, 1978.
12. Ibid.

Ideological Confrontation

This confrontation between the state/party and the Catholic church resulted in the extinction of the Catholic radio station on January 25, 1978,
by a decree that was supported by several legal citations: (a) Article 7
of the Constitution, providing for the separation of church and state;
(b) a resolution of the Third Plenary Meeting of the Central Committee
of the MPLA, providing that all information and propaganda be controlled by the Central Committee of the MPLA; and (c) the assertion
that the Catholic radio station was created under provisions of the concordat between Portugal and the Catholic church, which is not binding
on an independent Angola.

In his Benguela speech Lúcio Lara also discussed the question of the
Catholic Radio. He mentioned that on May 27, 1977, when the group
led by Nito Alves attempted a coup and briefly controlled the National
Radio, the Catholic station was also transmitting the rebels' "traitorous
message." It was necessary to send troops to stop it. But, he added,
that is not the reason for confiscating the Catholic Radio. It just did not
make sense to Lara and the MPLA that while the government and party
promote science others should spread antiscientific and obscurantist
concepts.

A primary school teacher wrote a letter to the editor of the *Jornal
de Angola*, complaining about the teaching of a Catholic catechist who
opposed the official history lesson:

> On a certain day I was giving the first history lesson to a fourth
> grade class. The lesson told of the appearance of human beings
> on the earth and how they lived. During the lesson one of the
> pupils who attends catechism class asked the following question:
> "Comrade professor, didn't God create man?"
>
> Then I answered that it was not true and explained how man
> had appeared on the earth, his origin, scientifically, and another
> pupil said that the catechist and the priest said that it was God, by
> means of Adam and Eve, and if it were not for him we would not
> exist. Seeing this pupil with such an absurd idea, I tried to rid the
> pupil of it scientifically, and he concluded that this story was all a
> lie and the class continued with questions along this line. At the
> end of the class some pupils went to the catechism class as usual
> and repeated what I had told them.
>
> On the following day we had another history lesson, which
> clashed with the Catholic religion — "The arrival of the Portuguese
> at the Congo and how they had spread the Catholic religion" —
> and they told me that they would call the catechist, who would
> explain to me or rather make me understand about God.

After a heated discussion between me and her in the presence of all the pupils she quit, and in order to put me in my place threatened to go to the Ministry of Education or to the political authorities.

Now I ask: how will we create a man who serves the People and the Revolution with false religious ideas? If I agree with the church will I not be contradicting the History of Angola? Won't I be lying to the children? . . . I ask the supreme authorities to take action in this case and alert all teachers to this kind of catechist.

My revolutionary greetings.

António Manuel de Jesus Romão[13]

The MPLA saw the ideological confrontation as that between science and religion. The party will give its message to the people as will the various religions. Who will win? Lúcio Lara was confident: "It is clear that the answer is simple: it is science that will win. Every place it has been that way and it will continue to be.

In preparation for the First Congress of the MPLA much political education was given to the people through speeches by MPLA leaders and by long articles in the *Jornal de Angola*. In such an article on November 17, 1977, the statement was made that "Marxism-Leninism is not a dogma or a religion."[14]

Reading these articles, however, their vocabulary, presuppositions, and "spirit" make it seem that the confrontation is not between church and state, but rather between two religions. Marxism-Leninism is not a religion only in the sense that it does not use the word "god" and calls itself atheistic. However, it still recognizes that there is a force or a power that has a determinative effect on the course of human history. It is called "dialectical materialism" and its study allows one to discover "the mechanism and the logic of the inevitable ruin of capitalism and the substitution of this by socialism, and the transformation of socialism into communism."[15]

The much-disputed pastoral letter of December 1977 also argues that Marxism-Leninism has the characteristics of a religion:

Para. 22. Paradoxically, the Marxist system calls itself secular but, perhaps unconsciously, it presents itself as a new religion. . . . For it

---

13. Ibid., April 5, 1978.

14. A stimulating article by Wyatt MacGaffey, "African Ideology and Belief: A Survey," *African Studies Review* 24, nos. 2/3 (June–September 1981), contends that "the distinction between ideology and belief is invidious and should be transcended." This would argue that the question is not "Is Marxism-Leninism a Religion or an Ideology?" because the two are basically the same.

15. *Jornal de Angola*, July 24, 1980.

there is no absolute or Infinite, but matter is absolute and eternal; the Catholic dogmas are considered absurd, but it [the Marxist religion] imposes dogmatically the principles of historical and dialectical materialism. Heaven is an illusion, but they tire themselves out working for a Paradise on Earth; everything ends in death, but immortal honor and worship are rendered to those who have died in the cause; declaring war on all alienation, choices are imposed that do not allow the smallest challenge.

One could argue reasonably that when the MPLA changed from a movement to a party, it was actually changing from a liberation movement to a church. In fact in the discussion over the question whether church members could be members of MPLA-PT and the matter of excluding church members from membership in the party, MPLA leaders recognized the parallelism and commented that the Christian churches also had strict requirements for membership.

This parallelism between membership in the Christian church and the MPLA was also seen in the terminology used in discussing membership in the Youth Party. A headline in the *Jornal de Angola*, June 24, 1979, announced, "About 300 young people confirmed in JMPLA-Youth of the party." It was common practice in the churches to receive members by stages: acceptance as catechumens and, after a period of training and trial, reception as members by confirmation. The Methodist church has four types of relationship with the church: baptized child, beginner, member on trial, and full member. A similar set of steps is described in the *Christian Initiation of Adults* in the Roman Ritual, which includes reforms made by Vatican Council II.

The three steps are (a) after the initial conversion and expression of desire to become a Christian, a person is received as a catechumen; (b) having advanced in the faith and almost at the end of catechetical training, the person is admitted to the more intense preparation for the sacraments, and (c) with the completion of his spiritual training the person receives the sacraments (baptism, confirmation, and Eucharist) by which he or she is initiated. To join the party there are also three steps: sympathizer, aspirant, and militant.

Another parallel between the party and church is the recognition of the need for a constant effort to examine, correct, and purify persons, and then recognize those who deserve being acknowledged as sympathizers, aspirants, and militants. The MPLA-PT calls this process "rectification." The churches' parallel would include revival, confession, and examination of new members.

The intensity of the Movement of Rectification is shown by a report in the *Jornal de Angola* of September 6, 1979, recording the results of 3,737 assemblies of rectification and 5,433 assemblies of sensitization in 888 work places, in which 548,253 workers participated. Of this number 8,299 were classified as militants, 7,617 as aspirants, 3,584 as sympathizers, and 4,702 as members of the JMPLA-Youth. Out of more than half a million the total of 15,916 militants and aspirants were organized into 1,097 cells and nine party committees in work places.

Since the political sensitization and rectification process was carried on in factories and other work places it is not surprising that the 24,202 total included only 1,474 women.

The care with which the party chooses its members is a challenge to the church, which in many instances has become lax in selecting its membership and in keeping up-to-date records.

Common Goals:
New Man and New Society

As the party is similar to the church in its methods of preparing and organizing its membership, so they have similar goals: producing the new man and a new society.

Jesus, in conversation with Nicodemus, a ruler of the Jews, explained that "unless one is born anew, he cannot see the kingdom of God" (John 3:3). The Apostle Paul repeats the same teaching in other words: "If any one is in Christ, he is a new creation; the old has passed away; behold, the new has come" (2 Cor. 5:17).

The party's aim of creating the new man in a new society is expressed repeatedly in party statements, such as, "The School is the forge of the New Man" and "Let us read and create a New Man," which was a headline about the literacy campaign.

The party and the church not only share the common goals of the new man and new society (which in the Christian church is most commonly called the kingdom of God) but they also share a strong moralism as they try to describe the character of the new persons and the new society. One of the columns of the *Jornal de Angola* on May 27, 1976, was entitled "Egotism: An Evil to Be Combatted." It argued that "egotism is something to be combatted by *campaigns of clarification* and other means, not only to avoid its spreading, but that it might disappear in the shortest period of time." The party did not use the church's definition of egotism as "original sin," but both church and party would agree that out of that evil many others appear.

To form the new man the party must start with youngsters so the foundations are laid in the program of the Pioneers, the organization for children of primary school age. The Ten Principles of the Pioneers of the MPLA are as follows:

1. The MPLA Pioneers are disciplined and vigilant.

2. The Pioneers criticize fraternally the errors of their comrades, and accept criticism of themselves.

3. The Pioneers do not speak behind the backs of people and are not offended when they are criticized.

4. The Pioneers are not proud. They are workers and modest. They know that all that they do is as nothing compared with the sacrifices of the people.

5. The Pioneers have the courage to defend their opinions wherever they are. They do not hide them for fear or shame.

6. The Pioneers do not desire for themselves what everyone cannot have.

7. The Pioneers look forward, advancing into the future, trying to be better, more educated, more courageous, more disciplined.

8. The Pioneers' motto is "Everything for the People."

9. The Pioneers feel that the victories and defeats of other peoples of the world are their own. They are internationalists.

10. The Pioneers will stop fighting only when there is nothing more to do. They know that there will always be something to do.

(Approved in July 1973).[16]

A parallel set of Ten Commandments for Christian youth could be found in the New Testament, for example:

1. Young Christians are "sober and watchful" (1 Pet. 5:8).

2. Young Christians "examine themselves" (1 Cor. 11:28) and "confess their sins" (James 5:16).

3. Young Christians "keep their consciences clear, so that when they are abused," the abusers are put to shame (1 Pet. 3:16).

4. Young Christians "do nothing from selfishness or conceit, but in humility count others better than themselves" (Phil. 2:3).

5. Young Christians are "always prepared to make a defense to anyone who calls them to account for the hope that is in them" (1 Pet. 3:15).

6. Young Christians do not covet (Rom. 13:9).

---

16. *Jornal de Angola,* February 22, 1976.

7. Young Christians "strain forward to what lies ahead, pressing on toward the goal for the prize of the upward call of God in Christ Jesus" (Phil. 3:13–14).

8. The young Christians' motto is "I shall love my neighbor as myself" (Matt. 19:19).

9. Young Christians "rejoice with those who rejoice, and weep with those who weep" (Rom. 12:15).

10. Young Christians will "fight the good fight and finish the race" (2 Tim. 4:7).

This parallel is constructed artificially. It is more likely that Christians would find their principles in such biblical passage as the Ten Commandments (Exod. 20), the Beatitudes (Matt. 5), or the Fruits of the Spirit (Gal. 5:16–25).

As the Apostle Paul condemned the evil practices that he called the desires of the flesh before he described the fruits of the Spirit in his letter to the Galatians, so the MPLA-PT uses lots of space in the *Jornal de Angola* condemning what it considers the most serious sins in Angola. Most of those articles could have been reproduced from Christian pulpits or publications. The list of sins is long. Some of the most frequently mentioned are alcoholism, greed, indiscipline, prostitution, racism, tribalism, obscurantism, absenteeism, and laziness. In reference to the last two they even quote the Bible: "If anyone will not work, let him not eat" (2 Thess. 3:10).

Dr. Agostinho Neto asked two questions in a much-quoted speech that he gave in Dar es Salaam before independence: "Who is the enemy?" and "What is our objective?" The MPLA-PT gives "the enemy" many names: imperialist, capitalist, bourgeois, etc. The objective is to eliminate the enemy.

The Christian gospel recognizes that people have enemies, and Jesus reminds his disciples that "you have heard that it was said 'Love your friends, hate your enemies.' But now I tell you: love your enemies and pray for those who persecute you" (Matt. 5:43–44).

The party and government of course recognized that the Angolan people longed for peace, and began each radio and TV news program with the affirmation "The Angolan People want Peace." They have refused, however, to accept the church's affirmation that reconciliation is the path to peace. Rather the government's slogan has been "harmony and amnesty." Some leaders of FNLA accepted the government's offer of amnesty and returned from exile, accepting government jobs.

Since the war between the government and UNITA was so long and violent, the government refused for years to consider any negotiations, and much less reconciliation, with the party led by Jonas Savimbi. Reconciliation requires the prior acceptance of the other person as an equal and therefore having the inviolable right to be treated as an authentic interlocutor.

Conclusion

The critical confrontation between church and state in Angola was due to the fact that both parts based their positions on faith and both had convictions of how people should live in society. Aware of the confrontation, the government sought to develop representative organs to allow for the broader participation of Angolans in political life.

The year 1980 was designated the "Year of the First Extraordinary Congress and of the Creation of the People's Assembly." In August 1980, the Constitution was amended to replace the Council of the Revolution by the People's Assembly. Article 34 stated: The deputies are representatives of all the people without any distinction based on race, social class, or religious, ideological or political status." However, Article 37 states, "The People's Assembly shall promote the execution of the objectives of the People's Republic of Angola as defined by the MPLA-Workers' Party."

According to this constitutional revision there are no religious restrictions on who may be a member of the People's Assembly, but this still does not open the door to Christians to participate fully in the decision-making functions of government. It is still the party that chooses the leaders of Angola and that establishes the "objectives of the People's Republic of Angola," which the People's Assembly must promote.

In the first thirteen years of Angolan independence church-state relations have become less confrontational. Immediately after independence the state confiscated the schools, which had been the church's main means of evangelism and Christian education. Many church leaders, lay and clergy, were imprisoned without trial for suspected subversive activities, or even thoughts. After the death of President Agostinho Neto and the assumption of power by Eduardo dos Santos and the Special Party Congress of 1980, the relations between church and state became less confrontational, and this trend continued gradually until 1986 when the first list of "recognized" churches was published.

Since then the relationship has been more stable, at least with the recognized churches. The tensions and confrontations are now more regional, with relations generally better in Luanda and more tensions or confrontations in provinces or localities where the officials tend to be more "papist than the pope."

Several factors certainly contributed to the change in government policy toward the church and religion, but two deserve mention: (1) the church was not fading away as Marxist doctrine had predicted. In fact with most of the population of Angola gathered into the main cities the crowded, active churches could not be ignored; (2) the MPLA leaders could not free themselves from the Christian education that most of them had received in their youth.

Chapter 14

The Church Adapts
to Independence

The church in Angola adapted several times to new sociopolitical situations. It was planted, or replanted, at the turn of the nineteenth century when Angolan kings and chiefs ruled in the vast regions of Angola outside the main cities of Luanda and Benguela. Portugal established effective control of the whole country in the first quarter of the twentieth century, and the church had to adjust to that fact. In the transition period 1961–74, the church was tested in the heat of the colonial war and by a variety of reforms. On November 11, 1975, the church was called to adjust to a Marxist revolution.

The Methodist Response

The first church officially to state its position in relation to the new Angolan government was the United Methodist Church, meeting in its Annual Conference in the Quéssua mission, Malanje, January 27–29, 1976. It declared solemnly that it supported the independence proclamation and identified itself with the political position of the government *without reservation.*

The Methodist church also showed its unconditional support of the government by publishing on the front page of its newspaper *O Estandarte* a picture of Dr. António Agostinho Neto, describing him as "uncontested President of the Popular Movement for the Liberation of Angola–MPLA, who was solemnly and unanimously elected by the Angolan People from Cabinda to the Cunene as President of the People's Republic of Angola on November 11, 1975."

Rev. Gaspar de Almeida, director of the Estandarte, *and Emílio de Carvalho,*
first Angolan bishop of the United Methodist Church in Angola

Other Angolans criticized the Methodist church and especially
Bishop Emílio de Carvalho for this unconditional support of the MPLA
government. The criticism came from two directions: from those who
supported one of the other movements and challenged the assertion
that Neto had been elected by the Angolan people. Other criticism came
from those who believed that it was not proper for the church to assume
such a partisan position in relation to any political movement.

The Catholic Response

Independence forced the Catholic church to adjust to a greater change
than any other church in Angola. A mission executive described the situation of Catholic missionaries, which could just as accurately be applied
to the whole Catholic church:

> The missionaries had to make a change of almost 180 degrees.
> From a situation of being protected by the state they passed to the
> precarious position of opposition to the official ideology and polit-
> ical system. Presently they are much closer to the people, sharing
> their insecurity and many of their financial limitations.[1]

---

1. Torres Neiva, "Angola: Uma Igreja de Fronteira," *Encontro*, no. 116 (September 1981):
11.

Not being under the protection of the government after independence, the bishops were freer to speak out courageously than they were under the colonial regime. In their pastoral note of November 22, 1976, they stated their position on the new nation and its government forcefully.

The bishops first congratulated the nation on the celebration of the anniversary of its independence and hoped that the young Angolan nation would rapidly build a worthy future with prosperity and justice, liberty and equality for all its people.

The pastoral note then lamented the tragic situation caused by the war: profound divisions among the people; family and tribal hatred; accusations, revenge, and retaliations; massacres, kidnapping, and pillaging; deteriorating economy and the specter of hunger and disease; disorganization of some essential public services with accompanying inconvenience and deprivation.

The bishops rejoiced especially at the guarantees of religious liberty in the fundamental law of the nation. However they added that it was important that these constitutional provisions be implemented or they would become inoperative. The pastoral note alleged that they were being violated with impunity in various ways, such as:

(a) aggressive atheistic propaganda in schools and public meetings;

(b) affronts to believers because of their religious convictions and practices, in contradiction to the Constitution (Art. 18);

(c) accusations of reactionism for the simple fact of professing the Christian faith or participating in acts of worship;

(d) frequent profanation of temples, sacred objects or images, and even of the Eucharist with obvious impunity by the offenders;

(e) destruction of missions and other ecclesiastical institutions with the passivity or even the connivance of some responsible persons;

(f) invasion and violation of missionary houses and even episcopal residences by official agents who used arms rather than proper credentials to justify their acts.

The Spiritan magazine *Encontro* of May–June 1976, published in Lisbon, reported specific violations of religious liberty perpetrated by Cubans. In Dongo a church was profaned and Communion utensils were used as ashtrays. Sacred images were mutilated in Matala, and in Caconda Cubans in a sacrilegious parody marched through the streets spilling the Communion elements on the ground. The Church of Our Lady of Fatima in Sá da Bandeira was also profaned by Cubans.

The Catholic bishops continued their Note deploring the arbitrary detention and prolonged imprisonment of priests based on unproved suspicions, in violation of Article 23 of the Constitution. They also referred to the case of Rádio Eclésia, the Catholic radio station, which according to the bishops had been forced to transmit programs, including some that contradicted Christian doctrine.

The question of the nationalization of schools was raised because the bishops contended that a monopoly requiring an education contrary to the will of the parents was a violation of the Declaration of Human Rights (Art. 26, 32).

In spite of these criticism the bishops claimed that they were not protesting against the construction of a socialist society that would be open to humane and Christian values. They argued that the church's well-known social doctrine clearly recognizes the evils and injustices in the capitalist system and demands that natural resources and riches created by work and intelligence should be at the service of the whole community to promote justice and equality among all. The church could not, however, accept an ideology that denies the existence of God and is radically incompatible with fundamental principals of the Christian concept of the human person.

The pastoral note concluded with three affirmations concerning the relation of the church to the new nation and its government: (1) All citizens should unite in building the new nation and stop the fratricidal war. (2) The missionaries are absolutely at the service of the people, especially of those in greatest need, and wish to collaborate with the constituted authorities in human development and national reconstruction. However, they will not be involved in party politics that divide, since the missionaries' function is to unite. (3) The Catholic bishops trust in the understanding and good will of the political leaders to avoid friction, solve differences, and find the best ways to lead all the Angolan people to reconstruct this promising country.

The Episcopal Conference of Angola and São Tomé (CEAST) increased from eight to fifteen dioceses from 1975 to 1984. Even more striking than the increase in the number of dioceses was the change in personnel. Fifteen of the sixteen bishops who composed the CEAST in 1988 had been consecrated since April 25, 1974. The only bishop who was a member of the Episcopal Conference during the colonial period was Dom Francisco da Mata Mourisca of Uige. In spite of the addition of so many new members CEAST has been able to function effectively, maintaining unity and cohesion.

CEAST has also sought the unity of the Catholic church in Angola by coordinating activities between itself and the Confederation of Religious Orders. This effort has been greatly facilitated by the military confrontations, which forced all church workers, whatever their nationality or religious institute, to become one family.

The unity of the Catholic church allowed it to respond effectively to the severe emergency needs caused by the war, the dislocation of peoples, and the economic chaos that accompanied independence. Caritas de Angola was the organization through which the emergency aid program was administered. The International Catholic Conference of Caritas had been organized in Germany at the end of the nineteenth century. Caritas of Portugal, which began in 1945, was active in Angola during the colonial period and worked most intensively there from 1961 to 1974. After independence Caritas de Angola was formed, and it assumed the responsibility of distributing the aid that Caritas organizations in other countries sent.

The *Jornal de Angola* de April 23, 1976, reported the amounts of aid distributed in tons: food, 95,160; medicines, 3,010; blankets, 13,790; and clothes, 3,300. These goods were distributed by diocesan committees all across Angola among the thousands of internal refugees caused by the civil war among the three movements still fighting for power in 1976.

WCC Aid

A three-man delegation from the World Council of Churches (WCC) visited Angola from June 20 to July 4, 1976, to consult with churches and government officials concerning needs of the newly independent country as it faced the task of national reconstruction and to learn of ways in which churches outside could cooperate. On their return to Geneva they presented their report and almost immediately financial grants were made to the Methodists, the Baptists, the Church of North Angola, the Kimbanguist Church, and the Church Council of Central Angola. The Commission on Inter-Church Aid, Refugee and World Service (CICARWS) sent out appeals to member churches of the WCC for material aid. Since the Protestants in Angola did not have a unified and effective organization to distribute emergency aid, it was agreed that 75 percent of the aid sent by the WCC would be distributed by the government's Secretariat of State for Social Affairs and the rest by the churches.

The pastoral letter of January 1975, "The Church and Angolan Culture," entitled its first section "An Authentic Incarnation Here and Now." Twelve years later in the pastoral letter "Evangelization and Baptism" the bishops continued the examination of the same theme:

> We have used such terms as "indigenization," "adaptation," "acculturation," etc., to express the reality and the implications of the encounter of the gospel message with the most varied cultures.

Sociologically the word "inculturation" appears today to translate most accurately this dynamic. Inculturation means, in fact, the insertion of the life and message of Jesus Christ in a specific cultural context, so that this life and message might both be expressed in the elements of the culture in question, and exercise on it an inspiring, normative, and unifying function that could transform and recreate it, making a new creation.

The Catholic church in Angola has recognized the need for inculturation and thus has welcomed some changes in the style of worship with the use of new songs and choruses, accompaniment by drums and guitars, as well as swaying and dancing, but it is very cautious, not to say conservative in approving new liturgies and formulas that incorporate African cultural forms.

Dom Zacarias Kamwenho, bishop of Sumbe, who has been president of the CEAST Commission on Liturgy and Culture, gave an interview in 1975, in which he commented:

A few days ago a catechist told me: "We're tired of praying in Portuguese, we want to be taught like the catechists in the South" (referring to the dioceses of Nova Lisboa, Benguela, and Silva Porto). I had to explain that even in those dioceses there is still no Angolan liturgy. We have translations that are only steps toward a renewed liturgy. The people truly want to hear the wonders of God in their own language.

We must recognize that the Roman liturgy is not a caricature; it has a well-defined character, a definite value on which we should construct our Angolan liturgy. To understand profoundly the Roman liturgy is indispensable for a renewal or we will make strange and pretty experiments that tomorrow will be trite and vacuous.[2]

The experience of the Catholic church in Zaire shows that the process of inculturation is approached with caution by the Holy See. In 1961 the Zairian bishops recognized that "the liturgy introduced into Africa was not adapted yet to the real character of the peoples, continuing to be foreign to them." In Kampala Pope Paul VI spoke about this matter in 1968: "A present question that arouses much discussion confronts your task of evangelization, that is, the adaptation of the Gospel, the church, to African culture." In response to this opening the Zairian episcopate began the official process in 1969, requesting approval for the Zairian Rite of the Mass. It was used *ad experimentum* in various dioceses in Zaire and was altered in several ways by Rome. Finally on April 30, 1988, af-

---

2. *Encontro* 8, no. 78 (November–December 1975): 27, 56.

Onjango (Palaver-house)

ter twenty-seven years, the Congregation for Divine Worship in Rome
approved the Roman Missal for the dioceses of Zaire.[3]

Onjango

Another example of the adaptation of the Catholic church to Angolan
culture is the experiment in the Sumbe diocese called *onjango*. The word
in Umbundu means "palaver-house." Each Umbundu village had such
a structure: a circular structure with a diameter of about twenty-five feet
with a center pole of about twenty feet supporting a conical grass roof.
The wall reached only two-thirds of the way to the roof, permitting people to see in and out. The village elders gathered there to talk socially
and also to decide any questions over which they had jurisdiction. This
was both the social and the judicial center of the community.

Under the direction of Dom Zacarias the local church communities
in the diocese of Sumbe have been organized following the traditional
pattern. Their objective is to emphasize the role and the responsibility of
each Christian in the community. The Christians take responsibility for
the various ministries of the church: catechism, liturgy, social services,

3. *Além-Mar: Revista dos Missionários Combonianos,* no. 355 (November 1988): 9.

hospitality, etc. Thus groups of active Christians are formed, seeking to bring the community to live a faith involved in the everyday problems of the people.

The pattern of *onjango* in the Catholic church since independence is practically the system used in Protestant churches in Angola from the beginning. The hierarchical organization of the Catholic church placed authority and responsibility at the local level in the hands of the priest, and he entrusted the catechist with a small part of his responsibilities. In most Protestant communities the authority and responsibility were in the hands of local elders, lay men and women who functioned as Christian *onjangos*. The ordained minister was called upon to help resolve more difficult disciplinary problems and to administer the sacraments. As we have seen, however, the sacraments were not as central to the life of the Protestant communities as to the Catholic.

An entry in the author's diary written on a trip to the Bocoio area in June 1956 for a catechists school indicated that the *onjango* was seen by those Umbundu church leaders thirty years ago as a pattern for the church.

> Thursday night around the fire the men had an interesting discussion comparing the "old-time" village and a present-day "Christian" village. The main loss suffered in the transformation is the lack of social solidarity which was present in the village-*onjango* system.

Some observers have compared the *onjangos* in the Catholic church in Angola to the *comunidades eclesiales de base* (CEBs), or "base communities," which have become important features of the Catholic church in Latin America and especially in Brazil. One observer described the significance of the CEBs: "This is not the case of expanding the present ecclesiastical system based on the ecclesiastical and clerical axis, but the emergence of another form of being the church, set on the base of the Word and the laity."[4]

It is too early to make a judgment on the results of the Onjango system in Sumbe, but whatever it is called, it does appear to be a move from a system that was essentially sacramental and clerical toward one that gives greater place to the Word and the laity.

Reorganization of Protestant Churches

Independence was not simply a declaration made by the MPLA on November 11, 1975, or the lowering of the Portuguese flag and the raising

---

4. Leonard Boff, *Eclesiogênese* (Petrópolis: Editôra Vozes, 1977), 10; Eng. trans.: *Ecclesiogenesis* (Maryknoll, N.Y.: Orbis Books, 1986).

of the MPLA flag. It was a complex of factors that changed the whole life of Angola and consequently transformed the churches, which embraced more than half the population of the country. The establishment of a secular state disestablished the Catholic church and thus put all the churches on the same level. The reduction of the European population involved the decrease of the foreign missionary population. Many rural mission stations were abandoned because of the intensification of the civil war. Hundreds of thousands of rural residents fled to urban centers. Political power became more centralized in Luanda because of the official policy of "centralized democracy" and also because the war impeded the establishment of effective political control in many outlying regions.

For the first time Protestant churches were recognized as valid Angolan institutions, although it took several years for the recognition to become legal. The first step was for the churches that were Angolan to be distinguished from the missions, which were considered foreign institutions. The Portuguese never gave *de jure* recognition to any Protestant organization and did not grant even *de facto* recognition to the churches. They only appeared in a section of the missions' annual reports as "Ecclesiastical Activities."

This anonymity had provided a certain shelter under which the Protestant churches established solid social structures without having to spend time and energy satisfying all the bureaucratic requirements that the colonial government would certainly have imposed if the churches had been given official recognition.

In Protestant villages the church elders, in addition to directing the religious activities, played the traditional roles of magistrates and community organizers. They administered schools, supported teachers, and promoted agriculture, public health, and literacy. In larger villages and pastoral centers church leaders administered boarding schools and clinics. They built the necessary installations for these services and handled the finances. In some cases missionary personnel provided encouragement and special financial contributions, but the church leaders generally administered the institutions and programs.

The colonial government, which had professed its Christian faith, refused to recognize the non-Catholic communities. The new government, controlled by a professedly atheistic party, was ready to deal with the various religious communities. This forced the churches that had functioned in the shadow of the missions to analyze themselves, decide on a name, and define their structure and program.

Worldwide churches such as the United Methodists and Seventh-Day Adventists had no need to rethink their name or organization, but most Protestant churches had to undertake a process of self-analysis and formulate a written statement of their history, structure, and program. In some cases the decision about the name required considerable debate.

The Evangelical Church of Angola (IEA)

The Missão Evangélica de Angola, with stations in Cabinda and south of the Congo River along the Atlantic coast, had been related to six mission agencies at various times in its history, but was popularly known by the name of Matthew Z. Stober, who served it for more than fifty years. After independence the leaders chose the simplest name, A Igreja Evangélica de Angola. From the four mission stations of Ambrizete, Sazaire (Quimpondo), Cabinda, and Mboca, the church reorganized itself into nine regions: Maiombe, Malombe, Cabinda, Soyo, Tomboco, Nzeto, Quindeje, Ambriz, and Luanda, with its general secretariat in the city of Cabinda. For several years Rev. Pedro Manuel has been the general secretary of the IEA.

The Evangelical Baptist Church of Angola (IEBA)

From the three BMS stations of São Salvador/Mbanza Kongo, Bembe, and Kibokolo scores of small congregations were gathered among the Bakongo in the north of Angola. After the colonial war began in 1961 almost four-fifths of the population of northern Angola became refugees in Zaire. As refugee Christians they played an important part in church life in Zaire, but they always hoped to return to Angola. In 1968, to prepare for this return, they formed the Association of Baptist Churches in Exile (ACEBA). The experience gained in ACEBA from 1968 to 1974 was valuable for the Angolan Baptist leaders who after independence organized the Igreja Evangélica Baptista de Angola. As was common among the Protestant churches after independence the former BMS congregations spread beyond their traditional regional limits but at the same time became more centralized organizationally. Instead of having headquarters in one of their original mission stations, they established an office in Luanda. Their first general secretary was the Rev. Pedro Manuel Timóteo, who was succeeded by the Rev. Álvaro Rodrigues.

The Angola Baptist Convention (CBA)

The Baptist congregations not founded by the BMS during the colonial period were related to the Portuguese Baptist Convention and later to the Southern Baptist Convention in the U.S.A. They were scattered around Angola, mostly in urban centers. The convention is divided into three associations: Luanda, Uige, and Huambo. In 1991 the general sec-

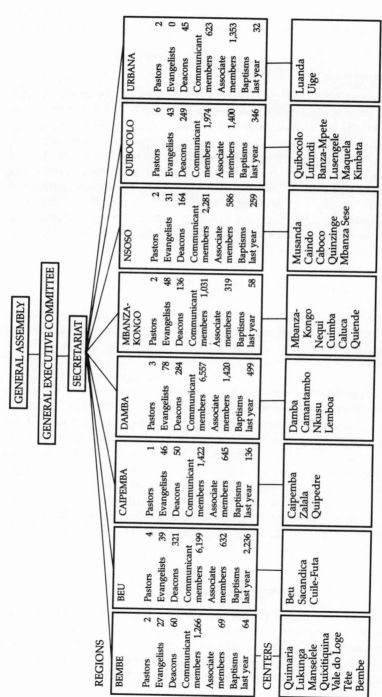

THE STRUCTURE OF THE BAPTIST CHURCH IN ANGOLA

After ninety-nine years the Evangelical Baptist Church ordained
its first pastors in 1977. Courtesy of the Baptist Missionary Society

retary of the Angola Baptist Convention with an office in Luanda was
the Rev. David N'Kosi.

The Evangelical Reformed Church in Angola (IERA) and
the United Evangelical Church in Angola (IEUA)

The Protestant communities that issued from the work of the North Angola Mission had difficulties in making the transition from mission to
church for several reasons. First, the Rev. Archibald Patterson had kept
the reins of the mission firmly in his own hands from the founding of
the mission in 1922 until he was forced to leave Angola at the outbreak
of the colonial war in 1961. Even during the war (1961–74) while Patterson was in England the Angolan leaders of the church looked to him
for guidance and support. However, with Patterson's long absence and
advanced age and the poor communications, his leadership became increasingly tenuous. At the invitation of the refugee community in Zaire
he did visit Kinshasa in 1972 and attended the ordination of Luiz João
Alexandre and Domingos Ventura.

Second, the leaders of this church who were close collaborators of
Patterson had acquired their knowledge of the Bible and the Christian
faith through on-the-job training. They had little or no academic education. Third, the North Angola Mission community was split three ways
during the 1961–74 period: many fled to Zaire, some spent long periods

hidden in the wooded hills of northern Angola, and others stayed in or near their homes in Uige, Sanza Pombo, and Quimbele.

The NAM community in Zaire organized themselves into the Igreja do Norte de Angola (*em exílio*). As the members of this church returned to Angola in 1974–76, they added the word "evangelical" to their name, becoming A Igreja Evangélica do Norte de Angola (IENA).

After April 25, 1974, Patterson visited Angola to hand over the work. August Jaquete, an experienced catechist and Patterson's chauffeur, was ordained during Patterson's visit and given the title of director of the mission. Pedro de Oliveira, who was also ordained at that time, was named by Patterson to be superintendent. The Rev. Manuel da Conceição was chosen to be superintendent of Kinkuni and Quimbele as well as president of the executive council. The Rev. Domingos Alexandre was named secretary of the council and director of the Bible institute. The latter was not satisfied with his appointments and expressed his dissatisfaction before Patterson departed from Angola for the last time. This discontent contributed to a division within the North Angola community when Alexandre led one part of the community to form a separate church, the United Evangelical Church of Angola (IEUA).

In 1978 the Evangelical Church of North Angola met in general assembly at Kimbunga-Lau, where the government representative accused the IENA of being a "tribal church" since the word "North" seemed to restrict the organization to one region or tribe. The executive committee met to consider other names. "Anglican" was suggested, as Patterson had belonged to the Church of England, but he had not used the name in Angola. The word "Reformed" was proposed and approved, so the Evangelical Church of North Angola in 1978 changed its name to the Igreja Evangélica Reformada de Angola (IERA).

Edmond Racloz, an agricultural missionary of the AME, had been visiting Angola and other African nations for an inter-mission organization, the Coordinating Committee for Agricultural Projects (CCPA) which included the AME and the Département Missionnaire des Églises Protestantes de la Suisse Romande (DM). The IERA inquired through Racloz whether one of the Swiss missions would be willing to support it. The AME and DM discussed the question in 1981 and agreed that the Département Missionnaire would do so. The IERA also has maintained contact with the Igreja Reformada de Holanda and in 1980 became a member of the World Alliance of Reformed Churches.

The fifty-year-old community with the new name was ready to choose a new generation of leaders. It seemed appropriate that the first new leader should have been born in Angola and trained in Zaire. Malungo António Pedro was born in Sanza Pombo in 1946. His family emigrated to Zaire before 1961. Malungo grew up there and did the secondary course in commerce and industry. He also took courses in the

Christian faith in the Kinshasa Mennonite mission from 1963 to 1968, including correspondence lessons and classes at the Center for Christian Information. He worked in the Church of North Angola (in exile) in Kinshasa, becoming vice-president. Having proved his dedication and competence to the Mennonites, they invited Malungo António Pedro to take charge of their large bookstore in the Zairian capital. He married Noemia Manuel, the daughter of the Rev. Manuel da Conceição and Juliana Ines, in 1969, and they built a house in Kinsuka, a suburb of Kinshasa, where they gathered a Mennonite Brethren congregation beginning in 1972.

The young couple returned to Angola in 1975, and Malungo António Pedro worked as secretary for Christian Education of the Church of North Angola in Sanza Pombo. In 1976 they moved to Uige and later the same year relocated to Luanda, where Pedro reopened the Bible Society agency, which had been closed since the Portuguese director, Anibal Machado, left Angola. For a brief period he worked in both the Bible Society and the IENA, which in 1977 opened an office in Luanda, but the Bible Society found a full-time secretary, the Rev. João Makondekwa and Pedro confined his work to what was by then the Evangelical Reformed Church of Angola.

CIEAC to IECA

A common factor in the reorganization of Protestant communities after independence was the shift from regional churches to national denominations. In the colonial period the only churches that took the whole of Angola as their field were the Catholic and the Seventh-Day Adventist. Other churches confined their activities to regions, which were recognized by unofficial comity agreements. Independence released forces that encouraged the regional churches to change into national denominations. The most notable example was the transformation of the Council of Evangelical Churches in Central Angola (CIEAC) into the Evangelical Congregational Church of Angola (IECA).

The decision to become a national denomination was taken in the face of traditions that opposed denominationalism. The ABCFM and the CFMSBNA were both supported by Congregational churches in North America, but they never used the denominational term in Angola. They described the churches they founded in Central Angola as "Evangelical." John T. Tucker expressed this nondenominational position:

> Denominationalism has always been at a minimum in the Angolan field. Home sectarian battlefields were not shifted to Africa; enough to proclaim the "Gospel of our blessed God." The word "Congregational" has no meaning to the thousands of Christians

in the hinter-land of Benguela. They call themselves and all other believers, *Vakua Yesu* (Those of Jesus), or *Vakua Kristu* (Those of Christ). From early days the West Central African Mission has been a united and uniting mission.[5]

In harmony with this nondenominational position the WCAM provided leadership and financial support for the Angola Evangelical Alliance, which tried to keep alive the hope that the regional churches using a the common name such as "Evangelical" or "Church of Christ in Angola" would not proliferate into a multitude of denominations, as in Europe and North America.

One example of the commitment to comity or regionalism was the willingness of the Council of Evangelical Churches in Central Angola to integrate their members who had moved to Luanda into the Methodist church, the regional church in the capital. The CIEAC agreed to have the Rev. Eduardo Daniel Nunda from Chilesso minister as a Methodist pastor, serving the Umbundu-speaking congregations in Luanda. This was not a unique experience. Several groups of Bakongo from BMS churches in the north of Angola functioned in Luanda as Methodist classes.

During the 1960s the Umbundu members in Luanda requested several times that their congregations be associated with the CIEAC in Dôndi instead of with the Methodist church. These requests were consistently refused by the CIEAC in faithfulness to the principle of comity.

After independence the Umbundu people, who were the largest ethnic group in Angola and the most widely spread geographically, followed the general trend of moving to urban centers to escape the civil war. Thus members of CIEAC church were increasingly found in cities and towns all across Angola.

Another factor that decreased the regional character of Angolan society was the centralization of public administration by the new Angola government. The Protestant missions and churches had been responsible to district or area authorities and had little reason to deal directly with government services in Luanda. With the government in the hands of the MPLA, a Marxist party, the churches wondered what that would mean for their work. Everything was so new that local and district officials could not answer the questions. Therefore the churches all over Angola had to deal more with Luanda. When the Rev. Floriano Ukuahamba of the CIEAC was assigned to Luanda, he was not only pastor of the Umbundu congregations, but also represented the CIEAC in the government offices.

One of the most politically dangerous factors that argued for a change in the name of the CIEAC was the flight of its principal leaders

---

5. John T. Tucker, *Drums in the Darkness* (New York: George H. Doran Company, 1927), 59–60.

from Dôndi to the bush with UNITA in February 1977. They included: the Rev. Ricardo Uliengue Epalanga, general secretary, Artur Cinco Reis, general treasurer, the Rev. Eliseu Buta, principal of the United Seminary, Professor Eduardo Oseas Baptista Chingufu, director of Currie Institute, the Rev. Abias Muecalia, director of the center of publications, Dario Catata, director of agricultural work, and Teixeira Chipaco, nurse of the Dôndi hospital. When the military took control of the Dôndi mission, except for the leprosarium, the headquarters of the CIEAC moved from Dôndi to Huambo. This produced the anomalous situation of the CIEAC having its headquarters in Huambo and its officers mostly in the bush with UNITA.

Pastor Ricardo Epalanga attended the Fourth Congress of UNITA held in the bush near Huambo and commented that he was able to see Christian brothers and sisters from such churches as Chilesso, Chissamba, Camundongo, Bunjei, Capango, Hualondo, Muié Catota, and Pereira d'Eça. He also wrote: "I heard that some of the church leaders in Huambo want to name an Interim Committee in order to contact the [mission] boards. At this moment I don't want to suggest anything. Let the brothers do as they deem best. We here in the bush are going to continue doing our work in accord with the existing facilities until we return to our points of departure."[6]

In 1977 the Rev. Henrique Etaungo Daniel was elected general secretary of the CIEAC.[7]

Meeting in February 1978 the CIEAC considered changing its name, but the minutes recorded only that the matter was referred to the Faith, Order, and Discipline Committee. The committee brought its recommendation to the General Synod meeting of January 3–9, 1979, and the new name was adopted: Igreja Evangélica Congregacional de Angola (IECA). The reasons for the choice of the new title were not explained in the minutes except to say that "the name Congregational was adopted to conform more closely to the organization and practice of Our Church."

Undoubtedly the church had important reasons for changing its name, but this explanation does not reveal an understanding of congregational polity. A congregational church is one in which the local assembly of believers has authority over its spiritual life, doctrine, organization, choice of leaders, finances, and property. In the newly named community in central Angola the general synod and regional synods were responsible for most aspects of the work for which a congrega-

---

6. Personal correspondence with author.

7. The CIEAC/IECA has had four general secretaries in thirty years. The smooth transition from one to another is a sign of the stability and functioning democracy that have characterized this community: Rev. Jessé Chiula Chipenda (1957–68), Rev. Ricardo Uliengue Epalanga (1968–77), Rev. Henrique Etaungo Daniel (1977-1983), and Júlio Francisco Muehombo (1983–).

tion would have had authority if the name were being properly applied. However with the multiplication of Protestant denominations in independent Angola, the title "Congregational" had the advantage of being distinctive.

The Evangelical Church of Southwest Angola (IESA)

The Protestant church planted by what was popularly known as the Swiss mission did not change its name after independence, even though it included a regional term, which the IERA and CIEAC had feared might be prejudicial. It had adopted the name Igreja Evangélica do Sudoeste de Angola (the Evangelical Church of Southwest Angola) in 1964 and has maintained it until the present time. The IESA was also the only church that kept its headquarters in a rural mission. This was undoubtedly because Kalukembe, its central station, was the site of the only large Protestant hospital to continue functioning after independence.

Pastor Eliseu Simeão, the first and only president of the IESA, has served longer than the executive officer of any other church in Angola.

The Pentecostal Assembly of God and the MEPA

The congregations started by the Church of God mission in the district of Cuanza South during the 1950s continued to grow during the transition period in spite of leadership problems. The pioneer missionaries were expelled in 1959, which left the community without missionary leadership. Also, according to comity principles the work had been started in an area where there were no other Protestant missions and very little educational opportunity for Angolans, which meant the first converts were mostly unlettered. Furthermore, the first missionaries were not there long enough to provide much biblical training.

To complicate the situation missionaries from the Assemblies of God in Portugal, who arrived in the early 1970s, took a very paternalistic attitude toward the Angolan church leaders. This led to tensions and conflicts that in the explosive atmosphere of the colonial war produced accusations and counteraccusations of collaboration with terrorists or with PIDE.

As a result, at independence two churches were formed. The Assembleia de Deus Pentecostal includes the majority of congregations and has missionary personnel and support from the Assemblies of God in Portugal and Brazil. It was among the first twelve churches recognized by the government and joined the Association of Evangelicals of Angola.

The Evangelical Pentecostal Mission of Angola (MEPA) has its headquarters in Porto Amboim with Pastor José Domingos Caetano as representative. It has not been recognized by the government, but is a member of CAIE.

The Brethren Assemblies

The Plymouth Brethren (CMML) planted the seed of the gospel in Bié and Moxico at the turn of the century, and Christian communities sprang up among the Umbundu and Chokwe peoples. During the colonial period the Brethren never developed an ecclesiastical organization embracing all the assemblies, as this was against their ecclesiological principles. Therefore, the Brethren were the least prepared to obey government orders that each church respond to a series of questions concerning its history, structure, doctrine, and program. As a consequence, even though the assemblies are some of the oldest Protestant congregations, they were not included in the first group of twelve churches recognized by the government.

Union of the Evangelical Churches of Angola (UIEA)

The congregations founded by the South Africa General Mission (SAGM), which had changed its name to the Africa Evangelical Fellowship (AEF), chose the name Union of the Evangelical Churches of Angola for the ecclesiastical organization in which they were united.

The SAGM comity region had been roughly between 14 and 16 degrees latitude south, with missionaries stationed at Muié, Catota, Sá da Bandeira, and Moçâmedes. Muié and Catota were areas of intense military activity after independence and missionaries were forced to abandon those stations.

The Moçâmedes/Namibe–Menongue railway became the axis of the UIEA congregations, and the Bible Institute that had functioned at the Catota mission was moved to Menongue. In the common practice of postindependence Angola the UIEA moved out of its regional base and established Ganguela churches in Moxico, Huambo, Bié, and Luanda.

The UIEA maintains that each congregation is autonomous, i.e., congregational, but the exigencies of the postindependence period have required an increasing centralization, and the head of the church has been given the title of "director." Pastor Silva Kapamba has held that post since 1979.

United Methodist Church (IMUA)

The United Methodist Church, as part of a worldwide organization, did not have to go through the process of self-analysis, choosing a name, or creating new structures in order to adapt to independent Angola, but it did go through a difficult time of change.

As the Catholic church created several new dioceses since independence, some members of the Methodist church in the Malanje area requested that the Angola Annual Conference be divided in two. The request was approved by the General Conference meeting in the United States in 1984, and a process was set in motion to prepare for the creation of a second annual conference. Bishop Emílio de Carvalho opposed the process at several points, creating tensions and even open conflict between the bishop and some Malanje Methodists.

The dispute had certain similarities to the division of the Uige diocese of the Catholic church to form the diocese of Mbanza Kongo. Regional loyalties and hostilities have existed within the Kikongo, as they have within the Kimbundu. Also the war had made transportation and communications difficult between Luanda and Malanje, as between Uige and Mbanza Kongo. Many more people became actively and even violently involved in the Methodist dispute than in the Catholic because the Protestant system is more open, and many more people had a voice and indeed a vote in the decisions. A Methodist bishop does not have the same authority as a Catholic bishop. All the bodies that had to approve any change — the General Conference of the United Methodist Church with worldwide authority, the Central Africa Conference and the Angola Annual — are composed of half lay and half clergy members.

After the decision to create a second annual conference was settled, the choice of the bishop became a matter of dispute. This was resolved in August 1988 when the Rev. Moisés Domingos Fernandes was elected bishop of the Eastern Annual Conference by the Central Africa Conference. He was born in Malanje April 17, 1938, and received his theological degree from the Seminario Evangélico de Teología, Matanzas, Cuba. Bishop Moisés is married to Luciana da Silva Clemente Fernandes, and they have eight children.

Igreja de Jesus Cristo Sobre a Terra
(Kimbanguist Church)

The beginnings of Kimbanguism were described in chapter 4, but in Angola during the colonial period it was not an organized church with a recognized structure and defined doctrine. It developed both in the process of recognition as a church in Zaire in 1959, reception as a member of the World Council of Churches in 1969, obtaining permission to function in Angola after April 25, 1974, and participating as a founding member of CAIE in 1977. It claimed on the information presented to CAIE that it had two hundred thousand members, which would make it the largest church in the Protestant community in Angola.

The Kimbanguist Church in Angola recognizes the Rev. Diangienda-Kuntima, also known as "Papa Joseph," third son of the Prophet Simon Kimbangu, as Spiritual Head (Chefe Espiritual) of the entire international Kimbanguist community. His residence and the business headquarters of the church are in Kinshasa, but the spiritual center of the church is at the sacred shrine in Nkamba, the New Jerusalem, in the Lower Congo district of Zaire where the mausoleum of Simon Kimbangu is located.

Leadership in the Kimbanguist Church is hierarchical, and the church claims a theological basis for such a structure:

> The trinitarian God is hierarchical in structure. This is seen in the fact that the Eternal or God the Father commands his Son Jesus Christ to come to redeem humanity from sin. Christ in obedient submission joyfully accepts this mission. . . . St. Paul testifies to this: "Have this mind among yourselves, which is yours in Christ Jesus, who though he was in the form of God, did not count equality with God a thing to be grasped, but emptied himself, taking the form of a servant . . ." (Phil. 2:5–8). The Holy Spirit in turn recognizes and submits to the authority of Christ.[8]

This hierarchical community demands strict discipline, but this does not mean an excessive clericalism. The laity have important responsibilities among the Kimbanguists. For example, a person who commits a grave fault and is placed under discipline may confess to his pastor, but the Kimbanguist church encourages such persons to make an individual confession to a group of persons. The role of "witnesses to the confession" is to intercede with the Lord in favor of the penitent, with whom they feel themselves in solidarity.

Kimbanguist Sacraments — Baptism.   The four sacraments recognized and practiced in the Kimbanguist church are baptism, Communion, marriage, and ordination.

Baptism by prayer and imposition of hands is called the baptism of the Holy Spirit of which John the Baptist spoke before Christ's ministry began: "I [John] baptize you with water for repentance, but he who is coming after me is mightier than I, whose sandals I am not worthy to carry: he will baptize you with the Holy Spirit and with fire" (Matt. 3:11). For Kimbanguist theology Jesus marks both the end of the former practice of baptism with water and the coming of the era of baptism with the Holy Spirit.

---

8. Rev. Diangienda-Kutima, "The Essence of Kimbanguism," *All Africa Lutheran Consultation on Christian Theology and Strategy for Mission*, Monrovia, Liberia, April 1980 (Geneva: Lutheran World Federation, 1980), 226.

In the Kimbanguist church children are not baptized before they reach the age of reason (about twelve years of age). They must pass through the catechumenate before receiving baptism. They are then permitted to receive Communion. It is customary for Kimbanguists to bring their children to church at the age of three months to be blessed by the pastor, in imitation of Christ who was blessed by Simeon (Luke 2:22–38). Although this rite is not in itself a sacrament, it is nonetheless important because it forms a stage in the process of becoming a full member of the Christian community.

Communion. Communion in the Kimbanguist church was defined only in 1970:

> For the blood of Christ, diluted honey is to be used. This was John the Baptist's food. For the body of Christ, a cake made of potato, eggs, maize flour and green bananas. After the prayer of benediction, the honey and the cake become in reality the Blood and Body of Christ. To receive Communion, for Kimbanguists, is very much more than to remember Christ; it is really and truly to eat and drink the Body and Blood of the Lord.
>
> In order to underline the sacrosanct character of Communion, the sacrament is celebrated only three times a year at dates carefully chosen by the church because of their significance:
>
> 25 December, the feast of the Nativity;
>
> 12 October, anniversary of the death of Simon Kimbangu;
>
> 6 April, anniversary of the beginning of Simon Kimbangu's Christian ministry, and the occasion of the feast of Easter.[9]

Marriage. By the sacrament of marriage, man and woman are united before God and the people by the church. The bride and groom must be Christians, and at the time of the marriage must not be under discipline. In practice, the religious marriage is only celebrated after the so-called customary marriage. Before the religious rite the pair cannot either cohabit or have sexual relations. The Kimbanguist Church recognizes only monogamous marriage and admits no polygamists to its membership.

Ordination. Ordination is the sacrament by which the church raises some of its members in the name of Christ to the dignity of ministers of worship or deacons. Ministers alone are entitled to administer the sacraments and carry out such important rites as the blessing of children and interment.

---

9. Ibid., 235.

The Kimbanguist Moral Code.

The Kimbanguist moral code requires . . . a strict and life-long practice of the ten commandments of God. Every Kimbanguist is bound in particular to love his neighbor, in accordance with Jesus' command. He must refrain from engaging in any commercial activities on Sunday, the Lord's day. He must not drink alcoholic drinks, dance, take drugs, smoke, be a polygamist, commit adultery or fornication, eat pork (the unclean spirits that Jesus cast out took refuge in the herd of swine). The Kimbanguist may not wash or sleep naked (for he must be decently clad in the presence of the Lord who is with us night and day). It is a duty to take off one's shoes in every place of worship (since Christ is present in every place where his name is invoked; Moses did so at his meeting with God on Mount Sinai), and to put aside for the moment money and objects of value at the time of prayer (as a symbol of humility before the Lord). The member of the church must avoid rendering evil for evil, and must endeavor to settle without delay and without violence any quarrel he may have had with another person. Women and girls must cover their heads in places of worship. They must also avoid wearing indecent clothes such as mini-skirts or short dresses or any other garment which exposes most of their body. Kimbanguists must refrain from having resource to talismans, magic, sorcery, divination, for these practices are ascribed to satanic power. They are also forbidden to belong to any secret society.[10]

When the Kimbanguists were applying for membership in the World Council of Churches they received strong support from the "peace churches," such as the Mennonites, and also from pacifist organizations. Since then they have defined their position as that of a church that professes nonviolence but not "passive pacifism." They do not object to their members entering military service in Angola.

Tocoism — The Church of Our Lord Jesus Christ in the World

Simão Toco, the founder of the Church of Our Lord Jesus Christ in the World, was transferred by the Portuguese government from one detention site to another in Angola in the 1950s and finally was sent in exile to the Azores, as described in chapter 4. In 1962, in the second year of the colonial war, the Portuguese thought that Toco might be used to influence his followers and other Angolans to express opposition to the

---

10. Ibid., 249.

"terrorists" and to support the government. So he was brought out of exile and received by the authorities in Luanda. During the year he spent in Angola he was a controversial figure since some Portuguese thought that he would be useful to the government and others, particularly the Catholic church, considered him dangerous, if not politically, at least religiously.

Toco's followers considered his presence as a real victory, claiming that thousands of Angolans were converted to Tocoism. They also reported that Toco had gone with his elders, Domingos Quibeta, João Sivi, and Luvuale Dabid, through the war-torn area in northern Angola, reaching the border and calling his people who had taken refuge in Zaire to return to Angola. To house them Toco is supposed to have built the town of Taia-Nova near Maquela do Zombo.

According to his followers, Toco presented a peace plan by which young Tocoist men, "spiritually prepared," would go into the war area and gather up all the armaments. The government was not willing to take the risk, and so Toco was returned in exile to the Azores. While a lighthouse keeper on São Miguel, he maintained a steady correspondence, giving spiritual counsel and restructuring the church in Angola.

Simão Toco returned to Angola on August 31, 1974, and was jubilantly received by his followers and interviewed by the press. Soon, however, he and his movement were again in the midst of controversy. His house was attacked in July 1975 as the fighting in Luanda between FNLA and MPLA forces became more intense. The MPLA was accused of being responsible for the attack. The *Jornal de Angola* of July 3, 1975, had the headline "House of Spiritual Leader Simão Toco Assaulted" and included an interview with him. When asked if he thought it had been the FAPLA (the MPLA armed forces), he responded:

> I do not know if it was Dr. Neto who gave this order. I don't know. Dr. Neto was my colleague. I did not study more because I did not have the money. I spoke with Dr. Neto, with Dr. Savimbi, and Holden Roberto. And I told them: You must be careful with this Angola. I have not studied; you are educated, but take care of this Angola. Unite yourselves, you three, to form one group, or you will destroy Angola. Dr. Neto said, "O.K., my colleague! but your career is different." That was the reply he gave me. They did not understand me.

To conclude Simão Toco said: "I will not speak any more to the world! A war will break out! This is folly. The real war has not started yet. I can die, but remember this: another war is coming!"

A year later, after independence, protests were made against what were being called reactionary sects: Kimbanguists, Tocoists, and Jehovah's Witnesses. In that turmoil the Tocoist Tabernacle of the Lord was destroyed. Toco went into hiding for fourteen months. The government responded to the protests by condemning the Witnesses, but looked sympathetically on the Kimbanguists and Tocoists.

Before the recognition process came to its fruition Simão Toco died on January 1, 1984. There followed a struggle for power within the church, leading to the creation of two main factions that entered into armed conflict. As a result the government did not include the Church of Our Lord Jesus Christ in the World among the twelve recognized churches, and religious activities of the Tocoist Church were suspended until the divisions within the hierarchy were resolved. This was accomplished in 1988 with the election of Luzaisso António Lutango and Panzo Firmón as general representative and second representative of the Church of Jesus Christ in the World. Subsequently the secretary of state for culture announced publicly that the suspension of activities had been cancelled.[11]

Official Recognition of Churches

On March 8, 1978, the Political Bureau of the Central Committee of the MPLA-PT instructed the Ministry of Justice to elaborate a process for the registry of churches and religious organizations, and it prohibited the establishment of new churches and organizations. In a separate sentence it ordered the prohibition of youth, women's, and work organizations of a religious nature.

The Ministry of Justice published Executive Decree 19/80 which provided the form to be used by each church or organization that wished to apply for recognition.

On May 13, 1986, the National Office for Religious Subjects in the Secretariat of State for Culture called representatives of nineteen churches to meet on May 17. The following churches or organizations were informed that they had not been approved:

- The Lassist Church of Prophetic Christianity
- The Church of the Twelve Apostles
- The Evangelical Church of Mennonite Brethren in Angola
- The Church of the Apostles of Jesus Christ
- The Lutheran Church of Angola in Zaire
- The Evangelical Pentecostal Fraternity in Africa
- The Prophetic Church of Christ in Angola

---

11. *Jornal de Angola*, May 12, 1988.

- The Church of Christ in Union with the Holy Spirit Way International
- The Church of the Mission of the Holy Spirit in the Christian Church
- The Scripture Union in Angola
- The Church Kia-Kua-Nza
- The Mission for the Evangelization of Africa in the Portuguese Language
- The Church of the Blacks in Africa
- The Church of the Universal Holy Hope
- The Islamic Community in Angola
- The New Apostolic Church
- The Evangelical Lutheran Community in Angola
- The Evangelical Community in Angola

The *Diário da República* of January 24, 1987, included Executive Decree No. 9/87 of the Ministry of Justice giving the names of the following twelve churches that had been "recognized" and could then proceed with the process of "registry":

- The Church of Southwest Angola
- The Evangelical Congregational Church of Angola
- The Catholic Church
- The United Methodist Church
- The Evangelical Church of Angola
- The Evangelical Baptist Church of Angola
- The Evangelical Reformed Church of Angola
- The Church of Jesus Christ on the Earth (Kimbanguist)
- The Pentecostal Assemblies of God
- The Seventh-Day Adventist Church
- The Angola Baptist Convention
- The Union of Evangelical Churches of Angola

Among the items of information that the government requested on the application for recognition was the date of founding of the churches in Angola. All the Protestant churches responded with the date in which their first missionaries arrived in Angola; the Catholic church gave the date of 33 C.E.

New Protestant Associations

The Protestant community had become more and more divided during the transition from colony to independence. The Aliança Evangélica de Angola, which had included all the Protestant missions except the Seventh-Day Adventists, had been prohibited from meeting from 1961 to 1974. It did maintain an office in Luanda, which distributed circular letters sporadically, but this was a very tenuous tie among the widely scattered missions and churches. The other all-Angola Protestant meetings, the Congress of Portuguese Language Congregations and the Congress of Evangelical Youth, were also prohibited.

The Portuguese government used the war as a reason for restricting travel of Protestant leaders. Foreign missionaries had to request travel permits from Luanda, and even if granted, they frequently arrived after the date for which they were requested. Angolan church leaders were at the mercy of local officials, who could limit their travel and the holding of area church meetings. All such restrictions limited the ties that were needed to create or maintain regional and national Protestant relations.

Worldwide and continental divisions in Protestantism affected the Angolan Protestant community as well. The World Council of Churches was considered an enemy of Portugal because of its financial contributions to African liberation movements, including the FLNA and the MPLA. The missions/churches related to the WCC were especially suspect by the Portuguese, and some of the missions that were antagonistic to the WCC expressed their antagonism publicly to establish more favorable relations with Portuguese officials. The Lausanne Evangelical meetings became a world rallying point for the anti-WCC Protestants. Mostly through the encouragement of Dr. Rodolphe Bréchet, some Angolans attended the Lausanne meeting in 1974.

In Africa this division was represented by the All Africa Conference of Churches, with relations to the WCC, and the Association of Evangelicals of Africa and Madagascar, with Lausanne ties.

Angola Association of Evangelicals (AEA)

April 25, 1974, meant the lifting of many restrictions on the Protestant churches of Angola, and so they asked themselves, "How will we work together now?"

The first answer to the question was given by representatives of six churches that met in Benguela on December 27–28, 1974: the Evangelical Church of Southwest Angola, the Assemblies of God, the Brethren, the Angola Baptist Convention, the Evangelical Congregations in Africa (AEF), and the Evangelical Christian Church. Their purpose was "to exchange views and to examine the opportunity of founding an organization joining various churches of conservative-evangelical doctrine." Pastor Eliseu Simeão of Kalukembe was elected to preside, and Pastor António Tiago Pereira of Huambo and Júlio António Afonso of Moçâmedes were chosen secretaries. The first item on the agenda was to agree on the doctrinal statement for the new organization. They accepted the statement of the Association of Evangelicals of Africa and Madagascar with only one amendment to the first article. Instead of describing the Holy Scriptures as "supreme authority" they changed it to "only authority." So the doctrinal statement read:

CONFESSION OF FAITH

What we believe:

The Association of Evangelicals of Angola maintains the conservative evangelical doctrinal position, which includes the following items of faith:

1. The Holy Scriptures, as given originally by God, divinely inspired and infallible, worthy of all trust and as the only authority in matters of faith and practice.

2. One God, eternal, in three persons, Father, Son and Holy Spirit.

3. Our Lord Jesus Christ, who is God revealed in the flesh by his virgin birth, his sinless human life, by his divine miracles, by his substitutionary and expiatory death, by his bodily resurrection, by his ascension, by his mediating work, and his coming in person in power and glory.

4. The salvation of lost, sinful man by the spilled blood of the Lord Jesus Christ, by faith, independently of works, and by regeneration of the Holy Spirit.

5. The Holy Spirit who, living in the believer, enables him to live a holy life to testify to and work for the Lord Jesus Christ.

6. The spiritual union of all those who, having believed in Jesus Christ for their salvation, were regenerated by the Holy Spirit and who therefore form the church, the body of Christ of which He is the head.

7. The personal existence of Satan, who seeks to supplant God and frustrate his purposes, but whose end is eternal condemnation.

8. The resurrection of the body, of all the dead: the believers for eternal blessedness and nonbelievers to judgment and eternal punishment.

The Angola Council of Evangelical Churches (CAIE)

Two years after the Association of Evangelicals of Angola was formed, a second Angolan interchurch Protestant organization was founded in February 1977. The United Methodist Church and the Council of Evangelical Churches of Central Angola sent invitations for a meeting to twelve churches — eight of which sent delegates. For the organizing meeting held in the United Methodist church in Luanda, the Rev. Daniel Ntoni-Nzinga of the Evangelical Baptist Church was elected president and David João Manuel Nkosi, secretary.

While the first preoccupation of the Association of Evangelicals of Angola was the elaboration of a doctrinal statement, the meeting of the eight churches in Luanda stated is objectives in these terms:

1. to strengthen and to develop the cooperation of churches in the realms of evangelization, Christian education, theology, and training of Christian executives in service responsibility, documentation, information, and communications;

2. to guarantee and to reaffirm the unity of the churches in expression and common witness of its faith in Jesus Christ;

3. to be the link and voice of the churches with the Angolan state and with national and international ecumenical organizations.

The AEA had acknowledged its relationship to the Association of Evangelicals of Africa and Madagascar, but the group meeting in Luanda, taking the name of Angolan Council of Evangelical Churches (CAIE) applied for membership in the All Africa Conference of Churches (AACC). On a world scale the AEA related to the World Evangelical Fellowship (WEF), while CAIE from its beginning acknowledged its ties with the World Council of Churches (WCC).

The founding members of CAIE were:

- The Council of Evangelical Churches of Central Angola
- The Evangelical Christian Church of Luanda
- The Evangelical Church of Angola
- The Evangelical Baptist Church of Angola
- The Evangelical Church of the North of Angola

- The United Methodist Church of Angola
- The Evangelical Pentecostal Mission of Angola
- The Kimbanguist Church

To draft a more complete statement of purpose and structure for CAIE the representatives of these churches chose a committee of five: Bishop Emílio de Carvalho, United Methodist Church; Rev. João Makondekwa, Evangelical Baptist Church; Rev. Arago José António Mateus, United Methodist Church; Rev. André Conga da Costa, Evangelical Church of Angola; and Rev. Daniel Ntoni-Nzinga, Evangelical Baptist Church. At the meeting in May 1977, when the committee of five brought in its report, CAIE elected its first regular officers: president, Bishop Emílio de Carvalho (UMC); vice-president, Rev. Henrique Etaungo Daniel (CIEAC); and general secretary, Rev. Daniel Ntoni-Nzinga (IEBA).

How many Angolans did AEA and CAIE represent? We noted at the end of chapter 3 when recording the religious census of 1960 that religious statistics are unreliable, but they probably roughly reflect proportions of the population.

If 18 percent of the population was Protestant at independence, probably 14 percent were related to CAIE churches and 4 percent to AEA churches.

Catholic Adaptations

The Catholic church, like the United Methodist and Seventh-Day Adventist churches, had no need to reexamine its structure to adapt to independence. Its organization was designed by canon law determined by the Vatican rather than by each local church. However, some adjustments were made by the Catholic church to meet the needs and opportunities of the new period in Angolan history.

The diocese of Pereira d'Eça/Njiva had been created in August 1975, but no bishop was appointed at that time. The bishop of Sá da Bandeira, Dom Eurico Dias Nogueira, named the Rev. Carlos Mittelberger as vicar general. On July 3, 1988, the Rev. Fernando Guimarães Kevanu was consecrated the first bishop of this diocese in the extreme south of Angola. The new bishop was born in Odime, Cunene on August 14, 1936, and ordained a priest on July 2, 1970.

Only three mission stations in the diocese had missionary personnel in 1988: Môngua, with the residence of the new bishop and a community of Sisters of the Most Holy Savior (Irmãos do SSmo. Salvador); Chiulo, the site of the hospital and leprosarium staffed by five Medical Missionaries of Mary and Father Alexandre Collin; and Cuamato, with Father

Belchior Valipo. Since 1986 it has been impossible for missionaries to travel to the various local congregations, but catechists gather from most points to meet in Môngua with the bishop each month.

In 1973 at the centenary of the founding of the Lândana mission, the first Catholic station in this modern missionary period, Cabinda was defined as an episcopal vicarage (*vigararia episcopal*). The first resident bishop was Dom Paulino Fernandes Madeca who, as auxiliary bishop of Luanda, had been vicar general of the diocese of Cabinda.

Dom Paulino was born in Povo Grande, Cabinda, on November 28, 1927, and ordained a priest on July 20, 1958. After eight years as episcopal vicar, he became resident bishop on October 1, 1984.

Showing the good relations between the Catholic church and the civil authorities in Cabinda, at the time of the consecration of the bishop the provincial commissar returned to the church the buildings that the government had confiscated in 1977. Cabinda claims the highest proportion of Catholics of any diocese of Angola — 84 percent.[12]

Not until November 8, 1984, was the diocese of Mbanza Kongo created. It actually was the first diocese ever created in Angola, almost four hundred years earlier in 1596, then called the diocese of Angola and Congo and located in what was then known as São Salvador. The new/old diocese was carved out of the diocese of Uige. The reasons given for the creation of this new diocese reveal some facts about that area:

1. The large area of the diocese of Uige.

2. The great difficulty of communicating between the provinces of Uige and Zaire, forcing the bishop to fly between them by way of Luanda, which doubles the distance.

3. The population of the province of Zaire is the same ethnically — Kikongo — but rooted in a long civil and religious history it feels superior to others.

4. The civil authorities of Mbanza Kongo do not recognize the jurisdiction of the bishop of Uige in the province of Zaire and consider it as illegal interference in its territory.

5. For this reason the bishop had to raise that area to the status of an episcopal vicariate, conceding great autonomy.[13]

The first bishop of the new diocese, Dom Afonso Nteka, received episcopal consecration at the hands of Pope John Paul II in Rome on January 6, 1985. He is a Capuchin priest, born in Damba on March 13, 1940,

---

12. *Acção Missionária* 47, no. 535 (February 1985): 5.
13. *Boa Nova* 61, no. 705 (February 1985): 12.

and ordained to the priesthood in 1971. He has studied in Angola, Italy, and Belgium, and graduated in catechesis and pastoral studies from the Lumen Vitae Institute in Brussels. Dom Afonso Nteka has translated the Missal, the Ritual, and a biblical catechism into Kikongo.

The Catholic church adapted itself to independent Angola by creating new dioceses and also by transforming missionary congregations or institutes that had functioned in Angola as districts of Portuguese provinces into Angolan provinces. The most important example of this process was the action of the General Council of the Spiritans, which created the Angolan province in June 1977. After consultation with all the Spiritans in Angola Father Bernardo Bongo was elected provincial superior. Thus after more than a century missionaries of the Congregation of the Holy Ghost in Angola no longer were tied by bonds of obedience to the province of Portugal, but were related directly to the general house in Rome.[14]

Father Bongo was born in the area of Bimbe in Angola on June 18, 1943, and after studying in the primary school of the Bimbe mission he entered the minor seminary of Quipeio. After completing high school, he entered the Congregation of the Holy Ghost, doing his novitiate in Portugal in 1963–64 and completing his philosophy and theology courses in the Superior Missionary Institute. Father Bongo was ordained presbyter on October 18, 1969, and was sent as professor to the minor seminary of Viana de Castelo in Portugal. In 1972 he went to Spain to work in a program of "Missionary Promotion." His desire to return to Angola was satisfied in 1974 when he was sent to Huambo, where he contributed to the strengthening of the major and minor seminaries.

The 1988 Catholic Yearbook for Angola reported that the fourteen dioceses in Angola were being served by 1,348 missionaries. Catholic and Protestant use the term "missionary" differently. Protestants use the term to refer to full-time foreign workers, while Catholics include all full-time workers: Angolan or foreign, priests, deacons, religious brothers and sisters, and lay missionaries. Accordingly in 1988 there were 1,348 Catholic missionaries and about 50 Protestant missionaries in Angola.

The Catholic church lives by the sacraments, which can (with a few exceptions) be administered only by ordained priests. Therefore the reduction of priests from 560 at the beginning of 1975 to 335 in 1988 was a sharp blow to the church.

The number of nuns in Angola also decreased slightly at the time of independence from the total of 911, but by 1988 the number of sisters had increased to 985. The most significant change in Catholic personnel during the first ten years of independence was the increase in Angolan nuns: from 158 in 1975 to 331 in 1985. Moreover, most of these are now

---

14. *Encontro* 14, no. 90 (November–December 1977): 4.

Teresian Sisters Joana Wandi and J. Chingambile in the Catholic mission of Kalukembe

being trained in Angola. At independence there were only seven novitiates — centers for the training of nuns in Angola; in 1988 thirty-one women's orders had novitiates in Angola.

Twenty-one new religious orders for women have entered Angola since independence, but especially notable is the story of a new order created within Angola.

The Congregation of the Sisters of Saint Catharine began simply as a group of young Angolan women related to the work of the Missionaries of Our Lady of LaSalette. The first seed was sown in a brief catechetical course for young women by Father Roberto Harder in 1951. At that time no one was thinking about forming an organization. The idea arose in 1964 when a group met in the Ganda mission and showed an interest in pastoral activities and the religious life. The following year at the Hanha mission the idea of an association of women catechists was formulated. Two years later, in 1967, nine young women, headed by Madalena Valeta, had their first experience of a religious and apostolic life in community. Bishop Daniel Junqueira of Nova Lisboa/Huambo encouraged the experiment and approved the group as a secular diocesan institute. When the new diocese of Benguela was created, its first bishop, Dom Armando Amaral dos Santos, approved the statutes of the institute in 1971. The next bishop of Benguela, Dom Óscar Braga, took the necessary steps, and on August 22, 1982, the diocesan Congregation of the Sisters of Saint Catharine was formed, and at the same time eight women made their perpetual vows. The motherhouse was opened in Lobito with Sister Madalena Valeta as head. By 1985 there were fifty-one sisters: eleven with perpetual vows, eleven novices, and twenty-four postulants.

Equally as important as the number of congregations and vocations among Angolans are the roles that Angolan religious are playing in the life of the church. In August 1987 two sisters of the Spiritan community were sent as missionaries from Angola to Cape Verde: Sister Carolina, a native of Golungo Alto, and Sister Salome, of Negola in the Huila province. Padre Anastácio Cahango, who presided at the Eucharist, reminded the congregation gathered for this special missionary service in Viana that "a religious community that sends missionaries shows that it is a community that is:

- Mature and attentive to God's Word;

- Poor, with evangelical poverty: freely you have received, freely give;

- Open, as the church is open;

- Anxious for the Kingdom: all who call on My name will be saved."[15]

New Protestant Churches

One of the most obvious changes in the church in Angola has been the proliferation of new groups. The Catholic church is strict in guarding its unity, but it has the flexibility to allow new orders, congregations, and institutes to arise and be recognized when there is a special ferment in the church. Before independence thirty-eight contemplative and apostolic institutes and orders worked in Angola. During the first ten years of independence that number had grown to sixty-five. Each has its own special carisma, but they all recognize the authority of the hierarchy.

The Protestants, without the same central authority, have experienced a proliferation of religious organizations in Angola which are difficult to number. They vary from churches that have a history of hundreds of years and a worldwide reputation for spiritual vitality and ecclesiastical responsibility, such as the Lutherans, the Mennonites, and the Salvation Army, to small dissident groups that may have sprung from personality conflicts or a disciplinary problem in older communities, from a serious search for new truth, or from a religious experience that is difficult for an observer to judge.

Recently the Catholic episcopal conference in Zaire published a pastoral letter entitled "The Catholic Faith and Sects." The government

---

15. *Boa Nova* 63, no. 733 (December 1987): 31.

of that neighbor of Angola decided to suspend the activities of 357 churches and sects, mostly of Christian origin.[16]

The Church in Diaspora

All Angolan Christians had to adapt to the new conditions of their country after independence, as did in fact all Angolans. This was true even of Angolans who were outside their country. Hundreds of thousands of refugees fled Angola during the colonial war, and although the majority of them returned after independence, others left, crossing the borders into Namibia, Zambia, or Zaire to escape the ravages of the civil war. There were also some thousands who abandoned their villages or towns to take refuge in remote rural areas controlled by UNITA.

The Church in the Bush

The Church in the Bush has its headquarters in Jamba in the southeast corner of Angola, as does UNITA. In the mid-1980s when UNITA was constructing its capital, Jamba, the first three permanent buildings were the hospital and the Catholic and Protestant chapels facing each other.

The predominance of the Catholic church and its close tie with the civil authorities during the colonial period left the Angolan Protestants and their churches in a minority position, both numerically and in socio-political status. The Portuguese authorities interpreted the fact that the leaders of the three nationalist movements, Agostinho Neto, Holden Roberto, and Jonas Savimbi, were all reared in Protestant communities as proof of the anti-Portuguese and subversive orientation of the Protestant missions. The regional system (comity) of the Protestant work coincided with the regional bases of the three liberation movements: Kikongo–BMS–FNLA, Kimbundu–Methodist–MPLA, and Umbundu–CIEAC–UNITA. The tables were turned in the early years of the civil war in central and southern Angola when the Protestants felt that UNITA was their movement and the Catholics felt in the minority. A Catholic observer commented:

> In the zones controlled by UNITA some of the leaders of the Protestant communities assume political and military administrative functions also. Due to a certain historic resentment against the Catholic church, which was in some ways protected by the colonial government while the Protestants had difficulties and were even impeded from having their religious services, there was created a certain antagonism toward some Catholic missionaries and

16. *Acção Missionária* 49, no. 574 (August–September 1988): 4.

Father Bernardo Bongo, missionary in Jamba.
Courtesy of Província Portuguesa da Congregação do Espirito Santo.

leaders. There was an attitude of discrimination and intimidation.
All this caused fear among many Catholics so that in these new
circumstances in which they were living they hesitated to practice
their religion. Some catechists even hid their Catholic Bibles, their
missals, and the catechism that they had saved.[17]

The Catholics continued to feel this discrimination as missionaries
who had been kidnapped and brought to Jamba were not allowed to
stay and work there. The situation changed in 1984 when Father Bernardo Bongo, the provincial of the Congregation of the Holy Spirit,
chose to go to Jamba and work. Shortly thereafter four foreign Catholic
missionaries were allowed to stay and carry on their ministry in UNITA
territory.

In 1988 there were six Angolan priests in Jamba — Bernardo Bongo,
Damio da Silva Ulundu, Jorge Manjense, José Barros, Justo Félix and
João Baptista Catombela — and two Angolan sisters — Elisabeth João
and Regina Bimbi. In addition there were five foreign Catholic missionaries: two priests and three sisters.

These thirteen Catholic workers were living in the parish of Santa

17. "Uma Igreja esquecida e activa na mata," *Boa Nova* 53, no. 726 (March 1987): 25–26.

Maria Mãe de Deus in Jamba but visiting five centers that spread from 22 to 340 miles from Jamba.[18]

In contrast to the reports from the Catholic church in Jamba, which focus especially on the clergy and "religious" workers, the Protestant reports focus more on the contributions made by Protestant nurses, doctors, teachers, and agriculturalists.

The Protestant work in the UNITA area is directed primarily by the leaders of the CIEAC who left Dôndi in 1977 since a considerable proportion of the refugee population is from the Benguela highland where that community had its main centers. A visitor to Jamba in 1988 reported that twenty-eight pastors from the former CIEAC were working in that area and ten from other churches. Elders of Assemblies of the Plymouth Brethren are also very active, as well as members of several other churches, such as the UIEA, the IESA, and the Seventh-Day Adventists.

With the centers of population spread out over more than six hundred miles, transportation being difficult, and many of the leaders residing in Jamba, this is another case in which catechists and other lay men and women are ministering on a daily basis to the spiritual needs of the people.

In April 1988 the Catholic and Protestant leaders of Jamba signed a joint appeal to the churches in Portugal to help in building peace in Angola. This was one sign of the good relations between the various religious communities in that part of Angola.

Refugees in Namibia

The Ambo peoples straddle the Angola-Namibia border; like other frontiers in Africa it was drawn according to conflicting interests of colonial powers without consideration of human or ethnic factors. The people, however, did not pay much attention to the border when too much or too little rain, family relations, educational opportunities, or colonial politics prompted them to move north or south across the border. Churches have existed on both sides, but no one church straddled the border except for the Kikongo Baptists, who were rooted on both sides of the North Angola–Zaire border.

The Lutheran church planted in Namibia by German missionaries and later supported by Finns was expelled from Angola during World War I. The Catholic church took over the Lutheran missions north of the border and established, with Portuguese colonial support, a swath of territory that was to be preserved from Protestant activity. Kwanyama Lutherans who moved from Namibia to Angola brought their faith with them, but when their activities such as organizing regular worship or

---

18. *Encontro*, no. 190 (June 1988): 16–20.

teaching catechism were discovered, they were threatened, imprisoned, or expelled from Angola.

Some Kwanyama Protestants suppressed their Lutheran identity and integrated themselves into Evangelical missions that were established in Angola at Bunjei, Dôndi, and Kalukembe. As a result, in the 1950s and 1960s the Bunjei mission had two pastorates along the southern border of Angola served by pastors who had their initial training in Namibia, but studied also in Protestant missions in Angola to learn Portuguese and become acquainted with the ecclesiastical and theological orientation of the Evangelical churches in Angola.

After independence Kwanyama Lutherans were not included in the first group of recognized churches, but since the old capital of the Kwanyama kingdom, Onjiva, is in Angola and the Lutheran church has been rooted in that people for a century, it is likely that they will be recognized.

Speaking of refugees in Namibia we are not referring to the Kwanyama, who have been moving back and forth across that border. Rather we are recording the fact that in 1975–76 hundreds of Angolan Christians fled across the southern border into Namibia with the Portuguese who were frightened by the interparty violence that spread from Luanda south during that period. Most of the Portuguese kept going south, finding their way to South Africa or Rhodesia, sometimes embarking in Windhoek or Johannesburg for Portugal.

Angolans, Catholics and Protestants, were gathered into refugee camps by the South African government — the largest being Rundu. Others found their way to urban centers. The Rev. Isaías Canutula de Almeida, who had been pastor of the IECA, in Lobito served Angolan Protestants in the border area of Namibia for many years. Mr. and Mrs. José P. Rodrigues, white Angolan missionaries of the AEF, have worked with Angolan refugees in Namibia since 1981. They began mostly with Angolans who came from the Ganguela and Chokwe peoples, among whom the AEF worked in Angola. Since then the work has spread into the Kaprivi strip.

Mr. Rodrigues reported that on New Years' Day 1987, "some forty-three people joined the church through baptism and about thirty-four have made their decision for the Lord as their Saviour." Most of these were Angolans who would want to return to their homes when the war ended.

Refugees in Zambia

The largest concentration of Angolan refugees in Zambia is located seventy-two miles west of Solwezi in the Northwestern Province. The Maheba refugee settlement has an area of about 225 square miles. It was established by the Zambian government, Lutheran World Federation, and the United Nations High Commissioner for Refugees in 1971. Maheba reached its largest population in 1978 with 15,000. In 1981 Maheba had 9,705 Angolans, 647 Zairians, and 147 Namibians.

In 1980 nine denominations were working in Maheba: (1) the Africa Apostolic Church, (2) the Christian Missions in Many Lands (Brethren), (3) the Evangelical Church, (4) the Kimbanguist Church, (5) the Mission Church, (6) the New Apostolic Church, (7) the Roman Catholic Church, (8) the United Church of Zambia, and (9) the Watchtower (Jehovah's Witnesses). At that time the nine denominations had thirty-four local churches within the settlement.[19]

Maheba is served by two Catholic missionaries who had worked in Angola, Father José von Rickenbach and Father Martinho van Koolzijk. Father von Rickenbach, a Swiss missionary of the Congregation of our Lady of LaSalette, arrived in Zambia in 1977, and at first could only visit the camp for six hours at a time. In 1980, with the help of Misereor, the German Catholic funding agency, he built a small residence, which included a chapel. Since then he has built eight chapels for the Catholic congregations, each with its own catechist.

Each chapel has a council with representatives of the various activities of the community: liturgy, catechism, development, charity, etc. On the first Saturday of each month a general council meets with all the chapel councils.[20]

In 1985 Father van Koolzijk, a Spiritan missionary who worked forty years in Angola, mostly in Vila da Ponte/Kuvango, arrived at Maheba. He had been kidnapped by UNITA in 1982, and when UNITA would not allow him to stay and work in Jamba he returned to Holland and requested to be sent to Zambia to continue to work with Angolan refugees. The two missionaries speak Portuguese and Angolan languages, which facilitate their ministry: Father José, Umbundu, and Father Martinho, Ganguela.

Cabindan Refugees in Zaire

Cabinda is separated geographically from the rest of Angola by the Congo River and a few miles of Zairian soil. Cabindans claim that the

---

19. Elias Mateus Isaac, "The Development of the Church among the People of Maheba Refugee Settlement: A Case Study of the Roman Catholic, Christian Mission in Many Lands, and United Church of Zambia Communities in the Settlement," unpublished research paper submitted for the diploma in theology, Makerere University, Kampala, 1985.

20. "A vida num Campo de Refugiados Angolanos," *Encontro*, no. 183 (November 1987): 20.

treaty of Simulambuco of 1885 provides a legal basis for their independence from Angola.

The declaration of independence of Angola on November 11, 1975,
both quickened the Cabindans sentiment for their own independence
and aroused fears that Catholics might be persecuted. So according to
Cabindan estimates 60 percent of the population of 100,000 fled to Zaire.
Since they were practically all Catholics, four priests accompanied the
refugees.[21]

They established a pastoral center at Tshela and worked in refugee
camps in Zaire, which had been organized with the aid of the United
Nations High Commission for Refugees. In addition to helping meet
the physical and social needs of the refugees, the Catholic church successfully promoted vocations and provided seminary training. In the
1985–86 academic year fifty Cabindan seminarians were studying in
Zaire:

Major Seminary:	theology	Kinshasa	6
	philosophy	Boma	2
	philosophy	Kinshasa	3
Minor Seminary:		Tshela	5
	humanities	Tshela	<u>34</u>
Total:			50

In 1980 the Cabindan refugees began to return to their homeland because the civil war between the Cabindan nationalist organization FLEC
and the government of Angola was de-escalating.

In 1988 the Catholic church ordered the four priests who were in
Zaire with the Cabindan refugees to return to their diocese in Cabinda.

Conclusion

The church in Angola has adapted to independence since 1975 in a
variety of ways. The Catholic church has created new dioceses and consecrated new bishops. New religious orders have entered Angola and
some old ones have created their own Angolan provinces. The church
has discussed what "inculturation" and "Africanization" mean theoret-
ically and how they might be applied practically in Angola. Protestant
churches have been renamed and restructured. They have formed new
alliances within Angola and outside. Many new religious groups have
entered Angola or have emerged from the colonial underground. The
church in urban centers is bulging with old and new members who are

---

21. *Encontro*, no. 166 (March 1986): 14–16.

seeking security in a time of many perils and hope in a day of doubt and death.

Many adaptations were made in response to a variety of forces: political, economic, and social. It is the church's hope that within such exigencies it has also responded to God's will as the Apostle Paul urged the Christians in Rome:

> Do not be conformed to this world, but be transformed by the renewal of your mind, that you may prove what is the will of God, what is good and acceptable and perfect. (Rom. 12:2)

Chapter 15

Testing Our Presuppositions

The church has now come into existence evangelistically but not theologically.... Thus the church [in Africa] as the Body of Christ must be its own major theological theme, in all situations, in all places and at all times, otherwise it ceases to exist, it ceases to make its presence and message relevant, and it runs aground in the stream of history.

— John Mbiti[1]

Four presuppositions about the church underlie this study:

1. The church is one.

2. The church is human and divine.

3. The church is the people of God.

4. The church's mission is to proclaim the Reign of God.

We are ready to test these assumptions by what we have learned about the church in Angola.

First Presupposition:
The Church in Angola Is One

In my conversations with clergy and laity in the churches in Angola all have agreed that the church is One, before God, or theologically. Yet, in practice, or ecclesiastically, from watching the churches in action I have

---

1. John Mbiti, "New Testament Eschatology in an African Background," *Readings in Dynamic Indigeneity*, ed. Charles Kraft and Tom Wisely (Pasadena, Calif.: William Carey Library, 1981).

taken their affirmation to mean: "The one church is ours and any other churches that agree to join us."

On the ecclesiastical landscape in Angola the great structure on the right is the Roman Catholic church, which claims almost half the population of Angola. It is certainly one. In fact it is the one institution in Angola — religious, social, political, or economic — that gives unity to Angola. Its fourteen dioceses cover the whole nation.

Scattered around the 481,351 square miles of Angola are eleven Protestant churches that have been recognized by the government. They range in age from the IEBA, which was planted in M'Banza Kongo, the capital of the kingdom of the Kongo in 1878, to the Kimbanguist Church, which legally entered Angola after April 25, 1974. The sizes of the recognized churches are difficult to determine, but the largest may have as many as a hundred thousand communicant members and the smallest less than ten thousand.

Around and between the eleven recognized are another twenty or so churches, the oldest being the Plymouth Brethren, which has been witnessing in Angola for more than one hundred years. It was not recognized with the first twelve, because it had always rejected any type of denominational organization and so was not able to fulfill the requirements of the government. That is, it did not have a national structure that could be held accountable by the government. The Brethren have since remedied that and will probably be recognized the next time the Justice Department issues a list of recognized churches. On the other end of the time scale of unrecognized churches are some who have recently entered Angola from neighboring countries.

The landscape is not quite as chaotic as would at first appear since many of the Protestant churches are associated into two organizations: the Associação de Evangélicos de Angola (AEA) and the Conselho Angolano de Igrejas Evangélicas (CAIE). AEA has seven member churches, and CAIE has fourteen. Both AEA and CAIE have offices in Luanda. The total membership of the CAIE churches is about four to five times that of the AEA churches.

The Bible Unites

The unity of the divided church in Angola has been more evident in the last few years as the Catholic church has followed the teachings of Vatican II: "This sacred Synod earnestly and specifically urges all the Christian faithful, too, especially religious, to learn by frequent reading of the divine Scriptures the 'excelling knowledge of Jesus Christ'" (Phil. 3:8). "For ignorance of the Scriptures is ignorance of Christ."[2]

---

2. Dogmatic Constitution on Divine Revelation, no. 25.

In 1988 the Episcopal Conference ordered forty thousand Portuguese Bibles from Difusora Bíblica, a Catholic organization in Lisbon dedicated to encouraging Bible study. A more ambitious effort to promote Bible reading by Catholics was the translation and publication of the New Testament in Umbundu in three printings between 1978 and 1985. The translation was done by Bishops Francisco Viti, Zacarias Kamwenho, and Eugénio Salessu and Fathers José Soma and Faustino Chilanda. The Old Testament in Umbundu is also being published in fascicles.

Another major contribution to making the Holy Scriptures available to Umbundu-speaking Catholics has been the publication of two large volumes: the *Assembleia do Senhor* and *Ulima Wéyovo*. The first is a missal that includes the liturgy for all the sacraments as well as a paraliturgy that can be celebrated without a priest, following the order of the Mass with the exception of consecration and communion of the Eucharist. The bulk of the book, pages 81 to 1,367, gives the passages of Scripture for each Sunday and saints' days in a three-year cycle, following the official lectionary. The second volume, even larger, is a daily missal with liturgy and Bible readings for every weekday of the year. Those who use these books personally will be reading the Bible everyday in their own language, and those who attend the public services will hear the Scripture readings.

The church is united in its recognition of the Holy Scriptures as a means of divine revelation, but a deep division still exists between Catholics and Protestants as regards the role of tradition and the teaching, or magisterium, of the church in divine revelation.

Ecumenical Encounters

The tenuous unity of the church in Angola has also been evident in the irregular and superficial nature of the participation of Angolans in various types of ecumenical encounters. Some progress has been made since this process has been institutionalized in the Catholic church by creating ecumenical commissions in most dioceses; the Episcopal Conference of Angola and São Tomé (CEAST) has a Commission on Ecumenism, whose first president was Dom Pedro Luís Scarpa.

The regional organizations of CAIE, which function in each provincial capital, are called Ecumenical Commissions of Cooperation. "Ecumenical" in this term refers to the participation of representatives of all the member-churches of CAIE, but it also indicates that there is an openness to other churches. For example the Ecumenical Commission of Cooperation of Moxico reported in 1988 that in addition to the members of CAIE the following churches cooperated in various activities: Catholic, Union of Evangelical Churches of Angola, Brethren, and

Seventh-Day Adventists. For Catholic-Protestant encounters to move beyond the present stage of occasional celebrations of the Word it will be necessary to put in practice the counsel of Vatican II:

> We must come to understand the outlook of our separated brethren. Study is absolutely required for this, and should be pursued with fidelity to truth and in a spirit of good will. When they are properly prepared for this study, Catholics need to acquire a more adequate understanding of the distinctive doctrines of our separated brethren, as well as of their history, spiritual and liturgical life, their religious psychology and cultural background. Of great value for this purpose are meetings between the two sides, especially for discussion of theological problems, where each can deal with the other on an equal footing. Such meetings require that those who take part in them under authoritative guidance be truly competent. From dialogue of this sort will emerge still more clearly what the true posture of the Catholic church is. In this way, too, we will better understand that attitude of our separated brethren and more aptly present our own belief.[3]

A series of three international meetings was held in Europe over a period of seven years, from 1977 to 1984, involving Roman Catholic and Evangelical participants discussing mission.[4] The report of this dialogue has been distributed to some Angolan church leaders in harmony with its final suggestion:

> We believe that the Evangelical-Roman Catholic Dialogue on Mission [in Europe] has now completed its task. At the same time we hope that dialogue on mission between Roman Catholics and Evangelicals will continue, preferably on a regional or local basis, in order that further progress may be made towards a common understanding, sharing, and proclaiming of "the faith which was once for all delivered to the saints" (Jude 3). We commit these past and future endeavors to God, and pray that by "speaking the truth

---

3. Decree on Ecumenism, no. 9.

4. "Evangelical" in this case refers not to Protestants in general, as the word is popularly used in Angola, but rather to a part of the spectrum of Protestantism that lies somewhere between the "ecumenical churches" and the "fundamentalists." In Europe and North America they are called "Conservative Evangelicals." The Catholic participants in the dialogue were named by the Vatican Secretariat for Promoting Christian Unity and included Sister Joan Chatfield, Monsignor Basil Meeking, Father Dionisio Minguez Fernandez, Father Parmananda Divarkar, Father John Mutiso-Mbinda, Bishop Anselm Sanon, and Father Thomas Stransky. The Evangelical participants were drawn from a number of churches and Christian organizations. They were not official representatives of any international body. They included Prof. Peter Beyerhaus, Rev. Gottfried Osei-Mensah, Rev. Peter Savage, Rev. John Stott, Dr. Kwame Bediako, Bishop Donald Cameron, and Father Philip Rosato.

in love, we are to grow up in every way into him who is the head, into Christ" (Eph. 4:15).[5]

Such a dialogue in Angola waits upon some courageous leaders who will give high priority to such an effort and be willing to spend the time and energy that would be required.

The Church in Angola as a Broad River

The government's process of recognizing churches has made each ecclesiastical organization more self-conscious and has required the churches to spend personnel and resources on establishing its identity. This need has been intensified by the destruction or abandonment of mission stations, by which many churches had been identified since their beginnings in Angola. Simply looking at the long list of recognized and nonrecognized churches in Angola, however, does not give a clear picture of the church in Angola. The church in Angola is not so well represented today by lists of names or by organograms, but rather by the image of a broad river with several currents.

The Catholic Current.   The most visible current is the Roman Catholic, which appears deep and strong, but some leaders are concerned that it is only a surface appearance. This concern has led them to explore such concepts as Africanization, inculturation, and incarnation. Of all the currents in this river the Catholic is the least immersed in Angolan culture for several reasons:

1. the name "Catholic" puts pressure on each local church to preserve the "universal" character of its doctrine, liturgy, and practice;

2. the bishops and many priests have received much of their training outside Angola, and they indeed have achieved their present positions because of having been raised outside their Angolan culture;

3. the number of foreign missionaries is very high, at least in comparison with the Protestant churches. (In 1991 there were six hundred Catholic foreign missionaries and fifty Protestant.)

4. all changes in doctrine, liturgy, and practice must be approved by the Holy See in Rome.

One of the curious phenomena that raise questions about the validity or likelihood of inculturation of the Catholic church in Angola is the

---

5. "Evangelicals and Roman Catholics Dialogue on Mission," *International Bulletin of Missionary Research* 10, no. 1 (January 1986): 20.

The Catholic bishops of Angola in 1989.
Courtesy of Província Portuguesa da Congregação do Espírito Santo

Seated: Dom Manuel Franklin da Costa (Archbishop of Lubango), Dom Fortunato Baldelli (Apostolic Delegate), Dom Alexandre do Nascimento (Archbishop of Luanda), Dom Francisco Viti (Archbishop of Huambo), Dom Eduardo André Muaca (Bishop Emeritus of Luanda).

First row, standing: Dom Óscar Lino Lopes Fernandes Braga (Bishop of Benguela), Dom Fernando Guimarães Kevanu (Bishop of Ondjiva), Dom Zacarias Kamwenho (Bishop of Sumbe), Dom Paulino Fernandes Madeca (Bishop of Cabinda), Dom José Próspero d'Ascensão Puaty (Bishop of Lwena), Dom Francisco da Mata Mourisca (Bishop of Uige), Dom Pedro Marcos Ribeiro da Costa (Bishop of Saurimo).

Second row, standing: Dom Afonso Nteka (Bishop of Mbanza Kongo), Dom Pedro Luís Scarpa (Auxiliary Bishop of Luanda), Dom Eugénio Salessu (Bishop of Malanje), Dom José de Queirós Alves (Bishop of Menongue), Dom Pedro Luís António (Bishop of Cuíto Bié).

growth in number and strength of the Legion of Mary in Angola. As the name suggests it is patterned organizationally after the military regime of the old Roman Empire. The form and content of the regular meetings are strictly prescribed and allow for little spontaneity.

Does this popularity indicate that there is a stronger element of discipline and rigor in the Angolan culture than is usually recognized? Or as one priest suggested, the Angolans appreciate the Legion because it includes the element of secrecy, which is also part of traditional circumcision or age-societies.

Another phenomenon that raises questions about the inculturation of the Catholic church in Angola is the international protection that it enjoys. Protestant leaders have been asked what they thought of certain Catholic pastoral letters and why they do not issue similar statements or support the bishops' letters. A common answer is, "We do not have the pope, the Vatican, and a strong worldwide church behind us. We are in a much more vulnerable position."

Three factors give some hope that the Catholic church may become more incarnated in Angola. First, if the church recognizes that the catechists are not just substitutes for the priests who are in short supply or prevented by the war from reaching their posts, then the lay leaders may be a significant channel through which Angolan culture may "transform and re-create the church, making a new creation."[6]

A second possibility is that the growing number of Angolan nuns may find that they are playing a double role: helping the church change its understanding of the position of women in church and society, and serving as roots into Angolan culture that can bring its lifeblood into the church.

Third, some Catholic leaders may have courage to explore the reality of the Protestant churches in Angola and especially those that have already achieved a certain degree of incarnation, even though some may call it syncretism. In such exploration and sharing there may be found a greater will and way to incarnate the church in Angola.

Protestant "Mission" Churches.   A second current that flows in the church in Angola is composed of the Protestant "mission" churches that arrived earliest in Angola: IEBA, IEA, IMUA, IECA, Irmãos, UIEA, IESA, IERA, and IEUA. They came to Angola from evangelical and pietistic religious movements that were strong in Europe and North America at the end of the last century and the beginning of this. From a distance this current looks quite homogeneous, but up close it shows variations that produced the two Protestant associations: the AEA and the CAIE.

This division is a sign of the lack of incarnation on the part of the Protestant churches for it did not arise from different Angolan responses to the gospel message. Rather it is a reflection of different alliances and tendencies in the mission agencies from which the missionaries came.

The Pentecostal Current.   The third current — the Pentecostal — arrived more recently, but has grown quite rapidly, as have similar currents on all continents in the last fifty years. It is represented in Angola by the Assemblies of God and MEPA. They look back especially to the Acts of the Apostles (chapter 2) and the descent of the Holy Spirit on the first Christians, believing that the presence of the Spirit with its gifts of wisdom, knowledge, faith, healing, miracles, prophecy, tongues, and the interpretation of tongues (1 Cor. 12:4–11) are still the most important signs of the true Christian life.

---

6. Pastoral Letter, "Evangelização e Baptismo."

David B. Barrett, who has been called "the Linnaeus of religious taxonomy," has estimated that of the 5.1 billion people in the world in mid-1988, 1.7 million were Christians by self-declaration. Roman Catholics formed the single largest group of Christians, totaling over 926 million. All Protestants — not including 52 million Anglicans, who do not consider themselves Protestants — number about 312 million. Pentecostals and charismatics, Barrett estimates for mid-1988, totaled 332 million. By the year 2000, Barrett projects, there will be 562 million Pentecostals and charismatics — by then higher in count than the combined total of 61 million Anglicans and 386 million Protestants.

The Assemblies of God claim 200,000 members in Angola today — a claim challenged by some members of that church. However, there is reason to believe that Pentecostals will increase in number in Angola as they have done in other parts of the world, and especially in the southern hemisphere.

The five values of Pentecostal theology seem particularly appealing to Africans: experience, orality, spontaneity, otherworldliness, and biblical authority.[7]

The Apostolic Churches. The Apostolic churches form a fourth current in the Angolan ecclesiastical river. They have some features of the mission churches since most of their leaders have come from those Protestant communities. They also have characteristics of the Pentecostal movement, emphasizing the gifts of the Spirit. Four such churches are members of CAIE: the Church of the Apostolic Faith, the Church of the Apostles of Jerusalem, the New Apostolic Church, and the Church Full of the Word of God (Full Gospel Church). A fifth Apostolic church, the Church of the Twelve Apostles, has applied for membership in CAIE. None of these churches has been recognized by the government. As David Barrett describes them:

> The word "apostolic" by these churches does not imply primarily the western meaning of a church that follows the pure doctrine of the New Testament Apostles in an unbroken continuity of church order down the ages, but rather in the sense of a church for which apostolate (or mission) is its primary *raison d'être*. Thus every single member of the Vapostori or Bapostolo (Apostles) — the African Apostolic Church of Johane Maranke, found from South Africa to the river Congo — is called an apostle in the New Testament sense of one commissioned to witness to the resurrection of Christ and to spread his Gospel. Contemporary theology of mission regards

---

7. Russell P. Spittler, "Implicit Values in Pentecostal Missions," *Missiology* 16, no. 4 (October 1988): 409–26.

this latter emphasis on apostolate as the chief mark of the authentic church.[8]

The Messianic Churches. The fifth current in the church in Angola today is that of the Messianic churches: the Kimbanguist and Tocoist. The determining feature of a Messianic church is the presence of a person who replaces Christ, such as the two Simons: Kimbangu and Toco. The present leaders of these churches would deny that the two founders considered themselves messiahs, but it is clear that many of their followers see them as such. Dr. Marie Louise Martin, a Swiss theologian who is herself a Kimbanguist, admits that there are "simple people in the Kimbanguist Church for whom Kimbangu means more than Jesus Christ."[9]

It has been suggested that

perhaps the theological meaning of the real position and role of Simon Kimbangu is explained best by a wood-engraving, to be seen at N'Kamba-Jerusalem [the most sacred shrine of the Kimbanguists in Zaire], which portrays Simon Kimbangu as Simon (sic!) of Cyrene who carries the cross of (a black) Christ. This engraving... is saying: Through the proclamation and healing miracles of Simon Kimbangu, but especially through his suffering, Christ became a living and concrete reality for the Congolese. Simon leads them to Christ, carrying His cross. But "more than that: He is the representative of Christ in Zaire, the "icon" in whom believers may recognise the true features of Christ.[10]

Common Witness to Unity

The unity of the divided church in Angola is more evident in the early 1990s than it has ever been, with the increasing use of the Bible and more frequent ecumenical encounters.

Once the various currents in the church realize that they have much more to gain than to lose from a common witness to Jesus Christ, many new opportunities for common witness will be discovered. A few can be mentioned here that have born fruit in other countries:

1. Common Witness in Bible Translation and Publication. Now that the *Instituto Nacional de Línguas* in Luanda has issued its study on the alphabets of the national languages, it would be very helpful for the Catholic

---

8. David B. Barrett, *Schism and Renewal in Africa: An Analysis of Six Thousand Contemporary Religious Movements* (Nairobi: Oxford University Press, 1968), 173.

9. Marie Louise Martin, *Kirche ohne Weisse* (Basel: Friedrich Beinhardt Verlag, 1971), 208.

10. D. J. Bosch, Book Review in *Missionalia* (Pretoria) 1, no. 2 (August 1973): 97.

and Protestant churches that are doing Bible translation and publishing to adopt a common alphabet for each of the national languages. This could lead to common translations of the New Testament in some national languages as there is already an interconfessional translation of the New Testament and Psalms in Portuguese published by the Bible Society and the Difusora Bíblica in Lisbon.

The church has been working recently on Bible translations in Kikongo, Kimbundu, and Umbundu, the three most popular national languages of Angola. This would be an appropriate time to adopt common alphabets and consider the publication of interconfessional translations.

2. *Common Witness in Community Service.* The report on the Evangelical and Roman Catholic dialogue on mission affirms: "There seems to be no justification for organizing separate Roman Catholic and Evangelical projects of a purely humanitarian nature, and every reason for undertaking them together. Although faith may still in part divide us, love for neighbor should unite us."[11]

The community service program that serves all of Angola most efficiently today is the Catholic organization Cáritas de Angola. It is related to Cáritas Internationalis, whose president is Cardinal Dom Alexandre do Nascimento, archbishop of Luanda. Each diocese has a Cáritas Commission with a priest, brother, or sister as the executive officer. In addition some dioceses, such as Sumbe, have made a special effort to have Cáritas organized in each parish and mission.

CAIE has a relatively small program of social assistance that reaches some needy people through its provincial Comissões Ecuménicas de Cooperação. Since CAIE's network is limited, by agreement with the government's Ministry of Social Assistance, CAIE distributes only 25 percent of the material aid that arrives from donor agencies, and the government distributes 75 percent. All churches receive some resources from donor agencies to use for emergency assistance, but Caritas and CAIE have the broadest networks in Angola. The Seventh-Day Adventists are currently negotiating with the government to be allowed to work in Angola as a development and relief agency.

3. *Common Witness in Social Thought and Action.* The pastoral letters of CEAST have provided the clearest and most specific analysis of the social situation in Angola since independence. In 1984 CEAST and CAIE issued separate statements on the subject of peace. The Catholic Pastoral Note on Reconciliation, after reviewing the story in Genesis of the fall of

---

11. Basil Manning and John Stott, eds., *The Evangelical-Roman Catholic Dialogue on Mission* (ERCDOM) (Exeter: The Paternoster Press, 1986), 85.

Adam and Eve by which humankind was alienated not only from God but from one another, continues:

> There is no other alternative for salvation than the return of the heart to the Lord and to his neighbor, created in the image and likeness of God. This return of the heart of man to God was accomplished by Jesus on the Cross and continues to be effective in the church, which He himself left as the continuation of His visible presence in the midst of humanity. The gift of the grace of God, this radical change of heart, first presupposes and requires of man an honest and courageous adherence to the truth, the only way to reconciliation; because reconciliation requires the previous acceptance of the other as an equal person and, therefore, with the inviolable right to be treated as an authentic interlocutor. This is the genuine path to reconciliation....
>
> Reconciliation and Redemption constitute two faces of the same saving reality....
>
> All those who desire the survival and dignity of our country will not hesitate to employ all their efforts so that the war comes to an end and the great Angolan family is truly reconciled. Angolans long for peace to which they have a right because there is no alternative: either there will be the extermination of the majority of the population or a reconciliation of this tortured Nation. Dialogue is the only way for people to resolve their problems and to live in harmony. Reconciliation demands dialogue among all involved in the conflict. The refusal to do so would result in a disaster that would only benefit third parties and damage the rights of the Angolan family.[12]

Later in 1984 CAIE issued a memorandum of the churches on peace, justice, and development in the People's Republic of Angola with the title "Jesus Christ, the Prince of Peace, Reconciles, Unites, and Leads the Peoples on the Way to Peace and Calls Us to Do the Same." It argued:

> The church, as the body of Christ, has a potent mobilizing capacity that should be put at the service of the Angolan people to achieve peace, which we need in the fight against underdevelopment. To achieve the goal we can use the following methods:
>
> 1. To employ the dynamism of Angolan Christians to give a common witness in this divided society, confronting with steady vigor, renewed by the divine spirit, the threats to peace and survival and fighting for justice and for human dignity.

---

12. Sections 4, 5, and 7.

2. To promote the participation of Angolan Christians in the rigorous combat against all forms of division in the church of Jesus Christ and the Angolan people because such divisions are destructive in our society.

3. To dialogue with all entities (national and provincial) considered important, whose responsibilities and actions are crucial for the achievement of peace in the People's Republic of Angola and in all of Southern Africa.

4. To increase the exchange of information and visits with churches and related organizations that have any responsibility in the present situation in Angola.

The CAIE memorandum on peace and reconciliation ended by quoting Luke 12:58–59: "As you go with your accuser before the magistrate, make an effort to settle with him on the way, lest he drag you to the judge and the judge hand you over to the officer, and the officer put you in prison. I tell you, you will never get out till you have paid the very last copper."

The CEAST and CAIE statements on reconciliation and peace have points of convergence and important points of divergence, but it would seem a valuable exercise in reconciliation for the two Christian organizations, or some representatives of Christian bodies in Angola, to at least experiment with the possibility of making a common statement on reconciliation and peace. Not only would such a process give a positive witness to the unity of the church, but it might reveal some practical means of dialogue that could be applied to the social and political divisions in Angola.

4. Common Witness in Worship. Celebrations of the Word on the occasion of the Week of Prayer for Christian Unity in January or during Holy Week or Pentecost are the most frequent sign of Christian unity seen in Angola since independence. In some places joint Bible study has been initiated. A next step in this area could be more regular occasions of common worship and of Bible study at various levels: among the clergy, groups of women, young people, or catechists.

5. Unworthy Witness. To conclude its section on common witness the ERCDOM report discussed briefly an unworthy kind of Christian witness, usually called "proselytism." They briefly mentioned three aspects of proselytism that apply as much within the Protestant community as between Protestants and Catholics:

First, proselytism takes place when our motive is unworthy; for example, when our real concern in witness is not the glory of

God through the salvation of human beings but rather the prestige of our own Christian community, or indeed our personal prestige.

Second, we are guilty of proselytism whenever our methods are unworthy, especially when we resort to any kind of "physical coercion, moral constraint or psychological pressure," when we seek to induce conversion by the offer of material or political benefits, or when we exploit other people's need, weakness, or lack of education. These practices are an affront both to the freedom and dignity of human beings and to the Holy Spirit whose witness is gentle and not coercive.

Third, we are guilty of proselytism whenever our message includes "unjust or uncharitable reference to the beliefs or practices of other religious communities in the hope of winning adherents." If we find it necessary to make comparisons, we should compare the strengths and weaknesses of one church with those of the other, and not set what is best in the one against what is worst in the other. To descend to deliberate misrepresentation is incompatible with both truth and love.[13]

Second Presupposition:
The Church Is Human and Divine[14]

The church, like any social institution, is composed of men and women, human beings, and so it is a human institution. However, these human beings have been called and gathered by God. In consulting church workers in person and through their writings for this book I have heard or read repeatedly affirmations such as, "We were such weak vessels, but God used us to plant and nurture the church."

During twenty-seven years of war the church has gone through countless experiences that dramatize its human-divine nature. The Catholic mission of Chinguar along the Benguela railway is a simple illustration. The mission is now directed by sisters of St. Joseph of Cluny after three priests who served the mission were killed. In 1984 Father Arnaldo Habraken, a Dutch Spiritan, was assassinated. In 1987 two priests who were on their way to Chinguar — Nicolau Lightart, a Dutch Spiritan, and Adriano Kasala, an Angolan diocesan priest from Huambo —

---

13. Manning and Stott, ERCDOM, 90–91.
14. This is called the "theandric dimension" of the church. Whoever looks at the church with eyes of faith is most impressed by the quality that is most significant, comprehensive, fundamental, and extraordinary, that is, its being *theandric,* or human (*anthropos*) and divine (*theos*) (Battista Mondin, *As Novas Eclesiologias* [São Paulo: Edições Paulinas, 1984], 309).

were killed in an ambush near Katchiungo. The most serious human frailty, death, struck this relatively small Christian community three times in three years, yet the result has been a remarkable quickening of faith. Every day, not just on Sundays, the church is filled with Christians to hear the Word of God, to receive the Broken Bread, and to pray for peace.[15]

Another sign of the church's dual nature that has taken a special form during recent years in Angola is the increased number of religious vocations in the Catholic church. The common wisdom during the colonial period was that Angolan women would not heed the call to the celibate religious life because of the African culture's emphasis on the woman's role as wife and mother. Although the total number of Catholic nuns in Angola has decreased from 899 in 1975 to 803 in 1987, the number of Angolan nuns has more than doubled from 158 to 331. Some observers cynically interpret this as a search for security in a time of social upheaval. Of course motives for such decisions are impossible for anyone to decipher completely, but the presupposition is not that the church is divine. It is human *and* divine.

God does not act in the church simply to call the clergy or the religious. It is the Christian faith that every person who hears God's call and responds with repentance and faith becomes a new person: still a man or a woman, but also a child of God.

Another way of stating the presupposition that the church is human and divine is to say that the church is the continuation of the incarnation of Jesus Christ, the Body of Christ.

At every stage of the history of the church in Angola we have noted signs of the human and divine. In planting the church, human and at times petty rivalry motivated the missionaries who strived to get an advantage over another mission. Yet in spite of these motivations and the death of scores of workers by disease and violence, the church was planted in all the regions of Angola by the end of the first quarter of this century.

As the church developed, colonialism interfered, giving advantages to part of the church that hindered that part's spiritual growth and impeding other parts, which increased their faith and sense of responsibility. But the church grew in number and spirit through the colonial period.

As we have looked at the various rites, activities, and services of the church in Angola we could identify in each the human and the divine. The sacraments, which are understood and practiced in different ways within the church, combine both human and divine elements. Preaching and interpreting the Word are done with the conviction that God is

---

15. *Encontro*, no. 185 (January 1988): 20.

speaking to the church, but in the knowledge that our human capacity allows us to see only in a "mirror dimly." The church at prayer has communion with God, but with the Apostle Paul we have to confess "we do not know how to pray as we ought" (Rom. 8:26). The church's charity is in response to God who first loved us, but it is combined with our self-interest.

Since independence the churches have been full and the celebration of the Word and sacraments enthusiastic. A visitor to Angola gave a glimpse of the worship life of the church in Angola:

> Liturgical participation is lived with an intensity to which we are not accustomed in Europe. In the great ceremonies time doesn't count. Everyone sings with enthusiasm. Everyone is involved. The great solemn offertories, with people going to the altar dancing rhythmically and singing, carrying the most diverse gifts, are inspirational. The ordination of young António Pedro Gonçalves in the cathedral of Malanje on January 3, 1981, lasted four-and-a-half hours filled with faith, enthusiasm, inspiring songs, offerings, and much love.[16]

The ordinations of Abias Cauto, Pedro Mango, and Tomás dos Santos Belo by the Evangelical Congregational Church in Huambo on July 31, 1988, could be described in similar terms. After a four-and-a-half-hour service in the Church of the Pilgrims 150 persons continued the celebration at an Agape meal served in the social hall of the IECA headquarters.

Participating in worship in the church in Angola is an experience in which the congregation is led to believe that God is not only present but active. We would be blind, however, if we did not recognize that very human needs and desires are being satisfied in the same experience: words of hope overcome, at least for a time, the gloom of despair; warm fellowship helps cure the wounds inflicted by death and family separations due to the war; the rhythm of song and dance bring comfort in a time of insecurity and tension.

At times the Catholic doctrine of "infallibility" and the Protestant belief in the "inerrancy of the Scriptures" seem to exaggerate the divine nature of the church at the expense of the human. If these positions are carefully examined, however, especially in an atmosphere of dialogue, they are compatible with the presupposition that the church is both human and divine.

---

16. Casimiro Pinto de Oliveira, "A Igreja em Angola, hoje," *Encontro*, no. 124 (May 1982): 9.

Third Presupposition:
The Church Is the People of God

Angolan Christians knew what it was to be part of a people. They needed to learn, as do all Christians, what it means to be the people *of God.*

This lesson was appealing to Angolan Christians because the Bible story used language that they understood. God called Abraham to leave his land and his relatives and his father's house to go to a different land — a common experience for many of the seminomadic peoples of Angola. God promised that Abraham and his family would prosper and that his descendants would be a blessing to all nations. This God was understandable to the Angolans because God was the God of a family — the God of Abraham, Isaac, and Jacob.

> With it He set up a covenant.... I will give my law in their bowels, and I will write it in their heart: and I will be their God, and they shall be my people ... (Jer. 31:31–34). Christ instituted this new covenant, that is to say the new testament, in His blood (1 Cor. 11:25) by calling together a people made up of Jew and Gentile, making them one, not according to the flesh but in the Spirit. This was to be the new People of God. For those who believe in Christ ... are finally established as "a chosen race, a royal priesthood, a holy nation, a purchased people.... You who in times past were not a people, but are now the people of God" (1 Pet. 2:9–10).[17]

The first Angolan Christians moved their families to the rural mission stations where they had heard the gospel, but soon they were too many so they started Christian villages near by. Kinship ties were very strong so there were not many individual, isolated Christians. In those areas where villages were large everyone was a member of an extended family, and this pattern was followed in Christian villages. To be a Christian usually meant being a member of a Christian family.

As Protestant and Catholic missions reached into the same area some traditional villages were divided into three parts: Catholic, Protestant, and traditional. The basic community was divided, but still everyone belonged to a family community as well as to a religious community. Some relatives were divided by religion, but loyalty to a faith tended to strengthen family ties.

The comity process, by which each of the early Protestant missions confined its activities to one ethnolinguistic group, also contributed to the church's sense of being a people. The church in each area was united

---

17. *Dogmatic Constitution on the Church*, 9.

by family ties and by a common language. Christian villages, missions, and even denominations became small Christendoms.

We usually associate "Christendom" with the synthesis between the gospel and the culture of Western Europe, which began with Emperor Constantine (274–337 C.E.). During the Middle Ages Christianity became the folk religion of Europe. That synthesis was the work of the thousand-year period during which the peoples of Western Europe, hemmed in by the power of Islam to the east and south, had the gospel wrought into the very stuff of their social and personal life, so that the whole population could be conceived of as the *corpus Christianum*.[18]

Christendom had been disintegrating in France and Portugal for some time when the Catholic Spiritans arrived in Angola in 1866 and founded the Lândana mission in Cabinda in 1873. The first BMS missionaries who arrived in São Salvador in 1878 came from a Great Britain where industrialization, urbanization, and secularism had eroded Christendom. Yet when those early missionaries arrived in Angola they saw themselves as ambassadors for Christendom as well as for Christ.

What happened in Angola and in most of Africa south of the Sahara was that the Christian missions produced little Christendoms. The mission station became a colony of the *corpus Christianum*, which then spread to the Christian villages. Missionaries, even those who went out dedicated only to evangelism, soon found themselves involved in educational, medical, agricultural, and industrial programs. Thus the whole of life was oriented around the gospel, which had been the goal in the heyday of Christendom. Colonialism was destroying African traditional culture and society, and the Christian communities inherited many of their functions, such as legitimization of leaders, maintenance of law and order, and celebration of rites of passage.

Angolans made the transition from their traditional cultures to little Christendoms in part to preserve their sense of being a people. The church was planted in Angola at a time when the traditional African cultures were disintegrating, and they took refuge in a pattern of society that had been eroding in Europe and the Americas.

Angolan Christians are caught now between wanting to adapt their faith to African culture and trying to hold on to the Christendoms in which their roots are planted.

The nostalgia for African culture has moved the church in two directions: inculturation and syncretism. The church in Angola made some innovations to adapt its liturgy and ceremonies to African rhythm, music, and style. The Catholic church is rather cautious in this area, as shown by the few innovations that have been approved by the Angolan

---

18. Lesslie Newbigin, *The Household of God* (New York: Friendship Press, 1953), 1.

bishops so far. The experience in Zaire, where the changes are more advanced, shows that this will be a long, slow process.

Many commentators classify the Kimbanguists and Tocoists as "syncretic sects." It is difficult to make a clear definition of the difference between "inculturation" and "syncretism." The former term is used if the commentator agrees with the elements of African culture that are being adapted to the Christian faith. The latter term is used pejoratively if the adaptation is deemed improper.

However, both the traditional culture and Christendom have been corroded by industrialization, urbanization, and secularism so the church in Angola, as a people, cannot easily identify itself as African, in terms of traditional African culture, nor as European, in the sense of the theology, ecclesiology, and sociology of Christendom. The church in Angola is faced with the challenge of finding what it means to be the people of God.

The process of recognition of the churches established by the government could detract Protestants from facing seriously the question of what it means to be the people of God. They have had to invest personnel and resources in establishing a denominational identity. They are no longer simply *Vakua Kristu*, or "Evangelicals," but are now Reformed, Congregational, UIEA, IEA, MEPA, New Apostolic, or Salvation Army. The phrase "people of God" also calls Angolan Christians, as well as Christians throughout the world, to recognize that the church is primarily a community. Since the church is, according to the second presupposition, human and divine, it needs structure and therefore becomes not only a community, but an institution.

One of the temptations of the church in Angola in this period is to emphasize the institutional character of the people of God, because to be recognized by the government and thus be able to function freely it is necessary to prove that the church has structure and institutional responsibility. In the Protestant community at least there is some criticism by the laity that the church leaders, who are almost all clergy, are emphasizing, if not abusing, the authority they have been given by the official recognition of the churches.

The word "laity" reminds us that its root, *laos*, in the Bible means "people" (1 Pet. 2:10). Angolan Protestants more easily recognize that the laity is the people of God because from the beginning the majority of Protestant missionaries have been lay men and women. In the early 1960s when the number of Protestant foreign missionaries was declining, of the total of 165 there were 32 ordained missionaries and 133 nonordained. Eighty percent of the missionaries were laymen and lay women. The Plymouth Brethren, who had the largest number of missionaries, had no ordained personnel, Angolan or foreign.

The ordained missionaries working in the other Protestant communities had special preparation and responsibilities for the work of the church, but the ordained minister was not recognized as being superior to those of other professions: doctors and nurses, teachers and administrators, agriculturalists and industrial arts specialists. All were part of the people, the *laos*.

The tradition in the Catholic church in Angola has been quite different. The missionaries were clergy or religious.

In the beginning of the 1990s in spite of the havoc of war and the debilitation of starvation the church seems stronger than ever because that is where the Angolans can still meet with family, speak their own language, and tap into their roots. The church is where they are still a people.

The process of recognition of the churches established by the government has given the Protestants another means of identification. Instead of being just Evangelicals they are now Baptists, Congregationalists, Reformed, Apostles, Lutherans. However, these identities are not as strong as the old ones of family, language, and land.

The strength of the old ties is shown by the development of the IECA. It had been the Council of Evangelical Churches of Central Angola, with congregations from Lobito to Bié along the Benguela railway. With its new identity as Congregationalists (IECA) it is in fact more ethnic since it has followed the Ovimbundu wherever they have gone and now has churches from Lobito to Luau on the Zaire border as well as in Lubango, Namibe, Luanda, Malanje, and Saurimo. It will continue to spread because Ovimbundu are in every corner of Angola.

The shape of the church in Angola tomorrow depends in part on what happens to the national languages. Will the Catholic church prepare and publish missals in other languages as it has in Umbundu? What will be the language of the children who have grown up in Luanda, Lobito, or Huambo since independence? Many Angolan parents want their children to learn their mother tongues. Will they achieve this desire? In part the future of the church in Angola depends on the answer to this question.

Edwin W. Smith's book *The Shrine of a People's Soul* tells a truth that the pioneer missionaries recognized:

> Every language is a temple in which the soul of the people who speak it is enshrined. Differences of speech reflect deeper differences of tradition, environment, outlook. This is true even while we acknowledge that fundamentally the human heart is one. There are differences between men in temperament, in ways of thinking and expression. It is not meaningless to speak of the soul of a people in this sense; and that soul finds expression in the language. The soul of a people is a precious thing. It is sin-

ful to exterminate them bodily, it is not less sinful to destroy their individuality.[19]

The first and third presuppositions are closely related: The church is one and the church is the people of God. Differences of family, language, region, and religious tradition have created different peoples. Therefore there are many churches in Angola. The church is truly one only if it is the people of God. Yet the Bible shows that God used family, language, nations, and religious traditions to call and shape a people.

The Fourth Presupposition:
The Church's Mission Is to Proclaim the Reign of God

This whole book has been about the church, and more specifically, the church in Angola. The author obviously believes that the church is important, but according to this fourth and final presupposition, the church is not the end or the goal of God's creative and re-creative work in this world. The church is the means to proclaim the Reign of God, which is the aim toward which God's creation is moving.

Jesus began his public ministry preaching the gospel of God, and saying: "The time is fulfilled, and the kingdom of God is at hand; repent, and believe in the gospel" (Mark 1:14–15).

This fourth presupposition is essential to understanding the church in Angola, for this church as all others is tempted to believe that the church is not only the means but the end of God's activity. We are tempted to pay so much attention to the church that we do not glimpse the grandeur of God's Reign. The Catholic church, impressed that it has the authority and sacraments to open the gates of God's Reign, focuses its concern on vocations for the survival of the church. The Protestants, preaching repentance and the new birth, tend to identify God's Reign with their personal religious experience.

In more practical terms the leaders of the church in sincere dedication can become so concerned for the survival and well-being of their churches that they forget that the church is a means and not an end. This led some missionaries to participate in mean competition and rivalry with other missions, believing that the survival and growth of their church justified any means. Vatican II corrected a commonly held preconciliar belief that the church and God's Reign were identical. The Constitution on the Church said more modestly that the church is "the initial budding forth" of God's Reign (no. 5).

---

19. Edwin W. Smith, *The Shrine of a People's Soul* (London: Edinburgh House Press, 1930), 44.

An American Catholic theologian, Father Richard P. McBrien, reflected in "The Future of the Church":

> Indeed, the world is called to become the Kingdom of God, not to become the church. Insofar as the church is already the embodiment of fellowship (*koinonia*), it serves as an anticipatory sign for the rest of the world of that final, perfect community, which is the Kingdom. But signs are always temporary and provisional. When the reality they signify is immediately and directly experienced, the sign is no longer required. When the Kingdom comes in all its fullness at the end, the sacrament of that Kingdom will yield its specific identity and merge with the rest of mankind in the enjoyment of that eternal banquet of the Lord. In that sense, there is no ultimate future for the church. Its destiny is to disappear.[20]

---

20. *The Remaking of the Church: An Agenda for Reform* (New York: Harper & Row, 1973), 140.

Postscript

Since the publication of this book in Portuguese in 1990, a peace treaty was signed on May 31, 1991, in Lisbon. The civil war has ended, but confusion, hostilities, suffering, and violence continue. By the time this edition is published elections will have been held. It is impossible to predict either the results of the polling or the political outcome. However, the Church in Angola, which has faced so many radical shifts in society, economics, and politics, will be caught in another vortex of change.

Pope John Paul II visited Angola in June 1992, and as the huge crowds followed his itinerary and the government showed him every courtesy, it is difficult to believe that a few years ago the president of Angola had predicted that the Church was soon to disappear.

How will the Church in Angola demonstrate in the coming months and years that the Church is One, that it is human and divine, that the Church is the people of God?

And, looking beyond Angola, how will the Church in the whole world proclaim the Reign of God?

Acronyms

AACC	All Africa Conference of Churches
ABC	American Board of Commissioners for Foreign Missions, archives, Houghton Library, Harvard University
ABCFM	American Board of Commissioners for Foreign Missions
ACEBA	Association of Baptist Churches in Exile
ACOA	American Committee on Africa
ADEBCO	Association of Baptist Churches in the Congo
AEA	Aliança Evangélica de Angola, Evangelical Alliance of Angola; *also* Associação de Evangélicos de Angola, Angola Association of Evangelicals
AEF	Africa Evangelical Fellowship
AMA	American Missionary Association
AME	Alliance Missionnaire Évangélique, known popularly as the Swiss Mission in Angola
BMS	Baptist Mission Society
CAIE	Conselho Angolano das Igrejas Evangélicas, Angola Council of Evangelical Churches
CBA	Convenção Baptista de Angola, Angola Baptist Convention
CBFMB	Canadian Baptist Foreign Mission Board
CBFMS	Canadian Baptist Foreign Mission Society
CCFMS	Canadian Congregational Foreign Mission Society
CCPA	Commissão Coordenadora dos Projectos Agrícolas, Coordinating Committee for Agricultural Projects
CEAST	Conferência Episcopal de Angola e São Tome, Episcopal Conference of Angola and São Tomé
CEB	Comunidade eclesial de base, Base Communities
CEDECO	Centre de Développement Communautaire
CFMSBNA	Congregational Foreign Missionary Society of British North America

CICARWS	The Commission on Inter-Church Aid, Refugee and World Service (WCC)
CIEAC	Conselho das Igrejas Evangélicas de Angola Central, Council of Evangelical Churches of Central Angola
CMML	Christian Missions in Many Lands
CMS	Church Missionary Society
CONCP	Conferência da Organizações Nacionalistas das Colónias Portughesas, Conference of Nationalist Organization of Portuguese Colonies
DGS	Direcção Geral de Segurança, General Security Administration (Portugal)
DM	Département Missionnaire (des Églises Protestantes de la Suisse Romande), Missionary Department of French-Speaking Swiss Protestant Churches
EBBF	Église Baptista Bas-Fleuve, Lower Congo Baptist Church
ERCDOM	*Evangelical–Roman Catholic Dialogue on Mission*
FAPLA	Forças Armadas Populares da Libertação de Angola, Popular Armed Forces for the Liberation of Angola, MPLA armed forces
FNLA	Frente Nacional da Libertação de Angola
GRAE	Governo Revolucionario de Angola em Exílio
IASA	Instituto de Assistência Social de Angola, Institute of Social Assistance of Angola
IEA	Igreja Evangélica de Angola, Evangelical Church of Angola
IEBA	Igreja Evangélica Baptista de Angola, Evangelical Baptist Church in Angola
IECA	Igreja Evangélica Congregacional de Angola, Evangelical Congregational Church in Angola
IENA	Igreja Evangélica do Norte de Angola, Evangelical Church of North Angola
IERA	Igreja Evangélica Reformada de Angola, Evangelical Reformed Church of Angola
IESA	Igreja Evangélica do Sudoeste de Angola, Evangelical Church of Southwest Angola
IEUA	Igreja Evangélica Unida de Angola, Evangelical United Church in Angola
IJCSK	Igreja de Jesus Cristo segundo Simão Kimbangu, Church of Jesus Christ on the Earth by the Prophet Simon Kimbangu
IMUA	Igreja Metodista Unida em Angola, United Methodist Church in Angola

IPE	Institut Pedagogique Évangélique, Evangelical Pedagogical Institute (Protestant Normal School)
JMPLA-Youth	MPLA Youth
LMS	London Missionary Society
MEPA	Missão Evangélica Pentecostal de Angola, Evangelical Pentecostal Mission of Angola
MFA	Movimento das Forças Armadas, Movement of the Armed Forces (Portugal)
MPLA	Movimento Popular de Libertação de Angola, Popular Movement for the Liberation of Angola
MPLA-PT	MPLA Partido de Trabalho, Labor Party
NAM	North Angola Mission
OMA	Organização das Mulheres Angolanas, Women's Organization of Angola
OPA	Organização dos Pioneiros Angolanas, Organization of Angolan Pioneers
PCA	Partido Comunista Angolano, Angolan Communist Party
PIDE	Polícia Internacional da Defesa do Estado, Portuguese Political Police
PLUA	Partido da Luta dos Africanos de Angola, Party of the Struggle of the Africans of Angola
SAGM	South Africa General Mission
SDA	Seventh-Day Adventists
UCBWM	United Church Board for World Ministries
UCC	United Church of Christ
UIEA	União das Igrejas Evangélicas de Angola, Union of the Evangelical Churches of Angola
UNESCO	United Nations Educational, Scientific, and Cultural Organization
UNITA	União Nacional de Independência Total de Angola, National Union for the Total Independence of Angola
UNTA	União Nacional dos Trabalhadores Angolanos, National Union of Angolan Workers
UPA	União da Populações de Angola, Union of the People of Angola
UPNA	União da Populações do Norte de Angola, Union of the People of Northern Angola
WCAM	West Central Africa Mission
WCC	World Council of Churches
WEF	World Evangelical Fellowship

Index

433

DATE DUE

OCT 2 6 1994			